A Playground Of Broken Hearts

Also by Andrew Wild

Books About Music
Pink Floyd Song by Song (Fonthill, 2017)
Queen On Track (Sonicbond, 2018)
The Beatles: An A-Z Guide to Every Song (Sonicbond, 2019)
Solo Beatles 1969-1980 On Track (Sonicbond, 2020)
Crosby, Stills and Nash On Track (Sonicbond, 2020)
Dire Straits On Track (Sonicbond, 2021)
Fleetwood Mac in the 1970s (Sonicbond, 2021)
Eric Clapton Solo On Track (Sonicbond, 2021)
Eric Clapton Sessions (Sonicbond, 2022)
Phil Collins In The 1980s (Sonicbond, 2022)
The Allman Brothers Band On Track (Sonicbond, 2022)
A Mirror of Dreams: The Progressive Rock Revival 1981 To 1983 (Kingmaker, 2024)
Live Aid: The Greatest Show On Earth (Sonicbond, 2024)
The Beatles On Track 1962-1966 (Sonicbond, 2025) – with Alberto Bravin
The Beautiful South + The Housemartins On Track (Sonicbond, 2025)

Biographies
Play On: The Official Biography of Twelfth Night (Twelfth Night, 2009)
One for the Record: The Official Biography of Galahad (Avalon, 2013 / 2nd edition, 2018)
His Love: the Art, Music and Faith of Geoff Mann (Sonicbond, 2023)

Books About Films
James Bond On Screen (Sonicbond, 2022)

Books About Comics
The Perfect Marvel Comics Collection – 1939-1985 (Rumble Strips, 2022)

Local History
108 Steps Around Macclesfield (Sigma Press, 1994 / 2nd edition, Rumble Strips, 2018)
Exploring Chester (Sigma Press, 1996 / re-publication, Rumble Strips, 2018)
Ever Forward (MADS, 1997)

As Editor
Stored In Clocks And Mortal Shadows: Geoff Mann's Poems 1973-1993 (Twelfth Night, 2024)

Plays
The Difficult Crossing (Stagescripts, 2016)
A Difficult Man (Rumble Strips, 2021)

A PLAYGROUND OF BROKEN HEARTS

THE PROGRESSIVE ROCK REVIVAL 1984 TO 1989

ANDREW WILD

This book is for Amanda, Rosie and Amy, and for everyone in the Last Eleven.

KINGMAKER PUBLISHING

First published in Great Britain by Kingmaker Publishing Limited in 2025

Copyright 2025 Kingmaker Publishing Limited

www.kingmakerpublishing.com

Copyright Andrew Wild

Andrew Wild has asserted his moral right under the Copyright, Designs and Patents Act, 1988, to be identified as the author of this work.

Edited by Gregory Spawton

Proof reading by Professor Geoff Parks

ISBN 978-1-8384918-8-8

Printed in Great Britain by Biddles Books Ltd, King's Lynn, Norfolk

Thank you to Rupert Akerman, Maarten Avontuur, Joe Banks, Rachel Barrett, Mike Barrington, Greg Belton, Julian Berkeley, Simon Branch, Kenny Brown, Stephan Brüninghoff, Mark 'Busby' Burrows, Joe Cairney, Nick Clancy, Gareth Cole, the Collected Underground, Mark Colton, Bob Daniels, Colin Dean, Kiki Dee, Marco de Niet, Ann and Tony DiPascale, Julie Etherden, Paul Fairweather, Noah Fanzerbutz, Felipe Fleury, Peter Forster, Darrell Foster Kirsop, David Futter, Carl Glover, Gordon Graham, Steve Grey, Mark Guenther, Jurriaan Hage, Oz Hardwick, Jonathan Hoare, Andy Inman, Stuart James, Mark Jepson, Michael Johnson, Steve Johnson, Dave Jones, Lucy Jordache, Roger Key, Stephen Lambe, David Leigh, Bruce Levick, Kevin Mackenzie, Robert McIlwraith, John McMurtie, Betty McMahon, Phil Macy, Gus Mark, Simon Middleton, Tom Mohr, Phil Morris, Marina Organ, Manola and Piersandro Pallavicini, Chris Phillips, Rob Portengen, Cliff Proctor, Jules Robinson, Emma Roebuck, AJ Samuels, Günter Schote, Nick Shilton, Peter Sims, Alistair Smith, Denis Smith, Sam Smyth, Simon Springall, Adrian Sunderland, Richard Swan, Kevin Thompson, Bert Treep, Joanne Tyrrell, Gary Uzzell, Nat Webb, Hellen Widdowson, Marc Wijnands, Glenn Williams, Robin Willcocks and Mary Wren.

Special thanks to Mike Bentley, Stephanie Bradley, Mark Drake, Jon Dunnington, Jerry Ewing, Mark Hughes, Andrew Humphreys, Albert Jagger, Darran Kellett, Mark McCormac, Roger Morgan, Russell Morgan, Guy Tkach and Jerry van Kooten.

Bonus points: Peter Moltesen and Professor Geoff Parks.

Author's note

Most of the quotes used in this book are taken from over 85 interviews and/or direct communications with the author. These are identified within the text by their use of the present tense. The author and editor express their grateful thanks to everyone named here.

Mat Anderson, John Arnison, Nigel 'Axe' Atkins, Julian Baker, John Barnfield, Nick Barrett, Rick Battersby, Lorenzo Bedini, Philip Bell, Stewart Bell, Stephen James Bennett, Mike Bentley, Mark Bloxsidge, Ken Bowley, Clint Bradley, Stephanie Bradley, Ronnie Brown, Hugh Carter, Rik Carter, Neil Cockle, James Colah, Barry Connell, Paul Cook, Paul Dennis, Brian Devoil, the late Malcolm Dome, Francis Dunnery, Jon Dunnington, Marc Elton, Tim Esau, Jerry Ewing, Paul Ford, Andy Glass, Ashley Goodall, Andy Grant, Nigel Harris, Mark Hawkins, Niall Hayden, Mike Holmes, Martin Hooker, Deborah Hopper, Mark Hughes, Nigel Hutchings, Brian Jelleyman, Jim Johnston, Nigel Mazlyn Jones, Cori Josias, John Jowitt, Mark Kelly, Alan King, Steve Leigh, Greg Lines, Euan Lowson, Mark McCormac, Chris McMahon, Paul McMahon, Niall Mathewson, Paul Menel, Tony Mills, Diz Minnitt, Clive Mitten, Ian Mosley, Graeme Murray, Peter Matuchniak, Hew Montgomery, Peter Nicholls, Stuart Nicholson, Clive Nolan, Martin Orford, Rog Patterson, Ed Percival, Mick Pointer, Andy Poole, Alan Reed, Andy Revell, Howard Rogers, Steve Rothery, Andy Sears, Steve 'Fudge' Smith, Tim Smith, Gregory Spawton, Mark Spencer, Nigel Spennewyn, Mike Stobbie, David Stopps, Nik Szymanek, Barrie Taylor, Tim Taylor, Ian 'Bush' Telfer, Mark 'Spindle' Trayton, Pete Trewavas, Keith Turner, David Valentine-Hagart, Dave Wagstaffe, Greg Walsh, John Walters, Phil Wheal, Alan Whittaker, Rob Wilsher, Steven Wilson, Sean Worrall, Martin Wright, Keith Young.

All secondary quotes use the past tense. Unless referenced directly in the text, the sources for secondary quotes are referenced at the end of this book.

Contents

9   Foreword by Jerry Ewing

15 Dramatis Personae

18 Introduction: Freaky Times On The Event Horizon

21 1984: A Bleeding Heart Poet In A Fragile Capsule

91 1985: Dawn Escapes From Moon Washed College Halls

141 1986: Egos Check Cheques In Transit

178 1987: Building Hope On Shifting Sand

192 1988: Indifferently Ticking In Cold Deserted Mansion Halls

206 1989: Watch The Old World Melt Away

214 Going Underground: The 1990s And Beyond

222 Calling All The Heroes

294 Closure: Impressions Lost And Overstepped

304 Sources

309 Bibliography

Nick Barrett in the Marquee dressing room, 17 June 1984 (Photograph by Roger Morgan)

Foreword

by Jerry Ewing

Now, where was I?

Ah yes, *Court Jester* fanzine…

In the foreword to the first volume I spoke of the impact of the events that unfolded in *A Mirror Of Dreams*, and how, reading and re-reading the book, and indeed the coverage of the 1980s prog scene we've featured in the pages of *Prog* magazine, that's something which really rings true for absolutely everybody involved in some way. Not just the musicians, but the people behind the scenes and of course you, the fans.

These really were life-changing and life-affirming times. A point rammed home by the fact that we're still here together, reading this book, celebrating these treasured moments, and *still* going to see many of the bands written about in both volumes, as well as many new ones that have sprung up, and continue to arrive on an almost daily basis. I'll be brutally honest and admit that I never thought I'd end up quoting Kiss in a prog book, but here we go: *'This is my music, it makes me proud / These are my people and this is my crowd'*

Anyway, *Court Jester*. So, when I last left you, I'd just seen Marillion at their now celebrated Marquee Christmas 1982 gigs and had been inspired by the band's newsletter, *The Web*. Back in 1982 I didn't know a huge amount about fanzines beyond the fact that they existed, as I'd seen them advertised and had bought a few via the classified pages in *Sounds*, the weekly music paper that for many years had been my go-to source for music, to which I had more recently added *Kerrang!* magazine.

Growing up in Sydney, Australia, *Sounds* had opened up a whole new musical world to me, which, until that point, had largely been dictated by home-grown acts of my early years - Skyhooks, Sherbet, AC/DC, Rose Tattoo and Cold Chisel. Despite the country's rich prog heritage, little of it had come my way. I was also vaguely aware there was a band called Yes from the UK who dressed a bit funny, but that was about it. But suddenly, albeit three months late, I was discovering about like-minded bands from around the world, all of which seemed so very far away back then.

It wasn't just the music either. It was the stories too. Great 'on the road' pieces from writers called Geoff Barton, Phil Sutcliffe and Garry Bushell and a photographer called Ross Halfin, with bands called UFO and Judas Priest. I'd never heard these bands - there was no internet to go and check them out on - but that didn't matter. I was fascinated. And I wanted in.

Remember your school's career officer? Imagine the look on their face when I rock up and announce I want to be a music journalist. Blank incomprehension, followed by "Come back when you've got something useful to say, Ewing. Oh, and get your hair cut!"

So, here I was, knowing what I wanted to do but with no idea how to go about it. It was becoming increasingly apparent I had a reasonable grasp of the English language - I was on the editorial team for the school magazine, *The Taylorian*. Snobby schools like wot I went to (stop sniggering at the back) had that kind of thing, you see. At least it was a step in the right direction. And now, having had my inner prog fire lit by those Asia and Marillion shows in late 1982, I started investigating.

As mentioned in the first volume, the excellent *Afterglow* was the daddy of the prog fanzines and a massive inspiration to me. *Exposure* too, while I also had copies of Brian Tawn's great *Hawkfan* and one

Marquee membership card
(From the collection of Russell Morgan)

of the Yes fanzines. They all served as influences as I began to put together what would become *Court Jester*, and from humble beginnings it gradually developed into something I'm pretty proud of now. I remember Dad printing off 50 copies of the first issue at his work. They sold out in two days. Back he went to the photocopier again and again, as it became apparent people seemed to like what I was creating, judging by the deluge of mail that suddenly began arriving through the letter box at Highfield Way in Chorleywood!

My sister Sarah, these days an artist of some repute and of whom I am immeasurably proud, browbeat me, or certainly got our late mother to browbeat me, into allowing her to create the cover art for issue 2 - so anyone out there with that issue, hold on to it. It's a fine example of the artist's very early period! Gradually a team was built, which included my dear friend Stephanie Bradley, a good school friend Rick Cook and eventually an artist of some note, Chris Dignan, whose designs featured on *Court Jester* from issue 3, as well as a team of contributing writers who, if I'm not mistaken, included a Clive Rudd and another Stephanie (whose surname shockingly escapes me now).

Part of running an effective fanzine was establishing a connection with the bands themselves, and Marillion aside, who were already operating at a level where the mainstream media were offering them coverage, *Court Jester* certainly seemed to be in the thick of things.

I can still remember being sent a complimentary copy of Pallas' major label debut *The Sentinel* by the Harvest Records' press office, interviewing Alan Reed in the Marquee bar, going round to IQ's infamous Kensal Rise flat to interview them when *Tales From The Lush Attic* came out, and regular Sunday afternoon telephone conversations on an old rotary wheel telephone with Nick Barrett and Brian Devoil, catching up on the latest news and gossip. And of course attending lots and lots of gigs.

The Marquee was the spiritual home of the '80s prog scene, but over in Aylesbury in Buckinghamshire you also had Friars, for so long such an important venue in the development of interesting rock music. And, closer to home, The Verulam Arms in Watford, whose main claim to fame at that point was that The Stranglers had played there in the early '80s, began putting on prog gigs.

Subsequent conversations with him put both myself and Steven Wilson at many of the same shows by the likes of IQ, Twelfth Night, Solstice and others, albeit unknowingly. We lived about four miles apart from each other at the time, apparently.

Foreword

From the IQ newsletter, July 1986 (From the collection of Guy Tkach)

In fact, the very last issue of *Court Jester* we published contained a review of a demo by a local band called Karma, featuring a young guitarist by the name of Steve Wilson!

The period which the aptly titled *A Playground Of Broken Hearts* covers certainly began in amazing fashion.

The first three quarters of 1984 were again spent largely at The Marquee, watching the likes of IQ, Twelfth Night and Pendragon seemingly go from strength to strength, joined by newcomers like Airbridge, Liaison, Trilogy, Quasar and Tamarisk, all looking to make similar headway to the bands they were supporting.

The first signs that the road ahead might not be as enjoyable and trouble free was when Geoff Mann decided to leave Twelfth Night. I recall this coming as a devastating shock to me and many fans, and those final shows at The Marquee in 1983 on 4 and 5 November are firmly ingrained in my memory. Like many other fans, I remain forever grateful that they were preserved for posterity on *Live And Let Live*.

Looking back now, I suppose that was the first crack in the garden wall. Later, Euan Lowson would leave Pallas, Peter Nicholls would leave IQ, Fish would even leave Marillion. These were steep learning curves for young and devoted music fans relatively unaware of rock music's penchant for revolving doors.

And yet there was more than enough to suggest things were as great as ever too. IQ's second full-length album *The Wake* remains a phenomenal piece of work, as is Pendragon's *The Jewel*, while the 1985 *Fire In Harmony* compilation album shed deserved light on other acts. Pallas and Twelfth Night found themselves headlining Hammersmith Odeon; and Marillion, of course Marillion, took prog to No. 1 in the album charts and had hit singles aplenty.

Within the grander scheme of a genre that has now been going for almost 60 years, the scene within a scene that's written about here does indeed falter. Why? A myriad of reasons, but I certainly believe that the interference of the major record labels later in the '80s did no band outside of Marillion any good.

Once the creatives had been replaced by accountants running record labels in the late '70s and early '80s and the balance sheet became king, there was no place for bands with ambition and who just did not fit into an easily marketable category. As with anything they get involved in, they see a band doing well, they all dive in to grab something similar, they don't really know what to do with, they try remoulding it, and when it all fails, discard it and move on to the next supposedly big thing. Dreams dashed. Confidence shattered.

A PLAYGROUND OF BROKEN HEARTS

**Pendragon badges
(From the collection of
Günter Schote)**

**Andy Revell, 1984
(Courtesy Twelfth
Night Archive)**

As Andrew wrote in *A Mirror Of Dreams*, I went to Lancaster University in late 1985, which is roughly when the final edition of *Court Jester* saw the light of day. It was certainly the biggest and best issue we'd created by that point, thanks in no small part to Chris Dignan's art direction and Stephanie's organisational skills (right, who said 'bossy'? Come on, own up!). And I'm pretty certain it wasn't intended to be the last. But the logistics and cost of trying to keep a popular fanzine going at university, coupled with other distractions like drinking, going out at night and sleeping my days away, meant that, sadly, *Court Jester* was no more as of 1985. But I still have my signed copy of Pallas' *The Wedge*, which I won in a competition when the band played at Lancaster's The Sugar House in 1986.

While my fanzine days were over, writing about music definitely was not. At university I met a fella by the name of Dave Shack, whom I used to write a rock column with for the student newspaper. Today Dave manages Iron Maiden with Rod Smallwood. Back then he was, and indeed still is, a likeable and friendly lad from Leeds with great taste in music but less taste when it came to football. To cut a very long story short, it was thanks to knowing Dave that I ended up being a staff writer on *Metal Forces* magazine in 1989 when Dave was Editor, and eventually Deputy Editor under the stewardship of my great friend, the late Malcolm Dome. And whilst much of the day to day music was metal orientated, slowly I became more and more reacquainted with the progressive rock that had filled my life so plentifully half a decade earlier. In fact it was hearing Dream Theater's debut album *When Dream And Day Unite*, which to my ears sounded like Metallica jamming with Rush, that acted as a big catalyst in reconnecting me, along with the fact that Malcolm had obviously been writing about the entire '80s prog scene for *Kerrang!* while I was away having fun and games at college.

In 1992 I accepted a job offer of becoming Associate Editor of *Metal Hammer*. At the time the magazine was still owned by the German publishers who had launched it back in 1983. It still had the word 'metal' in the title, but its editorial remit was broader than its main rival *Kerrang!* and albums by old pals like Pendragon (*The Window Of Life*) and IQ (*Ever*) started landing on my desk.

Dennis Publishing acquired the magazine in early 1994 and kept myself and the Art Editor on board to relaunch the magazine in the UK. Dennis Publishing brought with them more resources and a broader outlook, by which time I'd been introduced to the music of Porcupine Tree. And in 1997, in a kind of "Hang on a minute lads, I've got a great idea" moment, I announced to

my work colleagues Dave Ling, Andy Ryan, Monir Khan and Christina Neal, the idea of a new music magazine!

The premise for *Classic Rock* was that there was this massively successful area of rock music that was completely being ignored by the likes of *Q*, *Mojo*, *Kerrang!* and *Metal Hammer*, largely because it wasn't deemed hip enough. And yet the likes of Rush, Yes, Marillion, Rainbow, Deep Purple and more were the soundtrack to our working week in the office, not to mention the plethora of fluffy AOR acts Dave Ling would only be allowed to play when Andy and I were at the pub (which admittedly at the time was quite a lot).

Dennis didn't understand the idea at first and rejected my first pitch, but then this is the company where, having acquired *Hammer*, one member of the board of directors enthusiastically said to me he was looking forward to a magazine with "women chained to motorbikes and that kind of thing", only to look crestfallen when I suggested that perhaps times had changed a bit!

When it was simplified into the form of a Venn diagram they got it, and *Classic Rock* was greenlit. Prog was a major part of *Classic Rock* back then. I interviewed Steve Hackett and Marillion's Steve Hogarth for issue 1, as well as looking at how the music had influenced more modern rock acts such as Radiohead and Spiritualized, no doubt infuriating the gatekeepers of the day! History now shows that Dennis sold *Classic Rock* and *Metal Hammer* to Future Publishing in 2000, and although I was by that time working on the men's magazine *Maxim*, I continued to write for both, so it seemed the obvious choice when, in 2008, I had yet another idea...

Prog magazine was born of conversations with like-minded colleagues, including Nick Shilton, who

A PLAYGROUND OF BROKEN HEARTS

had been our go-to prog guy on *Classic Rock*, and is now a proprietor of the publishers of this very book, and who to this day recalls the phone call when I told him Future Publishing were on board and we had a new magazine about prog rock to get out! It seems amazing to be sat here some 17 years later, writing this, working on issue 158 of *Prog* magazine. But hey, here we are. That's the reality…

Equally amazing is that many of those friends of mine from those heady days of the 1980s are still with us and, seemingly, going from strength to strength. At the time of writing, Solstice have just romped home in the *Prog* Readers' Poll and IQ are on the verge of releasing a great new album, *Dominion*. Pendragon and Pallas are still with us, while Twelfth Night still do robust business with their back catalogue. Fish might be drawing his career to a close, but Marillion remain a unique phenomenon in the music world.

And Abel Ganz, Galahad, Trilogy, Quasar, Comedy Of Errors, Haze, Jadis, Pride Of Passion, Multi Story, No-Man, Airbridge, Tamarisk and more are either still with us or have been active of late.

Progressive rock may be in a better state of health than at any time since 1989, but to see so many artists from the '80s continuing to thrive suggests that we were all right in the first place. There is something quite magical about this music, especially for those of us lucky to have witnessed what happened in the 1980s.

It's not just the bands either. Stephanie (the one whose surname I do remember!) has now had to put up with what she refers to as my "incorrigible" outlook on life for over 40 years. And yes, she would have got less for murder! Martin Brimicombe, Martin Orford and Alan Reed are pals, I still enjoy a catch up with Brian Devoil and Nick Barrett, with Mike Holmes and Peter Nicholls, with Graeme Murray and with Andy Glass, the Marillion lads and that there Fish fella.

It's not just the musicians - it's lovely to still bump into Roger, Alice and Russell from *Afterglow* and Marina from *The Organ* at gigs, to see them still working hard to promote the music too. I did sadly lose touch with a lot of people from those *Court Jester* days, but on the off chance Rick Cook, Chris Dignan, or indeed anyone else who was involved, is reading this, do get in touch, it would be lovely to hear from you. I'm certainly lucky that today I can count a fair few readers of *Prog* as friends. Not many magazine editors can lay claim to that.

When *Prog* magazine put the '80s prog revival on the cover at the end of 2023, I remember a conversation I had with Dave Everley, who wrote that cover feature, on the nature of success. Not everyone from the '80s era of prog scaled the giddy heights of celebrity. And yet the majority of those bands are still here, still performing, still recording, still selling out gigs to adoring fans.

Would you have preferred the instant yet so often fleeting brush with fame and fortune, only to find yourself inevitably consigned to the bargain bin of history soon after? Or to still have a working musical career over 40 years down the line? I certainly know what I'd rather.

Congratulations to everyone involved. Enjoy. And I'll see you at the bar.

Jerry Ewing
Prog magazine
London, February 2025

Dramatis Personae

Mat Anderson: drums - Pendragon (1984-1986)

John Arnison: Marillion's manager (1982-1998)

Nigel 'Axe' Atkins: Twelfth Night auditionee (1983)

Julian Baker: guitar, vocals - Pendragon (1978-1980)

John Barnfield: keyboards - Pendragon (1978-1984)

Nick Barrett: guitar, vocals - Pendragon (1978-now)

Rick Battersby: keyboards - Twelfth Night (1979-1981, 1982-1986)

Lorenzo Bedini: guitar, vocals - Airbridge (1980-1983)

Phil Bell: Sounds scribe

Stewart Bell: keyboards, vocals - Citizen Cain (1989-now)

Stephen Bennett: keyboards: Airbridge (1983); LaHost (1984-1986)

Mike Bentley: Pallas aide de camp

Mark Bloxsidge: bass, keyboards, vocals - Trilogy (1982-1985, 2022-now)

Ken Bowley: bass - Solstice (1985, 1986)

Tim Bowness: vocals - No-Man (1987-now)

Clint Bradley: guitar, vocals - Beltane Fire (1984-1986)

Stephanie Bradley: Marillion team

Ronnie Brown: keyboards - Pallas (1979-1987, 1996-now)

Hugh Carter: bass - Abel Ganz (1980-mid-1990s)

Rik Carter: keyboards - Pendragon (1984-1986)

Gary Chandler: guitar, vocals - Jadis (1982-now)

Nigel Child: guitar - Pride Of Passion (1984-1987, 2023-now)

Neil Cockle: keyboards - Marillion (1978-1979)

James Colah: keyboards - Pendragon (1986)

Barry Connell: drums - Liaison (1980-1985, 2018-now)

Paul Cook: drums: IQ (1982-2005, 2009-now)

Barbara Deason: vocals - Solstice (1985)

Paul Dennis: guitar, vocals - Trilogy (1981-1985, 2022-now)

Brian Devoil: drums - Twelfth Night (1978-1986, 2007-2014)

Francis Dunnery: vocals, guitar - It Bites (1982-1983, 1984-1990)

Marc Elton: violin, keyboards, vocals - Solstice (1980-1985, 1986, 1992-1997)

Tim Esau: bass - IQ (1981-1989, 2011-now)

Jerry Ewing: editor, Prog

Fish: vocals - Marillion (1981-1988)

Paul Ford: vocals, guitar - Multi-Story (1981-1986, 2014-now)

Derek Forman: drums - Pallas (1976-1998)

Peter Gee: guitar, bass - Pendragon (1980-now)

Andy Glass: guitar, vocals - Electric Gypsy (1978), Solstice (1980-1985, 1986, 1992-1997, 2007-now)

Ashley Goodall: EMI executive

Andy Grant: vocals - Chemical Alice (1981-1982); Tamarisk (1982-1984, 2012-now)

Nigel Harris: drums - Pendragon (1978-1985)

Mark Hawkins: bass - Solstice (1980-1985)

Niall Hayden: drums - The Lens (1977-1978)

Steve Hogarth: vocals, keyboards, guitar - Marillion (1989-now)

Mike Holmes: guitar - The Lens (1978-1981); IQ (1981-now)

Dave Holt: guitar - Pallas (1976-1979)

Deborah Hopper: vocals - Pride Of Passion (1984-1987, 2023-now)

Mark Hughes: IQ and Twelfth Night archivist

Nigel Hutchings: Marquee manager in the 1980s

Brian Jelleyman: keyboards - Marillion (1979-1981), Pride Of Passion (1984-1985)

Jim Johnston: keyboards - Comedy of Errors (1984-1990, 2021-now)

Doug 'Rastus' Irvine: bass, vocals - Marillion (1978-1980)

Nigel Mazlyn Jones: Solstice's producer (1984)

Cori Josias: vocals - Marillion (1987)

John Jowitt: bass - Ark (1988-1990); IQ (1990-2010)

Mark Kelly: keyboards - Marillion (1981-now)

Alan King: vocals - Electric Gypsy (1978)

Sandy Leigh: vocals - Solstice (1983-1985)

Steve Leigh: keyboards - Chemical Alice (1981-1982); Tamarisk (1982-1984, 2012-now); Quasar (1987-1988)

Greg Lines: Pendragon's former manager

Euan Lowson: vocals - Pallas (1979-1984)

Geoff Mann: vocals - Twelfth Night (1981-1983)

John Marter: drums - Marillion (1983)

Niall Mathewson: guitar - Pallas (1979-now)

Peter Matuchniak: vocals, guitar - Janysium / Mach One (1980-1985)

Mark McCormac: Marko's Marillion Museum

Electra McLeod: vocals - Twelfth Night (1980)

Chris McMahon: bass, keyboards, vocals - Haze (1982-1988, 1998-now)

Paul McMahon: guitar, vocals - Haze (1982-1988, 1998-now)

Paul Menel: vocals - IQ (1985-1989)

Diz Minnitt: bass - Marillion (1981-1982); Pride Of Passion (1984-1987, 2023-now)

Clive Mitten: bass, guitar, keyboards - Twelfth Night (1978-1986, 2008-2014)

Hew Montgomery: keyboards - Abel Ganz (1980-mid-1990s)

Roger Morgan: Afterglow fanzine

Russell Morgan: Afterglow fanzine

Ian Mosley: drums - Marillion (1983-now)

Jonathan Mover: drums - Marillion (1983)

Graeme Murray: bass, vocals - Pallas (1976-now)

Peter Nicholls: vocals - IQ (1981-1985, 1989-now)

Clive Nolan: keyboards - Pendragon (1986-now)

Martin 'Widge' Orford: keyboards, vocals - IQ (1981-2007); Jadis (1989-now)

Marina Organ: The Organ fanzine

Shelley Patt: vocals - Solstice (1982-1983)

Rog Patterson: guitar, vocals - Twice Bitten (1982-1986)

Ed Percival: guitar, vocals - Airbridge (1981-1983)

Mick Pointer: drums - Marillion (1978-1983)

Andy Poole: bass, keyboards, guitar - Big Big Train (1990-2018)

Alan Reed: vocals - Pallas (1984-1988, 1993-2010, 2022-now)

Andy Revell: guitar - Twelfth Night (1978-1986, 2007-2010, 2012-2014)

Sue Robinson: vocals - Solstice (1982)

Howard Rogers: vocals, bass - Liaison (1980-1985, 2018-now)

Steve Rothery: guitar - Marillion (1979-now)

Andy Sears: vocals - Twelfth Night (1983-1986, 2007-2012)

Steve 'Fudge' Smith: drums - LaHost (1984-1985); Pendragon (1986-2006)

Gregory Spawton: bass, guitar, keyboards - Big Big Train (1990-now)

Mark Spencer: vocals - LaHost (1984-1986)

Mike Stobbie: keyboards - Pallas (1976-1979, 1987-1996)

David Stopps: manager of Friars, Aylesbury

Nik Szymanek: drums - Trilogy (1981-1985, 2022-now)

Barrie Taylor: drums - Moriarty (1983-1985)

Dramatis Personae

Afterglow ad

Tim Taylor: guitar - Citizen Cain (mid-1980s)
Ian 'Bush' Telfer: Marquee manager in the 1980s
Mark 'Spindle' Trayton: guitar - LaHost (1984-1985)
Pete Trewavas: bass, vocals - Marillion (1982-now)
Keith Turner: bass, vocals - Quasar (1979-now)
David Valentine-Hagart: guitar - LaHost (1984)
Dave Wagstaffe: drums - Quasar (1985-1989)
Andy Ward: drums - Marillion (1983)
Martyn Watson: bass, vocals - Twelfth Night (1986-1987)
Alan Whittaker: guitar - Moriarty (1983-1985)
Rob Wilsher: keyboards - Multi-Story (1981-1988, 2014-now)
Steven Wilson: guitar, keyboards, vocals - Pride Of Passion (1987), No-Man (1987-now)
Brian Wood: vocals - Pallas (1976-1979)
Sean Worrall: The Organ fanzine
Martin Wright: drums - Solstice (1980-1985, 1986)
Keith Young: guitar - Liaison (1980-1985, 2018-now)

Introduction
Freaky Times On The Event Horizon

At the end of 1983, the second wave of progressive rock in the UK was seemingly at its peak.

Marillion were leading the way with the success of their March 1983 album *Script For A Jester's Tear*. After the album's release they sought to change their line-up and sacked founding member and drummer Mick Pointer. They spent much of the summer sacking various replacements. Nevertheless, in December 1983 they were busy recording their second album.

Of the other bands that formed a wedge behind Marillion, Pallas were at the apex. Regrouping after the aborted Brave New World tour, their album *The Sentinel*,

Left: Fans waiting outside The Marquee in 1984 for shows by Solstice and Pallas (Photography by Robin Willcocks and courtesy of Phil Macy)

Pride Of Passion performing at The Marquee in 1985 (Photograph by Andy Inman)

recorded not without difficulty the previous August and September, was ready for release. Their fellow passengers on the tour, Solstice, had maintained a stable line-up for eight months, with Sandy Leigh proving to be a capable and captivating singer. Solstice's plans for an album of their own were coming into focus.

Twelfth Night had recruited a talented and ambitious new vocalist, Andy Sears, to replace their charismatic frontman, Geoff Mann. Sears was a formidable musician and writer and was bursting with ideas.

IQ's *Tales From The Lush Attic* had pushed them forward as a band to watch: their promise would be realised with their magnificent second album, *The Wake*.

Pendragon had yet to release an album. Founder John Barnfield would leave the band in the early weeks of 1984, but Nick Barrett's irrepressible work-rate ensured that the band stayed on the road with big plans for the future.

These six bands would perform over 400 gigs between them in 1984 alone.

And many other acts were starting to play more shows at The Marquee, creating a buzz and feeding the scene.

For both the musicians and their fans, it was a great time to be alive.

A PLAYGROUND OF BROKEN HEARTS

Adverts from *Sounds* and the *NME*
(From the collection of Guy Tkach)

1984:
A Bleeding Heart Poet In A Fragile Capsule

This, for better or worse, is 1984, yet... Pallas seem to have allowed Eddie Offord to hurl them back into the nether-reaches of his heyday (and also the period of the band's most influential origins). If this album had hit the streets a dozen years ago on the strength of these tracks alone it would have been hailed as a revolution! But, like I said, this is 1984...

Dave Dickson, *Kerrang!* issue 62, February 1984

'We don't write pop love songs, we leave that to Duran Duran and the Kajjes.'

Fish, *Sounds*, February 1984

Even as Marillion moved into larger venues, gigs at The Marquee, the undoubted epicentre for these new prog bands, continued apace in 1984. Shows by Solstice (7-8 January) and IQ (12 January) kick-started the new year. Twelfth Night began an extensive period of touring with their new singer: over 40 concerts around the UK from 5 January through to the end of March.

Phil Bell at *Sounds* conducted Andy Sears' first major national press interview on 15 January, during a run of two shows at The Marquee, resulting in a favourable feature in the weekly music paper soon afterwards.

Twelfth Night are certainly more 1984 than any of the seventies connotations that go with [the 'progressive' tag]. That's fact, not fiction, and it must be exhilarating for the band that the music-loving public en masse are at last beginning to accept them after years of graft.

Pendragon's headline set at The Marquee on 25 January marked their last gig with keyboard player John Barnfield. Barnfield did not want to give up his day job.

'I had been juggling a computing job with Gloucestershire County Council,' he says, 'and had started a new relationship. It was becoming increasingly difficult to keep all the balls in the air. It was never to do with the band or conflicts with music, it was for personal reasons where I simply could not keep all those things going. Eventually I knew I would be holding the band's aspirations back.

Clive Mitten backstage at The Marquee, 15 January 1984 (From the collection of Russell Morgan)

Contact issue 7 (From the collection of Darran Kellett)

PENDRAGON 'Contact' 7

Fellow Dragons,

Welcome to C7. Since you last heard from us there has been (as you may already know) a line-up change, namely that John Barnfield (Barney) has left owing to personal reasons. We would like to take this opportunity to wish him all the best for the future.

Barney played his last gig as a Pendragon member at the Marquee, which was a sell-out. Thanks to all those who went, and apologies to those who were unable to get in. For future Marquee dates advance tickets will be available from us.

You will be pleased to know that another keyboard player has emerged from the depths of Southend - namely Rik (Wakeman?) Carter. Rik has been playing piano for twelve years and rock keyboards for a year.

You may remember in the dim and distant past of Contact 6 we mentioned that the band are doing a T.V. appearance in February. Well, hold onto your hats, here come the details: the programme is, in fact, a competition for the best band in the West Country. Six bands are competeing, the last on stage being Pendragon. The prize is a £10,000 promotional video.

The show itself is being filmed at Goldiggers in Chippenham (Wiltshire) on February 29th. FREE tickets are available from us - just send an S.A.E. to the address below.

The actual show will be broadcast on March 5th, titled "Best Band West", on H.T.V. West at 10.30p.m. We are hoping that it will be shown at a later date in other regions.

We would like to thank T.Wilson and T.Vance for repeating the Friday Rock Show session in January.

The best item of news we've got for you is that Pendragon have ten dates supporting Marillion on their national tour including, wait for it, THE HAMMERSMITH ODEON. The dates are as follows:-

Feb;Wednesday 22nd:Norwich St. Andrews Hall   Tuesday 28th:Bristol Colston Hall
    Thursday 23rd:Oxford Apollo   Mar:Friday 2nd:Brighton Dome
    Friday 24th:Cardiff St.Davids Hall   Monday 5th:Leicester De Montfort Hall
    Sunday 26th Plymouth Skating   Thursday 8th:Southend Cliffs Pavilion
    Monday 27th:Exeter University   Saturday 10th:Hammersmith Odeon.

    MONDAY MARCH 19th - THE MARQUEE (headline)
    (tickets available now for £2.25. Send S.A.E.)

We are holding a competition. The person with the right answers to the following little brain teasers will have the chance to win either two free tickets for the Marquee on March 19th or a free t-shirt with the tour dates printed on the back.
1) Who is the mystery band member in the photo below? (alias the duck).
2) Name any one of the three tracks broadcast on the Friday Rock Show session.
3) Complete the Pendragon lyric "and once again we'll ...."

All answers must be in by Monday March 12th and the winner will be picked out of the top hat.

Finally, thanks to:- Jon Arnison and Marillion, Keith Goodwin, Julian Cull, Robin Prior, Simon Young, all at The Marquee, Greg, Billy, Alan and Norman, Chris and Mel.

Cheers then, Nick + Lorraine

61, Middle Street,
Stroud,
Glos.
GL5 1EA.

1984: A Bleeding Heart Poet In A Fragile Capsule

Twelfth Night, 15 January 1984 (From the collection of Russell Morgan)

Below: Andy Sears, Fforde Grene, Leeds, 21 January 1984 (Photograph by Aire Valley Photography/Twelfth Night Archive)

Pendragon had always been about friendships and the music, and I didn't want that to end on a sour note.'

Barnfield remained on good terms with the rest of the band and is still close friends with Nick Barrett. He was replaced in the coming weeks by Rik Carter.

'When Barney left,' recalls Nick Barrett, 'I think we put an advert in *Melody Maker* and nobody applied apart from Rik Carter. It was incredible to find someone who was really into the prog thing and wanted to join Pendragon. He obviously thought we were much bigger than we really were.'

'Rik Carter had been a fan,' says John Barnfield, 'going to see us at The Marquee. He was eager to step in, so the band moved forward fairly seamlessly.'

'I was a big fan of the band,' Carter says, 'and used to see them whenever I could at The Marquee. I first saw them when me and a couple of mates went to see Marillion at The Marquee in

Andy Sears, Bedford College, 27 January 1984
(Photograph by Roger Morgan)

September 1982 and Pendragon were the support band. I also saw them at a place in Brixton called the Ace [May 1983] and at The Dominion with IQ and The Enid [12 November 1983]. I made a couple of bootlegs of gigs myself which I used to listen to a lot – so when the time came to audition I knew a lot of the stuff, which I think stood me in good stead. As soon as I saw the ad in *Melody Maker*, 'Pendragon require keyboard player', I just knew that it was going to be me. It was embarking upon an exciting new venture – much better than working in insurance and commuting to London every day, which was soul-destroying.'

Nick Barrett: 'Rik moved down to Stroud from Southend-on-Sea. He was a great keyboard player. He didn't have a lot of kit, but he used what he had to the fullest degree. He had the cheapest Moog that you could get and a Logan String Melody. These were all old keyboards. When we recorded the song *Fly High, Fall Far* you can hear this humming. That's the Logan whirring away to itself in the background.'

'When I joined the band,' Rik Carter says, 'they thought it best for me to replicate John Barnfield's set-up as far as possible, so I bought a Korg Polysix and a Moog Opus ('Opeless' as we called it…) and a Sequential Pro One, which got nicked early on and replaced by a Moog Source. I also had the Logan – yes, it was very noisy but had a great sound. I ended up selling it to Martin Orford of IQ and you can hear it all over *The Wake* album.'

Twelfth Night continued their trek around the UK.

Andy Sears: 'This was the *Live And Let Live* tour. On one hand, it was a way of making sure that the momentum didn't disappear, and, on the other, it was a good way of us getting to know each other and working together.'

1984: A Bleeding Heart Poet In A Fragile Capsule

TWELFTH NIGHT, VERALUM ARMS, WATFORD JAN 26th 1984

Quite obviously the question on my lips tonight was 'What's he gonna be like?' He, for those of you who don't know (and consequently must be deaf, dumb and blind), is one Andy Sears, new lead vocalist with Reading hotshots Twelfth Night. Tonight's gig was about two weeks into the tour, so he'd had some time to get settled in, before I cast a more than wary (let's not deny it) eye over him and the band as a whole.

So, what's the new boy like? Well, he possesses a damn fine voice, which is very powerful. The moment he hits the stage it's clear that he's simply oozing with energy and simply raring to go. His stage presence is very expressive, sometimes even balletic. He is far more of a ROCK performer than Geoff ever was, and he's got a good sense of humour, so he was easily on terms with the audience. It was clear that he didn't want to be looked upon as a Geoff Mann clone, and clone he certainly is not, portraying the likes of *Creepshow* and *Sequences* in his own style.

I sometimes felt that he was overdoing it a bit on stage, but I'm sure as time goes on he will have got his whole show together a lot more. Any of tonight's mistakes were totally understandable under the circumstances. What really impressed me about the man was the way he managed to hold the whole show together when the power went towards the end of *Sequences*. Alone on a darkened stage, he led the crowd in a purely vocal version of *Love Song*, handling the whole situation superbly.

As for the rest of the band, they played tighter tonight than at any previous gig I'd seen. Their new image will definitely help them (something several up and coming new bands could take note of) and Andy fits in well with the band image. The set was basically a typical TN set, although there were some splendid re-workings of *Human Being* and *Creepshow*. Naturally, the musicianship was of a very high standard. Clive's totally Russian intro to *Fact And Fiction* was very impressive too. It was nice to see the band maintain a friendly feeling with the crowd throughout the whole show.

So, Twelfth Night mk 9 definitely get the thumbs up from me, especially Andy Sears, who I'm sure will prove to be one of the best performers fronting a new band. As I've said, the band's new image and their Pink Floyd-cum-Ultravox type sound will surely lift this band to the stature they deserve. In fact, on present showing, whilst Marillion seem to be on a slip down to the 'fugazi basement', it would appear that Twelfth Night are sneaking up the back stairs to the floor above.

Jerry Ewing, *Court Jester* **issue 6, 1984**

The album documenting Geoff Mann's final shows with Twelfth Night would be released by a newly-formed independent record label, Music For Nations. MFN was founded by Martin Hooker.

'After six years working at EMI, I set up a label called Secret Records, which was predominately a punk label,' explains Martin. 'We had enormous success all over the UK and Europe and had nine consecutive chart albums out of nine releases. I was keen to move more into the heavy metal/hard rock area and as a result I discovered the band Twisted Sister, whose Secret album also immediately went

A PLAYGROUND OF BROKEN HEARTS

Twelfth Night, Cambridge, 1 February 1984
(Photographs by David Futter)

into the UK charts. Following on from this success I decided to start a metal label and Music for Nations was born at the end of 1982, with the first release in early 1983.

'I had seen Twelfth Night perform live and was extremely impressed. They already had a small but loyal following and it's massively important for that type of act to be able to tour constantly and perform good shows. They had excellent songs, were very intelligent as individuals and had a good idea of how they wanted to go about their career. I didn't have any progressive bands on the label at that time, so it was an obvious way to go. I considered Twelfth Night to be the best unsigned band around in the progressive field. It was an easy choice.'

Hooker agreed a two-album licensing deal with Twelfth Night and the band booked three days at Livingstone Studios in Wood Green, north London, to mix the album. *Live And Let Live* was released on 27 January 1984 and was reviewed by the major music papers as well as the band's local evening paper.

GOOD NIGHT: TWELFTH NIGHT *Live And Let Live*

Music For Nations MFN18

It was a hell of a shock that cold Wednesday night in October '83. I'd arrived in Reading to interview the progressive masters Twelfth Night, and just as the Walkman was about to roll, drummer Brian Devoil broke the news.

'Our singer, Geoff Mann's decided to leave,' he said simply, and my prepared questions went out of the window and I sat back stunned and silent. Later they told me that they planned to play two final dates with Geoff at The Marquee in

1984: A Bleeding Heart Poet In A Fragile Capsule

Nick Barrett in early 1984
(Photograph by Brian Cairns)

November and hoped to release a live album of the event.

This is the result - a well recorded 40-minute slice of Twelfth Night's finer works which gives a fair impression of the emotional 'Farewell Geoff' gigs.

The Ceiling Speaks boots the LP off authoritatively with its long triumphant intro and powerful hook, while the gentler side of the band comes to the fore on the mellow *The End Of The Endless Majority*.

Side one's highlight is the dazzling mini-opera *We Are Sane*. Bassist Clive Mitten acts out his intriguing military blah-blah sequence and the track builds steadily with Mann's provocative and eerie falsetto vocal chopping into the frightening office scene. The musical backdrop increases in power, guitarist Andy Revell turning in rapid six-string statements amid the swirling, swooping synths of keyboardist Rick Battersby, and the whole thing chugs along marvellously. Essential listening.

Fact and Fiction, always a bit of a let-down on the album of the same name, is much improved here. Check the likeable, almost commercial verse and the neat link into the aggressive, orgasmic hook, and also hook an ear around the instrumental *The Poet Sniffs A Flower*. Genesis, BJH, etc. would be highly amused. Which leaves us with the lengthy *Sequences*. Probably the most inaccessible track on the LP, I have no doubt that given time it would have matured into a more impressive offering, but here it sounds muddled despite the clear-headed and bustling instrumental break. Still the lyric (as with all Geoff Mann's work) is provocative and well worth pondering.

Live And Let Live is a fitting end to Mann's career with the band and for once Twelfth Night have produced an album with clout, balls and emotion.

Paul Strange, *Melody Maker*, **March 1984**

Nick Barrett mused over making a change to Pendragon's format around this time.

'The thing is,' he said at the time, 'if we could find ourselves a suitable front man or an extra musician [so that] we could change different sounds more regularly, we'd be very interested! I'm a guitarist not a vocalist so therefore I find it a bit hard sometimes.

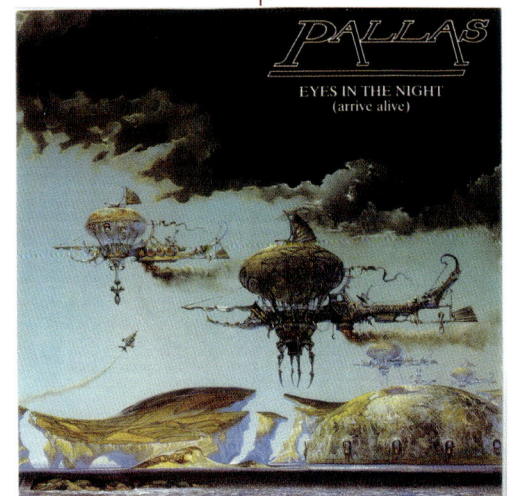

Eyes In The Night
(From the collection of Piersandro Pallavicini)

I do enjoy it but I think we've gone as far as we can. You can't push anything much further! I wouldn't like to disappear into the background, [but] two front people would be nice, sharing!'

Indeed, Pendragon auditioned a candidate for the role.

Nick Barrett: 'Initially, everyone told us that we needed a frontman. But in the end that turned out to be a strength for us, because we didn't need to bother with the wigs and the make-up, the hats and the cloaks. It actually became a plus, because people actually would listen to us and give us more of a chance. Having said that, we did try to find a front person. We had Paul Ford from Multi-Story audition for us. I think he was the only one.'

'I understand or was told that Nick had checked me out at one of our gigs,' Ford says. 'I was invited to Stroud, to Nick's place. The whole band were set up in one of the rooms. Multi-Story were unsigned at this time and Pendragon were well established, so I thought, 'Why not and see what comes of it?' Nick was obviously looking for a singer and frontman to open up more creative avenues.'

'I remember this,' says Rik Carter. 'Right after I joined, Paul came down to audition. We played *Victims Of Life* and he sounded really good, but I don't think Nick was ever really into the idea of not being the frontman himself. I do remember him telling Paul that he wouldn't be doing any onstage talking! So destined to fail really…'

'Paul was amazing,' says Nick Barrett, 'but we didn't think his voice was right for us. He started singing *Victims Of Life* with all these Jon Anderson vocal lines and it was great, but we'd never imagined it that way. And, to be honest, we couldn't help laughing. It just didn't work out, but he was a lovely guy. There were a couple of other people who we were due to have down for auditions and we just couldn't really arrange anything. Maybe it's fate but we just couldn't find anybody.'

Barrett remains Pendragon's sole frontman, 40 plus years on.

Pallas' single *Eyes In The Night* would creep into the low end of the UK singles chart at the end of January.

'We just about got to *Top Of The Pops*,' Euan Lowson says. 'But that did pretty well in the heavy rock charts for a prog rock band. We were torn about which direction we wanted to take. EMI wanted singles, but there was a lot of material we had for *The Sentinel* that never saw the light of day. It could have been a double album. Some of our better stuff was substituted for newer tracks we'd written specifically for singles. I think some of the songs were reworked for later albums.'

With the Manor no longer available, Marillion were in London, finishing their second album with frantic and energy-sapping recording and mixing sessions at studios across the city: Angel, Odyssey, Wessex, Maison Rouge, Eel Pie, Abbey Road and Sarm.

Simon Hanhart: 'The band had matured since the first album and of course Ian Mosley was now involved, which changed the sound and the character to a degree. I think 'difficult second album problems' crept in a little. After the success of *Script*, the pressure was on and perhaps there was some overthinking. The recording overran, and we ended up having to work in many different studios, seven in total I think, which made the process somewhat disjointed. I mixed the album in four different rooms, which isn't ideal. (Maison Rouge, Odyssey, and both rooms at Wessex) But the band were definitely on an upward trajectory and the new line-up was working well – amazing things were on the horizon!'

Punch And Judy would be completed in time for a 30 January release as single. Engineer Dave Meegan, exhausted from the mixing sessions, was sent to hospital to recover.

'It's about the unreality of the pop song,' Fish said. '*Punch And Judy* is about a couple who think that's what it's all about. They get pulled into the Mills & Boon romantic fiction stuff, get married and ten years later the guy realises that the spark of love between them is only a tiny percentage of the relationship. It sounds really pretentious, but it's social comment.'

The B-sides are the re-recorded versions of *Market Square Heroes* and *Three Boats Down From The Candy* featuring drummer John Marter, the only tracks he recorded with the band. EMI would have been disappointed at the song's four-week chart run, entering at number 29 and then dropping in successive weeks.

Mark Kelly: 'They were also unhappy about the huge studio bill run up by our late album delivery. *Fugazi* cost over £120,000, almost twice as much as *Script*, while failing to match its sales. Back in London, storm clouds were gathering over Manchester Square.'

The single received mixed reviews. *Sounds* suggested that the song was 'brilliantly sharp and at the same time so bittersweet'; *Record Mirror* described Fish as '[boxing trainer] Terry Lawless on a Frank Bruno training session'.

But, first, TV promotional duties saw Marillion on the ITV kids' show *Razzmatazz* (6 February), once again on *Top Of The Pops* (9 February) and then the *Oxford Road Show* (10 February). These were scheduled around final mixing sessions for the album.

Naturally, a tour followed. The 24-date UK-wide trek would open in Leeds on 11 February with the upbeat new song *Assassing*. Most of the new album would be performed, along with some old favourites. Pendragon would provide support at concerts in mid-size venues in Norwich, Oxford, Plymouth, Exeter, Bristol, Brighton, Leicester and Southend, concluding with three nights in London.

Pallas' album *The Sentinel* was also released that month. It spent three weeks in the album charts in late February and early March, reaching number 41, the highest album chart placing of any of the six main prog bands other than Marillion.

The CD reissue from 1992 re-orders the tracks and adds *East West*, *March On Atlantis* and *Heart Attack*.

1984: A Bleeding Heart Poet In A Fragile Capsule

Marillion on stage in Aberdeen and Edinburgh, 18-19 February 1984 (Photographs by Peter Forster)

This is much closer to the band's original plans for the album. 2011's *XXV* was written and recorded as a direct sequel to *The Sentinel*.

'In comparison to other prog rock albums released this year,' suggested Russell Morgan in *Afterglow*, 'particularly from Marillion and Twelfth Night for instance, it's plain to see that Pallas come across as the Seventies band in the Eighties. The fantasy related lyric, the keyboard dominated music pigeon-hole Pallas with both wings, giving the two-fingered salute.'

The opening *Eyes In The Night* is a reworking of the older song *Arrive Alive*.

Graeme Murray: '*Eyes In The Night* was written in a 'fit of pique' on getting a crop of record company refusals. It was spawned at the same time as *Paris Is Burning* and *Stranger On The Edge Of Time*. [We wrote] these three singles in one evening. What can I say? Heads down and rock, sing along you buggas, get the picture? Somewhat improved in Atlanta with a new middle eight for the instrumental and a new intro. The song isn't a great favourite with the band on record as it has been around for so long, but is great stuff live for winding the pace up during the show. Changing the title of the track… was done out of necessity, legal things and all that.'

Cut And Run, working title *The Spy Song*, dates back a couple of years. Ronnie Brown explained how the song was developed.

'The plot behind *The Spy Song*,' he noted, 'is loosely based on Orwell's *1984* with the 'thought police' in mind. In the live show Euan portrays 'a state executioner', whose job is to track down and execute enemies of the state, i.e., people who think for themselves. The musical marriage of the song was born out of the original verse-chorus pattern, written two years before, and a piano piece which I had put forward. The two ideas worked well together and combined to form a very complete sounding 'backbone' for what was later to become *Cut And Run*. The real fun began [in] the studio in Atlanta. Before we recorded the backing track for the song, we recorded roughly twelve to fifteen different arrangements onto cassette, trying different [combinations] of verse, chorus and bridge passages, before all five of us settled on the version which can now be heard on *The Sentinel*. We wanted to combine a 1960s spy movie feeling with a *1984* overall flavour. To obtain this combination, I used various brass arrangements, over the *Cut And Run* bridge sections and also the slight adaptation on the *James Bond Theme*. I feel it is also interesting to point out that, at one time, we even had a little brass piece in the song, which was so authentic, that it sounded like we had flown in the Earth Wind & Fire horn section. It was later replaced by Niall's Glen Miller sax section, which was done with his trusty E-Bow. The orchestral arrangement at the end comprises of strings, brass and church organ counterparts. The original piano piece was symphonic in structure, having theme and development sections, with use of all the instruments; the song is eventually brought to a very stirring conclusion.'

At the time of release, *Rise And Fall* was Graeme Murray's favourite track on the album.

'Though I'm not sure why!' he said. 'The story line actually preceded the music, being the history of the Atlanteans and explaining the Sentinel's existence, i.e. the domed computer that saves the Earth from Armageddon in Atlantis. Euan and I enjoyed the challenge of taking the story and turning it into lyrics. We felt that a spoken monologue would complete the dramatic feel to the track and would tie it up well with Atlantis in which we had already planned to use commentary.'

In concerts, Euan would portray a warrior from the 'people of the West', singing on his knees on the battlefield, dying from his wounds and fallout. The track ends with an astonishing solo from Niall Mathewson.

Graeme Murray: 'I feel great satisfaction with this track as I feel it really bridges the gulf between prog rock and heavy metal, which is something I like to think Pallas' music does, more so than any other band to date.'

Shock Treatment is the only song on the album which was written during the sessions in Atlanta.

'We took enough material over to complete a double album,' said Euan Lowson, 'but on listening to everything over it was felt that several tracks would benefit from further development at a later stage, and also that the album would be more complete and better balanced with the addition of a shorter and quite direct track. We obviously wanted a track that would tie in with the loose overall concept, and as *Cut And Run* was the Orwellian Hunter song, the logical conclusion was that the victims' point of view be put forward. A working title was the next problem and when *Shock Treatment* was suggested, the vital link fell into place. We felt the song should reflect the confusion, frustration and rage that would be felt by a victim of the 1984 system, and the relentless pace of the number conveys this panic very well.'

The idea for *Arc Of Infinity* came to Niall Mathewson early one morning.

'I actually woke up with the idea swimming about in my mind,' he said, 'but it didn't actually click until the second slice of toast. I took the tune to Ronnie. [He] and Graeme had written an instrumental section for keyboards around a pacey drum pattern and this seemed to fit well with the part that I had written, and also with the story that was now taking shape. Euan and Graeme came up with some beautiful lyrics. Like many of our songs, there were several levels of meaning behind them. One interpretation is the idea of the last survivors on a dying planet who set sail aboard the ark into deep space to find a new home in the stars. Their course was set on the arc of infinity. When we came to record it in Atlanta, we wanted to create the feeling of space. I had also wanted to lay back the guitar, treating it more as a textured tone than a lead instrument, with lots of reverb and a sound that leaned towards the higher harmonics. If you listen, you can hear them ring. Ronnie had the chance to layer his keyboard tracks many times, giving a huge and very full sound, something he'd wanted to do for a long time. I used the Roland guitar synth during the 'look on through space' section with the oscillators set slightly apart to give a breath of strings to the proceedings. Also hats off to Graeme for some tasteful harmony lines, and Derek for the finger bells.'

Atlantis was born out of a jam session in June 1981.

'*Atlantis* appeared out of thin air,' Euan Lowson explained. 'That [opening] one-and-a-half-minute section of music conjured up such vivid images of the dome rising up through storm-tossed and turbulent seas that a condensed version of the saga was written in literally less than half an hour. Over the next six months to a year, *Atlantis* was gradually

1984: A Bleeding Heart Poet In A Fragile Capsule

honed into shape.'

This lyrical idea would eventually be worked into the entire concept of *The Sentinel* album.

'The song, on the surface, is fantasy,' Lowson said, 'but below that is a reflection of current conflict and potential destruction.'

Chris Watts in *Kerrang!* was very favourable: 'Having been temporarily taken under Eddie Offord's wing and having been exposed to the American market, Pallas have benefitted greatly in musical terms. Anyone in possession of the band's decidedly dodgy *Arrive Alive* self-produced album will notice a remarkable leap. Whereas *Arrive Alive* was barely above the turgid level, this new platter is a cohesive collection of length and breadth, from the might of *Ark Of Infinity* and *Atlantis* to the snappy single orientated material including *Shock Treatment* and a re-working of *Arrive Alive* itself - the latter under scrutiny for possible single material. It's an album of variation; given the time and money to experiment slightly Pallas have uncovered a rare tomb of gold.'

To coincide with the release of *The Sentinel*, the band were pictured on the front cover of *Sounds*, 11 February 1984, with a 3000-word feature and interview inside.

As the roads became icier and the landscape more barren, the manic driver of the hyper-charged Capri ground the ball of his foot into the accelerator. He leered over his shoulder at the demure PR lady and announced with a roar: 'I havnae had a crash for ages. I think I'm about due for one.' I pretended not to hear and concentrated on sucking a boiled sweet, something I always do to unblock my ears when the sound barrier is breaking. Slamming the car into top as we tore round a hairpin, Mad Graeme urged the machine through the banks of frozen snow.

We were deep into the Aberdeen tundra, bound for Ice Station Echt where Pallas rehearse in a farmhouse which was almost completely cut off by snow a fortnight ago. Suddenly we did a 90-degree turn on iced cow poo. Nobody was injured, but you get the idea of what sort of a Monday it was turning out to be.

The Sentinel shows that [Pallas] have pulled themselves out of the shadow of Marillion and established themselves as frontrunners in their own right. Did working in America live up to their expectations?

Euan: 'I think it probably surpassed our expectations because we didn't really know what to expect. It was quite a culture shock, both being in America and actually having the opportunity to have two months solid studio time.'

Do you think you benefited from being in the studio?

Graeme: 'It was really good because we were able to immerse ourselves in the whole thing, as opposed to *Arrive Alive* which was just one gig. We'd never had the chance to build tracks up from scratch before, and we learnt a lot as regards recording techniques. We'd never had the luxury of time in a studio.'

It was a brave move to choose a producer who must surely be regarded as 'progressive' inasmuch as he was involved with Yes and ELP...

'He definitely brought things out of our music,' proffers Euan. 'One major thing that surfaced on this album was vocal harmonies. Not the bland, Americanised vocal harmonies you can expect, as we thought.'

'He was also very interested in what we were doing—he had a feel for the sound that we wanted . . . we like a certain sort of ambience,' explains guitarist Niall Mathewson. 'He was aware of that.'

Let's go back to more exciting things - things like progressive rock! Mention that in the Pallas camp and you're more likely to be greeted with rolled eyeballs rather than reefers, and a derisive snort rather than the offer of a bowl of muesli.

Graeme explains: 'It appeals to the people who were into Yes and Genesis and are now looking for something new from the music they have liked since the early 70s, and it also appeals to kids who have maybe listened to big brother's albums and are looking for bands of their own… instead of listening to old Genesis albums. If you look at the album charts, you'll notice that all those old albums still sell steadily. There's obviously a market there, but we feel that it's about time the oldies moved over and made room for some new bands. We all go through musical fads and phases, and at certain times in one's life one latches on to bands and then (after puberty!) moves on to other things.'

Do you think that Pallas are a band who people are going to get into and then pass on from?

Euan: 'No. I think amongst ourselves we all realise we've got to develop yet as musicians - and hopefully that will continue as we carry on as the same five-piece unit. And we have people of all ages at gigs.'

There exists within Pallas a mutual rapport and camaraderie the likes of which I have encountered very rarely in a band. Unusually, they are all possessed with a quiet, telling humour - and an infectious enthusiasm for life which rubs off on you straight away.

But although they may have set off fire extinguishers in Solstice's dressing room and generally remained unimpressed by the kilo bags of aforementioned muesli (and a cow in the dressing room for milk.), Euan adds honestly, 'They were a good bunch.'

It's hard to even equate Pallas with the progressive rock revival ('revival' as in 'artificial respiration', because their completely down-to-earth attitudes and ideas are so far removed from the many bands who make up that particular media creation). However, it's not my place to defend bands' reputations - they'd be the first to admit and agree with that.

IQ were booked at The Marquee again on 23 February, their fifth headliner.

'So, is everybody hot enough?' Peter Nicholls asked the audience that night. 'Some of you here probably read the music magazine *Sounds*. If you do, you've probably heard the recent results of the readers' poll. In the new bands section in sixteenth position there was a band by the name of IQ [the audience applauds]. For all those that voted for us, it wasn't me either. By way of saying thank you, this is a new track. We played it for the first time at the last Marquee. This one is in a slightly re-arranged and written form and I probably can't remember the words for this one either. I've got a crib sheet down here, so I want to see that first. This one is… this!'

Mike Holmes leads them into *Widow's Peak*, one of the key songs from the band's next album, still

1984: A Bleeding Heart Poet In A Fragile Capsule

IQ promo in 1984 (From the collection of Guy Tkach)

Below: IQ at The Marquee in 1984 (Photograph by Mark Drake)

over a year away. It would be worked on further in the weeks and months to come. The intensity of the final number, *The Enemy Smacks*, was leavened by encores of the band's Glenn Miller medley and Peter Nicholls' tongue-in-cheek *Sweet Transvestite*.

The second leg of Genesis's *Mama* tour took in 30 dates across the US and Canada in January and February 1984. Five dates back in the UK at the NEC in Birmingham closed out the tour. The first of these, 25 February, coincided with a Twelfth Night show at JBs in Dudley. At least two fans are known to have rushed across Birmingham after the Genesis show to catch the end of Twelfth Night's gig.

In an unusual move, no doubt encouraged by a first prize of a £10,000 promo video, mid-way through their support stint on the Marillion tour

A PLAYGROUND OF BROKEN HEARTS

Pendragon at The Marquee
(Photograph by Mark Drake)

Pendragon, 1984 (Photograph by Brian Cairns)

Pendragon took a night off, 29 February, to take part in a 'battle of the bands' at the Goldiggers Club in Chippenham. This was broadcast by the local HTV television station on 5 March as a TV show called *Best Bands West*. Pendragon performed *O Devineo* (spelling as credited on TV).

Nick Barrett: 'There were a lot of people there, which was fantastic. The audience reaction was brilliant but it wasn't really seen by very many people.'

A Bristol-based covers duo eventually won the contest.

In Pendragon's absence, Marillion's support slot at Southampton Gaumont that night was filled by the highly-regarded Middlesex-based four-piece Liaison.

Audience member Phil Morris tells the story of the first time he saw Twelfth Night, at Avery Hill College in Eltham on 2 March 1984: 'It was a health and safety nightmare. First having to be asked to stand back from the low stage to avoid the entrance explosions, and then, during *The Ceiling Speaks*, Andy Sears' tambourine flew out of his grasp and hit me square in the balls. I thought I'd scored my first piece of genuine rock and roll memorabilia, but a very gracious and apologetic Mr Sears requested its return at the end of the song, as it was his only one.'

Twelfth Night performed two more back-to-back shows at The Marquee, 3 and 4 March. The following evening, in Leicester, Marillion's concert would be professionally recorded. Three tracks found a place on 1984's live album *Real To Reel*; two more are included on the US-only EP *Brief Encounter*; *Chelsea Monday* appears on the 1988 album *The Thieving Magpie*.

Over four days in March 1984, all of the big six bands would be active in London.

On 9 March 1984, a rare video document from inside The Marquee shows Twelfth Night performing their current set. This went out live in Finland, Norway, Switzerland, France and Germany, and was also recorded for subsequent broadcast in the UK as part of a TV series *Live From London*. Five miles west, Marillion were headlining the first of three consecutive nights at the Hammersmith Odeon, supported by Pendragon.

'For me, to be playing on the same stage as all my favourite musicians have played on over the years was magical,' Peter Gee recalled. 'It was a night I will never forget. During *Leviathan*, I was meant to give the rest of the band a cue and er… I forgot, with the result that half the band changed into the next section and the other half didn't. We then thrashed around on a D chord till Rik saved us by putting on the arpeggiator on his keyboard! It is still the closest we have come to stopping mid-song on stage.'

That same evening Pallas recorded three songs in a live-in-the-studio session for the *Friday Rock Show*: *Cut And Run*, *Shock Treatment* and a *Rise And Fall/ Heart Attack* medley. These were broadcast on 30

1984: A Bleeding Heart Poet In A Fragile Capsule

March 1984.

Solstice performed at The Marquee on 10 and 11 March and, amidst all of this, the dark, brooding *Fugazi* saw release on 12 March, a week later than originally planned.

'I actually came across 'fugazi' in Mark Baker's book (*Nam*),' Fish said. 'And I just thought, 'What a fucking great word!'. It became a bit of a call word within the band: 'How are you doing?' 'Ohhh, totally fugazi.' The original title of the album was going to be *Afterthoughts Glow Afterwards*, but that didn't feel comfortable. *Fugazi* fits perfectly with the whole span of the album.'

The first 90 seconds of *Assassing* are pure Peter Gabriel, all Middle Eastern style rumblings and mystic brooding. Fish's lyrics are typically wordy, but the 'my friend' hook is extremely catchy and Steve Rothery's guitar solo is both edgy and aggressive. Ian Mosley is brilliant throughout. The tight single edit removes much of the fluff. The short, arrhythmic paranoia of *Punch And Judy* follows. *Jigsaw* is perhaps overlooked after the two hit singles which precede it. It's probably the best song on the album, much closer to the progressive rock of *Script For A Jester's Tear*. The arpeggio bears a remarkable, if presumably coincidental, resemblance to Twelfth Night's *Sequences* and the powerful, emotional choruses ('Stand straight, look me in the eye and say goodbye…') give way to a fluid, soaring guitar solo from Steve Rothery, the undoubted highlight of the track.

Emerald Lies is a mini-suite of different elements and showcases superb work by Ian Mosley and Pete Trewavas. From 3.31, this is classic progressive rock, with flowing, uplifting chord changes under Fish's relatively understated vocals. *She Chameleon* is one of the oldest songs on the album, performed live as early as June 1982, but in a very different musical arrangement. It is atmospheric, with eerie keyboards and distinctive drumming. The dark and complex *Incubus* is menacing and, if we skip over the awkward 'nursing an erection' lyrics, the theme of betrayal is powerful and dark. From 3.57, the song changes utterly, to a delightful off-kilter waltz with an utterly gorgeous romantic guitar solo. The track builds to a satisfyingly powerful conclusion.

A PLAYGROUND OF BROKEN HEARTS

IQ in Aberdeen, 16 March 1984
(Photograph by Kevin Mackenzie / ticket from the collection of Kevin Mackenzie)

The closing track, *Fugazi*, features many tempo changes through its eight minutes. It sometimes feels like several songs stitched together but the 'Where are the prophets? / Where are the poets?' ending is uplifting and fulfilling.

'*Fugazi*, for reasons both good and bad, is still probably the hardest Marillion album for first-time buyers to grapple with,' writes Mick Wall. 'The material is not to blame, the seven numbers contained on *Fugazi* represented the band's most elevated and determined work to date; nor can the playing be faulted. The fault all too clearly lies in the production, which is constantly busy and colourfully ambitious, but curiously soulless and tainted by the whiff of a strange introspection that often obscures the album's best moments. Where [Nick] Tauber's work on the first Marillion album had highlighted the band's vulnerable, early sound, throwing a careful light over fragile backwards waltzes like *The Web* and *Chelsea Monday*, dressing the rest up with a coat-of-arms stamp that gave meaning to every scattered pause in the music, every sigh, every swing, given twice the money and twice the time and with twice the expertise at his disposal, what Tauber had effectively managed to do to tracks like *Incubus*, *She Chameleon*, and *Fugazi* was to produce a sound which the band found unacceptable.'

The sleeve once again is full of potent imagery. The jester lies in a bed-sit, poppy in one-hand, half-spilled glass of wine in the other. Three bleak albums lie nearby: Pink Floyd's *The Wall*, and two by Peter Hammill: *Fool's Mate* and *Over*.

That same day, EMI released a two-track video EP, containing *Grendel* and *The Web*. Marillion were in Chippenham recording an enthusiastic, if road-weary, set for BBC's *Sight And Sound In Concert* series at the Goldiggers Club.

'Remember this gig well as it was tagged on at the end of a gruelling tour that had been booked well before the actual album was ready,' Fish wrote. 'We ended up with it being released almost as it finished. I was pretty fragged and last thing I needed was a live TV appearance. There's lots of stories around this performance/event. Trashing the BBC crew and Steve Blacknell the presenter at Pop Quiz in the bar the night before as we introduced them to the dreaded Grendel cocktail as a forfeit to wrong answers! Walking up the streets of Chippenham in the dawn to find a hospital for my badly cut and damaged elbow after falling off a balcony in the early hours while trying to throw a fertilizer bag full of water over the manager. I forgot to let go and followed the bag over the rail to the concrete below. Only the Grendels softened the blow!'

IQ performed at The Marquee on 13 March. For

their final encore they played a raucous version of The Tubes' *White Punks On Dope*. A recording of the show reveals a loud voice shouting, 'Come on, Pete, get yer top off!' Nicholls responds, saying, 'I'm not taking my shirt off. You lot saw enough of me last time!' The audience start chanting, 'off, off, off'. 'No. You'll have to be content with my bottom from last time, that's all you're getting. There's a, there's a very funny smell around here. And it's none of us, I'll tell you. In view of this we'd like to bring things down to a more ordinary level now. In keeping with IQ gigs at The Marquee, we'd like to play you a song which isn't one of ours. So everybody better join in, alright?'

What follows is a remarkable punk/prog crossover with Nicholls pushing vocals to breaking point.

At the end of that week they travelled to Scotland for bookings in Aberdeen, Inverness, Bathgate, Hamilton and Bannockburn. During the tour they were interviewed by Tom Russell of Radio Clyde, who would, a few weeks later, help Pallas to find a new singer.

Immediately after their own March dates at The Marquee, Solstice headed to the West Country where they would record their debut album with producer Nigel Mazlyn Jones in a converted rectory.

'I had been a full-time singer-songwriter since 1972,' Mazlyn Jones says, 'and by 1983 was trying to get off the road forever gigging away from home, so I could spend more time with my wife and two young children. Throughout the 1970s other artists asked me to record them and these occasional mobile recordings developed into also giving workshops in recording giving access to younger musicians. I'd always wanted a permanent base where I could make in-depth recordings. We knew friends who lived in a large, old Georgian rectory in Boyton in Devon. They suggested using the rectory as a possible recording venue. I started recording there. Musician friends came to record and friends' teenage kids' bands made demos. It was great fun and financially just about viable, so I invested in more equipment.'

Mazlyn Jones and his family moved into the rectory and started to take bookings.

'In early 1984, Solstice asked me to produce them. They had heard my second album, *Sentinel*, at Margaret Phillips' house in Tring where the band often jammed, rehearsed, wrote songs and ate.'

Mazlyn Jones attended a Solstice gig at The Marquee.

'The sound was rough, intense and edgy,' he recalls. 'The gig was packed out and the band sweated but gelled well, making a good vibe overall. I thought the violin and guitar pairing and their intuitive playing with Sandy's soaring voice worked great. There was a folky edge to it all, reminding me of the electric folk of Fairport and Pentangle but harder edged and more intense. The drums and bass were very solid. There seemed to be loads of potential in the band. I wanted to help. I am not and have never been a prog rock artist, just a folky guy inspired by various songwriters and players. I concentrated on 12-string intricacies and acoustic sounds, loving exploring adding effects to my live sound. Then met other players from other genres who seemed to like my approach to music and worked with me now and then. It was fan mags and articles in music press that lumped me into the genre title 'prog rock'. They didn't know which other bin to dump me in. My fault. Been fun though, mostly. But the die-hard folkies never ever forgave me to this day. Pass me the tankard, I feel a shanty coming on.'

We'll live a hermit-like existence for a few weeks in the seclusion of a small studio. We are grateful to [Nigel] Mazlyn Jones for agreeing to produce the album, and look forward to an inspiring experience. We'll be recording more material than we actually need, so at this stage we can't be sure of the songs which will be on the album, but we can confirm, without hesitation, that our tribute to the progressive rock revival *Don't Tell Me* **** will not appear.

The album will be released to coincide with a national tour by the band in May and June.

Solstice newsletter, 1984

'That's the Holy Grail, isn't it, for a band?' Andy Glass mused. 'To do a 12-inch album? But it was just out of our budget until the day we got a little publishing deal. They gave us an advance, and we thought, 'Right, we will use this to record an album… this is our opportunity to do it…' Our days at Hedgehog House were immersed in music and one of the artists we adored was Nigel Mazlyn Jones and, in particular, the albums *Sentinel* and *Ship To Shore*… just beautiful albums. We listened to him a lot. Nigel was contacted and he said, 'Yeah, I'm interested in producing your album'… We were thrilled about that. So, we had a bit of money and we had Nigel Mazlyn Jones.'

'Both Marc and Andy were familiar with Nigel's work,' says Martin Wright, 'and felt he would be a good fit to produce the album. We all believed we were finally doing the album that we had wanted to do for so long.'

Andy Glass: 'His studio was down in Cornwall in this idyllic vicarage… a residential studio, what more could you ask? We booked two weeks, which is what our budget would allow. At the end of two weeks, I think we essentially had the drums down and guide tracks. So, immediately there was an issue.'

Martin Wright: 'I loved the time I got to spend in Cornwall. The drum tracks were done very quickly, and I was pretty happy with them.'

'Martin Wright was a lovely guy and an easy drummer to work with,' says Nigel Mazlyn Jones. 'We spent enjoyable hours perfecting the drum kit's sound before recording started. I never started the studio charges clock running for recording until setting up of equipment was finished throughout the whole process. Same for miking up a lead guitar cabinet, combining it with the DI signal while searching for the lead guitarist's best sound so they can create the most inspiring overdubs. Marc had to use an overhead mic plus his DIs for violin overdubs, which he found frustrating being used to using only DIs. The backing tracks went well, and we all agreed what to keep and use to go forward. Some took two takes and some more. Their live feel was embedded in the backing tracks, so everyone was happy. From setting everything up so each player was happy to finishing backing tracks was about four days.'

'Everything was set up in the main room, and there were wires through a wall into this little box room, which was where the mixing desk was,' Andy Glass said. 'We were all pretty much on the dole at the time, so recording time had to be worked around signing-on days. The guy who owned that house was a bit of a stoner as well. And then we had to get back to Milton Keynes to sign on.'

Andy Glass: 'Myself and Marc made many a trip to Cornwall that summer. We'd jump in his Austin Maxi for the long drive, popping in on the remnants of Stonehenge Free Festival for supplies along the way. Loved those road trips.'

Sessions were planned to last for three weeks, but problems between the band and Mazlyn Jones stretched the project to more than five months.

'The band were in a wonderful, atmospheric old building in the middle of nowhere, well away from their reality, so they could really focus on themselves, their friendships and their music,' said Mazlyn Jones. 'They were a family to themselves and had their own support system. I was up against it from the start though, as it was pushing the limit for an eight-track recording desk. I must admit that I wasn't the paragon of diplomatic communication. If I'd worked 23 hours, was knackered, and they'd all had a wonderful supper, chilled out, were having a nice time and cracked open a bottle, then there would have been a gulf of understanding.'

These extended sessions generated high studio bills, which the band could ill afford.

'More overdubs were added over the next few weeks,' Mazlyn Jones explains. 'Some overdubs took a long time as the players searched for their definitive performances that would be as good as their backing tracks demanded. As the overdubs and mixes stretched their costs, I allowed the debt to stretch ahead to help them out. They left the studio with a finished album, a deal and an advance owing me and the studio a debt of £1,300. They were younger than me with little studio recording experience and some of them had to learn more about studio processes to produce the results they knew so well in their live work. From the outset I explained the method and process using two eight-track machines and we all agreed this would work for their first album. We had estimated basic costs of between £1,500 and £2,000 but that didn't include unforeseen problems or changes as the album developed. I leaned a long way over to ensure the costs were kept low. They agreed and promised future staged payments from giros and future gigs. I drew up a letter where the band agreed to pay me each week until the debt was settled. That never happened and so my income stalled. This broke us financially. We had no other income. I was not a gigging musician but a fledgling studio producer engineer. With the band's agreement I arranged for the contracts to be checked by a solicitor and tried to make sure the band did not get ripped off. I got them an advance of £3,000 and took £500 of that towards the studio debt.'

With the album finished and the band now touring, the story now took a darker turn, when the owner of the rectory decided to wash his hands of Mazlyn Jones and the very idea of a residential recording studio.

'He locked the rectory doors, leaving directions with a neighbour to 'call the police if Nigel turns up',' Mazlyn Jones says. 'I had been gigging and when I got back found myself locked out of my family home and studio and a note on the door saying I was 'banned'. He was bored with me and the studio, and it was time for him to move on and sling me and my family out.'

Mazlyn Jones was able to break in and retrieve his family's possessions.

'I found a full-on sophisticated witches' circle in the loft above my family's bedroom,' he says.

The trauma and debt had lasting repercussions for Mazlyn Jones.

'That Solstice album bankrupted me,' he said, 'ruined the studio, cost me a divorce, rammed my life into the ground and it took me ten years to recover from financially and emotionally. But I've made my peace with Solstice and I still look back on those sessions fondly.'

Martin Wright: 'I liked Nigel despite the fact he sued us for money and kind of respected his reasons.'

As Pendragon played once more at The Marquee, 19 March, Sandy Robertson reviewed Pallas' *The Sentinel* in that week's *Sounds*.

As I recall, the movie *The Sentinel* was a weird tale concerning a gateway to the bowels of hell which had to be guarded in order to prevent all manner of fiends of the pit escaping into the everyday world. I'd expected this first studio offering from Aberdeen team Pallas to be pretty damn hellish, too, what with their rep as heroes of the progressive revival, and the LP being masterminded by ELP/Yes controller Eddy Offord. But let's be fair.

Readers of last issue's Pallas story will have noted that the band, while not denying where their musical interests lie, are keen to escape the boundaries of categorisation, and in truth, the record at hand reflects this ambition. The opener, *Eyes In The Night*, blends hard rock with harmony, and while it's certainly cliché-laden, it must be said that there's a definite sprightliness to the sound, if not the style.

And this sets the tone for much of the disc: *Cut And Run* may borrow heavily from groups like Genesis (Gabriel era) in both the keyboard and vocal departments, but it bursts into a sweeping, uplifting melody a la synth, reminiscent of the best cowpoke cinerama epics, and yet quite light and - more importantly - modern. ELP (say) could never have managed anything so unencumbered and devoid of pomp.

This isn't to say that Pallas are a) my personal choice for innovators of '84 or b) likely to attain the huge success of their mega predecessors. But who knows, really? *Rise And Fall*, closing the first side, is lethargic/derivative/overlong, and includes a hilarious voice-over that'd embarrass Manowar, with only a deft guitar part at the end to commend it. Which makes me think it might go down a storm in the stadium wastelands of the USA.

For boyz who protest agin being dubbed prog-rockers, they certainly do make all the bad moves: cluttered Patrick Woodroffe cover art/full of science-fiction Trojans in gas-masks, ya dig? A foldout, too, with lyrics... on Harvest of course! Remember Forest and Third Ear Band? You don't? Well...

But a lot of people do, I guess. *Shock Treatment*, *Ark Of Infinity* and the Yes-cribbed *Atlantis* make up the flip, and sound just like you'd expect 'em to. And yet ... as with the previous cuts, an occasional snatch of guitar or synthesiser will jump up and make you think that Pallas, with such technical ability and quirky notions are - must be - capable of so much more!

Judicious editing could transform them into a fine pop band, possibly... but that might lose them the audience they've already won.

Still — they're no worse than Duran Duran. And maybe that's who they wanna be! Their biog describes the lengthy, tedious cuts on side two as 'Snappy, singles-oriented material' (!). Oh, well - it's only pomp'n'roll...

Dave Dickson of *Kerrang!* reviewed *The Sentinel* in issue 63 (22 March – 4 April).

I may have mentioned this before but the point is worth repeating: the great Theodore Sturgeon once stated that 90 per cent of everything is crap, and this applies as much (if not more) to the record industry as it does to the rest of creation.

The problem we're faced with here is just where does Pallas' debut album fit into this scheme of things? Is it part of the majority (bilge), or is it amongst the coveted few (brilliant)? The only answer I can come up with is to sit the thing on the fence, which is a cop-out, I'd be the first to agree, but then *The Sentinel* has a foot entrenched in each camp so really, there's no other place for it.

The basic problem is a disconcerting one of time-shift which is very much of Pallas' making. There are six tracks on this album, of which three, *Eyes In The Night*, *Cut And Run* and *Shock Treatment*, are singles contenders jaunting along for the most part at a goodly pace and generally rocking out with the best of them. The other three, however, *Rise And Fall*, *Ark Of Infinity* and *Atlantis Suite* although fine tracks, sound SO dated.

Pallas have allowed themselves to be buried under a mound of (admittedly) very slick production that nevertheless reeks of that early seventies 'art rock' feel with which Offord had so much success when producing bands like Yes and ELP (my God, even Yes had the suss to bring in Trevor Horn - the producer of the eighties sound! - to knob-twiddle on *90125*).

Pallas may argue that I've missed the point and that this isn't supposed to be taken seriously, that this is 'escapist' music - which is fine, but why can't we escape into the future (or even the present)? Why do we have to be dragged back through time when, Goddammit, the band have the potential to give it all to us now?!!

Pallas prove they have this potential on those three tracks I mentioned at the beginning. They're also very good to watch live, but I get the impression that EMI had them over a barrel with this album and that they were pretty much told what to do, i.e. leave it to the producer, boys, he knows what he's doing, cue long list of hit albums Eddie Offord has produced. Offord was probably in his element with those great memories flooding back to him. Maybe this shows a lack of character on the band's part, maybe they simply didn't have a choice, maybe I'm wrong, who knows? But tell me this, who the hell decided to get a Roger Dean clone to design their artwork? That's just plain asking for trouble.

If it sounds like I've got a real downer on this album that would be misleading, because it is undoubtedly superbly performed and the production, of its type, is wonderful. Pallas have been given a rich, textured sound and I wouldn't hesitate to recommend this to any fan of the early seventies art bands, but for others, I'm not so sure. What I'd say to them is buy the brilliant

Eyes In The Night (Arrive Alive) single (which I remember plugging when it was plain old *Arrive Alive*), a song that strongly deserves to be a hit, and then go and check out the band live.

I hate to be non-committal because this album is far too good to be slagged but, on the other hand, there's too many question marks hanging over this band at the moment for it to warrant unbridled praise. Approach with caution.

That same issue included a full-page ad for *Fugazi*, which entered the UK charts at number 5 on 24 March. Howard Jones - Marillion's support for two nights at The Marquee in July 1982 - was at number 1 with his just-released debut album *Human's Lib*.

In late March, Pallas set out on their biggest tour yet: three weeks of theatre dates across the UK between 24 March and 12 April. The Infinity Tunnel was a mirrored onstage effect that gave the appearance of a never-ending tunnel. Euan would flit in and out during the performance. The band's first date, in Aberdeen naturally, was reported in detail in the next issue of the band's newsletter. Somebody somewhere may not have known the difference between feet and inches:

Although having planned the production for many months, it wasn't until the short production rehearsals at the Glasgow Apollo two days before the first gig that the band and production first met. Unfortunately it became immediately apparent that the risers on either side of the tunnel were not built to the correct dimensions, the drum kit barely fitted on. Hasty arrangements were made to rush side extensions to Aberdeen for the first gig, but the height couldn't be altered until the show got to Birmingham.

The costumes were just as had been designed, but the new Sentinel helmet caused Euan a few difficulties as he couldn't properly see where he was going. The production took much longer to put together than had been thought and the show only had one complete run-through before the gear was dismantled and trucked to a windswept and wet Aberdeen. The band's faithful tour coach, Vic, was now too small and ill-equipped to sleep the fifteen band and crew. So accommodation and transport was a Trathens Starider hired for the tour, which drove through the gales with the two artics of gear.

Playing your first theatre gig at home in front of all your relations, friends and enemies is certainly a nerve wracking experience; but the home crowd's enthusiastic response certainly helped overcome the first night nerves. After Aberdeen it was on to the band's second home Glasgow, this time to the Pavilion theatre, a much more civilized venue than the decaying Apollo. Of all the gigs on the tour the atmosphere here was the most electric, re-creating the feeling of the old days at the Dial Inn around the corner. The intensity reached an unbearable climax during the final sequence of *Crown Of Thorns* when a number of people in the front row fainted. The first-aiders quickly dragged the victims away, but some returned only to pass out again. Hard on the heels of this climax came the opening sequence of Atlantis with the awe-inspiring sight of Euan, in the guise of the Sentinel, emerging red-eyes glowing, from the smoke-filled strobe-lit 'infinity tunnel'. A magic piece of rock-theatre

1984: A Bleeding Heart Poet In A Fragile Capsule

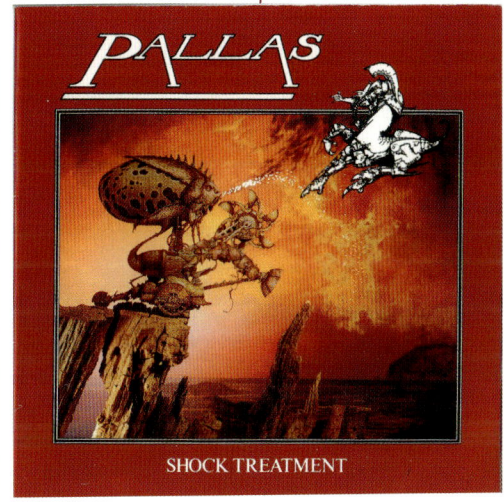

Shock Treatment
(From the collection of Piersandro Pallavicini)

UK tour ad from *Sounds*, 17 March 1984
(From the collection of Guy Tkach)

which had the crowd in ecstasy. The encores took on a great party atmosphere with old favourite A Bit Of Culture having them dancing in their seats.

Pallas' second single for EMI, *Shock Treatment*, was released to coincide with the tour, and would give the band their highest-ever singles chart placing, reaching number 82 in mid-April. On 27 March 1984, Pallas would play at the Hammersmith Odeon, with Twelfth Night supporting.

The next Pallas newsletter noted that they, 'will be first to admit that this wasn't quite the blockbuster that they'd hoped for. Nerves had got the better of them, with the flow and communication so apparent at Glasgow strangely lacking. That said, audience reaction was phenomenal with two encores and a curtain call. Critical reaction varied from highly complimentary in *Music* and *Soundcheck* to downright poisonous: - Phil Bell's review in *Sounds*. However good or bad the gig may have been, it was a valuable experience and changes made as a result certainly made a difference. The next two gigs at Hanley and Manchester were the last on the first leg of the tour with the full production. With the minor running order and presentation changes enacted, and the production firing on six cylinders.'

Despite the new exposure that Twelfth Night were

enjoying there was still no long-term recording contract on the horizon. But there were some green shoots. Both Tony Smith from Hit & Run and Barclay James Harvest's manager, David Walker, attended the Hammersmith show and expressed an interest in working with Twelfth Night.

Pendragon supported Pallas at the Manchester Apollo three days later, as reported in the Pallas newsletter: 'The Manchester Apollo was particularly memorable, if only for the Ronnie Reagan death hoax!'

This refers to comments made onstage in Manchester by Euan Lowson. These would have major implications for Pallas in the weeks to come.

As the tour progressed, Pallas and Pendragon performed together at Rock City in Nottingham on 4 April. The Scottish band received important promotion in that week's *Melody Maker*. Writer Derek Oliver starts, ominously,

A PLAYGROUND OF BROKEN HEARTS

Andy Revell, Twelfth Night
Harrow College, 29 March 1984
(Photograph by Aire Valley Photography/Twelfth Night Archive)

Pallas at the Edinburgh Playhouse, 2 April 1984
(Photographs by Peter Forster)

with a half-apology.

'Before we go any further, I'd better lay the cards face up on the table and state quite openly and proudly that Pallas are a progressive rock band,' Oliver wrote. 'Yeah go on, turn the page if you must, hide your face in the acceptability of this week's fave rave, pretend that it's all some kind of passing joke. A flick of the wrist would be the easiest remedy for all you level-headed critics of dangerous, provocative pop. However, if challenges are required, then read on… music fans. Admitting influences can often blight a flourishing reputation. Look what happened to Adam Ant when his dated respect for Alice Cooper crept out into the open. Heartfelt affection for past musical trends - stepping conveniently over the chic, baggy-suited-trad-jazz buffoons - is definitely treated as something approaching near lunacy. But why? Why should an appreciation of Barclay James Harvest, Greenslade, Peter Hammill, Henry Cow et al be scoffed at with such malign distaste? There probably isn't a universal reason: hip kids simply

require hip trends and, if they bothered to think about it hard enough, hip trends (take a bow Mr. Businessman) require hip kids. Natural induction or corporate policy? The answer is visible but the eyes are squinted.'

Oliver suggested that Pallas' hometown gig at the Capitol Theatre [24 March 1984] had 'mark[ed] the end of one rather traumatic period for Pallas and heralds the start of a new and decidedly optimistic future'.

'Ye Gods!' Graeme Murray is quoted as saying. 'It honestly frightens me to death when I think back. It came to the point after so many false promises from record companies where we just had to take the future into our own hands. We knew that our material had a big market, Marillion's album proved it, but the companies were still very reluctant to take a chance. So we had a meeting and decided that we could either split up or put every penny we had into the recording of *The Sentinel*. I went home, thought about it in the evening and came back the following day with the same choice as everyone else. It was so frightening yet strangely exciting. We all knew that the music was good enough but to actually put ourselves on the line was the ultimate sacrifice. From there we started to sell everything that wasn't essential; equipment, cars, junk, anything that could raise a few pounds. Our manager and myself took out second mortgages on our houses and we managed to get an overdraft facility from the bank. It was unbelievable yet essential to our survival.'

Parallels with Marillion were shunned.

'God, I hate those bloody comparisons,' Euan Lowson said. 'It springs from the press more than anyone else. The fans don't equate the two of us on that level at all and they are the people who count in the long run. The music press need to sell papers - they like glamorising and picking out what in their view are anomalies. It's also incorrect to say that we're following in Marillion's footsteps. If they bothered to investigate the histories of each band they'll find out that we've been around the longest, but Marillion always had the distinct advantage of being based in or near London. They got the deal first but I think it was simply down to exposure at that stage. We're definitely not jumping on a bandwagon and in a way I think we're a more underground band.'

Derek Oliver concluded: 'Pallas may be a large step behind Marillion at present, but I've got a feeling that Fish and co. could be on the verge of a tumble judging by the contents of *Fugazi*. On the other hand Pallas have a potentially longer career in front of them. Whatever: progressive rock (if you really want labels) does have a future and does have something positive to offer. Forget preconceived opinions and take a peek with Pallas.'

Oliver also reviewed *The Sentinel* in the same issue.

> By definition Pallas ought to be classed as progressive rock. That is the movement they have been most closely associated with and those are the fans who have stuck with them through thick and thin.
>
> But they have about as much in common with Yes and Genesis as Black Sabbath have with The Smiths or JoBoxers. An instantly identifiable sound of their own that is so breathlessly original and fresh that I suspect Marillion will soon be quaking in their boots. This is true progression

and not ambient regurgitation.

The 'sound' is the vital element although the sentiments may be slightly dated. Built on what could fundamentally be described as a solid, hard rock backing, fuel-injected with the subtlety and delicacy of the American pomp brigade, most notably that of Styx and Kansas. But what really puts Pallas on a plateau of their own is the sense of aggression and urgency.

Eyes In The Night meets this criterion perfectly. A romping rocker brimming over with the overblown pomposity of Queen (early) and Styx, not forgetting the solid metallic guitar solo... totally melodic yet bitingly effective. In fact the standard of guitar work by Niall Mathewson is both stunningly original and almost revolutionary in its clarity.

Cut And Run and *Shock Treatment* follow suit. The former built around sharp movements with a recurring theme reminiscent of the *Mission Impossible* soundtrack.

Rise And Fall in my view is a much more satisfying attempt at the epic. Razor sharp riffs dart to and fro across the Styxian keyboard pomposity.

Armed with the efficiently effective vocal strains and intriguing lyrics of Euan Lowson, Pallas have turned the progressive cards by becoming leaders of a more commanding and believable movement. Marillion's *Fugazi* may have a lot of explaining to do.

That same week, Twelfth Night benefitted from a two and a half page feature in *Kerrang!* issue 65 (5-18 April 1984). Chris Welch's article starts with the line 'Welcome to Nukeshire'.

The message, daubed on a road sign on the M4, pointed the way to Reading, epicentre of the nuclear destruction industry and home of Twelfth Night, a band of the Eighties who reflect the decade's mixture of paranoia and business-like urgency. Stuck in the Berkshire nuclear triangle, they are concerned about the Bomb, as their lyrics show. But they also burn up with energy and optimism.

Shrewd, keenly intelligent, Twelfth Night are pioneering their own kind of music and creating a DIY rock industry in the process.

The article features a blooper, with Welch asserting that Geoff Mann wrote the lyrics to *The End Of The Endless Majority*, a track that was, and always would be, an instrumental.

Twelfth Night's Clive Mitten has a few stories of the road from 1984.

'One night I came out of The Marquee, still in my make-up, heels and leopard skin dress and fell over into a pile of rubbish bags, only to be picked up, dusted down and escorted home by two ladies of the night. They recognised me and knew where I lived...'

Mitten's former colleague in Twelfth Night, Geoff Mann, made his first solo appearance on stage at the IQ gig at The Gallery in Manchester, 12 April 1984.

Peter Nicholls: 'I had spotted Geoff in the audience and pulled him on during the encore of Alice Cooper's *School's Out*, inviting him to sing along. The fact that Geoff didn't know the words and had been enjoying a quiet drink or two made it a somewhat chaotic rendition, but it was received in the spirit of fun that it was intended!'

Support was provided by local band Moriarty. Moriarty had released a three-track demo tape called *Elementary* the previous year and started picking up support gigs, of which this was the first.

'We got chatting to the IQ guys,' recalls guitarist and vocalist Alan Whittaker. 'They liked our set and invited us to play at The Marquee with them. We crashed at their house as well. We always liked IQ… we were blown away when we first saw them.'

Kerrang! continued to profile the new prog bands, including IQ in issue 66 (19 April – 2 May 1984).

'IQ are destined for success,' wrote Paul Roland. 'From their first tour - supporting The Enid in May '83 - to the release of their stunning debut (vinyl) LP just before Xmas, all the signs have been in their favour. That self-financed album, *Tales From The Lush Attic*, sold out its initial pressing of a thousand copies within eight weeks, through mail order and gigging alone. The recent airing of one track on the *Friday Rock Show* doubled their following overnight and stocks of the second pressing are already running low. Despite the LP's rehearsal room atmosphere - it was recorded and mixed in four days! - it strikes you immediately that the band's strength lies in the accessible complexity of their rhythms. Unlike their predecessors, IQ retain a refreshing spontaneity whilst dazzling the senses with incredible time signatures. IQ are a young band, but they know that success does not come easily. They are not in a hurry, they take the breaks as they come and seem content just to stay together and build a following on merit rather than hype.'

With their UK tour concluded, Pallas flew to Israel for three dates.

'[Pallas manager] Harry Maloney had some contacts over there,' says Graeme Murray. 'He wanted to get the band out of the UK and to spread the word.'

Euan Lowson smiles at the memory.

'A week in Israel, at the Liquid Club in Tel Aviv. It was a busman's holiday. I remember that we visited the pressing plant in the Palestinian sector in Haifa or Jaffa, where they were pressing copies of *The Sentinel* at the time. It was Passover whilst we were there, so being of a different religious background, that was all very interesting. How I could have gin and tonic on my first night, but not on the second night? It had to be gin and bitter lemon. Graeme and I had to eat omelettes in different rooms because we couldn't have mushroom and cheese together. And there were a lot of very famous people there that had travelled back from America for Passover, because it's a very important festival.'

The trip was written up in the band's next newsletter.

Those of you who attended the Sentinel tour may have been intrigued by the last dates of the itinerary: the Liquid Club, Tel Aviv. Well, sure enough, after a two-day break in London, Israel was Pallas' destination. This was their first gig abroad, and was certainly quite a challenge, especially for Ronnie since the only gear of his that the promoter could afford to freight over was the irreplaceable Novatron. Ron would have to quickly programme different synths. It was also a challenge for the band, playing to a totally fresh audience - but at least the weather would be fine.

With those thoughts in mind we left Luton airport for a five hour flight to Israel. On the flight we learned that it was Passover in Israel and this would mean certain food restrictions. We got the little gear we had through customs easily and were met by the promoter with his van bedecked with Pallas posters in Hebrew. We were told they described us as 'advanced rock'.

Arye, the promoter, took us to the club, which could have easily been an Israeli branch of The Marquee. It was uncanny having travelled so far to be in such familiar surroundings! Then on to the hotel where the food restrictions became apparent. We'd expected no bacon, but no bread, mushrooms, imported drink or BEER! Fortunately all the above could easily be obtained outside the hotel, but a bar with no beer, what a thought!

The album was released to tie in with our visit, and already *Eyes In The Night* was a radio favourite, if only it had been played as much on Radio 1! EMI is licenced to CBS in Israel and the album was hand-pressed before our eyes at their small factory. CBS had arranged plenty of press and radio for the band, but this was no hardship as the weather was diabolical with storm force winds and rain!

The first night at the Liquid Club was going to be a totally unknown quantity, but thanks to the promo-work the band could now assume the audience knew something about them. The club was very busy and the *Blade Runner* theme heralded the band onto the stage, a quick 'Shalom' from Euan and off into the same set as the British dates. The visibly stunned Israelis soon warmed to their guests and the response was just like The Marquee. Some of the lyrics assumed a new poignancy notably *Ark of Infinity*, *East-West* and especially *Crown Of Thorns*.

The irony of playing the Easter-inspired song to a Jewish audience during Passover proved too much for Graeme who inadvisably dedicated the song to the Christians in the audience! This was not well received by a vociferous few, and the torrent of Anglo-Saxon abuse ensured that this faux-pas wasn't repeated the following nights. The crucifixion scene was met with stunned awe and more fainting; despite the controversy the response was earth shattering! The *Atlantis Suite* was met with similar awe, the encores brought the tension down to a jovial finale. The following nights were equally well received and the band's first foreign jaunt was a success. The success of the trip may result in a tour later on in the year, when hopefully the weather may be somewhat more middle eastern.

That newsletter feature doesn't include two of the more alarming stories from the band's cache of road tales.

Firstly, Graeme Murray: 'We were staying in a very posh hotel in Tel Aviv. We were sitting having breakfast outside and enjoying the high life. All of a sudden, a man fell out of the sky and splattered on the floor. He had thrown himself off the top of the hotel after breaking a window with a shoe polishing machine…'

And Euan Lowson: 'One night, Chris, our stage manager at the time, and I had been partying. We were outside the hotel about two o'clock in the morning watching the waves come and go, you know. And we were discussing the pattern of the waves, that every seventh wave was a big one. Jack Daniels was doing its job. We decided that we could probably time it right and scuttle across the rocks and go and see the dolphins in the marine park nearby. So we did, we dodged the biggest wave and saw the dolphins. But on the way back we lost count and got hit by the big wave and bounced up onto these big rocks. We were pretty badly bruised and cut up. The next morning Graeme, myself and I think it was Niall were due for an interview at a Tel Aviv radio station. You could say that I was feeling… worse for wear. The interviewer would ask us questions in English, we'd answer and she'd translate it to in Hebrew. She asked about *The Ripper*… 'The blood, the knife,' she asked, 'it's all staged, isn't it?' I had a moment of inspiration and said, 'No, it's real. I just get into that place and go with it.' Then the long translation into Hebrew after which she asks again, 'Oh come on, it's all fake.' So I pulled my shirt off and I'm covered in bruises and cuts from our fall on the rocks the night before. And then there's loads more Hebrew and three words of English: 'Crazy Christian fucker.' We sold out the rest of the club dates.'

Those three dates at the Liquid Club would be the band's last with Euan Lowson.

As Solstice played The Marquee on Friday 20 April, Pendragon's long association with Marillion came into play when Marillion's manager John Arnison set up his own record label, part-funded and distributed by EMI.

'John started a label called Elusive and we signed with him,' Nick Barrett explained. 'The first thing we did was the mini-album *Fly High, Fall Far*. We had no experience at all.'

Engineer Will Reid-Dick and producer Pete Hinton had worked with the likes of Motörhead, Thin Lizzy and Saxon.

Nick Barrett: 'Will was a good engineer and Pete was a fine people person, although he wasn't the right producer for our sort of music. In the end, we had to remix the record, which didn't go down too well with him. The recording sessions were done at Cloud Nine Studios, which was owned by Status Quo's Rick Parfitt. That excited Peter Gee, because he was a huge Quo fan. Not that Parfitt was around.'

'We only met Parfitt's ex-wife Mariella, who still lived in the main house, with the studio on the side of the house,' Gee recalls. 'The nearest I ever got to meeting Rick Parfitt was seeing them through their dressing room window when we were on the guest list and had come to see them play at Shepton Mallet. It was great that we got to record at Rick Parfitt's house as Status Quo were one of my favourite bands as a teenager.'

Fly High, Fall Far was recorded in just seven days in the last week of April.

'We had been playing the material live for so long,' Barrett said, 'that we knew exactly how it should sound. But that might have worked a little against us. It might have been better if we'd been less familiar with the tracks, and therefore been more able to let things develop in the studio. But we were convinced that we knew how it all should come out.'

'We recorded at Rick Parfitt's house,' says Rik Carter. 'An amazing place in Hydon, Surrey. Pete Hinton was a great laugh. I was a teenage headbanger so was a big fan of Saxon, who Pete had produced, and was very impressed to be working with him. It was my idea to do *Dark Summer's Day* because I thought it was a great song that the band had for some reason stopped playing. Nigel's drums on this are fantastic, very subtle, lovely swing.'

'I know that we were quite young and naive when

1984: A Bleeding Heart Poet In A Fragile Capsule

Peter Gee and Nick Barrett of Pendragon in 1984
(Photograph by Brian Cairns)

it came to recording the *Fly High* mini album,' Nigel concedes. 'Pete Hinton was very personable and made you feel at ease. We were aware that he was A&R with Carriere Records and had produced Saxon and other acts, and with engineer Will Reid-Dick at the controls we had the opportunity to sound really full and edgy with good definition. And on vinyl, instead of those thin sounding and unreliable tapes. We were staying in a little lodge house at the entrance. Mariella made us feel really welcome and catered for us with snacks and refreshments. We more or less set up 'as live', all in the same converted lounge with the control room at the side. We had a few minor problems in recording but most of them were first takes. One episode I do remember is approaching the end of *Victims Of Life*. I'm sure that we had a bad earth buzz on the monitors which was coming through the headphones and which was so distracting and low that I couldn't hear the instrumentation properly in that quieter end section with Rik's organ sound on the keyboard, just before the cymbal build and swell, onto the last two chords and crashes finishing the song. I didn't hear that section, I just felt and counted it – pretty seamless on the recording – with no timing issues. Also, we were towards the end of a 24-track spool of tape. Pete and Will thought that we would have just enough tape to complete the track *Fly High, Fall Far*. We just squeezed in that last keyboard arpeggio bit before the tape ran off the spools. In fact, Pete performed what he jokingly named an 'American fade' – he dropped the master levels in the last 2 or 3 seconds. I bet if you listen and turn the volume level progressively up on your sound source, you'll hear it suddenly drop off at the end. Generally, it was one heck of an experience, recording our first notable piece of music – a long lasting and collectible artifact. I may sound pompous, but I am proud to have been a part of it.'

'Recording *Fly High, Fall Far* was a wonderful and

very exciting experience,' says Peter Gee, 'right up to the final mix. This was done for us whilst we were out of the room by Pete Hinton. We were disappointed with it, as it was a very dry sound. We arranged to remix it with the engineer, Will Reid-Dick, and put lots of reverb onto it the second time around. We were pleased with the final result.'

It was originally Pete Hinton who came up with the name [for the track] *Fly High, Fall Far* when we were in the studio recording it. The lyrics were already written and we had suggested calling it 'Western World'. However, other bands had incorporated this into other song titles so that idea was dismissed. Calling it *But Love Is Free* just seemed downright daft. So we settled for *Fly High…*

Now, to the contents of the song. Well, it's basically about all the strange goings on in remote countries which you hear about from time to time. It's the sort of thing you read about in the papers or see on TV documentaries where somebody goes missing and then suddenly reappears, years later, claiming to have been held captive and, moreover, to have been badly treated while in prison. When the whole issue is finally exposed no-one ever admits to what has actually happened, save the prisoner himself.

The song is, I suppose, about an injustice to a person. It was inspired, to a degree, by the film *Midnight Express*.

As most stories seem to have a happy ending I decided not to break from tradition and the character does, in fact, escape his prison. Thus, the explosion of freewill bit represents our character, who has just escaped, being forced to use his own judgement and once again having to make important decisions about his life, e.g. where to run to next.

The 'but love is free' lyric could, I suppose, be taken for your but love is free, ooh yeah baby kind of thing. However, in the light of the situation, it really means that in a world where bribes and shady deals are commonplace, a little compassion and respect would cost nothing.

Anyway, I won't give too many of the lyrical meanings as I always think it's a good idea to let folk use their own imagination as to what a song could be about.

Cheers for now,
Nick

Contact issue 9

IQ performed at The Marquee on 26 April, and recorded three songs for their *Friday Rock Show* session the next day: *Just Changing Hands*, *Awake And Nervous* and the superb *Widow's Peak*.

Martin Orford: 'Well, if the recording and mixing of *Tales* was quick, then this was even quicker! But we were better at the whole process by then and the recordings from that session hold up quite well. It was nice to go to Maida Vale Studios, and it felt like we were becoming part of the establishment, even if we never did quite get there.'

Peter Nicholls: 'A BBC session! We were being acknowledged as a band that was starting to go somewhere. It was hugely significant and it felt very exciting.'

This version of *Widow's Peak*, a song that would become the cornerstone of the band's live set, is easily the equal of, in fact probably better than, the version later recorded for *The Wake*. The *Rock Show*

1984: A Bleeding Heart Poet In A Fragile Capsule

Solstice, The Marquee, 5 May 1984
(Photographs by Mark Willcocks)

Twelfth Night, 19 May 1984 (From the collection of Russell Morgan)

Twelfth Night at The Marquee (Photographs by Mark Drake)

version can be heard on the 25th anniversary re-release of *The Wake*.

Assassing was released as Marillion's next single on 30 April. The A-side is heavily edited, losing over three minutes. The otherwise unavailable (and very good) *Cinderella Search* was added to the B-side – the 12" version is a minute or so longer. The single would again be promoted by a second appearance on the kids' TV show *Razzmatazz*.

Solstice played two further dates at The Marquee on 4 and 5 May. These were intended to be launch events for their new album, but persistent delays meant that it would be several months before the album was ready for release.

The *Friday Rock Show* broadcast IQ's session on 11 May. A few days later they returned to The Marquee for a powerful and confident performance. Being such regulars at The Marquee, IQ had developed a penchant for playing a different cover version as an encore to add some variety and an element of unpredictability to their set.

'As we were gigging regularly at The Marquee,' says Peter Nicholls, 'we were keen to vary the set where possible each time. Given that we were very slow at writing new IQ tracks, throwing in covers as encores was an expedient way of having something new to play. The other thing to remember is that, although there was a handful of journalists in the music press who were on our side, for the most part we were fighting anti-prog preconceptions and we, and the other bands, were slagged off as being dated throwbacks. Within the band, we had very varied musical tastes and we were all fans of the music that was popular at the time... Culture Club, Duran Duran, Howard Jones, the Psychedelic Furs, Ultravox, all of that, so we wanted to show another side of the band, something that would challenge people's expectations of us. I think *Sweet Transvestite*, complete with costumes, was probably the most extreme example of that!'

Tonight, they turned their attention to Queen's *Now I'm Here*, which they delivered with their usual fire and energy.

'After nearly two hours of intense prog rock, the encore covers provided a bit of release both for us and for the audience,' Martin Orford explains. 'It also had a practical value and having a string of familiar rock covers we could wheel out at some of those rougher provincial gigs probably softened the hatred towards us from the locals and ensured we could leave the venue safely. It started as a bit of fun, but we became quite good at it.'

A memorable evening was rounded off in manic style with the frenetic crowd-pleaser *Stomach Of Animal*.

At the conclusion of their *Live And Let Live* tour, and after another three dates at The Marquee, 19-21

A PLAYGROUND OF BROKEN HEARTS

The Marquee 'bar lounge' on 19 May 1984, with publicist Keith Goodwin, Fish, Clive Mitten and others (Photograph by Lisa King/Twelfth Night Archive)

May, when they performed their classic *Sequences* for the last time, Twelfth Night signed a management and publishing deal with Hit & Run Music, joining Genesis and Peter Gabriel amongst others at the company. Hit & Run was owned by the legendary Tony Smith, manager of Genesis since 1973. For a while it had looked as though Twelfth Night would sign with Handle Artistes, managers of Barclay James Harvest. Part of the deal would have been to tour major venues in the UK and Europe in April 1984 as support to Barclay James Harvest, who were promoting their album *Victims Of Circumstance*. This possibility was put to a vote within the band, with the majority choosing to sign with Hit & Run.

'I remember well the anguish at the Hammersmith Odeon gig supporting Pallas,' says Rick Battersby, 'where we had to make the decision that evening. It was, needless to say, very stressful, particularly as the gig itself was huge for us.'

'I'm just glad that the casting vote didn't fall to me!' notes Andy Sears. 'I was particularly torn between the idea of getting out and touring with Barclay James Harvest almost immediately, or rubbing shoulders with the Genesis camp. Having to make that decision meant that we were all high on tension and nerves that night.'

'While the Handle deal offered an immediate carrot in terms of the European tour,' says Andy Revell, 'we were wary of being linked to BJH, feeling that they were a bit 'old hat'. Overall, we felt more confident in Tony Smith and his team, given their track record with Genesis and Peter Gabriel. I also think we clicked on a personal level with Tony Smith more than with the people at Handle.'

'We had the opportunity to support Barclay James Harvest on a huge European tour,' recalls Rick Battersby, 'but our management company decision meant that this opportunity was lost. I think we all later regretted that lost opportunity, although at the time I think we thought of it as maybe 'wasting' six months to a year of our time and we wanted to move more quickly. We definitely came to regret that decision. I don't think we were truly a support act in any case in the sense that we were pretty unique and who would we fit with? Hit & Run had the huge allure of managing Genesis and that was irresistible.'

'I think we found the Genesis connection

intoxicating,' comments Brian Devoil, 'but in retrospect it was probably the wrong decision.'

Their spot on the UK dates of the Barclay James Harvest tour was taken by Nigel Mazlyn Jones, taking time out from producing Solstice's album.

Later in May, MCA showed enough interest in Twelfth Night to pay for them to record some demos at Granny's Basement Studios in Fulham, London. The three songs recorded were *Blue Powder Monkey*, *Blondon Fair* and *Take A Look*. These had been first performed live at shows earlier that month.

Despite a strong showing with *The Sentinel*, and three charting singles, Pallas singer Euan Lowson left the band in mid-May, necessitating cancellation of a planned Marquee show in June. He was kicked out after 'becoming a little too complacent, not really contributing to the songs', according to a contemporary interview with Graeme Murray.

'At the time we were working at the studio and under pressure to follow up *The Sentinel*,' Murray says today. 'Euan would go off and wander in the forest around the farmhouse with his archery equipment to practise his Robin Hood skills and we would hardly see him. We were keen to work, but Euan's heart didn't seem to be in it.'

Lowson tells a different story, which doesn't contradict what Murray says but perhaps adds a more personal slant.

'I was unceremoniously turfed out on my backside,' he says, still visibly edgy at the memory after 40 years. 'I had offended someone. I think it was in Manchester [30 March] and there were some people there from Capitol, our American record company. We were about to do *East West* and *Heart Attack* and I made a joke about Margaret Thatcher, Ronald Reagan and buttons being pressed and the start of the nuclear holocaust. The people from Capitol were not best pleased and apparently they approached EMI and said, 'That album's not getting released over here if he's anything to do with the band.''

'This is true,' Graeme Murray confirms, 'and it wasn't helpful.'

Lowson: 'The rest of the guys and our manager came to my flat, and I remember thinking 'This isn't good…' It was 'fucking EMI' and 'fucking Marillion' and 'fucking Fish'… and 'but you're out'. The band were given the choice, and they chose self-survival. There were all sorts of stories put around to put it in a good light, 'Euan left to pursue other interests…' Lots of spin to try and keep everybody looking good. It was pretty shite, all told.'

'We were put in a very difficult position by EMI,' comments Niall Mathewson, 'in that they wanted him out of the band, and it was an 'us or him' choice. So, we were pushed into doing the pushing.'

Lowson went on to sing with Erg with former members of a Derby-based band called Minas Tirith.

'This was during the miners' strike,' Lowson says. 'Rehearsals were in a barn miles away from anywhere. We'd get turned back by the police, who thought we were flying pickets. We rehearsed for about eight months and we were ready to go and gig and record. Then the place was raided by armed police and the dog squad. They were after our management. Then we were invited to see a record company, it might have been Juice Records, just around Christmas time. They had the studio set up and we recorded all the material we had. And the record company manager said, 'You're away back to

A PLAYGROUND OF BROKEN HEARTS

Alan Reed
(Photograph by
Mark Drake)

Glasgow to see your family at Christmas. Why don't you stay over here tonight? I'll get your train sorted out up to Glasgow for tomorrow…' The rest of the guys left to head home and later on he came to me and said, 'We'd like to sign you but we're not interested in the band.' So that was within a year of what happened with Pallas. I thought, 'I can't do this to these guys…' So I said no. I went back to Glasgow and was unceremoniously hoofed [out] because the manager was livid that he was missing out on his 20% cut. So that was me done. And that's why I've done nothing else since. You don't lose the anger quickly. I went back to my original trade and met a lovely lady that's sorted my head out. And had a family. I'm quite reconciled and happy with the way things turned out.'

Back in the rat race, *Kerrang!* issue 70 (14-27 June 1984) speculated that Peter Nicholls would replace Euan Lowson in Pallas. This was fake news. A young singer from Bournemouth also threw his hat in the ring.

'I remember going to see Yes at Wembley Arena on their *90125* tour on 11 July 1984,' says Stuart Nicholson, long-time singer in Galahad. 'On the way I popped in to see Harry Maloney as I knew Pallas were looking for a new vocalist. I was 20 years old and a little overawed by all the gold discs on the wall for the likes of Uriah Heep, Motörhead and Manfred Mann's Earth Band. The large Atlantis helmet was just lying on the carpet in the hallway. I cannot remember much of what was said, apart from Harry saying to me, 'You do realise that Pallas are based in Scotland and you live on the south coast?' That didn't matter to me at the time, although it might have done if I'd have got the job, which was never going to happen as I had so little experience at the point. I think Alan [Reed] was already the main man. It was a great day all round as Yes put on amazing show at the arena with the 'new' line-up. It was the best laser show I'd ever seen, including a large laser globe spinning in the auditorium, which was pretty spectacular for 1984!'

If Pallas hadn't quite replaced Euan Lowson with Alan Reed by this time, then they soon would. As with many other musicians in the prog bands of the 1980s, Reed had first heard the classic prog bands through an older brother. Or, in this case, a friend's older brother.

'I was introduced to *Selling England By The Pound* around the age of 14,' Reed recalls. 'It was from a mate's older brother's collection. He had loads of Yes and Greenslade posters on his wall, and, to be honest, I was slightly awed and a bit frightened by the world they depicted. Genesis spoke to me in the way that only a very English, upper-middle-class world could to a working-class Scot. It felt as though

1984: A Bleeding Heart Poet In A Fragile Capsule

Alan Reed outside The Marquee
(Photograph by Roger Morgan)

they were from a different planet. But one that I could identify with. I then bought …*And Then There Were Three*… and was deeply confused by what seemed like a complete line-up change. Soon after I listened to Yes and became a huge fan. The *Old Grey Whistle Test* introduced me to ELP. I loved that they were so unapologetically over the top. Then I discovered Rush – and through them – the bass guitar.'

Reed attended the University of Stirling to study English. Here he formed a band. 'I sang, played bass, 12-string and a bit of synth. It was the early era of what came to be known as neo-prog. You had Pallas and Chasar in Scotland, and Marillion (who were part Scottish anyway). I was becoming aware of Twelfth Night, IQ, Pendragon, Solstice, Haze and so on.'

He soon joined Abel Ganz. And despite seeing Scotland's premier prog band a number of times, Reed had never met the guys from Pallas. But they knew of him…

'I was at a party near Aberdeen,' Reed says. 'I'd never been that far north before. A friend of a friend seemed to know the band a bit. So I gave him a copy of *Gratuitous Flash*. And forgot about it.'

Mike Bentley: 'Somebody I knew met Alan at a party. Alan gave him a cassette and I took it around to Graeme the next day. He contacted Harry immediately, who said, 'Check him out.' Tom Russell told us of an upcoming Abel Ganz gig, so we drove to Glasgow to watch.'

'We had heard recordings from an Abel Ganz album, and were suitably impressed,' says Niall Mathewson. 'So we went to see him playing with them in Glasgow. Again, we were suitably impressed.'

'I was performing with Abel Ganz at the Radio Clyde open air festival at Kelvingrove Park in Glasgow [27 May 1984],' Reed says. 'It went very well indeed. After we came off, Tom Russell, Radio Clyde's Rock DJ, took me aside and told me that Pallas were looking for a singer. I'd had no idea. I still thought of myself as a bassist who sang a bit, so the idea of joining a band as a singer seemed a bit of a cop-out. But Pallas was one band where I could see it working. I thought about it for a bit. My second year at university was ending, and I'd gone to the Glasgow Apollo with a few friends to see Quo's *End Of The Road* Tour [June 1984]. I was at home ironing when the phone rang. It was someone claiming to be Graeme Murray. After he eventually convinced me it was indeed him, he persuaded me to come up to Aberdeen for an audition. It was a bit nerve-wracking: a fairly long and drawn-out process. It culminated in a sing-off, a gig at the same venue in Aberdeen a week apart [in July 1984], between me and the other short-listed candidate.'

Harry Maloney had vetted audition tapes and two others were put forward in addition to Reed: Paul Ford and Paul Liversidge. Both went to meet the band at their farmhouse.

'I was living in South Wales, singing with Multi-Story,' Ford says. 'Pallas were in Aberdeen, so there was much more to consider than just the artistic and creative aspects. But I believe it could have worked well, particularly with the band's love and influence of Yes and as I had a vocal frequency range similar to Jon Anderson. I loved these guys, great musicians.'

Graeme Murray: 'Paul is a really nice guy. He was a bit shocked when he came up to see us for a few days. It was too cold for him.'

Evidently, Pallas' management and EMI ultimately decided that Ford sounded too much like Jon Anderson. Alan Reed and Paul Liversidge were therefore taken to the final stage of auditions: a live performance in Aberdeen on 5 July.

'I had been singing in some really good bands in my home town,' Paul Liversidge says. 'But I could see the future being mapped out as occasional gigs… fun but ultimately unfulfilling. I was honing my craft, and I knew that if I wanted to make a go of it I had to move to London. I had a great job in engineering but one day I thought, 'What the fuck. I can come back if I need to.' And to the immense chagrin of my parents I quit. I wrote and recorded a bunch of songs in my bedroom with the most basic of equipment, aided and abetted with my long-term buddy, Andy Sharp, and planned world domination. A few months later I saw an ad in *NME*, 'band seeking vocalist'. Nothing to lose, I sent a tape of me singing. They loved it. They sent me an album of theirs, asking me to learn three songs and would I come to Aberdeen for an audition. It was Pallas. I was a fan and, yes, I'd love to come! I duly learned the songs, met the band, got a bit drunk over a weekend and agreed to keep in touch. Now, I'm a Northerner but they hail from Aberdeen, which is way up north of the north. Penguins avoid winter there. Still, I thought, let's see what happens. After three weeks I hadn't heard from them, so I chalked it down to experience. Then, Graeme Murray called me asking me to come to play a 'let the fans decide' gig. To be honest I'd already decided that, beautiful though it is, Aberdeen wasn't for me. But I thought a gig would be mighty fun.'

Liversidge sang *Arrive Alive*, *Shock Treatment* and *Cut And Run*. Alan Reed, however, prevailed.

Niall Mathewson: 'We asked Alan if he would like to join Pallas, which he did. He certainly has a unique and instantly recognisable voice. I think the band felt that, with Alan, we could start expanding musically.'

Ronnie Brown: 'We liked Alan's voice. Despite his youth, he had a very mature sounding voice – husky, powerful where required and, we thought, soulful.'

Alan Reed was in and within a few weeks was performing his first gigs with Pallas. Paul Liversidge would later change his name to PL Menel.

'I was always known as PL,' he says, 'and a late friend of mine, Mark, always used to say 'Menel' after it in a singy, American drawl. I decided to mark his death, hence PL Menel.'

PL Menel will return to this story in due course.

Marillion undertook a short tour of Europe in May and June, performing in Germany and France, finishing at the Pinkpop festival in Geleen, near

1984: A Bleeding Heart Poet In A Fragile Capsule

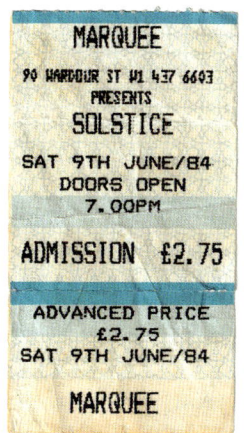

Tickets for Solstice and IQ at The Marquee, June-August 1984 (From the collection of Peter Moltensen)

Maastricht. Their popularity in northern Europe was beginning to build significantly.

'Places like Germany, France, Switzerland and Holland were all suddenly showing a big interest in getting us over to play,' said Steve Rothery, 'but we couldn't possibly afford to go to all of these places the way we had been doing, you know, four days on and four days off, back and forth all the time. We needed to co-ordinate a proper European tour. So when EMI suggested we should release a live record of some sort, we all thought about it and eventually said yes, all right we'll do it. But it would have to be a low-price budget-affair. We didn't think the band was anywhere near ready yet to release a proper double-live album. Originally, we saw the idea more as a live twelve-inch EP, something along those lines.'

Nine dates in Canada and the north-eastern US included three at Le Spectrum in Montreal, 18-20 June. These were recorded for a proposed live album, *Real To Reel*.

'*Fugazi* didn't sell as many as *Script*,' says Mark Kelly. 'We spent twice as much making it and it didn't sell as many copies. And it was, I think, John Arnison, to his credit, who suggested that we do a live album as a sort of interim thing to plug the gap.'

Simon Hanhart: 'Making *Real To Reel* was exciting. It involved my first trip to Canada and the USA. I went with the band to Montreal and recorded them at The Spectrum Club. The club had a little studio attached to it, which was ideal.'

The entire set from 20 June can be heard on the 2021 re-release of *Fugazi*.

'Canada at the start of that tour was great!' Fish said. 'Really happening! It was starting to go the same way as Europe and Britain had gone for us. You can always tell when an audience starts singing all the words to something like *Script*… If they can manage that then we know we've got real fans in the audience, and that's what was starting to happen for us most nights in Canada. But as soon as we crossed over the border and moved down into America for our gigs, things started to change again pretty quickly. We still had a hell of a long way to go over there, that much was obvious from the first gig, and by the time we got to the Ritz in New York we were left in no doubt at all as to just how lowly we were regarded in America in 1984. I mean, there must have been all of about a dozen people there for our show at the Ritz! It was another complete waste of the band's time and money even playing there.'

Marillion's tour continued with 11 shows in Germany, France, Spain and Switzerland in July.

The other prog bands continued to fill The Marquee, usually performing across two or sometimes three consecutive evenings to meet demand. In the second half of 1984, Solstice headlined on 8-9 June, 4-5 August, 31 August and 1-2 November; Pendragon on 17 June, 10-11 August,

A PLAYGROUND OF BROKEN HEARTS

Autographed IQ hand-out, June 1984 (From the collection of Guy Tkach)

21 September; Pallas on 21-23 June and 16-17 August; IQ on 5-6 July, 18-19 August, 11-13 October and 31 December.

A recording of Solstice's 8 June gig demonstrates that Sandy Leigh was an engaging, talented singer. Opening with a sparkling version of *New Life*, their set was strong, appealing and markedly progressive, with six songs lasting eight minutes or more.

At around this time (no one can remember exactly when), Solstice performed at Broadmoor psychiatric hospital, not far from Bracknell in Berkshire.

'The gig went under some strange label like the Tennis Club Social,' says Martin Wright. 'We were booked as a fan of ours was inside doing time for something or other and put our name forward. Upon arrival the security guys looked into my big drum flight cases and once cleared we were escorted by several screws to the room where we would perform. The band decided to wind up Phil [Wheal, sound engineer] by telling him that the most serious offenders would be chained up at the back with him at the mixing desk. Between the two sets we were fed steak, which we had to eat with plastic knives and forks, and were not allowed to leave the room without an escort. I needed a pee and broke the rule and got a serious bollocking. It was an early finish and upon leaving, security was surprisingly not as tight… we could have easily smuggled someone out in my big flight cases. We were back home by about 9.30pm.'

Phil Wheal: 'I do have a few memories I haven't repressed of that one. Being escorted back and forth to the loo by security, the sedative vibe of a lot of the audience, some very unusual dancing and I think most of us felt like we'd walked into a Lewis Carroll book. Definitely different. I was on the lookout for Peter Sutcliffe, and I remember asking something along those lines to one of the wardens. He made it clear that certain groups of inmates wouldn't get an invite to this party.'

Marc Elton: 'Some prisoners were chained to the back walls and the rest were all drugged up to the eyeballs. It beggars belief that they allowed us to spend an entire afternoon setting up several thousand watts of PA, backline and a massive drum kit without expecting us to be loud… I'll never forget the terrified looks of sheer astonishment from residents and screws alike as we opened the set at volumes evidently never before experienced in Broadmoor. I remember my bravado dissolving into awkwardness and confusion as the screws urgently pleaded with us to lower the volume. We looked on helplessly at Phil and Guy who were suffering multiple thromboses as they struggled to compromise with the demands until, finally, we were playing at the volume (and quality) of a village fête, with only the onstage monitors actually being used, and even

1984: A Bleeding Heart Poet In A Fragile Capsule

Solstice in Norwich, 2 June 1984

Twelfth Night rehearsing for the Dominion show, summer 1984 (Courtesy Twelfth Night Archive)

they were too loud. At some point the decision was made to bring *Find Yourself* forward in an attempt to salvage the situation and thankfully it did have a calming effect, although, at this point, the residents immediately started ballroom dancing with female inmates who had been bussed in from another wing. It was literally like tripping, yet, for once, we were the only ones who were completely straight. I think the wardens indulged us for a few more numbers before calling time. I'm not sure who was more relieved by our departure: us, the screws or the residents, but what I do know is that we couldn't get out of there quick enough…'

Andy Glass: 'That's got to be one of the weirdest gigs of all time!'

Twelfth Night had, for now, moved beyond the confines of Wardour Street. On 20 July 1984 they played their biggest gig as headliners to over 1,200 people at The Dominion on Tottenham Court Road. Twelfth Night, as you will recall, did not have a record deal at this point, making this an impressive and notable occasion. Tony Smith held court in the Dominion bar with several other music industry executives.

'That first Dominion show was certainly a culmination of everything that had gone on before,' comments Clive Mitten. 'I still remember Andy Sears being very excited before this show and roaring out from the dressing room like a wind-up toy when it was time for us to go on stage.'

A PLAYGROUND OF BROKEN HEARTS

Twelfth Night at The Dominion, London, 20 July 1984 (Photographs by Dave Jones)

1984: A Bleeding Heart Poet In A Fragile Capsule

Ticket for The Dominion, London, 20 July 1984 (From the collection of Peter Moltensen)

Backstage pass from The Dominion, London, 20 July 1984 (Courtesy Twelfth Night Archive)

Flyer for The Dominion, London, 20 July 1984 (From the collection of Peter Moltensen)

'It was the biggest gig we ever headlined', says Andy Revell. 'But it was an odd experience to be honest, being so far from the audience, who were seated in the theatre. It felt a bit impersonal. Certainly not as much fun as The Marquee!'

Fishy—Neo-Pompers In Health Hazard Shock!

Come and see Twelfth Night, they said. Always open-minded about these things, I said yes. But even the offer of a complimentary ticket was unable to tempt a friend into accompanying me. My comrades obviously have impeccable taste…

Any band touted as the new Marillion had a lot (a little?) to live up to. Could they come up with such gonzoid hairstyles? (NO - just the kind you would expect to see on Reflex - New Wave? Nein Danke!) Would they have a vocalist of comparably immaculate misconception as Fish? (NO - just a slippery eel who could barely squeeze into his leather pants - Straight legged loons? Nein Danke!) Would they be able to tackle similar epic topics in such a ham-fisted manner (sham Fish did)? (YES - 'This one's for all those people who ain't having too good a time of it, like in Africa' …No-brained bands? Nein Danke!) Would they wheel on a Strippergram to celebrate drummer Brian's birthday? (YES - and it got the biggest cheer of the night, so maybe the semi-lobotomised sub-Python/Young Ones Anne Nightingale listening audience had some musical taste, if not feminine awareness, after all) …

Still, they did have a few melodies: East Of Eden was catchy enough but, typically of the pomp genre, by the time it was over I was in need of a good shave, and my cardigan had come in and gone out of fashion at least three times. I would suggest that if they really want to score with the groovy youth, they ought to record my latest neo-psychedelic, occult inspired piece, Hesse, We Have No Mandalas. That would soon have 'em cross legged in the aisles.

Bruce Dessau, *New Musical Express*, 1984

The following day, 21 July, Marillion appeared at what was billed at the time as 'Quo's Last Show' as part of a six-act show at Milton Keynes Bowl. Jason & The Scorchers, Nazareth and, erm, Gary Glitter warmed up the crowd ahead of full sets by Marillion and Status Quo.

'We had a really good relationship with Status Quo,' says Ian Mosley. 'We were under the same management team and the Quo fans seemed to like us. Francis Rossi was always very friendly - we bumped into him in a hotel corridor somewhere and he said, 'Hello, Ian, how's that posh band doing then?''

A PLAYGROUND OF BROKEN HEARTS

'FISH's View of Milton Keynes on 21st July', from *The Web*: issue 13, August 1984

The breakfast room in the 5 Bells, Weston Turville was doing a neat impersonation of the Marie Celeste's gallery. I'd made breakfast for the first time in months, just sitting there hypnotised by events and poached eggs, just me and the butterflies that were coming out [of] the cocoons in my stomach as the hands on the clock crawled to midday.

At one o'clock we decorated the bar of the Bell Hotel, Aylesbury, silent refugees acknowledging the mutation of birds from butterflies with the type of eyes you normally see on the eyes of Alfred Hitchcock's victims. The bus was late.

Two o'clock, here come the vultures, 'just a small brandy', 'is the make-up box with the crew?', nervous smiles and stifled small talk.

When we manoeuvred into the site welcoming smiles defused the situation momentarily until the stage and its backstage intestines slammed the nerves back into the overload marker and we slid from the coach to the dressing caravan feeling like prodigal children about to face the judgement of 35,000 fathers.

The first gig on home soil since the release of *Fugazi*. Three thirty and beneath the rib cage there's an aviary going crazy. Gary Glitter's on after the exploding Sainsbury's effect on Jason & the Scorchers. Make-up time approaches. Smiles and handshakes to old friends that realise they're meeting a pre-gig stranger. The gig. It's run through in the head a million times and a million times something goes wrong. 'Paranoid? what not me, but are you sure the radio mike's ok?'

Four thirty. A large brandy. The face, the mask assembled. Comfort wreathed a cigarette. The mirror auditions the band and gives the thumbs up. Time to go and the parade to the catwalk begins.

Four forty. 'Are you sure the radio mike's ok?' The last drag on the cigarette and as it flutters into the backstage encampment the spring uncoils and propels five defendants to the sunlit dock.

On Sunday I didn't even manage lunch.

… FISH

IQ prepared a 12" promo single for release in July 1984, comprising an edit of *Awake And Nervous* backed with *Through The Corridors*.

Mike Holmes: '[These were] intended as promo for the USA (500 were pressed) but we never made

Quo's 'final show'
(From the collection of
Guy Tkach)

it to the States.'

Peter Nicholls, Paul Cook and Martin Orford were interviewed for Radio Kent and the as yet untitled *The Magic Roundabout* was given its live debut at The Marquee that month.

'One of the reasons we've not been plodding around on the live circuit for four or five weeks,' Peter said on stage, 'is that we've been writing some new songs. One of which we are going to play now. This being its first appearance on a live stage some of it will probably be a bit rough around the edges but hopefully you'll bear with us. I have to use my crib sheet, hope I don't forget too much. This one, in true fashion, doesn't have a title yet so it's this…'

In early August 1984, Twelfth Night demoed some of their new songs at Matinee Studios in Reading, and then travelled to Amazon Studios in Liverpool to record the *Art And Illusion* album across two weeks, starting on 13 August. The studios were in Simonswood near Kirkby, 10 miles from the city centre, and were owned by Hit & Run. Gil Norton was contracted to produce.

'I like the production on that album,' says Andy Sears. 'It certainly has energy. Gil Norton really captured a vibe. These days it's easier to hear the compression and limiting at work on the tracks, which adds a kind of urgency to the overall feel. Is it dated? What isn't after almost 40 years? Nevertheless, I think it holds its head up extremely well today. Gil was great to work with, as was Keith Andrews, the assistant engineer. We'd send the rest of the band off, and then work early evening through to midnight. Job done, we'd walk back to the local pub where we were all staying. I remember those walks back, through the streets of Kirkby, Liverpool. It was three years on from the riots, and though Toxteth lay some distance away from Kirkby, the street shops were nonetheless uniformly grilled and barred. It gave the place quite a sinister aura.'

'Working with a producer for the first time meant we started looking at the songs during the recording process, taking apart and reassembling,' Brian Devoil said. 'In the past we lacked that specialised objective ear.'

Andy Revell: 'All of the ideas are ours; they have just been brought into sharper focus. I think Gil brought a hard, bright, contemporary edge to our sound that I really quite like. Our songs have never been fluffy or even particularly comfortable in their meaning and I liked the fact that our sound had a harder edge, too.'

The tracks were mixed at Westside Studios, London. Only five songs, 26 minutes in total, were recorded for *Art And Illusion*: a deliberate strategy by the band.

Andy Sears: '*Art And Illusion* was supposed to be called *First New Day*. That would have made more sense. It should always have been a full album. Having said that, I'd only just come up with *Take A Look*, and the band were still feeling around it. *Blondon Fair* was ready. *Graffiti* would have worked, and *Blue Powder Monkey* hadn't yet been slaughtered. The original Battersby/Sears version was far more compelling.'

Clive Mitten: '*Art And Illusion* was the first step where we consciously moved away from being a prog band. It was seen as a taster of this new direction.'

With Twelfth Night in the studio, Solstice headlined at The Marquee on 4 and 5 August.

Pendragon embarked on a six-week UK tour in Gwent on 4 August, including two headline

A PLAYGROUND OF BROKEN HEARTS

Andy Glass at The Marquee, 5 August 1984
(Photographs by Oz Hardwick)

concerts at The Marquee on 10-11 August.

The band was gaining a higher profile, with these shows reported by *Sounds* and *Kerrang!*

PENDRAGON: Marquee

THIS STROUD crowd have been striding down the right road in recent months. Ditching dodgy visual embellishments, such as singer/guitarist Nick Barrett's silly top hat, means attention is firmly focused where it can only be with such a band: on the music.

Where it can only be because, as poseurs, Pendragon are hard-pushed to be exciting, though the vampin' verve in these casual country boys is decidedly on the up.

Groove-stricken gyrating is the most you're likely to see. No shocking antics here, especially considering the absence of any instrument-free party to portray any intricacies – bassist/guitarist Pete Gee, drummer Nigel Harris and new keyboardist Ric [sic] Carter complete the company.

However, scepticism still pervades over my opinion of the group. On newer numbers *Oh Divineo*, the lengthy *Circus*, *Pleasure Of Hope* and especially on *Fly High, Fall Far*, playing is promisingly punchier, more precise. But the main course of the menu, Pendragon's earlier pennings, is staple Seventies prog-rock, without the absolutely thoroughbred musicianship that, say, IQ can muster.

Songs like *Black Knight*, *Victims Of Life* and *Alaska* become bogged down in too much jazz-rocky accenting or Pavlovian epic evocation, and are left lackadaisical in the memorable melody dept.

Having said that, it is mood music. Pendragon invite immersion in rich textures, regimental rhythms and introvert instrumentation, and it would be naive to pretend the niche for such stylistics has vanished.

Phil Bell, *Sounds*

'The question I always find myself asking about progressive rock bands,' Geoff Gillespie wrote in *Kerrang!*, 'is, while they may be good at what they do, is what they do necessarily good? Well, in Pendragon's case, the answer is yes. Anyone in search of originality would have done well to have stayed away from [The] Marquee on this particularly hot and sweaty Sunday night, but who really expects originality from progressive rock? The unfortunate fact is that, unlike heavy metal acts, progressive rock bands have influences that can be traced back to specific groups, purely because there were so few of them to

1984: A Bleeding Heart Poet In A Fragile Capsule

Marc Elton at The Marquee, 5 August 1984 (Photograph by Oz Hardwick)

be influenced by. All this being said, however, Pendragon have a hell of a lot going for them. They are unique among second generation progressive rock acts in as much as they do not possess a vocalist who parades around the stage resplendent in make-up like old what's-his-name. What they do possess, however, is a warm, eloquent frontman/guitarist in Nick Barrett, and an excellent keyboard player in Rik Carter. Right from the *Dallas* intro tape up until the encore, *Alaska*, [a] packed Marquee treated the band to the sort of reception normally reserved for Hammersmith headliners, and the 'Dragons responded accordingly. Standout numbers were the fluent, flowing instrumental, *Excalibur, Oh Divineo*, with its pumping beauty, and *Out In The Night*, full of marvellous grandeur. The bass of Pete Gee and the drums of Nigel Harris anchored the set admirably, and indeed the band showed themselves to be instrumentally rock solid and capable of some moments of exceptional beauty.'

Pallas were given a full-page feature in the 11 August issue of *Sounds*. The feature was, like the *Kerrang!* article from November 1982, punningly titled 'Pallas In Wonderland'. Here they introduced 'diminutive' Alan Reed as their new singer, who was asked how he would influence the band's direction.

'What we're doing now is more direct, less of the meandering space-opera,' swears Alan enthusiastically. 'What went into 20 minutes is being put into shorter songs, so people aren't sitting around being bored. No way can we afford to be labelled progressive revivalists. If we were labelled with all those bands we'd be digging our own grave.'

Strong words from a man just into a band formerly seen as front-runners in the very field he's knocking. There's more!

Graeme: 'He's 20, and up until now he's been a punter. We can't be labelled as living in the past, 'cause now we've got a driving force that was playing with his Action Man in the 70s, not listening to Yes. We're an 80s rock band, and I don't see why rock music by definition can't be commercial.'

Nearly 40 years on, Reed can look back with circumspection.

'There was clearly an agenda that we didn't see,' he says. 'Yes, we said all those things, but stripped of the context it came out very different from our intentions. I think it catches what we were trying to do - move forward. But, along with the photoshoot, it presented us as abandoning entirely our previous prog roots in favour of a pop mentality. That wasn't on our agenda at all. Our naivety really shows through. We should have known better.'

Pallas played their first dates at The Marquee with their new singer on 16 and 17 August.

'I remember London being very hot and sticky,' Alan Reed says. 'There were fans placed at the back of the venue and they opened the rear doors to try and keep the temperature down. In the end all they

Pendragon at The Marquee, 11 August 1984
(Photographs by Dave Jones)

1984: A Bleeding Heart Poet In A Fragile Capsule

Handwritten postcard advertising Pendragon at The Marquee, 10-11 August 1984 (From the collection of Jon Dunnington)

managed to do was blow hot air in our faces! The Marquee on Wardour Street was an institution. It had been there since the 1960s and anyone who was anyone had played there. It was smaller than I expected but it was very central and a mecca for the discerning music fan. The guys who ran it, Nigel and Bush, were very affable, and it became our home from home whenever we were in town. I used to hitch down from Scotland and kip at our manager's assistant's place and lig there regularly. I met and saw all sorts of musicians there. There was also the St Moritz club down the road for out-of-hours drinking. There was a sort of understanding that you became a temporary member if you played at The Marquee… I met some very strange people there!'

IQ appeared at The Marquee on the next two evenings, supported by Geoff Mann and Jadis.

A new song, *The Thousand Days*, was added to the set for these shows. The band also played *Widow's Peak* and the still to be titled *The Magic Roundabout*, which Peter Nicholls jokingly calls *Slippery Sam Goes Chartered Accounting*.

It was around this time that, to relieve the tedium of endless road miles, IQ rearranged the branding stickers on the side of their hired van from 'Swan National' to 'Twat Lotion'.

'We had to borrow some letters from the other side of the van,' says Martin Orford. 'I seem to remember that we forgot to change it back after the tour and unsurprisingly lost our deposit from the van hire company. There are lots of stories about IQ and unfortunately most of them are true. We were truly disreputable most of the time.'

Solstice, meanwhile, finally completed their album *Silent Dance*.

'The recording of *Silent Dance* was a very protracted process that nobody really expected or wanted,' Martin Wright recalls. 'After the initial rhythm tracks were done very quickly – I did all my drum tracks in one day – it became very fragmented and took so much longer than anticipated.'

'Nigel [Mazlyn Jones] and Marc Elton didn't get on terribly well from the beginning,' Andy Glass said, 'and you can hear that in the final result because Marc's fiddle was a lot less prominent than you would expect. It was a fantastic experience but I ended up being the diplomat between those two firebrands. The result was not what we envisaged. We'd wanted a recording more akin to our live sound but ended up with something quite different. So it was a bit diluted, it didn't have that live energy and I think fans probably thought that too.'

August is festival season. The First Annual Scottish Rock and Pop Festival was held at East Kilbride Calderglen Country Park on 25-26 August. Pallas were placed mid-way through the Sunday afternoon schedule on a bill with Frankie Miller, Nazareth and others.

That same weekend, Marillion, Twelfth Night and IQ were booked to perform at a revamped Reading Festival. Issues with the traditional site at Thames Mead necessitated a move in venue to Lilford, near Thrapston, Northamptonshire, 100 miles from Reading. The festival was also renamed 'the 24th National 'Reading' Rock Festival'. Marillion were booked to headline the final day, in what would no doubt have been a triumphant return to one of the key moments in their history.

The full and eclectic line-ups, as advertised, were:

> Friday 24 August 1984: Hawkwind, Boomtown Rats, Eloy, Dumpy's Rusty Nuts, Playn Jayn, New Torpedoes, Chelsea, Wildfire. Special guest: Snowy White
>
> Saturday 25 August 1984: Jethro Tull, Hanoi Rocks, Nazareth, Twelfth Night, Thor, Silent Running, Terraplane, IQ, She, Roaring Boys. Special guest: Steve Hackett
>
> Sunday 26 August 1984: Marillion, Phil Lynott's Grand Slam, Helix, The Enid, Clannad, New Model Army, Opposition, Scorched Earth, Young Blood. Special guest: The Bluebells

At almost the last minute, the local council refused the licence.

'I don't know why they [did] it,' said Mike Holmes of IQ. 'I suppose it's because they're scared of the 'drug' problem. I think it's ridiculous, I can't see what they gain from it, particularly Reading, because that was never a violent place was it? I'm really pissed off about it anyway, because I really wanted to play it! Then we were really looking forward to playing Lilford, and that bloody got blown out…'

Many of the bands, Marillion included, transferred to the Nostell Priory festival near Wakefield, held over the same weekend. Marillion headlined the fourth day, Monday 27 August.

'So we all piled in the van and drove up to Wakefield for the Monday night show,' Ian Mosley recalled. 'Phil Lynott's Grand Slam went on before us, and we headlined. It was a really good gig, as I recall, nice warm night, Fish and the rest of the boys going mental on stage, thousands of people in the audience singing and waving.'

IQ were in Glasgow for a week recording new versions of three songs for a single. *Barbell Is In*, *Just Changing Hands* and *Dans Le Parc Du Chateau Noir*. Whilst there they recorded demos of two of their new songs, *The Magic Roundabout* and *The Thousand Days*.

Two weeks later, Marillion headed into Barwell Court Studios in Chessington, on the south-west edge of London, to write their next album.

'Barwell Court was idyllic and atmospheric, and we laboured away utterly ignorant of how close we had come to being dropped by EMI,' Mark Kelly writes. 'Indeed, we were growing confident and bullish about our relationship with our record label. We decided there and then that we were done with trying to please EMI.'

They were going to make a concept album.

'With *Misplaced Childhood* we thought, 'fuck singles'. We were actually trying to do the exact opposite of what EMI wanted. And then they pulled *Kayleigh* out of that and made a hit single out of it.'

With Solstice headlining a local show in Milton Keynes, Pendragon toured the West Country, performing shows in Exmouth, Sidmouth, Yeovil, Torrington, Okehampton, Taunton, Torquay, Exeter and Plymouth between 10 and 23 September.

They also appeared on TV.

'We were asked by a promoter to do a tour of the south west of England,' Nick Barrett said. 'One of the promoters managed to get us a spot on television. He said 'you can play live, one song.' It was about 6 o'clock in the morning. I mean musicians don't usually get up until at least midday, so early in the morning trying to play a song like *Fly High, Fall Far* was very difficult. Nobody really saw it at the

1984: A Bleeding Heart Poet In A Fragile Capsule

Solstice, Milton Keynes, 19 September 1984 (Photograph by Oz Hardwick)

time because it was for local TV.'

At the time of writing the video can be seen on YouTube.

Heads in Watford (the back room of the Verulam Arms) presented four 'prog rock nights' on successive Wednesdays in October, starting with The Host on 10 October, with Pendragon, IQ and Quasar in successive weeks.

IQ celebrated their new single, *Barbell Is In*, with three nights at The Marquee. The first of these was attended by Phil Morris.

'By autumn 1984 I had started my first job in central London,' Morris recalls. 'Indeed, on my first day at work I was off to see IQ on the first of a three-night run at The Marquee [11-13 October]. I like to think my employer was impressed by my commitment when I offered to stay late those evenings, but it wasn't worth going home before the gigs. Probably less so when I arrived for work the next mornings a little hard of hearing. I was going to so many gigs there that I became a member. This gave the advantage of being able to book tickets in advance. Otherwise it was only possible to turn up and queue, which as several of the bands were growing in stature became increasingly risky to ensure entry. It was also cheap enough to go to as many shows as you wished, so I took in every night the bands I adored played there. This included such legendary shows as IQ's on New Year's Eve in 1984 and their gig on the same day as Live Aid, when they showed the televised broadcast on a large screen between sets.'

Barbell Is In was released on 12 October 1984. A week later (and a week late) Twelfth Night's *Art And Illusion* album would also hit the shops, including Action Records in Preston, where it was bought by this author. The album included a loose sheet with lyrics and, at first glance, a photograph of Duran Duran.

Brian Devoil: 'I think when we did *Art And Illusion*, we were a bit more conscious of image. I mean it was 1984, so Duran Duran were very much the flavour of the month and we were a good looking band relative to our peers. Clive used hairspray to stick his hair up, which was wonderful until you went on stage at The Marquee and within two minutes it was flat again! One thing I particularly remember doing is a photoshoot with Sheila Rock. We had our girlfriends with us and they gave us a little bit of make-up, which was quite fun. We were trying for a more commercial sound and obviously it made sense. We did wear spandex trousers for a while as well.'

Gregory Spawton: 'As a front-row fan at gigs, I was confronted with Clive's spandex-trousered balls, right in my face. I wasn't sure about their increasingly 'glam' image then, and I'm still not certain it was a good call for them. Of course, I was a very serious young hippie kind of guy, who didn't have any understanding of the music business or why it may have been important, especially in those days, to use image to get a record deal. But sometimes I think it is best to let the music do the talking.'

Art And Illusion is brittle, brisk and brightly produced. There is, though, a feeling of being short-changed, with five songs (two of them older numbers repurposed) making up 26 minutes of music.

The opening *Counterpoint* is ballsy and energetic, complete with a catchy chorus and tight arrangement. It's not so far from earlier punchy tracks such as *Three Dancers* but with a new and meretricious commercial sheen. *Art And Illusion* is an aggressive Mann-era track. The song had been written in spring 1983 and was part of the band's set list for several months before Mann's departure. Here, Andy Sears rewrites the vocal melody and sings brilliantly. We'll have to forgive the dated sound of Brian Devoil's electronic drum rolls. *C.R.A.B.* is an old piece, snipped from a longer instrumental called *Entropy*, which dates from the early 1980s and was later incorporated into an encore medley. This is all calculated prog dynamics and works well in the context of the album, even if it adds nothing new to the oeuvre. *Kings And Queens* hints at a heavy rock style, chopping between quieter sections and loud guitars and drums. The closing *First New Day* is sparse, with just lush, willowing keyboards and metronomic drum machine. Andy Sears' hard-hitting social commentary and top-notch vocal performance decorate an unusual and highly effective track. *Art And Illusion* is, to date, the only entry the band has in the *Guinness Book of Hit Singles and Albums*.

Andy Sears: 'The album made the Top 100 national charts with absolutely no record company hype, promotion, or 'special sales'. That's something no other TN album achieved. That's something to celebrate.'

Art And Illusion marked the end of Twelfth Night's association with Music For Nations.

'Hit & Run made it very clear from the start that they intended to take the band away from us and get them a major deal,' recalls MFN's Martin Hooker, 'which was somewhat demotivating for us as a label. Rather than getting the one-on-one attention they enjoyed with MFN, the band went to being a small fish in a very big pond, and in my opinion never got the attention from Virgin that they deserved. Keep in mind that they'd just had a chart album, and were able to sell out The Dominion. With the right promotion things were set up for them to go on from strength to strength. However, things were handled badly by Hit & Run. Very sad and a terrible waste.'

The band played the three-date *Kerrang! Wooargh! Weekender* festival in Great Yarmouth ahead of their only professionally managed tour, which started in Reading on 16 October.

Pendragon tour flyer (From the collection of Jon Dunnington)

1984: A Bleeding Heart Poet In A Fragile Capsule

Barbel [sic] *Is In*
(From the collection of Guy Tkach)

Twelfth Night – Art And Illusion promo shot
(Courtesy Twelfth Night Archive)

'We travelled with the road crew on a tour bus, which was a laugh,' recalls Andy Revell. 'There was a living room, TV, bar, sound system, basic kitchen/galley, loos and, at the back, beds down each side with just curtains across each for privacy. Plenty of scope for practical jokes… After each gig the band would unwind with a few drinks while the crew dismantled the gear, which went into an articulated truck. At around 2.00 or 3.00 am the crew would be finished and would join us… for a few more drinks (it was the only way to sleep, honestly!). After a stop at the nearest motorway services for the obligatory fry-up, the bus would then be driven through the night to the next venue. There would always be the odd surprise in the morning. Like who appeared out of which bed and had to be put on a train back to the previous town. One morning I crawled naked out of my bunk, opened the curtain across my window only to find myself looking straight into the eyes of a curious old age pensioner complete with shopping basket - we had parked up in the middle of a Birmingham shopping centre.'

Twelfth Night were supported at every date by Midlands rockers Shy.

'In 1984,' lead singer Tony Mills told the author in 2009, 'our manager Barry Keen employed some agencies in London to acquire support slots on the UK rock circuit for us to promote our new album. Hit & Run offered us the TN tour. We were not aware of Twelfth Night before this at all. We were young at the time and the progressive side of rock had not come to us then. But we loved their music.'

A PLAYGROUND OF BROKEN HEARTS

SHOWSTOPPER PROMOTIONS PRESENTS

THE 1st KERRANG! WOOARGH! WEEKENDER

12 NOON FRIDAY 12th OCTOBER TO 5.00 pm SUNDAY 14th OCTOBER
AT LADBROKES SEA-SHORE HOLIDAY VILLAGE, GREAT YARMOUTH, NORFOLK.

LIVE IN CONCERT

motörhead

★ NAZARETH ★ TWELFTH NIGHT ★ SPIDER ★
★ PHIL LYNOTTS GRAND SLAM ★
★ WAYSTED ★ THOR ★ DUMPY'S RUSTY NUTS ★
★ KILLER ★

NEWSFLASH!!
B.B.C. Radio 1 recording the event for the FRIDAY ROCK SHOW.

D.J'S STEVE JOULE, ALLAN ROBSON, BAILEY BROTHERS etc

GIANT SCREEN VIDEOS FEATURING "MONSTERS OF ROCK". new releases from:
DIO, RUSH, BON JOVI, KISS, DEF LEPPARD, TWISTED SISTER, ZZ TOP.

NO HIDDEN EXTRAS ALL AMENITIES OPEN INCLUDING GIANT HEATED INDOOR POOL, AMUSEMENT ARCADES WITH ALL THE LATEST GAMES, POOL & SNOOKER ROOMS, TAKE-AWAY FOOD SHOPS AND MERCHANDISING STALLS, LATE NIGHT BARS, FILMS & VIDEOS. EVERYTHING UNDER COVER, FORGET THE WEATHER!!

3 ROCKIN' DAYS & 2 HEAVY NIGHTS
FULLY INCLUSIVE PRICE (EXCEPT FOR FOOD & DRINK – PUB PRICES) WITH ACCOMMODATION IN SELF CATERING LUXURY CARAVANS. LINEN SUPPLIED, NO ELECTRICITY SURCHARGE.

£30 INCL. V.A.T. SEND £10 DEPOSIT NOW FOR EACH PERSON WITHOUT DELAY.
Please note there are no day tickets, and the event is expected to sell-out very quickly.

OFFICIAL BOOKING FORM KERRANG WOOARGH WEEKENDER.
£30 PER PERSON INCLUSIVE. TO RESERVE BOOKING SEND DEPOSIT OF £10 PER PERSON WITH S.A.E.

NAME .... NUMBER OF RESERVATIONS:

ADDRESS... DEPOSIT PAID £

CHEQUES, POSTAL ORDERS SHOULD BE MADE PAYABLE TO SHOWSTOPPER PROMOTIONS, AND THE BOOKING FORM SENT TO SHOWSTOPPER PROMOTIONS. PINK ELEPHANT CLUB, SOUTHGATE, LONDON, N14. TEL. 01-886 8141

1984: A Bleeding Heart Poet In A Fragile Capsule

Thirty pounds, accommodation included, no electricity surcharge. Twelfth Night in Great Yarmouth

The imminent release of Pendragon's first album was celebrated by two dates at The Marquee, 19 and 20 October. Here, the band was interviewed by Mary Anne Hobbs for a feature in *Sounds* the following month. This also includes a rare report of The Marquee in its prime.

I dolefully searched my wardrobe for my flares but found they'd been donated to the cub scout camping club, and a large stain on my psychedelic blouse indicated even a feline fashion sense.

On my arrival at the gig, however, I was quite taken aback. I thought that to appreciate this style of music one had to secure at least an ounce of smouldering weed in the corner of the mouth and adopt a yoga position on the floor. How wrong I was! The stage was arranged with both kit and keyboards occupying the corners leaving maximum space for the guitarists to leap around in, and the audience was standing up! Surely I'd come to the wrong gig. This wasn't progressive rock.

At The Marquee there was [a] surprise in store for me. I didn't realise that progressive rock was such an energetic affair, and on surveying both band and punters alike leaping around and having a ball, it struck me that, like myself, many people had presumed far too much about something they really had no right to judge without experience.

The set was bold but classy, showing off instrumental expertise and a real flair for transposing mood into music. Much of the material ran a good deal deeper than many sex, drugs and rock 'n' roll songs creating a real atmospheric intensity relatively unique to themselves, and conjuring up a world of fantasy for their following. Their music rose and fell in intricate patterns, portraying power and passion in the favourite *Black Knight* and subtle romance in the newly penned *Please*. As yet Pendragon have very much of a cult following, but as they progress and branch out musically they hope they'll appeal to a wider spectrum.

Pendragon's music is a far cry from the progressive rock of a decade ago, and rather than being dated is somewhat timeless. Neither are they a second rate Marillion copy merely cashing in on the revival triggered by Fish and Co. All Pendragon ask is for you to come along and 'give them a try'.

IQ's performance at Heads in Watford on 24 October was filmed; this was released on *The Wake 25th Anniversary Collector's Edition* in 2010. As October moved into November, long-awaited debut albums by Pendragon and Solstice would finally be released.

Firstly, after many delays, *Fly High, Fall Far* entered the world on 29 October. The album was distributed by EMI and peaked just outside the UK Top 100. This four-track, 24-minute mini-album displays enthusiasm over sophistication. Nick Barrett's vocals are, of course, immediately recognisable. The title track is a basic slab of loud rock with swirling keyboards and a simple but effective guitar solo. Barrett's vocals are set back in the mix. *Victims Of Life* is classic early Pendragon: largely instrumental and with a definite *Duke*-era Genesis feel. *Dark Summer's Day* is melodic and melancholic, mixing keyboards (which finally come to the fore here) alongside the guitar, to create a beautiful piece.

Pendragon poster for The Marquee, 19-20 October 1984 (From the collection of Jon Dunnington)

Early period Genesis informs *Excalibur*, an elegant, multi-part instrumental, which allows Barrett to stretch out brilliantly on guitar.

Fly High, Fall Far is a mere morsel of the 'Dragon's fiery future. Unlike music for manic depressives courtesy of the greasepaint merchants who have shadowed prog rock with infernal gloom, Pendragon offer a light and refreshing alternative. A nicely produced and stylish sound complements a varied song selection. The raunchier title track *Fly High, Fall Far* shows a stronger rock influence in contrast with the gentle and pleasurable ebb and flow of the instrumental *Excalibur*. Especially as a debut, the album is highly commendable and will succeed, I'm sure, in dampening many a palate.

Mary Anne Hobbs, *Sounds*

Rik Carter: 'I would love to re-record *Fly High, Fall Far* and *The Jewel* with decent sounds and good production. I can't listen to either now. All I hear is this terrible, tinny production because none of us really had any proper studio experience at all – but we were young I guess...'

Solstice had started a seven-week UK tour on 26 October. This included familiar venues such as The Marquee (1-2 November), the General Wolfe (3 November), Bangor University (9 November), Maxwell Hall, Aylesbury (22 November) and Bristol Granary (15 December) as well as gigs as far apart as Glasgow and Penzance.

This was to promote *Silent Dance*, which was finally made available to fans on 3 November.

Hopefully some of the Cornish magick will come across in the music though it is hard for us to be objective about it after seven months. The album is being released on our own Equinox label and being distributed by Illuminated Records. If it isn't on the shelves of your local record emporium the catalogue number to quote is EQR-LP 001. It will be available at all our gigs and also by mail order from the usual address.

Things look bright for 1985, several record companies showed a positive reaction to *Silent Dance*, although they're still not ready to put their money where their souls are – it's up to all of you to demonstrate that Solstice have a future.

Solstice newsletter, October 1984

Silent Dance mixes progressive rock, folk and new age sounds into a formidable brew. The unique mix of Sandy Leigh's pure voice, Andy Glass' gloriously melodic guitar solos and Marc Elton's soaring violin combine to create music that is difficult to characterise yet easy to enjoy. The opening *Peace* is a strong composition, even though it keeps threatening to morph into *State Of Independence*, with its 1980s synthesisers and Jon Anderson feel to the vocals. The compelling, flowing *Earthsong* has deep bass lines and delicious vocal harmonies and *Sunrise* echoes Renaissance, Curved Air and the more pastoral moments of Led Zeppelin to great effect. The superb *Return Of Spring* is vivid and invigorating: an instrumental showcase for Marc Elton's expressive violin playing. *Cheyenne* add multiple vocals to sharp guitar playing. The hypnotic second half combines thumping drums and vocals in a language made up by Sandy Leigh designed to invoke the feel of Native American chanting. It could be an outtake from Mike Oldfield's *Incantations*. One of Andy Glass' favourites from this first incarnation of Solstice, *Cheyenne* was beautifully re-recorded in 2020 for the album *Sia* and, at the time of writing, is still featured in the band's set list. *Brave New World* is 100% progressive rock, the folk-tinged bastard son of Rush and Jon & Vangelis. The album closes with the soothing *Find Yourself*, a simple pop ballad. Sandy Leigh sings brilliantly, sounding more like herself here than on any other track on the album. The song fizzles out after four minutes, fading with 90 seconds of noodling.

Steve Rothery: 'I thought that [*Silent Dance*] was okay but hadn't captured their essence very well. I also thought they were trying a bit too hard to be alternative when the music business is a game you have to play, even if it's on your own terms.'

Twelfth Night's tour continued, with Shy supporting. At one memorable gig in the cavernous Manchester Apollo, Geoff and Jane Mann watched the whole show and Geoff jumped on stage to duet with Andy Sears on *Love Song*.

Although this author, who was present that evening, has no recollection, a third band performed that night, a local group called Moriarty. They had also played at The Marquee on 6 July 1984 supporting IQ.

'We were booked to play Liverpool and Manchester on this tour as we were a Stockport band with some local support,' says guitarist and vocalist Alan Whittaker. 'But on the way to Liverpool our drummer/driver Mark missed the motorway turn off for the gig, so we didn't play… Manchester Apollo was a big hall for us … so we had a good gig!'

The tour finished in London with a return to The Dominion on 6 November 1984 followed by Twelfth Night's only date outside the UK, at Marburg University near Frankfurt. The tour had been heavily promoted and visited significantly bigger venues, but attendances had been generally disappointing.

'That tour was probably make or break for us, although we maybe didn't realise it at the time,' recalls Rick Battersby. 'In retrospect though, it perhaps marked the beginning of the end. That tour really had to be completely memorable and while it was good, it wasn't good enough. It was clear that things were beginning to show the strain, internally, both with the management company and musically.'

With hindsight, this was a key turning point for Twelfth Night. The band's major deal was over a year away and there would be a 22 month gap between *Art And Illusion* and its follow-up. The momentum achieved during Andy Sears' first year with the band was irrecoverably lost. After the Marburg show, Twelfth Night would perform only another 18 gigs over the next three years.

As Twelfth Night's series of gigs wound down and Pendragon knuckled down to write songs for their first full-length album, Marillion played a seven-week tour of the UK and Europe to promote *Real To Reel* and to perform some new material written that autumn. By now, Marillion had leapt far ahead of the other contemporary bands and were playing arenas in France and Germany. Released on 5 November 1984, *Real To Reel* had been recorded in Leicester on 5 March and Montreal on 19-20 June. As is typical with live albums, some in-studio repairs were undertaken.

'Most bands when mixing live recordings replace, repair, overdub or completely re-record their songs

1984: A Bleeding Heart Poet In A Fragile Capsule

Andy Sears (Photograph by Mark Drake)

before mixing,' noted Mark Kelly. '… We've always been a bit coy about what we got up to in the studio with that album, and I'm here to tell you, hand on heart, that we didn't go that far. It certainly wasn't like we took the metaphorical halves of two separate cars and welded them together, but there were a number of repairs.

'Some were because of bad recording such as the bass, which was badly overloaded as it went to tape in Leicester. Others were plain old bum notes or out of tune vocals. It's one thing to experience a song in a hall with a few drinks inside you and a rowdy crowd singing along and quite another to hear the same mishap over and over again on headphones from the sterile and sober comfort of your living room chair.'

'We went to Rick Parfitt's studio in Weybridge for a few days to do some touch ups to the tracks,' engineer Simon Hanhart said. 'And then we mixed at The Marquee.'

Retailing at just £2.99, the album was a big hit, reaching number 8 on release.

'Luckily it made a little bit of a splash in Europe,' notes Mark Kelly. 'That was just enough to keep us going to the point where EMI were, 'OK, you can make another album.''

Ian Mosley's influence on the whole band is very clear: there is power and precision on *Real To Reel*.

'Having Ian in the band is like knowing you carry heavy insurance,' said Pete Trewavas, 'you feel safe. You don't have to worry about anything except your own playing, and he allows you to get away with it and run away with a few ideas on stage without being terrified the whole thing is going to collapse around your ears.'

'Playing with Ian means really having to be on your toes,' noted Mark Kelly. 'He's got a lot of imagination but he never hits a beat or a roll that shouldn't be there, he never wastes his moves, and his timing is impeccable. As a result, after Ian joined the band the rest of us improved as musicians virtually overnight! You can't play with someone like Ian for long periods of time without some of it rubbing off and having a positive effect. I mean, even though there's only one change in the line-up between the band that recorded *Script…* and the one that played on the *Real to Reel* album, if you listen to both records back-to-back it virtually sounds like two completely worlds apart, really.'

Pallas completed their 20 date *The Knight Moves* tour in November. The tour had started in Aberdeen, with the band's newsletter at the time explaining their rationale.

As you will be well aware this tour is a special return to smaller venues to introduce Alan Reed, the new frontman, to club audiences on an 'intimate' level so you can get to know him well. Alan has been with the band since late summer and it already seems as if he's been with Pallas since the start and the special debut gigs in August were a great success.

Another purpose of this tour is to introduce many new numbers which will be featured on the band's next two releases; the first of which will be in the form of a 12" single to be released in January. Those tracks will NOT be included in the next album which will be recorded after the next leg of the Knight Moves Tour which is planned for January. So there's plenty of new material to be aired!

The Game begins.

The Knight Moves.

Solstice's visit to Night Moves in Glasgow, 12 November, was reviewed in *Revelatory* issue 5.

Afghan coats and embroidered denim, faded, that had obviously seen better days, were in evidence. But the average age of those present was such that the majority probably aren't old enough to remember the original times.

Sandy Leigh flitted off and on stage depending on the track. She also took over on keyboards allowing Marc Elton to play his olive-green coloured violin. Manically. Frantically. Eyes staring, rolling. Facial contortion. Full of expression. Andy Glass, shoeless, bounced around the stage occasionally playing the stand-mounted double neck guitar. Superbly. Both Mark Hawkins and Martin Wright (bass and drums respectively) supported with skilful musicianship, yet shunned the obvious limelight and attention foisted on the up-front threesome. No self-indulgent drum, or tedious bass solos. Solstice had the crowd eating out of their hands.

November 1984 marked the highest concentration of gigs by the big six prog bands of the 1980s: 72 dates in that month. Twelfth Night completed their 18-date *Art And Illusion* tour between 12 October and 10 November, IQ toured the UK from 20 October to 22 December, 22 dates in total. Marillion were in the UK and Europe (3 November to 22 December), and Pallas were on the road from 1 to 21 November. Pendragon's only booking of the month was supporting The Enid at Hammersmith Odeon.

'It was my favourite venue,' says Pendragon's Rik Carter. 'I used to go there twice a week to see whichever metal bands were touring when I was a teenager: Motörhead, AC/DC, Judas Priest, UFO, Ted Nugent, Black Sabbath, ZZ Top, Rush…'

The *Real To Reel* tour, Marillion's biggest European tour to date, spanned seven weeks in November and December. This included their first concerts in Sweden (Stockholm), Belgium (Poperinge) and Luxembourg (Schifflange) as well as long runs of shows in the UK, France, the Netherlands, Denmark and Germany. What would become the first half of *Misplaced Childhood* (without *Lavender* as yet) formed the core of these gigs. The final series of UK dates, between 13 and 21 December, included support from the Cardiacs.

The 14 December show at Hammersmith Odeon was broadcast by BBC Radio and Westwood One.

1984: A Bleeding Heart Poet In A Fragile Capsule

Marillion (Photograph by Mark Drake)

This can be heard on *Early Stages: The Official Bootlegs 1982-1987*. *Sounds* covered the tour in the 15 December issue under the headline 'The Prog Prince'.

That same week, new wave band The Europeans performed back-to-back shows at The Marquee promoting their second studio album *Recurring Dreams*. Their singer: Steve Hogarth.

Marillion, Live In Glasgow, 19 December 1984

Maybe I'm getting jaded or just cynical in my 'old' age but somehow Marillion's two Christmas concerts in Glasgow did not inspire me as much as previous outings to their gigs. Don't ask me to explain why…

The Barrowland Ballroom may be the latest trendy venue, but to my mind it is an awful one. The temperature at the evening performance was on a par with The Marquee in July, and the front of the hall greatly resembled a rugby scrum – and due to the fact that it is a dance floor, you had to be about 6ft. 4in. before you could see anything!

The matinee performance followed by the evening one was an unusual idea. If like me you went to both you were left a physical wreck.

Assassing got the proceedings off to a flying start – no assassination of unsuspecting roadies this time! It was a powerful punchy version with the crowd singing along with every line. Next up was the unlikely inclusion so early in the set of *Garden Party*. People bounced and buns flew but no low flying cucumbers were seen.

Let's slow things down with the relative 'newie', *Cinderella Search* (well I hadn't seen it performed live before) – poignant lyrics of a fishy variety set to a sensual rhythm. Bouncy at the end though and if the crowd bounces, you've got to bounce too.

Some more oldies but goodies in the form of *Jigsaw*, *Chelsea Monday* (wonderful lighting on this) and the vitriolic *Emerald Lies* mesmerised me with the fatal attraction of a cobra's stare. Smooth and elegant while going straight for the

A PLAYGROUND OF BROKEN HEARTS

Fish, Utrecht, 22 November 1984
(Photograph by Rob Portengen)

jugular (or the emotion).

Marillion then introduced their new mega epic *Misplaced Childhood*. I'm a bit sceptical of concept albums with 20 min. epics on both sides. Lack of progression… (who said that! - maybe I'm just biased). It was good but it didn't inspire me to the extent of *Fugazi* or *Chelsea Monday*. Everyone else loved it!

A truly wonderful version of *Script…* followed with the Glasgow choir taking over most of the vocals. The set proper was then concluded by the rather seedy *Incubus* with the greasepaint mask being symbolically erased.

The evening show merited two encores, *Market Square Heroes* and *Fugazi*. *Fugazi* is perhaps Marillion's pièce de résistance with its labyrinthine construction and 'Runrigesque' ending.

On the whole I enjoyed the concert, but I was still slightly disappointed. C'est La Vie……

Fiona Dempster, *Revelatory* issue 5

Marillion's year ended with a return to Friars in Aylesbury.

IQ's concluded with a New Year's Eve booking at The Marquee. This was their 71st gig of 1984.

'We were asked by the Marquee management to play a New Year's Eve show there,' says Peter Nicholls. 'This was a huge honour for us, and we were thrilled to be invited to do it. By this time, we were regulars at The Marquee, it was our home venue.'

Indeed, this 31 December show was their 13th at the famous London venue that year, a total matched by Pendragon in 1984, with Solstice (11 gigs) and Twelfth Night (8) not far behind.

At this gig IQ played a new song, *Hollow Afternoon*, and attendees were given a specially recorded one-sided single as a souvenir (catalogue number IQ FREE B1).

Martin Orford: 'It was a song I'd written in its entirety, but it didn't get a great reception from the band. Although my chorus lyrics were retained, my rather wordy verses weren't well liked, so Pete wrote some different ones which we recorded. Mike didn't seem remotely interested in *Hollow Afternoon*, so I think I ended up playing the lead guitar on it. Given the antipathy towards it, *Hollow Afternoon* was never going to make it onto an IQ studio album, but at least it got a release of some sort.'

Peter Nicholls: 'We pressed up 500 copies and gave them out to everyone who attended. We

1984: A Bleeding Heart Poet In A Fragile Capsule

IQ at The Marquee, 31 December 1984
(Photographs by Albert Jagger)

wanted something special to give to people as a thank you for their support. It was Mike's idea; he was always good at coming up with things like that.'

The band's second set was comprised almost exclusively of the covers they'd been playing as encores that year.

'We had a reputation for playing unlikely cover versions for encores,' Peter recalls. 'Problem was, this had started to overtake us a bit, and people just wanted to know what the cover was going to be at each gig. So we thought this would be a good opportunity to play the covers for one last time and

A PLAYGROUND OF BROKEN HEARTS

IQ's rare *Hollow Afternoon* single
(From the collection of Russell Morgan)

IQ's 1984 Christmas card
(From the collection of Guy Tkach)

try to draw a line under it. We made the decision to play two sets: an IQ set followed by a second set of all the covers. There were rigorous rehearsals, we timed everything meticulously.'

Peter, Mike, Widge, Cookie and Tim performed *Relax* (Frankie Goes To Hollywood), *Suffragette City* (David Bowie), *Hey Hey, My My* (Neil Young), *Open Your Heart* (Human League), *School's Out* (Alice Cooper), *For Christ's Sake*, a Genesis medley, *God Save The Queen* (Sex Pistols), a Glenn Miller medley, *Sweet Transvestite* (from *The Rocky Horror Show*), *Ace Of Spades* (Motörhead) and *White Punks On Dope* (The Tubes). The clock ticked towards midnight.

'We'd arranged for Bush, the deputy manager at The Marquee, to join us onstage at 11:55,' Peter says, 'but he was late getting there. I suspect alcohol might have been involved. So we got everyone to sing *Auld Lang Syne*. Bush finally showed up in time to say, 'Happy New Year, everybody, from The Marquee, London!', and we launched into U2's *New Year's Day* at the stroke of midnight.'

'I was at university in Leeds,' says Stephanie Bradley, who attended the show. 'I went with my friend Lisa Wright who was on my course. We both went dressed up as Magenta from *The Rocky Horror Show*. Nigel Hutchings, the club's manager, had pulled us aside, and he said, 'I want you to go on stage at the stroke of midnight with these bottles of champagne, shake the bottles and spray them all over the audience.' Bizarrely the cork would not come out of my bottle. So this is my moment on stage at The Marquee and this bloody cork wouldn't come out of the bottle. I had one job to do…'

'Still now, all these years later, there are people who remember it as the best gig they ever attended,' Peter remarks, 'which is remarkable. I remember walking home to Harlesden afterwards, with a bunch of people who were staying over at mine. I guess it took a couple of hours to get there but I was floating. It was an amazing night.'

1984: A Bleeding Heart Poet In A Fragile Capsule

Martin Orford channels Lemmy
(Photograph by Albert Jagger)

Peter Nicholls
(Photograph by Mark Drake)

1985:
Dawn Escapes From Moon Washed College Halls

> I thought of him as a good friend at the time. It was like a switch had been thrown and he was someone else.
>
> Steve Rothery, in conversation with the author, 11 July 2023

At the end of 1984, Pendragon were voted fourth in the annual end-of-year *Sounds* poll, and Twelfth Night eleventh. And yet, for both bands a record deal seemed to be still out of their grasp.

Twelfth Night played two fan club shows at The Marquee on 5 and 6 January. All five songs from *Art And Illusion* were aired, along with some strong new material that shows Andy Sears' influence on the band's musical direction. *I Am*, *The Craft* and *Pressure*, all performed at those shows, were demoed at Matinee Studios in Reading along with three others: *Last Song*, *South Of The Wind* and *White Glass*. *Last Song*, *The Craft* and *Pressure* received more work in March 1985 at Soundmill Studios.

'This might surprise you,' notes Clive Mitten, 'but the catalyst for the sound we wanted in 1985 and what became *XII* was Frankie Goes To Hollywood's debut album *Welcome To The Pleasure Dome* [released October 1984]. I had heard and enjoyed ABC's album *The Lexicon Of Love* [June 1982], and, of course, *90125* by Yes [November 1983]. These were all produced by Trevor Horn and they really caught my attention with their crisp production and unusual sounds. Prog was dying and we needed to change. I wanted to mix the synth-driven poppy Trevor Horn sound with the arena style metal of Van Halen, with some of Andy's unique vocal stylings on the top.'

Record company interest was piqued. Charisma Records offered Twelfth Night a ten album deal.

'We were given a big advance,' Andy Revell says. 'And we were managed by Genesis's manager. But by then, I think we'd kind of lost our way a little bit.'

Solstice's tour to support *Silent Dance* had been a success, but founder bassist Mark Hawkins stepped out of the band in the early weeks of 1985.

Andy Glass: 'After the experience of recording the album, we became very intense about making sure everything was as good as it could be.'

Glass was listening to the likes of *Aja* by Steely Dan and Joni Mitchell's *Wild Things Run Fast*. This was the level of musicianship to which he aspired.

'We didn't feel that Mark was cutting it,' he said. 'This was a dreadful mistake on our part and the magic left the band after that. It's something I still feel awful about to this day. The long and short of it is that we felt that a new bass player was the right thing to do. And it was absolutely the wrong thing to do.'

Glass had qualified as an architectural technician after four years at Buckinghamshire County Council and now expected Solstice, with an album in the can, to move to full-time professionalism. Mark Hawkins had quit his job as a dental engineer in response.

Ticket for Twelfth Night at The Marquee, 6 January 1985
(From the collection of Peter Moltensen)

Adverts from *Sounds* and the *NME*
(From the collection of Guy Tkach)

Barbara Deason
(Photograph by Oz Hardwick)

Andy Glass: 'It required all of our time to be able to tour and play to that extent and we wanted everyone to be available and committed to that. I felt terrible about it at the time, but I really believed that firing Mark was the right thing to do. Like a fool, you know.'

Then, shortly afterwards, singer Sandy Leigh fell pregnant.

'Sandy was embracing a particular way forward with that pregnancy that wasn't compatible with being in a band,' Andy Glass said. 'Of course, we respected that. Sandy was another absolutely crucial part of what the band was at the time we made the album, and for several years before that.'

Barbara Deason would be their fourth singer in fewer than three years.

'I remember Marc and I auditioning for a replacement for Sandy round at his flat,' says Andy Glass. 'Another *Melody Maker* ad I think. It was painful. I'm not sure if that's how we found Barbara, but we definitely went to her place to meet and hear her. She was a good singer, and she fitted the bill. And we thought, 'Yeah, this is gonna be great!''

Mark Hawkins in turn was replaced by Ken Bowley.

'I knew nothing about Solstice at the time,' he told the author. 'I had recently finished my first tour as a professional musician with Gordon Giltrap and was doing a lot of auditions looking for the next gig. I was still collaborating with Giltrap on music for a TV series, but I had a yearning to be out playing live. The audition was in Milton Keynes, in some downstairs room at a community centre or some such place [it was at Peartree Bridge]. All I remember is that after it was over, I was loading up the car and had to go back downstairs for something I'd

1985: Dawn Escapes From Moon Washed College Halls

Solstice – first gig with Barbara Deason and Ken Bowley in Dunstable, early 1985 (Photographs by Oz Hardwick)

forgotten. Andy was gushing about what a great audition it was, and I was mildly embarrassed but quite gratified…'

The final Solstice line-up of the 1980s was in place, but would last only six months.

Andy Glass: 'If I was to go back and give myself some advice it would be to understand the importance of chemistry… It's such a rare thing to have band chemistry that really works and changing any element is a potential disaster… it certainly was in our case. That's where things started to unravel. It was a decision we made that had nothing to do with commercial interest or external pressures.'

With their new album written, Marillion recorded a high quality demo of the entire piece at Bray Film Studios near Maidenhead across several weeks in January and February 1985. *Lavender* would be added to side one at this stage. Formal recording sessions were due to begin in March.

Mark Kelly: 'We approached a few respected producers, including Glyn Johns and Rupert Hine, but none of them were interested, especially when they got wind of our plans to record a concept album. That sort of talk in 1985 was bordering on heresy. Eventually someone suggested Chris Kimsey, who we knew little about apart from the fact that he had worked with The Rolling Stones and engineered for ELP early in their career.

'He was invited down to Bray where we played him some of the album demos. He quickly understood where we were coming from and made some insightful observations about the music, which instantly struck a chord with us. We liked his personality too.'

IQ had been working on new material. At their first date of 1985, at the Granary in Bristol on 26 February, they would perform three new songs: *Outer Limits*, *The Wake* and *Corners*.

'Good evening, everybody,' Peter Nicholls told the Bristol audience. 'We've got a special little occasion tonight. We've been off the road for about eight weeks now and in that time we've been writing some new songs. So we thought we would come along tonight and let you hear one or two. Some more finished than others. These are some songs we thought we'd give Bristol the benefit of the doubt first. These are some of the tracks from the new album which we'll start recording in about two weeks' time.'

Music by Solstice (*Peace*) and Pendragon (*Fly High, Fall Far*), Haze, Liaison, Trilogy, Citizen Cain, LaHost and Quasar would be included on a compilation album called *Fire In Harmony*, released on 18 March 1985 on John Arnison's Elusive record label.

'It was a fun deal,' laughs Haze's Chris McMahon. 'Elusive agreed to pay each band an advance of their share of the royalties, which I think was £200, on condition that we spent the money on a recording session in their studio. We eventually got a royalty statement saying that we were due £187.50. They wrote off the £12.50 that we owed!'

Fire In Harmony (Elusive ARRLP 100) ****

AFTER MARILLION and co. comes the new new wave of progressive rockers, this sampler featuring the latest re-emergence of a musical form popularised by 'dinosaurs' Genesis and Yes. Honours go to the more experienced acts on the LP due to better production, Solstice's *Peace* mimics Yes, especially Sandy Leigh's vocals, while Pendragon's *Fly High, Fall Far* is one of the rockier inclusions.

Liaison offer *A Tale Of You*, a mellow ballad built around a melodic guitar refrain. Trilogy, Haze and Quasar also include a track each. The snag is, the showcase smacks of revival rather than progression. Only Citizen Cain's *Unspoken Words*, thanks to a quirky melody and George Scott's strident Scottish brogue, shows some individuality.

But, as with most compilations, it's difficult to judge any band on the strength of one track. LaHost's *Blood And Roses*, in particular, doesn't do justice to an excellent live act. Nevertheless, a commendable chance to hear the new face of prog rock.

Pete Picton, *Sounds*, 6 July 1985

At producer Chris Kimsey's suggestion, Marillion travelled to Berlin to record their third album, *Misplaced Childhood*.

'We had to do it in Berlin because it was cheap to record there,' says Mark Kelly. 'EMI tightened their purse strings considerably. We were about to be dropped. We didn't see the writing on the wall. Maybe it was just youth, hubris, whatever, I don't know. Blinkers.'

The Hansa Tonstudio in central Berlin had seen some important artists in recent years, including David Bowie (*Low*, *"Heroes"*, *Baal*), Iggy Pop (*The Idiot*, *Lust For Life*), Tangerine Dream (*Force Majeure*), Depeche Mode (*Construction Time Again*, *Some Great Reward*), Killing Joke (*Night Time*), David Sylvian (*Brilliant Trees*) and Nick Cave & The Bad Seeds (*The Firstborn Is Dead*).

'We had played *Misplaced Childhood* live a number of times by then,' says Ian Mosley. 'On our first day at Hansa we sat Chris in the middle of the studio and we played him the whole album from start to finish.'

Sessions lasted from March to May 1985.

'Berlin, before the Wall fell, was a microcosm of anarchy and unrestricted freedom, something we embraced with reckless abandon,' writes Mark Kelly. 'We would work every day from around noon until about 7pm and then break for dinner, which usually meant going out to a restaurant and eating and drinking for a few hours. We would then return to the studio and, depending on our alcoholic equilibrium, do some useful work or fool around recording music that was destined to be erased the next day.'

But a split was starting to open. During the Berlin sessions, Fish and Steve Rothery had argued about possible plans for solo albums.

'Hugh Stanley-Clarke [from the band's label EMI] flew over to listen to the mixes,' Rothery says. 'Both Fish and I punted solo project ideas to him. Fish had an idea based on the Geisterfahrer principle. This is a person who drives down the wrong side of the Autobahn to commit suicide by crashing into another car.'

'It's a German social problem,' Fish said. 'A lot of high falutin' businessmen who end up worshipping cars, say that the best way to commit suicide is to drive up the Autobahn, do a u-turn, and drive against the flow of traffic and into a truck. If you're driving about in Europe real late at night and you put on the radio, you hear Geisterfahrer warnings come out on the radio that say, 'between junction 3 and 17'. So, you pull over to the side, and you see this car going by, and a lot of cops are chasing it. It's quite a deadly little game. And I wanted to do this album about a guy who went on a journey from the

1985: Dawn Escapes From Moon Washed College Halls

Solstice at The Marquee, 24 March 1985, with Ken Bowley and Barbara Deason (Photographs by Robin Willcocks and Oz Hardwick)

time the car engine turns on. It was going to be a bit like Dickens' *Christmas Carol*, which was to take characters like a mechanic or a policeman, or another Geisterfahrer that succeeded and maybe they can all sit in the back seat, and you know, they can talk to him, and have this musical discussion about his life. And the guy switches on the radio and a cover song comes on that's relevant to his life, like a narration piece from an analytical sense.'

Steve Rothery: 'At the same time, I had an idea for a project called *Ravenscar*, which was gonna be more of a rock kind of thing. Hugh loved my idea and turned down Fish. And the next minute Fish has me pinned up against the wall in the downstairs bar at the Hansa Tonstudio accusing me of saving all my best ideas for my solo album. I wrote about 85 to 90% of *Misplaced Childhood*, so it was a little bit ironic to have this psychopathic Scotsman threatening violence and pinning me against the wall. And that's the moment I stopped thinking of him as a friend and just as somebody I worked with.'

Solstice booked time into Aosis Studios in London, 15 March 1985, to record a few demos with the new line-up.

Andy Glass: 'I remember we went into the studio in London. Ken Bowley had a LinnDrum, a drum machine. This was quite an exciting new thing at the time. So instead of using Martin, we used the LinnDrum and recorded a couple of things.'

Martin Wright: 'I am sure there was something I had going on that clashed with the date picked for recording in London, so Ken's suggestion to program the drums helped me out as well as saving studio time.'

They recorded a third version of *New Life*, a song that had been around for some years by now, and a

A PLAYGROUND OF BROKEN HEARTS

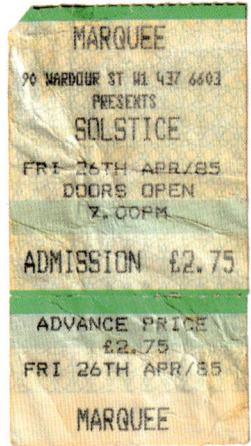

Solstice tickets from March and April 1985 (From the collection of Peter Moltensen)

newer composition called *Spirit*.

Andy Glass: 'I remember taking it back and playing it to Phil Wheal and clearly recall him just laughing at it. It crushed me at the time because I was still trying to be positive about how this was going to work… but Phil was right. I think at that point we knew deep down it was over.'

Pendragon and IQ were in the studio, too, during March and April 1985.

Pendragon were recording the tracks that would make up *The Jewel* at Soundmill Studios in Berkshire. All of the songs had been blooded in concert, with the exception of *Higher Circles* which was written in the studio to fill up a spare three minutes.

'The budget wasn't there for us to bring in an outside producer,' Nick Barrett said. 'Besides, we felt that we could do the job ourselves. That was a mistake. One of the problems was we had three weeks to do the album. That might not seem like a long time now, but it was almost an eternity back then. This meant everything came under the microscope, and suddenly nothing was good enough. We were ultra-critical of everything. It got to a point when we could no longer be objective and heard mistakes all over the place. We really did need someone else in the studio with us, to provide an outside perspective.'

Band members' different preferences for recording would cause friction.

'Peter would do his bass parts overnight,' Nick Barrett recalled. 'When I got in during the early morning, to do my vocals and guitar parts, he'd play me back what he'd recorded that night. He was totally fried, though, and when I'd hear what he had done, I knew it wasn't good enough. So I often told him the bass lines would have to be done all over again. It all made the recording process so torturous and difficult. There was a sense of doom in the studio a lot of the time, because we had nobody else to turn to.'

'We had three weeks to record and mix the album,' Gee says. 'So we had to work fast. But it was also very exciting. My main memory of recording *The Jewel* was that somehow I had managed to get Andy Latimer from Camel's home address, and so I wrote to him saying that we were self-producing our first album and asked if he would come and produce it for us? Much to my amazement, Andy wrote back saying he didn't feel that he could produce our album, but he would drop in to see us in the studio. So I was sat in the control room one morning recording bass takes, when the door opened and my all-time musical hero, Andy Latimer, walked in. I think Andy was actually there too when Nick was recording the guitar solo for *The Black Knight*, so no pressure there then! But Andy is one of the nicest people that I have ever met, as well as being very encouraging and complimentary about our debut album. What a great life memory, to have met your hero.'

Buoyed by that visit from Latimer, who 'ate the last piece of gala pie for our lunch', recording was completed on time. But when it came to mixing, Nick Barrett elected to withdraw.

'I had been working so hard on my parts that I simply had to bow out, and let Rik and Peter oversee things,' he admitted. 'The four of us had

1985: Dawn Escapes From Moon Washed College Halls

IQ in 1985 (From the collection of Guy Tkach)

choreography. We got some great sounds down to tape on *The Jewel*, but somehow managed to lose it all in the mixing. It just came out quite thin and a flat sound. It has a precision and detail to it, but it lacks the life and power of the *Friday Rock Show* recordings. I also think that we were all quite tired by the end of it and maybe had lost our way a bit in the mixing. We were learning as we went along, what worked and what did not work. But I am pleased with the music and the arrangements, if not with the actual final production and the sound itself. The album does been quite democratic in the studio. However, I was burnt out by then and had nothing more to offer. In the end we finished the album at 5am on the last day. When we listened back on the sound system in the studio it all came across so well. We really thought we had nailed it. But the trouble was that we didn't know what sounded good, and what didn't, by this point. It had been such a slog.'

'In those days we didn't have the money, time, or luxury of doing a rough mix and then coming back two months later to have another go,' says Peter Gee. 'We basically had one or two attempts within a couple of days to get it right. It was also 'live mixing' where there were two or three of us sitting at the desk, each in charge of five or six faders. Mixing was like a live performance, a type of sound better today, however, now that it has been remastered. But there was definitely a sense of pressure on us to get everything completed in the time available.'

IQ were recording their second album at Falconer Studios in London with sessions starting on 12 April.

'The writing process of *The Wake* started pretty much immediately after we released *Tales From The Lush Attic*,' recalled Mike Holmes.

'The main theme of the album is death,' Peter Nicholls explained, 'which was one of my preoccupations at the time of writing *The Wake*. The central character dies at the end of *Outer Limits*, the opening song, and the story is built around what happens to his soul from that point. There was a short story by Edgar Allan Poe called *The Premature*

A PLAYGROUND OF BROKEN HEARTS

Peter Gee of Pendragon at The Marquee (Photograph by Mark Drake)

IQ ticket from 18 April 1985 (From the collection of Peter Moltensen)

Burial which was lodged somewhere in my brain, and that was one of the starting points for *The Wake*. As with all stories, the concept was a mixture of various influences and ideas, and although death wasn't a particularly positive theme for an album, it worked well as a way of connecting the songs we were writing.'

Holmes would co-produce with Tim Esau.

'I have to say we were fairly naïve in terms of production values,' he said, 'and there was no real plan to make it sound significantly different from the previous album. I think the difference was that we had a bit more time to devote to recording and mixing *The Wake*, and also that we decided as a band that I would be the main producer, along with contributions from Tim Esau. This allowed me to have an overall vision for the feel of the album, rather than everyone pushing their own fader up in the mix, as we did for *Tales*.'

'*The Wake* was a bit less rushed,' suggests Martin Orford, 'though we certainly didn't have much of a budget for studio time. But the studio facilities were much better, and we were able to experiment with different keyboards and an Emulator 2, which was proper high-tech at the time. As a result, *The Wake* is a better sounding album than *Tales* and it contains some IQ classics, but *Tales* still shades it for me in terms of the songwriting quality.'

IQ returned to The Marquee on 18 April.

'Most of you might have noticed that publicly speaking we've been keeping quite a low profile since the beginning of the year,' singer Peter Nicholls said from the stage. 'Behind the scenes is the much nicer story. We've been hard at it and recording a new album. This album is entitled *The Wake*. For those of you with calendars and diaries with you, you might like to check off 3 June because, fingers

1985: Dawn Escapes From Moon Washed College Halls

Little Bold Shine (From the collection of Russell Morgan)

Below: IQ at *The Wake* playback, 24 April 1985 (Photograph by Albert Jagger)

crossed and if the music fairy is with us, that should be the release date of the LP. Well, coincidentally, the next track we are about to play is a new track from the album and, as coincidence would have it, this is entitled *The Wake*.'

Some of the band's demos from this period, along with a couple of live tracks, some interviews and finished songs from *The Wake* would be compiled by Peter Nicholls into a promo cassette called *Little Bold Shine* with a handwritten sleeve and examples of Nicholls' quirky humour.

The band completed their second album at the end of April 1985. Release was set for six weeks later.

Solstice performed a brace of gigs at The Marquee on 25-26 April supported by a new band called Pride Of Passion. Solstice's set list included most of *Silent Dance*, a couple of new tracks and some older songs such as *Guardian Of My Soul*, *Time For A Toke*, *The Journey*,

New Life and *Brave New World*.

Andy Glass: 'I did love Barbara's soulful take of *Guardian Of My Soul*.'

Indeed, *Guardian Of My Soul* is a highlight of a recording made at The Marquee on 26 April. This also includes a song accompanying a female Japanese singer. No one can recall her name now.

Martin Wright: 'There was a Japanese crew filming her. She was completely unknown to us. But we were happy for her to make a guest appearance on stage.'

Andy Glass: 'I don't actually recall this at all. Quite nice though. I assume it's her song.'

'I remember it being painfully loud onstage at times,' says bassist Ken Bowley, 'and Barbara having a near constant flow of port and brandy to ease her throat.'

Pallas' new singer Alan Reed was bedded in with a 12" EP called *The Knightmoves* released in late April or early May. This contained three new songs: *Strangers*, *Nightmare* and *Sanctuary*. *Strangers* and

A PLAYGROUND OF BROKEN HEARTS

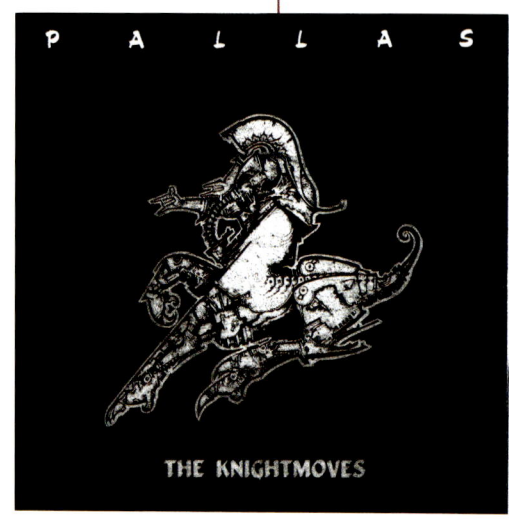

The Knightmoves
(From the collection of
Piersandro Pallavicini)

Nightmare were also released as a 7" single and as a picture disc.

'It was meant as a bridge between the two different line-ups,' Reed says. 'I'd already made it clear to the band that I wouldn't try and ape Euan in any way. That I'd do things differently. *Sanctuary* was the first thing we wrote from scratch as a band. It had the more 'modern' feel that we were trying to develop, whilst conforming to many of the prog elements we were known for.'

'We thought that the EP would be a transitory phase,' Graeme Murray told *Kerrang!* the following year, 'to prepare people for the album which is a bit of a change again, and give them a variety of tracks (anything from instantly accessible commercial rock to involved and evolved nine minute epic stuff) to show that we're developing some more styles yet are still in touch with the things that have gone before; a stepping stone.'

'We were looking for a producer for *Knightmoves*,' Reed said, 'and Mick Glossop was suggested by our A&R man at that time. We met, and we got on like a house on fire… basically, because he's a really wonderful guy, and because of the diverse musical fields he's worked in… but essentially he's a heavy rock fan… he has a good guitar sound and a good drum sound and he knows what live music's all about… but he's also worked with stuff like The Skids and X-Mal Deutschland, so he knows how to get rawness live on tape… he's a technology freak, so he understands all about Fairlights and sequencers and all those kind of things that we wanted to get involved in.'

Strangers is unapologetically commercial. It's relentlessly upbeat. Alan Reed effortlessly trills the bright chorus and Niall drops in a short but memorable guitar solo. The 7" single reached number 92 for one week in early May. Pallas' third and final Top 100 chart entry. *Nightmare* is atmospheric, eerie and 100% prog, utilising the sinister diminished fifth 'devil's chord', so beloved of Black Sabbath (and Rush on *YYZ*, one of the band's key influences). *Sanctuary* is surely one of the classics of the era and is a candidate for Pallas' best song of the '80s. The slow, flowing keyboards in the opening minutes are matched by a terrific vocal performance by Alan Reed. Its nine and a half minute length allows the music to expand and contract, its themes coalescing into a dynamic instrumental section, with Niall providing an enervating guitar solo, one of his best. If you are new to the Reed-era Pallas, then this is the place to begin.

Some copies of the EP were shipped with a limited edition single containing demos of *Mad Machine* and *A Stitch In Time*.

'It sold well,' said Alan Reed, 'considering the band had been away for such a long time, and it being the first release with myself doing the vocals. We were very, very pleased with the response, and I think we crossed over with it into an audience who hadn't quite heard of us before or who were put off us before.'

Marillion's biggest hit single, the effervescent

Supporting Uriah Heep (From the collection of Guy Tkach)

Kayleigh was released on 7 May 1985, six weeks ahead of its parent album. It's based around a shimmering guitar riff and has a rousing chorus which had been repurposed from an early arrangement of *She Chameleon*. Fish's unusually direct lyrics read as an apology to several of his past girlfriends. Fish took the name from an on-off girlfriend called Kay Lee.

> *Do you remember? Chalk hearts melting on a playground wall*
> *Do you remember? Dawn escapes from moon washed college halls*
> *Do you remember? The cherry blossom in the market square*
> *Do you remember? I thought it was confetti in our hair*
> *By the way, didn't I break your heart?*

About 30 seconds of Steve Rothery's guitar solo was chopped out for the single release.

'What makes me really smile,' recalls ex-*Sounds* journalist Phil Bell, 'is remembering when, many years later, I called my gas provider and the young lady said, 'Hi, I'm Kayleigh, how can I help?' And I said, 'Let me stop you there. You are named after a song by Marillion, aren't you?' 'Yes, how did you know?' she exclaimed. 'I used to know her,' I replied! None of the other bands had that kind of wide cultural impact, which is a pity really.'

'It is amusing when you meet them all around the world,' smiles Steve Rothery. 'It became one of the most popular girl's names. There are lots of Kayleighs out there.'

If Kayleigh is about lost love the B-side, *Lady Nina*, is about the sex trade.

> *One night you'll play Elizabeth Taylor*
> *The next night you're Marilyn Monroe*
> *Forever kissing frogs that think they're princes*
> *Oh, Lady Nina, where did all the romance go?*

Remarkably – and perhaps Capitol didn't read the lyrics too closely – *Lady Nina* would be released as the A-side of a US single in April 1986.

Pallas promoted their EP on a UK tour supporting Uriah Heep, visiting large venues in Manchester (15 May), Glasgow (16 May), Birmingham (17 May), Sheffield (18 May) and the Hammersmith Odeon (19 May).

The band's second visit to the Hammersmith Odeon—the first had been the half-empty double-header with Twelfth Night—included *Shock Treatment*, *Crown Of Thorns*, and *Cut And Run*, as well as two new songs. The rumbling *Dinosaur* would not move beyond demo stage. They ended their set with their tour de force, the magnificent *Sanctuary*, which merged into the closing section of *Atlantis*.

Alan Reed: 'It was with only a few sleepless nights of rehearsal and [after] a chaotic dress rehearsal/gig at Ritzy's in Aberdeen that we headed down to Manchester, and my first encounter with the concert hall stages of the UK. I must admit to being more than normally nervous on that first night, remembering all too well the fate of many a support act at Glasgow Apollo, my local gig, but the sight of

Graeme Murray and Alan Reed, somewhere on the road
(Photograph by Mark Drake)

Andy Revell in May 1985
(Photograph by Mark Drake)

evening was a problem caused by a member of Hammersmith Odeon staff, who, true to the tradition of 'No encores for support act', brought the house lights up just as we were halfway back on to the stage. A bit of a disappointment - but next time! And so to the party… deciding that it deserved formal dress, I turned up wearing full Highland regalia. My kilt caused no end of enquiries as to what I was wearing underneath, even to the extent of several EMIers chasing me around trying to grab hold of it and so many Pallas T-shirts rushing down to the front immediately put me at my ease. Glasgow was just that bit special. Maybe I'm biased but true to form, the Apollo audience well and truly let their hair down. Birmingham Odeon saw the band take total amnesia in the middle of *Dinosaur* and Ronnie's hi-tech MIDI keyboard system scrambled its brains, leaving the first half of *Sanctuary* to Niall and I, making the events of the evening just that little bit unusual. And so to Hammersmith - long and legion are the stories that say if anything can go wrong at a gig, it'll be in London. But luckily my fears were groundless. What can I say - I've never been so scared in my life and I enjoyed it immensely - a strange place to play at last, but I'm looking forward to the next time. The one thing that marred the *Sounds*' Tony Mottram crawling camera in hand along the floor to get a good shot… perhaps we'll get that cover story after all!'

Pendragon were also on the road: a dozen gigs across the UK, their first since December, included two dates at The Marquee on 17 and 18 May.

Twelfth Night's final UK tour comprised seven dates during the month of May, mostly at student venues.

Many new songs were added to the set list, with five of the 11 tracks subsequently recorded for the band's next album already in place. Only three songs from the Geoff Mann era (*We Are Sane*, *The Ceiling Speaks* and *Love Song*) were performed on this tour: changes were blowing through the Twelfth Night camp.

Twelfth Night, Birmingham University, 10 May 1985 (Photographs by Mike Barrington)

IQ and Pallas recorded sessions for the TV series *Live From London* this same month, both at the Camden Palace in London. Pallas recorded their set on 20 May. Fan Phil Morris attended.

'It's odd that the crowd noise on the soundtrack makes it sound like there were hundreds there: there were actually about 20 of us. I couldn't believe it, even for a Monday afternoon. I'd been to the IQ recording the week before where this one was advertised. I assumed the same crowd would go to another free gig… But what a day for live music: after Pallas I was off to The Dominion that evening to see China Crisis.'

'I haven't actually seen it all,' said Alan Reed. 'I've seen a bit of it. Everyone we spoke to who's actually done one of them has said the same thing: 'It was a load of crap.' I mean it was done in a Monday lunchtime with nobody there, so it's not really like a gig. I mean we were all suffering from hangovers and stuff after the Uriah Heep party the night before. Actually, one or two people have come up to me and said 'Hey, saw you on the telly, thought it was great', and so we've made one new fan out of it. I mean maybe it's turned off a few old ones, it's difficult to tell. Looking back, it probably wasn't the best thing to do, but we did it. And for people who want to see some of us on video, then at least they've got something now.'

Also that month, Marillion made two important TV appearances to promote *Kayleigh*. Firstly, the week after the single's release and with a promising chart entry at number 15, Marillion appeared on the popular tea-time chat show *Wogan* (20 May 1985). They followed that with an appearance on *Top Of The Pops* (23 May 1985). These helped to push the song into the Top 10 the following week, the band's highest chart position to date. It would stay there for an impressive seven week stretch and was still in the Top 30 as late as July.

Mark Kelly: 'We had a few dates to play in Spain and Portugal, so after appearing on *Top Of The Pops* and *Wogan*, we set off on tour. When we arrived back in the UK, Marillion was a household name. We were number two in the singles chart and number one in the album chart. *Wogan* was the appearance that put us in front of millions of people who would go out and buy *Kayleigh*. It transpired that they would not only buy the single, but would also name their unborn girls after the song.'

A few days later, Marillion performed at the first Rock am Ring festival in Germany. The second day, 26 May 1985, was headlined by Foreigner, with Marillion in the middle of the bill. They played a truncated 45 minute set comprising *Assasing, Script For A Jester's Tear*, side one of *Misplaced Childhood, Fugazi* and *Garden Party*. They played further dates in Spain, Portugal, France and Italy, split by another booking for *Top Of The Pops* with *Kayleigh* sitting at number 2 on 13 June.

Pallas' album *The Wedge* would be recorded in May and June 1985.

'*The Wedge* seemed to take ages,' recalls Alan Reed. 'The initial drum sessions were at Townhouse 3 in Vauxhall. It had previously been owned by The Who as Ramport and was an old church that was apparently haunted, though I never felt anything weird there. We spent about three weeks recording drums there. Then we moved to Tears For Fears' new place, The Wool Hall near Bath, for the majority of the recording. That was great. It was a new farmhouse conversion and away from the road to Frome.'

'We were treated wonderfully both by the staff and the locals from the picturesque village in which it is situated,' Reed said. 'Meals were provided by the village pub, the Woolpack and it certainly began to feel like a home from home. Ronnie, meanwhile, was grappling with the Emulator II. Like the Fairlight we used on the EP, it's a sampling keyboard - that is you record something into it and can then play it as a keyboard sound on any part of the keyboard. This time not only did we try for unusual keyboard sounds, Orchestral Stab, and percussion effects, but we went further using its built-in sequencer to construct unusual rhythmic patterns built from both percussion instruments and other instruments like in *Just A Memory* where we used a drum machine in conjunction with keyboard sequences to build a series of interrelating patterns which form the basis of the song. Having come to the end of our time in Bath, we were faced with a slight problem. We had run out of time and still the album was only half finished.'

Although Solstice performed at the Stonehenge

Free Festival in both 1983 and 1984, they stayed away in 1985.

'By the time 1985 came around everyone knew what was going to happen,' said Andy Glass. 'The Peace Convoy had been growing for some time. It was a convoy of trucks and buses that started getting a bit out of hand as those with a dubious agenda tagged along. It got very big. This gave Mrs Thatcher, who didn't like the whole idea of free stuff, a reason to say 'Right, we're going to stop this'. A large convoy was on its way to Stonehenge and the police were going to stop it… or try to stop it.'

Indeed, the so-called Battle of the Beanfield on 1 June 1985 pitched 1,300 police officers against 600 festival goers, resulting in dozens of injuries and over 500 arrests.

Andy Glass: 'I didn't really want to experience that so didn't go. That effectively brought to an end the whole free festival circuit and they passed a law [the Public Order Act 1986] which limited the number of vehicles that could come together in one place to ten or twenty or something like that.'

You can hear newsreel from that day on Solstice's 1997 album *Circles*.

'It's horrific,' Glass says.

Instead, Solstice were booked at the City Hall, St Albans, supporting ex-Fleetwood Mac guitarist Peter Green.

'I remember it with sadness,' says Andy Glass. 'Obviously I was excited and humbled to have a chance to share a stage and meet with the great man, but knew of his troubles. When I approached him backstage in the hope of exchanging a few words there literally seemed to be no one at home. Apart from sitting alone and unresponsive, he had those long fingernails both of which suggesting he was in no condition to perform or even play. My recollection is that the band, who included members of Osibisa and a second guitarist, carried him through the show. I was left with the feeling that he was being exploited. I may have been completely wrong about that of course and others in the audience seemed unaware of any shortcomings. He was definitely not a well man though.'

Kayleigh peaked at number 2, week commencing 9 June 1985, behind a charity single and as part of a typically eclectic British Top 10:

1. *You'll Never Walk Alone* – The Crowd
2. *Kayleigh* – Marillion
3. *19* – Paul Hardcastle
4. *Suddenly* – Billy Ocean
5. *Obsession* – Animotion
6. *A View To A Kill* – Duran Duran
7. *Out In The Fields* – Gary Moore & Phil Lynott
8. *The Word Girl* – Scritti Politti
9. *Crazy For You* – Madonna
10. *History* – Mai Tai

New albums by IQ and Marillion were released a week apart. The first to arrive, *The Wake*, on 10 June 1985.

The Wake is a work of stunning proportions, immediate, but needing a long time for real appreciation and interpretation, vast yet built around one theme (various attitudes to death and dying), spontaneous, yet flawlessly realised.

This album is in my mind nothing short of a classic, and now sits alongside *Still Life* and *The Lamb*, as one of my most prized records. The music has matured in all the right ways since the brilliant, but slightly over-complicated *Tales*, and the theme is subtly 'hidden' in the lyrics and the visually stunning cover artwork (by Pete), not stuffed down your throat, as with some albums.

The Stairway issue 1, November 1985

The Wake is an edgy album, often dark. It displays a remarkable evolution and huge improvement in production over *Tales From The Lush Attic*. The off-beat thrumming of the opening bass riff of the grandiose *Outer Limits* serves to put the listener on guard: just where is this going? The tricky 5/4 time signature in the confident verses shows a poised musicality: the production is lush, but one could argue that Peter Nicholls' vocals are mixed too far back. Towards the end of the track, as Nicholls pushes himself into his higher registers, his singing has power and character. This is matched by Mike Holmes' bright guitar lines in the extended fade-out. *The Wake* is a mature rocker which Nicholls really belts out. Mike Holmes delivers a powerful, overdriven solo in his best Steve Hackett manner. *The Wake* segues directly into the captivating *The Magic Roundabout*. Martin Orford's massed keyboards transform into a beautiful flowing melody. Tim Esau's fretless bass drives a vivid multi-section composition that isn't afraid to take its 1970s influences into 1985. Mike Holmes' sustained guitar solo lifts the track immeasurably.

This opening trio sees a band starting to find itself with enormous self-confidence. We hear them, well, progressing, in the true meaning of the word.

Corners is the cuckoo in the nest, with a rigid drum machine sequence, sitar-sounding guitar, backwards sounds and long fade-out. It reminds the listener of Tom Petty's *Don't Come Around Here No More*, which had been released just before recording sessions commenced. The prominent sitar sound on Petty's record was played by producer Dave Stewart.

'I bought a Coral sitar-guitar, which I've used on the song I wrote with Tom Petty and the Heartbreakers, *Don't Come Around Here No More*,' Stewart told *One Two Testing* magazine at the time. 'All the way through America I was scouring ads and music shops till I found one — I think it was in Atlanta, eventually. Somewhere like that.'

It's this same guitar, played by Mike Holmes, that can be heard on *Corners*. IQ's recording engineer Harun Coombes knew Stewart and was able to secure a loan.

The closing triple whammy of *Widow's Peak*, *The Thousand Days* and *Headlong* is perhaps the crowning moment of this first iteration of IQ. This intense sequence of brilliant songs can stand up against any of the other music of this period and lays the foundation for the 1990s re-emergence of IQ: confident, musical, effortlessly mature.

Widow's Peak is haunting, bombastic and passionate. Yes, it channels late 1970s Genesis in places, but IQ have the chops to pull it off, with shifting moods and tempos. We must mention Paul Cook's wonderful drumming here. *The Thousand Days* is simple, catchy and attractive. It's no surprise that this was one of the songs carried over into the later Paul Menel era of IQ. A keyboard passage leads into the last track: the melodramatic and emotional *Headlong*. A slow build-up, with Peter Nicholls singing brilliantly, leads to a wry nod to *Watcher Of The Skies* which includes a virtuosic keyboard solo from Martin Orford that starts à la Tony Banks before proceeding through a series of jazzy inversions. The majestic closing section is simply uplifting. A return to the main musical theme from *Outer Limits* ends the album on an optimistic note. Despite wearing its influences very much on its sleeve, *Headlong* is an out and out classic of 1980s' prog music. *The Wake* is the place to start for understanding the longevity of this excellent group of musicians.

Peter Nicholls: 'It isn't easy to describe what each track is about lyrically as the words were deliberately written to be a series of impressions, rather than a linear story. But very loosely: *Outer Limits* deals with the main character dying and there's an image of a narrow bridge which he has to cross. If he gets to the other side, he reaches a place of safety, let's call it Heaven, but if he falls from the bridge he ends up in Hell. *The Wake* is an angry song; his soul is confused and lost and doesn't understand what's going on. My original working title for this track was *Rant*. In *The Magic Roundabout* he's wishing he could communicate with his wife, trying to tell her everything will be okay. The main character finds his soul going through a trippy, other-world kind of experience in *Corners*. *Widow's Peak* refers to the character's widow. She finds out that he was buried alive and that's how he came to die. He's still trying to reach out across death. In *The Thousand Days* there's a turning point where his soul feels that, rather than wandering aimlessly, it might be re-born, which is what happens in the following song, *Headlong* which is all about giving the story a resolution: spirit, bear me away to the place of birth.'

Despite the high quality of the album, Nicholls does not have fond memories of the album sessions: 'The recording of *The Wake* was definitely not a happy time; I remember it being very tense. I can hear the tension in my singing on the album. During the [sessions], relationships within the band had really broken down and I was very uncomfortable with it all. I felt separated from the rest of the band. We couldn't talk to each other and it was a very dark time for us on a personal level, even though the music we were creating together was great.'

As with *Tales From The Lush Attic*, the cover was painted by Peter Nicholls.

'The main face was inspired by a film at the time called *Quest For Fire*,' he said. 'I used a photo from the film as a starting point. I only discovered several years later that some of the band members thought the face was mine, and that I'd decided to put a big picture of me on an IQ album cover! Of course that isn't true. The other images around the main face were added as representations of some of the lyrics on the album.'

Kayleigh was Marillion's most successful single in the UK, staying on the chart for a total of 14 weeks. It was a Top 10 hit across Europe, and became the band's sole appearance on the USA's Billboard Hot 100, hitting number 74 in October 1985.

Suddenly, Marillion were pop stars.

'I could never take it seriously,' Pete Trewavas says. 'I don't think any of us really could. I hated the way the press and attention was getting in the way of the music. From my point of view the music was everything. Maybe this was a naive point of view, but I thought that good music would shine through. Of course appearing on *Top Of The Pops* and being flown around the world was fun but only up to a point. Being in the teen magazines was a little embarrassing really.'

'We were out travelling around Europe doing promotion for the album,' says Mark Kelly. '*Kayleigh* was climbing up the charts. It went in the charts at 15, then it's up to seven. Then it went to four, then three. I can remember, we were in Spain doing some promotion when it went from three to two. Week after week it was going up one place at a time, which is unheard of really. Every other single we'd released had done the opposite, so it was a new experience in that sense and totally unexpected. It didn't really change us, but I think Fish noticed it the most. He was the one that was on the cover of *Smash Hits*. It was fun. But it wasn't crazy. We were famous enough that you'd get stopped in Sainsbury's but not so often that it was a pain in the arse.'

'I hated it,' says Steve Rothery. 'We'd walk around supermarkets and people would recognise me. I was oblivious to a lot of it, just looking at the cornflakes, you know? A bit later we were at Ronnie Scott's for the launch of *Clutching At Straws*. There was a journalist from the tabloids who was trying to get an angle, you know, a bit of sleaze. I couldn't imagine living in the spotlight.'

'I never thought of myself as a pop star,' laughs Ian Mosley. 'But doing *Top Of The Pops* was great. We were flown back on a Learjet in the middle of our French tour [13 June 1985]. That was big time.'

IQ's *The Wake* appeared for a single week in the UK album charts: number 72, week commencing 22 June 1985. The following week it would register at number 1 in the Metal albums chart in *Sounds*.

Mike Holmes: 'I remember just after we released *The Wake*, there was a real buzz about IQ at that time. [The album] went into the independent chart at number three and it was just getting rave reviews. It just felt that that was our time. I remember thinking then, you know, often you look back and think those were good days, and I remember thinking then, this is going to be one of those times when you look back and think, oh yeah that was a good time.'

Holmes mused on how important he considered commercial accomplishment for bands such as IQ.

'Ultimately I don't think a band can survive without it really,' he said. 'All chart success really means is that you're selling more records and getting through to more people. It's an ongoing thing, once people see you're in the charts it creates an awareness about you, and they know that you're there... they have heard of the name IQ. It's very important really.'

Misplaced Childhood would be released on 17 June 1985. As if proving the late David Longdon's assertion that 'the extended song format [is] like reading a book', writer Nathaniel Webb suggests that '*Misplaced Childhood* tells a single story structured like a novel, with an introduction, midpoint turnaround, moment of loss, and redemptive denouement.'

'*Misplaced Childhood* might have been an interlinked suite of songs,' explains Joe Banks, 'but it certainly wasn't *Tales From Topographic Oceans*. It was in fact a very modern sounding rock album, with the understated melodicism of Pink Floyd displacing the theatricality of Genesis as the band's primary influence - the opening riff to *Kayleigh* is pure Dave Gilmour, while the lyrical arc of the album is pretty similar to that of *The Wall*, albeit with a happier ending.'

The album ruminates on loneliness, lost love, substance abuse, the shallowness of fame, man's inhumanity to man, and a longing for the lost innocence of childhood. It begins with the soft keyboard fanfare of *Pseudo Silk Kimono*, Steve Rothery's sustained guitar lines and Fish's close-miked vocals. It's an ominous, engaging opening which draws you in brilliantly. And then, the shimmering guitar introduction to *Kayleigh*, effortlessly commercial and, with Fish's simple and direct 'Do you remember?' lyrics and bright chorus, a sure-fire hit. Kudos here to Pete Trewavas' delicate bass lines and Steve Rothery's flowing, articulate guitar solo. *Kayleigh* is a great song, as is the wonderful *Lavender*, which builds to a devastatingly gorgeous guitar solo, the Mother Goose nursery rhyme transformed into a touching love song. *Kayleigh* and *Lavender* somehow sit perfectly in a complex progressive rock album but have a wide commercial appeal. So far, so good. The eight-minute *Bitter Suite* continues a quite remarkable run of glorious music. It's split into five parts: *Brief Encounter*, *Lost Weekend*, *Blue Angel*, *Misplaced Rendezvous* and *Windswept Thumb*. Its lyrics are evocative—'She was a wallflower at sixteen / She'll be a wallflower at thirty-four / Her mother called her beautiful / Her daddy said, 'a whore''.

Themes from *Lavender* make an appearance in *Blue Angel*, a superb section in which Fish sings in a key which suits his voice as he seems to reflect on a meeting with a French prostitute. *Misplaced Rendezvous* is pure mid-period Genesis. *Windswept Thumb* briefly nicks from The Who's *Love, Reign O'er Me* before the album moves smoothly into the magnificent *Heart Of Lothian*. The *Curtain Call* section was an odd choice for the third single from the album, but it always sounded brilliant in concert, so who was right?

Side one of *Misplaced Childhood* is a remarkable achievement: 20 minutes of sustained brilliance.

Side two kicks off with the dark, anxious *Waterhole (Expresso Bongo)*. The transitions into and out of *Lords Of The Backstage* are clunky, but again here is a carefully arranged, dynamic song with an accessible chorus… 'I just wanted you to be the first one…'. The five part, complex ten minute *Blind Curve* has echoes of Pink Floyd, and deploys the band's not so secret weapon - Steve Rothery - to great effect, especially in the sneaky reprise of *Heart Of Lothian*. The next song is the sublime *Childhood's End?* (the title taken from a Pink Floyd song, a Van Der Graaf Generator song or possibly the novel by Arthur C Clarke). Whatever the source of the title, the song is self-affirming, cathartic and hopeful:

> *I looked out the window*
> *And I saw a magpie in a rainbow, the rain had gone*
> *I'm not alone, I turned to the mirror*
> *I saw you, the child, that once loved*
> *The child before they broke his heart*
> *Our heart, the heart that I believed was lost*

The band sound poised. There are moments of genuine elegance here. A switch of pace takes us into the energetic, triumphant *White Feather*, which fades rather than ending with a flourish. Concert performances would deliver the big ending that this song, and album, deserved.

Misplaced Childhood entered the UK album charts at number 1, remaining in the Top 100 for the next nine months.

'We had been told that on pre-order sales alone we stood a very good chance of *Misplaced…* going straight in at number one,' Steve Rothery said. 'So we were all pretty excited the day the charts were announced, waiting to hear how high we'd actually gone. But there's a world of difference between being told that you might have a number one album, and being told that you have got a number one album. When we heard we went mad! It was just such a dream come true! I think we were all walking on air for about the next three weeks.'

'It's funny, though,' Fish said, 'when you're still a kid you sit there and dream about what it must be like to be told your new album has just gone straight in at number one in the charts… your album… number fucking one! Then when it happened to me it just didn't seem real. I couldn't quite get to grips with what it meant. I don't think I stopped drinking for a week.'

Misplaced Childhood would also creep into the US Top 50, their highest placing there. It is still a wonderful album and a major work in the progressive genre.

Solstice's sole appearance at the Glastonbury Festival was on 21 June 1985. They performed at noon on the second stage as part of a typically eclectic bill headed by reggae band Black Roots.

Andy Glass: 'Our reputation had built over those years and we got that gig on stage two, which was quite a big deal.'

Ken Bowley: 'The night before there was a deluge and the site descended into a mud bath. Backstage, the PA amps and power distro were soaked and in the morning the sound crew were trying to dry everything out with hairdryers. So, we take to the stage and go through a brief soundcheck in front of our muddy audience and the stage's compère, then we launch into the opening song. About five minutes into the set the power died. We had no PA and no onstage amps. So Martin does the only thing he can do… a drum solo! Eventually the power was restored but by then there was only about 20 minutes left of our 45 minute slot. And to add to the fun, all the vehicles were bogged down so we were unable to get off the site until the following Monday when they were hauled out of the quagmire and towed back to the main road. Five nights in a tent in the middle of what looked like the Somme. Who said the music business wasn't glamorous…?'

IQ commenced a three week tour of the UK supporting Wishbone Ash on their *Raw To The Bone* tour.

'We all saw that tour as a great opportunity to reach new people,' Mike Holmes notes, 'and we were playing to 2,000 people a night so we were all really excited.'

'The Wishbone Ash tour was an easy tour, and great fun,' says Paul Cook. 'We had a short set, then we'd watch Wishbone Ash's set most nights. And drink lots of beer. I think we drove around the UK in our manager's old Volvo staying at bed and breakfasts of varying types.'

The band's set list changed slightly as the tour progressed but generally consisted of *Outer Limits, It All Stops Here, The Wake, The Magic Roundabout, The Thousand Days, Widow's Peak, Corners* and *Awake And Nervous*.

Seventeen dates over a three week period concluded with the band's only performance at the Hammersmith Odeon on 21 June.

Call a spade a spade, IQ are another progressive rock outfit, a term bands of this ilk may deride in public while showing little inclination to leave the movement. The music's aimed at the head rather than the heart, hence its college boy audience. But the 'timewarp' jibes are no more relevant than to the Style Council or the Jesus & Mary Chain gang.

IQ, especially, are sussed enough musically to have moved forward, booting the corpse of Gabriel on the way past. Evidence? A danceable *Thousand Days* or the reggae backbeat of the new single *Barbell Is In*. And a guitarist, Michael Holmes, wearing bondage pants? Shome mishtake, surely?

Admittedly they played the odd epic, dispensing their hooks like misers. But at least they have ideas and vitality. If Echo & the Bunnymen and Simple Minds are the successful progressive rockers of the Eighties, then IQ are the missing link stretching back to Yes.

Any support act than can pull a dancing crowd to the front of Hammersmith Odeon and top Sounds' Heavy Metal album chart with their new LP, *The Wake*, must have something going for them.

Pete Picton, *Sounds*, 6 July 1985

Singer Peter Nicholls, though, was considering his options.

'Sadly the writing was on the wall before the tour started, to be honest,' he says. 'It's hard to think about this now because it was all handled so badly, but essentially the recording of *The Wake* hadn't been easy and cracks were starting to show. I was going through some personal difficulties and was pulling myself away from everyone. We were young and didn't have the capacity to speak to each other, which I think is all it would have taken to clear the air and move forward, and I'm as much to blame for that as anyone else. Instead, before the tour started I asked our management company to mediate and arrange a band meeting. For some reason, they chose instead to inform the others that I had decided to leave after the tour. Needless to say, that was not the conversation I remember having. Nevertheless, the tour then progressed with the band expecting me to leave soon, probably resenting me for not telling them myself, and me confused about the meeting never happening. An awful and uncomfortable time all round.'

Immediately after the tour supporting Wishbone Ash, IQ headlined a further eight gigs around the country: Croydon, Whitehaven, Glasgow, Wishaw (near Motherwell), Bristol, Oxford, Thatcham (near Newbury) and Brighton.

Pallas were still recording their album, *The Wedge*.

Alan Reed: 'EMI were so impressed with results thus far that our budget miraculously grew, and we found ourselves zipping between studios in search of time to record. First of all, Aosis in Camden where we spent four days. After Aosis, we all went home for a week, being both physically and particularly mentally exhausted after more than two months without a break. Making my own way back to London for the last fortnight of recording, I miscalculated and arrived a day early, only to discover that a certain fellow EMI band were inhabiting the Townhouse to record their single. When I went to investigate, however, I found myself rushed to a couple of London nightspots to exchange criticism and discuss Tears For Fears' contribution to modern art with members of said band. I'm quite sure that this otherwise innocuous meeting is particularly responsible for my strange collapse from nervous

1985: Dawn Escapes From Moon Washed College Halls

IQ at the Pennyfarthing in Oxford, 13 July 1985 (Photograph by Albert Jagger)

exhaustion two days later and my subsequent night in hospital.'

Pallas moved to Power Plant Studios in Willesden for a week of sessions in mid-July. On one of these, 13 July, Alan Reed could hear some of the acts performing at Live Aid, which was taking place at nearby Wembley Stadium. Marillion were keen to take part in this famous concert but were too late to be added to the bill. They were, however, 'first reserves' if any of the scheduled acts needed to pull out. Fish attended and was interviewed on BBC TV by presenter David Hepworth just ahead of Elton John's set. He is pictured in the official Live Aid book. Brian Devoil and Andy Revell of Twelfth Night also attended that famous concert as punters.

'I had the chance to be there but turned it down,' says long-time IQ fan Sam Smyth. 'I was queuing in the dinner hall at college one day when some friends came over to say that they were going up to London that afternoon to get tickets, and did I either want to go with them, or did I want them to get me a ticket? I was really interested, but when they told me the tickets were £25 I changed my mind – as a student on a grant my weekly budget was £30, so to blow nearly all of it on a gig ticket seemed a bad idea. Wrong!'

Sam went along to The Marquee instead, to see the second of two back-to-back IQ bookings.

'We booked The Marquee [on 12 and 13 July] and we didn't know about this Live Aid thing,' Mike Holmes said. 'And then we thought it would be a really good gesture to do [it] anyway, because I think everybody's got to do their bit, haven't they? [The Live Aid idea] is wonderful, I think it's excellent, you can't really say anything against it, can you? I just wish people would think like that all the time, instead of 'it's this year's thing to do that sort of thing'. Me and Martin in particular have big arguments about

Adverts from *Sounds* and the *NME*
(From the collection of Guy Tkach)

Revelatory: After 26 gigs on the tour how do you feel?

Mike Holmes: Tired!

Martin Orford: Not too tired to play properly, it's good fun. But it's good to have a rest.

Revelatory: What was the reception like on the Wishbone Ash tour?

Martin: It was very good mostly. There were a lot of IQ fans turned up to see that tour anyway. But there were a lot who were seeing us for the first time.

Mike: Yeah, and there were things like Hammersmith which were out of this world.

Revelatory: Are you pleased with the way the album turned out?

Mike: Definitely. We were particularly pleased with the time we had to record it. Four weeks. It's the same with almost any recording you end up saying 'Oh, if only we had had another week it would be ten times better.'

Revelatory: Got any favourite tracks on the album?

Martin: *Headlong*.

Mike: I don't really know. Yeah I suppose it would be *Headlong*, but probably only because it's the newest and we're not pissed off with it yet.

Revelatory: What is the album about?

Mike: It's loosely a concept about death and dying and that sort of thing. But it doesn't have to be treated in a really morose way. It's just different aspects of this guy who dies and doesn't end up in either heaven or hell. A lot of things happen to him on the way.

Martin: I think it's good because it starts when he dies which is a good place to start a story and nobody's ever done it before with the exception

what we'd do if we got lots of money. He'd be a total Fascist and just spend it totally on himself! I'm sure that I wouldn't. I'd really like to rid the world of all known diseases with my beauty!'

Mike and Martin were interviewed for the *Revelatory* fanzine just ahead of taking to the stage.

of *Heaven Can Wait*. That is roughly what this is about. It's quite a happy ending actually, the guy dies properly and finally makes it.

Revelatory: How is it selling?

Mike: Very well, we've sold 10,000 in under a month.

Martin: I didn't know that.

Revelatory: What will you be doing tonight as it's the last night of the tour?

Martin: Going to bed for a long time.

The doors opened one hour earlier than usual at The Marquee to allow fans to watch Live Aid on a giant TV screen.

At around 8pm, after David Bowie had performed his Live Aid set, the screen was dismantled and IQ took to the Marquee stage. Pete wore make-up for the first time in a long while and the band performed the whole of *The Wake* (with the exception of *Headlong*). The encore included covers of *Ace Of Spades* sung by Orford and Pete Nicholls as Frank-N-Furter for *Sweet Transvestite*. The event raised £1,400 for the Live Aid appeal.

'We watched Live Aid on TV before we left home for London,' Sam Smyth recalls. 'They were showing it on a big screen at the venue between bands, so we got to see Phil Collins taking off on Concorde while we were at the show. We arrived home in time to see him play in the USA! Plus, as it turned out, we also got to see Peter perform with IQ for what would be the last time for five years.'

A week later, Pallas moved again, to Rooster Studios.

'This one was tucked into a basement flat just off Shepherd's Bush Green,' Alan Reed recalled, 'and was perhaps the most difficult place our equipment has ever had the misfortune of trying to get into. Naturally, our crew was in Aberdeen so we had to do it all unaided.'

With time against them, the band had to push through to meet their deadline.

'As the sun came up on the morning of the last day,' Reed says, 'I was still writing vocal parts! There's lots on there that got mixed down to texture levels. Unless you know, it's there! It still sounds pretty good to these ears. It got mixed at Amazon in Liverpool, which seemed like a breath of fresh air after London.'

The album would be released the following February.

In early July, Marillion booked a week at Abbey Road to write and recorded a new song, *Freaks*, for the B-side of their forthcoming single. This pounding song with its gated mid-'80s drums is perhaps autobiographical: the narrator has become famous and wishes for a quiet life back in his home town to get away from the 'freaks' who obsess about him.

It seems likely that the heavily reworked single version of *Lavender* dates from these sessions.

Twelfth Night's agreement with Charisma had been brokered by Tony Smith at Hit & Run. But, in July 1985, Charisma was sold to Virgin. Twelfth Night's new album, written and ready to go, was put on hold.

Pendragon's 20 July date at The Marquee was the last for founding drummer Nigel Harris, who left after seven years.

'I had mixed feelings about giving up the band,' he reflects today. 'We had all been through a lot, musically and otherwise, in those seven years. But reality and practicality took my concentration and marquee

marquee

1985: Dawn Escapes From Moon Washed College Halls

IQ at The Marquee, 13 July 1985
(Photographs by Albert Jagger)

Nigel Harris' last gig
(From the collection of Jon Dunnington)

Below: Nigel Harris
(Photograph by Mark Drake)

attention away from being able to input creatively any longer. I had a big mortgage on a 250 year old crumbling cottage, very little savings, and a desperate need to return to a steady, continuous income.'

'Nigel left a big gap, not just as a drummer but as a musician,' Nick Barrett declares. 'He had perfect pitch. He was phenomenally inventive as a drummer. But in the end it was the age old problem that we were unable to financially support ourselves. We were starting to get problems with the fraud squad because we signed on the dole as well as being professional musicians. We had no money to keep it going and, although we all gave it a good go, some people would end up getting to

the end of their tether. And they just had enough, you know? We'd play in somewhere like Leeds, then drive home through the night. I'd go straight into the farm where I used to work. It was bloody hard going. Nigel used to really need his sleep, and he wanted some stability in his life. In the end, he just wanted a normal job with normal hours and normal people.'

'I know that there was a slight animosity towards my decision,' Harris says. 'I had planned to leave a few months before, but I had continued my duties by recording *The Jewel*, whilst only recently commencing a three month job with a local firm trimming and finishing fibreglass mouldings. It was tough going during April to June 1985. I committed myself until the farewell gig at The Marquee in London. What a show to go out on! Thanks guys!'

Harris, described as 'an octopus with firecrackers in his pants' in the band's newsletter, was replaced by 17 year old Mat Anderson, a friend of Rik Carter.

'Mat joined on my recommendation,' Carter explains. 'We had been in a couple of bands together and bonded over a mutual love of Genesis.'

'I first met Rik at school,' Anderson says. 'We both went to the local grammar, Westcliff High School for Boys. I'd always loved the sound of drums and had been hitting anything I could get my hands on since the age of four. When I was around 10, I nicked a snare drum and splash cymbal that my parents had bought my brother and used to play along to the family record collection using a tambourine wedged into a paper bin and covered with a Subbuteo cloth as a kick drum. Fleetwood Mac's *Rumours* was my go-to. Eventually I saved up enough money to buy a three piece Hoshino kit in 1980 and I played every day for an hour. This had to be negotiated with the neighbours and I absolutely loved it. I used to put on Genesis albums and *Green* by Steve Hillage and learned by playing along to them. Looking back on it, this really sharpened my ear, though the lack of a teacher held me up later as I didn't know rudiments.

'I played in any band that would have me but, generally, no one was interested in playing prog. I was, and still am, a big Genesis fan and one lunchtime I could hear *Firth Of Fifth* being played on the piano in the main hall. I was delighted and amazed to hear someone playing it, as I loved the tune and the piano intro is no walk in the park. Of course, it was Rik. I sat and listened and then introduced myself. I was in awe as he was a couple of years older than me and the most competent musician I'd come across. At that point I'd been learning drums for about two years, but I was pretty confident of my abilities and keen as mustard to join a band with someone who loved and could play Genesis. We started playing together fairly soon after, in late spring 1982, and carried on in bands together up until late 1983 when schoolwork began to get in the way for me. By this time Rik had left school, I think.

'I saw Pendragon for the first time aged 16 at Cliffs Pavilion in Southend-on-Sea [8 March 1984] when they supported Marillion on the *Fugazi* tour. I only knew of them because Rik had joined them, and though I wasn't a huge Marillion fan I wanted to be there to see him. They were brilliant. What stood out for me were the chords – loads of minor and major sevenths that gave the music a slightly jazzy feel but through the sound of a rock band. I thought Nick's guitar playing was sublime and, of course, I've always been a huge fan of Rik's playing and sound. Rik told me Pendragon were looking for a drummer and I was massively excited. I spent a couple of weeks learning all of Nigel's parts whilst also revising for my A Levels. By the time the audition came I could play 90% of it beat for beat. The band were delighted so I got the job on the spot.'

Anderson moved to Stroud and performed his first gig with Pendragon at the Underground in Croydon on 6 August 1985.

'That was terrifying,' Anderson says, 'I felt that I didn't play very well.'

After slogging away on the European TV promotion circuit, Marillion returned to live duty with a festival date in Israel on 6 August. This was as part of the 85 Star Festival, held at the Ramat Gan Stadium in Tel Aviv. Originally planned for 50,000 punters over three days, only about 12,000 tickets were sold. The festival was reduced to a single day. Saddled with huge debts, the promoter fled the country and most of the artists were not paid. As Fish later wrote on his website: 'A ridiculous festival in Tel Aviv at the football stadium that was planned for three days and closed after one day because there were more people behind the stage than in front. Most of the bands on the list did not even bother to fly to Israel. We did fly and spent four days with chronic diarrhoea at the King David Beach Hotel.'

Pendragon's new drummer was introduced to the band's faithful at a one-off gig at The Marquee on Wednesday 14 August.

'I don't remember much about it,' Mat Anderson admits. 'My brother and a family friend came along and said how proud they were of me for joining the band.'

Peter Nicholls left IQ in mid-August 1985.

'I had many reasons for wanting to stay in IQ,' he said. 'I was very pleased with the album and it felt like the band was starting to get somewhere, but I wasn't happy and I needed to make the break. I'm sure that if I hadn't left, someone else would have. I know Martin Orford, our keyboard player, was also unhappy at the time. Something had to give, and I decided it had to be me.'

'To this day I'm still not quite sure what it was that made Pete decide to leave,' muses Mike Holmes, 'but he was obviously unhappy. He'd already moved out of the band flat into a bedsit, and I suppose that added another barrier between him and the rest of us. The point is we were still relatively young and none of us were great at communicating. I think now we'd sit down and say, 'What's going on?' but we just weren't emotionally mature enough at the time.'

'It had to happen,' Orford concedes, 'and if it hadn't been Pete, it could easily have been me. Four very different people living 24/7 in very close proximity was bound to turn into a powder keg in the end. It didn't really matter who went so long as someone did, because that was the only thing that was going to release the tension.'

Mike Holmes: 'I think part of the problem was that we all lived in the same small flat, socialised together, rehearsed together and went out to shows together. Add to that the fact that some people really didn't take to London living and weren't really living their best life. I'd always assumed that we all had a shared vision of what we wanted to do with IQ, and I guess looking back that wasn't actually the case. It did feel like something had to change, but I'm pretty sure IQ would have

A PLAYGROUND OF BROKEN HEARTS

1985: Dawn Escapes From Moon Washed College Halls

Peter Nicholls
(Photograph by Albert Jagger)

continued in some form.'

Nicholls went on to eventually form a new and decidedly non-progressive band, Niadem's Ghost, with three Manchester musicians: guitarist David Bennett from Nicholls' pre-IQ band The Same Curtain, bassist David Tomkins and former Slaughter and the Dogs drummer Brian Grantham.

IQ, with a major tour supporting Magnum booked for later in the year, started looking for a new singer.

Sounds published their advert for 'vocalist-frontman' that month.

> SUCCESSFUL ROCK BAND
> requires
> VOCALIST-FRONTMAN
> (non heavy metal)
> Band have major touring and recording commitments to fulfil.
> Please send tape, photo and biog to:
> Irate Management,
> 35A High St, Chislehurst, Kent, BR7 SA6.

Marillion were second on the bill, ahead of the likes of Bon Jovi and Metallica, at the 1985 Monsters of Rock Festival at Donington Park in Leicestershire. The headliners were ZZ Top.

'It was a very big day for us,' Steve Rothery said. 'The moment we walked on stage the crowd just all got on their feet and started cheering. I'd never seen anything like it. Playing second on the bill at Reading two years before had been similar, but this time everybody really had an excuse to go mad and really enjoy themselves. A number two single and number one album had probably gone to the fans' heads much more than to our own, and everybody just started going wild the moment we came on. It was like the return of the conquering heroes!'

At last, *The Jewel* was released on 19 August 1985.

Nick Barrett: 'We really weren't very happy with *The Jewel* because we had to record it so quickly. Before this, we'd record most stuff live, or at least quickly and cheaply, and not worry about mistakes. We wanted to get *The Jewel* right, so we were a lot more pernickety about things like bass drums being off or something being slightly out of tune. The trouble is, once you start going down that rabbit hole, you are there forever, particularly if you're inexperienced. If you're trying to make something which is perfect, then you give yourself more time to do it – if you want something with energy, then you don't. We had only about three weeks to record *The Jewel* and it was really hard, because we were rushing to finish and mix it. And we became absolutely sick of it. It was probably the hardest album we ever had to make. And the main reason is probably our lack of experience. In retrospect I'm very pleased with it because in time you forget all about the tuning and timing issues. When we remastered it and put it out again I thoroughly enjoyed listening to it. I thought the material on it was more mature and not so much sixth form, schoolboy chords. It had complexity to it, with Nigel's drumming, and Barney was a great writer. I still like it very much.'

The album opens with the positive, catchy *Higher Circles* which screams 'hit single' with its pop hooks and bright production. It might strike some listeners as cheesy Styx-lite AOR, but it's almost impossible to dislike. The brilliant *Pleasure Of Hope* successfully marries prog tropes of the 1970s and 1980s, with energy and phenomenal musicianship. Nigel Harris shines here. The full-on progressive *Leviathan* showcases this band's chops as players, channelling Rush and Yes, but with Nick Barrett's distinctive vocals, almost spat out such is the power and aggression of his delivery. The slower more pastoral sections contrast wonderfully with the faster, harder verses. It's easy to hear why this would become such an in-concert favourite even when it threatens to segue into *Market Square Heroes* from time to time. The flowing *Alaska* had been a highlight of the band's set for two years at this point. This new recording is a triumph, magnificent in every way, with flashes of jazz rock and truly stellar solos by Carter and Barrett. It's a gem of a track. *Circus* maintains the quality of musicianship, with hints of Genesis in Barrett's guitar and some truly astounding drumming from Nigel Harris. *Oh Divineo* is another oldish track, a thumpingly good mostly instrumental piece which blends Camel, Rush and Genesis. The album ends with the polished *The Black Knight*, which starts slowly and builds to an impressive, complex middle section and a remarkable three minute guitar solo which is the equal of any other from the similar bands of the era. *The Black Knight* lays down the roadmap of Pendragon's future path. Here we have the first signs of the mature style that the band would move towards with *The World* and perfect with *The Masquerade Overture* and *Not Of This World*.

Basically, I like Pendragon. Their music may be clichéd, but it is skilfully played and very pleasing to the ear. I was not massively excited about hearing *The Jewel* as I already knew practically all the material on it, but it was going to be interesting to hear how it sounded on vinyl. As I put needle to groove the awful *Higher Circles* blared out. This is quite obviously their bash at commercialism, but quite frankly there are other songs on the album which are much better potential singles material. After this is the excellent *Pleasure Of Hope* with its incredibly memorable Mini-Moog riff and its wonderful harmony rundowns. *Leviathan* follows in true 'Dragon / Genesis fashion, but there's no doubting that it's a good song, in fact it's a VERY good song! The beautiful *Alaska* closes side 1 on a sustained high, which is great spine shivering material incidentally.

Side 2 contains the excellent, the good, and the not so good. *Circus* is prime Pendragon, involving all the things they're good at: sweeping guitar solos, manic synth doodlings, magic chords and some classical theft.

Sandwiched between *Circus* and *Black Knight* is the boring *O Deveno* [sic] which involves too much worn-out rifferama. The album's closer *Black Knight* is a nice low-key number, but there are too many starts and stops which break the flow a touch.

Although they sound just a bit too much like Marillion *et al* to send me wild with delight, Pendragon have a very distinctive sheen to their music, and this facet of their sound is captured very well on this album. However, if Pendragon wish to progress any further, I fear that they are going to have to cut down on the musical clichés.

The Stairway issue 1, November 1985

Twelfth Night returned to The Marquee for a sold out three night residency, 19 to 21 August, which saw the band performing a set of new(ish) songs, with five of the first six unreleased at that point.

1985: Dawn Escapes From Moon Washed College Halls

Twelfth Night at The Marquee, August 1985 (Photographs by Mark Drake)

Below: Twelfth Night ticket from 20 August 1985 (From the collection of Peter Moltensen)

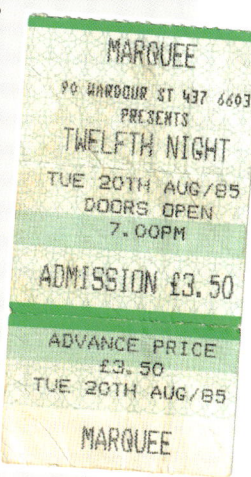

TWELFTH NIGHT Marquee, London

Not long ago someone asked me, quite by chance, in the rear bar of The Marquee, I think, if I liked Twelfth Night. Tasting the air in a moment of thoughtful consideration, I chose the easy way out: 'Yes,' I replied, 'but they're too qualified, too eloquent, too cunning.'

You know, I think they must have overhead me that night cos the latest version of Twelfth Night is radically different and considerably less unbalanced than at any other time in their career, the strange frontier of this Reading crue [sic] having been relocated closer to the heart of pop chart potential. The complete modernisation of TN rests neatly in the unified court of (bleugh, bleugh) Tears for Fears, U2, Simple Minds and China Crisis… they sometimes sound like whining prog rock fans. Appropriately, the songs have now been constructed for technical supremacy, random meandering has been binned and direct-drive rebellion is in vogue. It made me smile because it was all so much simpler.

But they are still saintly, saintly grammar school

A PLAYGROUND OF BROKEN HEARTS

Twelfth Night at The Marquee, 21 August 1985 (Photographs by Andy Inman)

rockers, digging refined heels into the exasperation of passionately wanting to be recognised as anarchic musical boot boys. Thinking loud and clear as I watch Clive Mitten reach for another intricately sculpted guitar, it occurs to me that perhaps the pretension has not been ditched but rechannelled into other (exciting?) areas. They would do far better to delete the puzzling array of sumptuous hardware and, at times, perplexing poses.

I don't want to deflate the success of this gig, one of a series of three. Success that includes widespread acceptance by scoop neck T-shirts, hush-puppied college kids and hardened hacks like myself.

Let's clap.

Derek Oliver, *Kerrang!*, 19 September 1985

Once again, Twelfth Night disappeared from public view for a lengthy period: this trio of gigs would be their last for nine months as they turned their attention, finally, to recording a new album. A record deal had been signed. It would tear the band apart.

To promote *The Jewel*, Pendragon started a 40 date, 11 week trip around the UK and into Europe with their new drummer, Mat Anderson.

'When I first joined,' Anderson says, 'the band had told me tales of life on the road with Marillion, but that level of tour support had gone, so my time was just driving around the UK in Olive, the band's touring van playing some fairly small venues. As a boy who'd spent his whole life in Essex, driving north was like visiting another planet. Scotland was another universe. The band very cruelly wound me up about playing Scotland to the point where I was

1985: Dawn Escapes From Moon Washed College Halls

Solstice with Rogers and Young, 31 August 1985 (Photograph by Oz Hardwick)

absolutely terrified of getting stabbed the minute we set foot there.'

The beautiful, wistful *Lavender* was extracted from *Misplaced Childhood* for single release on 27 August 1985. The relatively short album version had been extended by over a minute by a wonderful new guitar solo and reworked ending. It gave Marillion another Top 5 hit single and pushed its parent album back into the Top 10 for another five weeks.

As Marillion consolidated their commercial success, major changes were happening elsewhere, suggesting that the progressive rock revival was running out of steam. A news item confirming Peter Nicholls' departure from IQ appeared in the 31 August edition of *Sounds*. That same evening, Solstice played their last ever show at The Marquee.

'Ken and Barbara bought a different dynamic to the band, but it never quite captured the magic,' says Martin Wright. 'Audience reaction was not the same and the wonderful chemistry Sandy had with the audience was gone. I was friendly with Nigel Hutchings, who booked us into The Marquee, and I recall a conversation where he was seeing attendances for our gigs dropping off. He didn't want to pull the plug on us and encouraged us to go out on a high by announcing the last shows we were to do there in summer 1985. I felt the ship was rudderless after those gigs, with really no momentum.'

They were supported by Howard Rogers and Keith Young, lately of Liaison. Howard and Keith also played a short set with members of Solstice.

'I remember seeing Andy, Howard and Keith, along with Marc Elton, rehearsing a short set at some church in Milton Keynes ahead of the gig at The Marquee,' recalls Phil Wheal. 'They wrote at

A PLAYGROUND OF BROKEN HEARTS

Adverts from *Sounds* and the *NME*
(From the collection of Guy Tkach)

least one number for it which I remember was called *The Children Of A Better Age*, which I thought was quite cool as it goes.'

'Howard and Keith were my favourites and the best guitarist and singer on the scene,' says Andy Glass. 'Seeing them live recently didn't change my view on that.'

Marillion headed out on the road once again for a 21 date Ireland and UK tour, starting at the SFX Centre in Dublin on 4-5 September, the band's first Irish gigs. Finally, after three years, fan and collector Mark McCormac was able to see his favourite band.

'The three years since *Market Square Heroes* had passed so slowly,' he says, 'but it was certainly worth the wait. I remember my anticipation was sky high as I entered the dimly lit venue with lots of spotty kids in Marillion and Rush shirts, denim and leather. The venue felt like home and the audience like my tribe. The reality of the show far exceeded my expectations. The band were on fire, Fish full of charisma, regaled us with a mixture of dark tales and bad jokes. The crowd were transfixed and sang every word. It was like being on the terraces at a football match, except everyone was cheering for the same team.'

After their gig in Leeds on 5 September Pendragon and their crew stayed with their friend Jon Dunnington.

'I'd moved to Leeds earlier that year,' he says. 'I offered to let them bed down at my shared house not really expecting that they would take me up on the offer, but they gratefully accepted as money was short. They played this awful club in Leeds, Adam & Eve's, and didn't go down too well as it was really a haunt for goths. Someone broke into the van during the gig and stole my radio broadcast bootleg of Roger Waters at Radio City Music Hall [28 March 1985] that I had lent to Nick.

1985: Dawn Escapes From Moon Washed College Halls

A ticket for Marillion's cancelled show in Leicester (From the collection of Russell Morgan)

He later sent me a cassette of a Pendragon gig to make up for it. I still have the apologetic cover letter that came with the Pendragon cassette asking me not to copy it for anyone. We went back and had homebrew beer and lasagne, and they all slept on the floor of the lounge, except the only lady in the crew, Thel who did the lights, who got the spare room. The next morning they presented me with a signed and dedicated copy of Fly High, Fall Far and which I still treasure.'

Marillion's tour was cancelled after three dates. Fish's voice was having none of it.

'Fish was in a party mood,' Mark Kelly said. 'We were [in Dublin] for three days of production rehearsals before the first gig, and Fish was having so much fun he somehow forgot to sleep. By the time the first show came around… his throat or more specifically his vocal cords decided enough was enough and promptly shut down. We struggled (as he croaked) through a second night in Dublin and one in Belfast, but the game was up. The medical advice was that Fish needed to rest his voice, and if he didn't follow the advice to the letter, he was in danger of doing more damage, and permanent damage at that.'

With dates rescheduled for 1986, a 'Misplaced Marquee' fan club event on 10 September also seemed likely to be postponed. However, the band took to the stage for a short set and encouraged the crowd to sing along.

Ian Mosley: 'I remember afterwards getting a hard time from some of the fans saying that we'd sold out. I just thought, 'Oh, thanks a lot!''

A memorable booking for Top Of The Pops, broadcast on 12 September, saw Marillion miming to Lavender. With the tour called off, and not wanting to confuse their disappointed punters, Marillion ensured that presenter Mike Smith explained that they'd 'dragged Fish out of his sickbed' for the show. Fish then mimed happily, holding a flip chart with the words. Hilariously, Fish had written 'guitar solo' with a big arrow pointing at Steve Rothery and concluded with a cheesy grin rather than mime the last line.

Solstice, meanwhile, had ground to a halt.

'Our demise had begun with the departure of Sandy and Mark and the loss of that magical and rare chemistry,' says Andy Glass, 'which I failed to recognise at the time. Myself and Marc, and perhaps Martin too, were confident about the future but, as good as Barbara and Ken were, the magic was gone. We knew it and I think our audience knew it too.'

The final gig for this iteration of Solstice was in Milton Keynes. There was only one problem. Andy Glass did not have a guitar.

'We had the van, the old horse box, parked outside the house in Milton Keynes that some of us were staying in,' he says. 'All the gear was in it, stupidly. In the morning we found it had been broken into. Loads of stuff taken from it, including my guitar. And we had a gig coming up, a festival in Milton Keynes in a huge marquee by the lake.'

129

**Pendragon at The Marquee,
20-21 September 1985
(From the collection of Jon Dunnington)**

He went to visit Steve Rothery.

'I had bought my first house,' Rothery says. 'It was a little two bedroom cottage in Broughton Crossing just outside of Aylesbury. I was alone in the car and Andy drove past one day and stopped and we said hello. I asked him how he was doing. 'Oh, I'm working as a labourer to buy some more equipment 'cause our stuff was stolen.' He played the same guitar as me, a Yamaha SG2000. So I went to the house and I lent him my original Yamaha SG2000, the one I got when I was 18. 'Look, Andy,' I told him, 'whatever you do, guard this with your life. This is very special to me.''

Andy Glass: 'Steve, bless his heart, he lent me his guitar. And he said to me, as he handed it to me, 'You're welcome to borrow it, but please look after it, because it really means a lot to me…''

Andy used Steve's guitar for the Solstice show in Milton Keynes.

'A lot of people turned up for the gig,' Martin Wright recalls. 'Most of the ex-members were there. We played in a marquee and there were so many people we had to remove sides of the tent so everybody could see.'

After the gig, Andy locked Steve Rothery's precious guitar in his car.

'After the show there was a panic as we heard that four or five musicians' cars had been broken into,' Glass recalls. 'I was mortified to find that mine was one and that Steve's precious guitar was gone! I couldn't believe it. Steve was away touring and, of course, in those days there was no way of contacting him. So I wrote him a letter, which was the best thing I could think of doing at the time.'

Steve Rothery: 'I went off on tour, came back to a letter through the post box saying, 'Hey, Steve, I'm really sorry, but the guitar got stolen. But don't worry, I'll get you the insurance money…' which I still haven't seen, by the way.'

'Steve has never forgiven me,' Andy groans.

Rothery: 'Andy's a lovely guy, so I couldn't hate him for it. I was more annoyed with myself for trying to help someone out and it biting me on the ass, I suppose! Never, ever lend a guitar to a hippy!'

The guitar has never been recovered.

Pendragon continued their UK trek.

'I remember one gig in Peterborough, 22 September,' recalls drummer Mat Anderson. 'It was the first and only time I played on a drum riser. It was built from two blocks that gradually separated over the course of the gig. The harder I played the faster it went. My main memory is of being hungry all the time and never having enough money to buy food. I learned to sleep sitting upright which is a skill I still have. Very useful on long journeys, unless I'm driving. I felt under a lot of pressure to drum well every gig, which was a first for me. Gigs had been single events spaced out over weeks, and now here I was playing difficult parts every night. It was both a joy and a challenge.'

After several auditions IQ replaced Peter Nicholls with Paul Menel, as announced in *Sounds*' 12 October edition.

'I answered an ad from a band who loved my tape and wanted me to audition in London!' Menel recalls. 'Now you're talking. It was a popular beat combo called IQ. They sent me *Tales From The Lush Attic* and *The Wake*. I loved the music but hated the name. They asked me to learn all the songs and come down in two weeks to audition. No pressure then.'

Menel's audition was successful.

'Paul was obviously very different to Pete in his approach to the frontman role,' says Tim Esau. 'I would probably call it more traditional and not very 'prog'. We weren't too sure about the songs on the tape he sent in but thought his voice was among the best of the bunch, so invited him along for audition.'

'In truth,' concedes Martin Orford, 'most of the tapes we were sent were absolutely dreadful and Paul was the only serious contender, being a good singer who didn't sound like anyone else.'

'Paul was a very different kind of performer,' suggests Paul Cook. 'He was much more mainstream than Peter, a sort of rock'n'roll cliché. He did work hard as a frontman though and influenced the writing through his singing style and lyrics rather than anything else.'

'As it turned out, Paul and I had quite a lot in common as far as the bands and music we liked,' notes Tim Esau. 'I suppose, because of other things going on in the wider music industry trends at the time, we used that to suggest a slight change in direction in order to 'fit in' a little better than we had up to that point. Though we didn't really meet any resistance from the others, it was Paul and I who really pushed for this new sound on several of the new songs on the following two albums. Martin, in particular, seemed to be onboard with that idea, but at the same time both he and Mike, as principal songwriters, continued to fly the prog flag.'

Menel's musical tastes were influenced by his older brother.

'None of my family could play an instrument,' he explains, 'but it was a household full of music. My dad had been in the Royal Marines, and he would play their albums every Sunday without fail. He had a fine voice too, so he would sing along to Mario Lanza and Joseph Locke. We had an old Bush record player which played constantly: my sister's Motown, my brother's rock and northern soul. Silence didn't exist in my home! My dad influenced and encouraged my singing. He'd take me to the local church choir every Sunday. I loved showing off and singing loudly. The lyrics of the hymns I think first showed me how emotionally moving words can be. I had found my forte! My brother David, now sadly passed, was nine years older than me, so I heard *Led Zeppelin* when I was six and, boy, it left a mark! Jimi Hendrix, Ten Years After, The Who, Curved Air. What a soundtrack to my childhood! I miss David every day, but I cherish the love of music he gave to me.'

Menel immediately brought his ideas to the table. *Promises (As The Years Go By)*, *No Love Lost* and *Nomzamo* were written within a few weeks of Paul Menel joining. For IQ, then, a new focus. The double A-side single *Corners* and *The Thousand Days* was released that same month, with Mike Holmes' remix of *Corners* adding new drums and keyboards as well as shortening the track. A 12" variant added *The Wake*.

A PLAYGROUND OF BROKEN HEARTS

Pendragon: Nick Barrett and Rik Carter in Utrecht on 15 October 1985 (Photograph by Martijn Kuiper)

Corners (From the collection of Piersandro Pallavicini)

After three weeks of rest, Fish had recovered sufficiently to undertake a long tour of Europe in October and November 1985. They were supported at three of these gigs by Pendragon, who undertook their first European shows at the Muziek Centrum in Utrecht on 15-16 October and Teatro Tenda Pianeta in Rome on 22 October.

'Once again we will always be indebted to Marillion for opening the door to touring in Europe for Pendragon,' notes Peter Gee. 'The 2,000-seat Muziek Centrum was like a mini Royal Albert Hall, all in the round, with standing at the front and then seating all around on about three tiers. Right from the start the Dutch audience were really welcoming to us, and appreciative of us. We were blown away to discover that there was still a place where they really listened to, and cared about, their music.'

Mat Anderson: 'The Utrecht show came at a pivotal point for me. I was renting a room in Stroud, working part time at a DIY shop and spending a lot

of time indoors reading. I was pretty homesick. The Utrecht shows offered a sniff of rock'n'roll glamour and a chance to play on a big stage. I vividly remember the roar of the crowd when we came on stage – even though it was only a couple of thousand, you really felt it – and the first thing they heard was a tricky opening drum fill. I was shitting myself, shaking so badly I could barely play. Afterwards we were on a massive high, hence me ending up in a hotel room finishing a bottle of whisky with Fish.'

Rik Carter: 'My main memory of Utrecht is meeting a beautiful girl called Mandy who worked at the Holiday Inn where we stayed. Sigh…'

Pendragon played six songs each night, opening with *Victims Of Life* from *Fly High, Fall Far* and including three from *The Jewel*.

Yes, the first taste of playing abroad and it was a blinder! Two and a half thousand unbelievably enthusiastic fans per night, really made for a tremendous experience. We spent two nights at the 'luxurious' Holiday Inn, which probably makes the best scrambled eggs this side of the Equator; and just to round the trip off, after the last show, Mat had a drink or two in the company of the 'aquatic one' only to find out that once a bottle of Scotch is opened it must be finished!

Contact issue 14

Pendragon returned to Stroud to write and demo new material. It would be three years before their follow-up to *The Jewel*.

Pallas were on the road again. Their concert in Dundee, 28 October, was reviewed by Vicky Stanhope in *Revelatory* issue 5.

Alan Reed… is a striking contrast to Euan Lowson, both in appearance and style as he does away with the elaborate costumes and theatrics to concentrate purely on his vocals. As a result he avoids the aloofness that Lowson adopted and establishes a much better contact with the audience, by his more down to earth approach.

The new material was also an improvement and augers well for the release of their next album, with Alan's vocals giving their songs a new range. The new epic song *Sanctuary* was particularly impressive, mainly due to the atmospheric keyboards. Ron Brown has expanded his keyboard collection, enabling him to vary his playing more. His new portable keyboard allows him to perform alongside the guitarists which is good visually.

On the whole there was a considerable increase in the group's confidence since I last saw them on the *Brave New World* tour. They handled both the set pieces and the solo performances with ease. *Atlantis* was still a dramatic closing number, with an appearance of the Sentinel on stage and the fireworks at the front of the stage. They played a gritty version of *Arrive Alive* for one encore and then an Alex Harvey classic which went down well with the Scottish audience.

Pallas seem to have emerged from the upheaval of changing vocalist as a band who have developed a far more confident and original style.

Reed's appointment was consolidated by Pallas supporting hard rockers UFO on a 16 date tour of decent sized venues around the UK in the last two weeks of November, starting on 12 November in Exeter. Shy were added to the bill for most of these shows.

'Getting to see how much alcohol human beings could consume without dying was pretty mind blowing,' Graeme Murray observes, referring to the show's headline act.

Dates followed in Bristol, Brighton, Norwich and Cardiff. Howard Johnson of *Kerrang!* reviewed the Cardiff concert, 16 November 1985.

> Pallas' heavyweight bassist Graeme Murray sure bends those boards and the band's pompous ideas make it tough to wade through the songs. Mustn't beat about the bush, though; Pallas are simply purveyors of awfully tiresome progressive plod. They try to be Marillion (a cliché sure, but clichés stem from obvious truths) though Alan Reed's 'Fishy' vocals fail desperately cos there isn't a song in sight. There's a new album out in January, I believe. I won't be buying it and I shan't waste any more ink on Pallas. If you weren't there, you missed nothing. Count yourselves lucky, cos I missed the bar through watching 'em!
>
> *Kerrang!* issue 108
> (28 November – 11 December 1985)

The tour continued to Ipswich, Leicester and Aberdeen, where a future Pallas vocalist, Paul Mackie, was in the audience, then to Glasgow, Leeds, Manchester, Birmingham, Nottingham, Oxford and Southampton.

'When we were in Oxford,' says Graeme Murray, 'one of the EMI executives came to talk to us. 'Listen guys, I've got great news. I've been put in charge of the band and I'll be doing things from now on.' We were cock-a-hoop as he was a huge fan of the band. About three weeks later we went into Manchester Square to meet up with him, only to find out that he'd been sacked. We were devastated. There was no happy ending.'

Murray went to see the EMI executives to ask them why, as he felt Marillion were getting lots of support but Pallas none.

''Well, Graeme, it's like this… Marillion are a pop group and you're heavy metal.' I knew then that we were in trouble.'

The tour ended with the band's fourth and final visit to the famed Hammersmith Odeon.

IQ continued to bed in their new singer.

Mike Holmes: 'There's bound to be a difference in style between two singers, but more than that I think Paul was keen to work on new material and didn't really want to sing lyrics written by someone else. Paul brought different things to IQ, but I think he never really felt as passionate about singing those songs as Peter did.'

Fans who didn't get to see the band for themselves could order a double vinyl 'official bootleg' called *Nine In A Pond Is Here* by mail order or at gigs. This contained three sides of rehearsals with Paul Menel recorded just after he joined the band in October 1985. Menel sings two of the band's signature songs from *Tales From The Lush Attic* – *Awake and Nervous* and *The Last Human Gateway* – and two from *The Wake*, namely *Outer Limits* and the title track. There are also versions of three of the band's earliest songs, *Intelligence Quotient*, *It All Stops Here* and *Fascination*. The fourth side is a collection of humorous songs and instrumentals.

The decision by Peter Nicholls to leave IQ came as something of a shock, to say the least, to their growing number of fans. This is probably due to the lack of outward signs of Peter's dissatisfaction and IQ's growing maturity and success. Still as the prophet once said, 'One man maketh not a band', so while Peter went off to new pastures the band wasted no time in recruiting a new vocalist. Eventually they decided on Paul Menel, a 22 year old from Barnsley. As a novel way to introduce him to IQ fans and presumably to have another go at the old material, the band recorded this double official 'bootleg' album during rehearsals in October 1985 for their Autumn tour. Apparently it is a limited edition, though how limited I don't know! Its attraction to the buyer is increased by a side of previously unreleased material.

In a sense it could be said that this is an IQ 'greatest hits' album. Both album releases and the now-deleted tape are represented. Musically these see a more mature and naturally, aggressive approach as they are captured live. If you liked the originals you'll like these.

Now we come to the thorny problem of Paul Menel.

'Well,' I said to myself, 'Superficially he sounds a lot like Peter Nicholls.' However on closer inspection I found that his voice lacks the passion and commitment of Peter's. This may have something to do with the fact that he isn't singing his own lyrics and this is his debut album. Undoubtedly though the potential is there for him to fulfil the role very well. It will be interesting to see what sort of stage persona he has. As it is he hasn't done a bad job and I can't honestly see the changeover soundwise being as traumatic as it could have been.

The unreleased stuff, depending on your sense of humour, is either quite silly or a waste of vinyl. I think it's a bit of both. The first bit of IQ madness is the *Glenn Miller Medley* on side three, including *In The Mood* as you've never heard it before. Side Four is where IQ really go to town exploring various different avenues of music. *Flak* is basically on the rap/scratch dance beat mode. I find this kind of music tedious and even IQ can't dispel this notion. *The Story Of Cow And The Grocery Boys* opens with strange sound effects à la Genesis' *Waiting Room* before a thirties jazz style tune takes over. *Robo II* is a delightful acoustic guitar and harpsichord interlude. A short Python-esque sketch, complete with silly voices though not as funny, preludes *Funk Is In My Brain*. As you might expect from the title this is a funkier, dance track. It is quite interesting but outstays its welcome. *Stomach Of Animal* is obviously heavily influenced by the afro-funk style of Talking Heads, complete with Byrne-esque vocals! *Sno It Re Crep (Truth)* is all backwards tapes and is very short.

The side is a bit of a mixed bag, ranging from boring indulgence to evocative interpretations of different styles of music. Overall however, the good outweighs the bad enough to make it worthwhile.

The album will be bought by IQ fans inquisitive to hear the new vocalist. It could also serve as a useful, if expensive, introduction to IQ's music.

David Pickering, *Slogans* issue 19

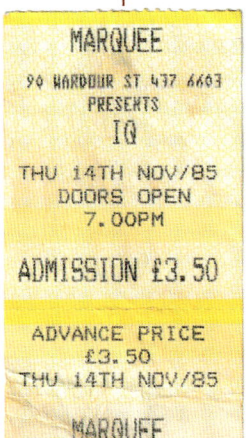

Ticket for Paul Menel's first gig with IQ (From the collection of Peter Moltensen)

Paul Menel in 1986: 'The idea was really twofold. Firstly, to get my voice across to the fans, singing the old IQ stuff and also to get onto vinyl some of the songs off the cassette album [*Seven Stories Into Eight*]. Because it was recorded in one day it was like 'sing now' and if anyone made a mistake we stopped and started the track again, which was difficult, especially in *The Last Human Gateway* because I hadn't learnt all the lyrics and was singing them off a lyric sheet. The album was never meant to be a Trevor Horn-type production – it was the product of a long day… and it shows!'

'I hated that album then and time hasn't eradicated that feeling,' Paul Menel says. 'I guess it was good to rehearse those songs together to help me to gel, but as a commercial enterprise or 'Let's do this for the fans!' type thing? It sucks the big one!'

Menel debuted at The Marquee on 14 November.

'I'm a confident person,' Menel says. 'I know my talents and skills and I know how to play to a crowd. But honestly that day I was a bag of anxiety and nerves. I can't remember how much toilet paper I got through. I remember walking in and out of the shops in Carnaby Street in a daze. It was all I could do to stop myself hopping on the Tube and heading back up north for a night of tomfoolery with my old mates. But this band were my new mates in waiting and I had a crowd to win over. I don't think people appreciate how difficult it was to sing songs you'd had nothing to do with writing. Super tortured artist? Me? Pretentious? Moi? No, it was never a 'woe is me' and a wringing of hands from this singer, but a little bit of love occasionally wouldn't have gone amiss. I won more fans over than I lost that first night at The Marquee.'

As part of an 11 song set, the new *Promises (As The Years Go By)* was a taste of the next two IQ albums: big drums, commercial choruses and sharp, radio-friendly production. At this stage, it was missing the catchy opening but it's a definite step away from the Nicholls era music. The final recorded version, two years away, sounds nothing like 1970s Genesis, but quite a lot like, say, Mike + the Mechanics.

The Marquee show was a warm-up gig for a five week tour supporting a rejuvenated Magnum at large venues across the UK, including Manchester Apollo, Sheffield City Hall, Birmingham Odeon and Hammersmith Odeon. Their set list comprised *Outer Limits*, *The Wake*, *The Magic Roundabout*, *Promises (As The Years Go By)*, *The Thousand Days*, *Widow's Peak* and *Corners*.

'Magnum were a joy to play with,' Menel says, 'ultimate professionals. I caught a bad cold early on that tour and their singer, Bob Catley, insisted I come on their touring coach to stop it spreading. Great memories, great people. Their fans, especially in the UK, took a bit of persuading that we were a good band despite Tim's eye shadow and lippy, but it was a difficult tour for me. Baptism of fire doesn't quite cover it. New and old songs to sing, new and old fans to win over, constantly living in a goldfish bowl. It was the first time that I asked myself if it was worth it, especially when you have a few of your own fans booing the new guy.'

Speaking the following spring, Menel said, 'The pressure was two pronged because as well as trying to convert people and play to IQ fans, I was trying to convince Pete's diehard fans that it was 'goodbye Peter, hello Paul!' I think that in a lot of respects it has worked. It was a good experience for me, straight in at the deep end. For me the best gig was Birmingham. Magnum are from there. We went on stage expecting stick from the crowd, but they warmed straight to us and the feeling of convincing an audience that you are good over forty-five minutes is brilliant.'

How did Menel respond to performing at the Hammersmith Odeon?

'It's really weird,' he said, 'because IQ primarily are a Southampton based band, but they've been taken to heart by the London crowd. It was brilliant to see that about thirty percent of the crowd were IQ-ites, and they gave us a good reception. Obviously people are still wary of me because I've only played the one headline gig, the farce at The Marquee; I was still learning the words! All being well, the next headline tour should quell any doubts that fans still have about me and the direction of the band.'

Promises (As The Years Go By) was one of three new songs demoed at the time, along with *Nomzamo* and *Stillness Of Life*. These would be recorded for the band's next album, with the latter being given a slight change of name to *Still Life*.

A re-arranged *Heart Of Lothian* was Marillion's third single from *Misplaced Childhood*. This less obviously commercial track, released on 18 November, just crept into the UK Top 30 and comprises sections from both *Bitter Suite* and *Heart Of Lothian*, which fades ahead of the final minute as heard on the album. The B-side is a live version of *Chelsea Monday* recorded at the Muziekcentrum Vredenburg in Utrecht on 15 October 1985. The entire concert, featuring a very enthusiastic Dutch crowd, would later be made available in the 2017 reissue of *Misplaced Childhood*. This includes a live performance of the whole of that album, and is perhaps the definitive record of Marillion at their in-concert peak with Fish.

Due to massive demand, the 11 November concert in Stuttgart was upgraded from the Liederhalle to the massive Hanns-Martin-Schleyer-Halle: capacity, 12,500. This was Marillion's largest headlining crowd to date. Then, to Japan, for five dates in early December.

Changes were afoot in the Pendragon camp: Mat Anderson and Rik Carter left.

'When I joined I had sat my last A Level two weeks previously,' Anderson explains. 'I had undiagnosed autism. I had no job, no offer of pay from the band and nowhere to live. I had never left home and had never toured. No one in my family worked in the music industry, so there was no one to explain that at the very least I should have had some offer of pay in writing, and that I could still tour without relocating. It was a bit of a baptism of fire, and looking back on it now I can see both how ill-prepared I was and equally how the band wasn't really set up to accommodate someone who was still a child. Thinking back, it was pretty extreme. It's not surprising that it quickly became too much for me. We did the best we could, but I do wonder how my life would have been different had I stuck it out for a bit longer.'

'I left for a few reasons,' Carter says. 'The main thing was money. I was never paid a single penny

Marillion on the *Misplaced Childhood* tour
(Photograph by Mark Drake)

during the two years I was in the band and ran up a huge overdraft on my bank account in order to survive. That was very stressful. Everyone was stressed about money back then. I wasn't happy in Stroud. It's beautiful but also weird and very insular. I definitely wasn't a fan of the newer poppier direction the band was going in either…'

'I can't remember which one of us decided to jump first,' Mat Anderson says. 'I know we were both unhappy. I can't speak for Rik, but I was broke and homesick. The whole experience was just too much for me at that age. I felt hugely relieved when I left. Looking back on my short time with the band, I wish there had been someone to give me a couple of pointers about how to navigate the situation. I think it would have made quite a difference. However, being with the band taught me so much about drumming, music and touring and I'm grateful for that. But I've never toured since.'

Rik Carter would go on to work with The Mission and All About Eve. The remaining duo, Nick Barrett and Peter Gee, recorded some new songs at Millstream Studios in Cheltenham, playing all of the instruments themselves. These three songs, *The Mask*, *I Walk The Rope* and *Time For A Change*, would eventually be recorded for *Kowtow* and the demos would be released on later reissues of the album.

Back from Japan, rare video footage of Marillion at The Marquee would be broadcast on BBC's *Whistle Test* on Tuesday 10 December. As part of a short set, Marillion performed *Bitter Suite* and *Heart Of Lothian*. Their song *Kayleigh* would be the 32nd best-selling single of the year.

This same night, the former singers with Twelfth Night and IQ played their debut gigs together with their new bands. Geoff Mann's The Bond and Peter Nicholls' Niadem's Ghost performed at the Gallery in Manchester ahead of a joint gig at The Marquee five days later.

'We were two friends on the same journey,'

1985: Dawn Escapes From Moon Washed College Halls

Marillion on the *Misplaced Childhood* tour
(Photograph by Mark Drake)

Nicholls says. 'We'd both left our respective bands for entirely different reasons. Geoff and I discussed this. We had both realised that the music in Twelfth Night and IQ was quite big and grandiose. We, as singers, were often looking to find our place within very intricate music. When we were free from those constraints we wanted to make the music more intimate, more manageable. We both wanted the vocals to be more of a key feature in our musical endeavours, to find our own places rather than sit in someone else's sound picture. I liked being part of a group, but in Niadem's Ghost I had a stronger say.'

On 12 December 1985, after several months of detailed contractual negotiations, Twelfth Night signed a worldwide, eight album deal with Virgin.

'I remember our manager, Patrick Williams, turning up to West Side Studios in Southall where we were rehearsing,' says Andy Sears. 'It was the 12th of the 12th at 12 noon. Who knows how long he'd been waiting outside for the clock to strike 12?

This wasn't just the story of Twelfth Night. For me it was also the culmination of all my efforts since 1979 when I had seen EMI's 'big door' slightly ajar. This time it had really opened, and with it our chance to make anything happen. But something had already left by that same door. It should have been our biggest celebration ever - but we didn't even go for a pint in the local. Five signatures later, and we were carrying on with the rehearsals, and after that, everyone to their respective lives. I remember thinking to myself at that point that we need to get the internal politics sorted now, or all of this has been a waste of time.'

Andy Revell: 'The Virgin record deal was the opening of a door we had been knocking on since 1980, when Brian and I first went to their offices in Notting Hill with an instrumental demo tape. The deal was for eight albums with a sizeable advance. It was a serious, long-term deal and we were all thrilled. Perhaps there was a little too much of a

139

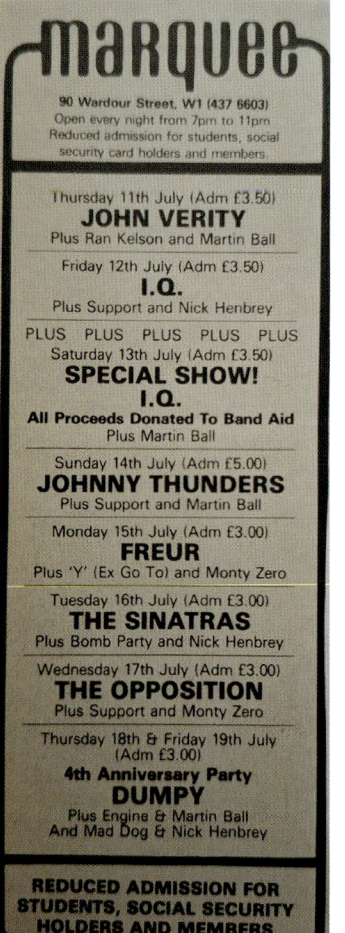

IQ Marquee ad July 1985
(From the collection of Marco de Niet)

feeling of relief amongst us, because it had felt like such a long and rocky road to get there. I think we all felt a bit of 'Thank God we have finally done it' rather than 'Fantastic this is where it really starts.''

The band were booked into Jacobs, a pair of state of the art digital recording studios near Farnham in Surrey. They were allocated producer John Walters.

'I was always interested in production,' says John Walters, 'and had huge admiration for arranger/producers such as Quincy Jones, George Martin and Arif Mardin, so I wanted to try my hand. Richard James Burgess and I had worked together on a few projects, usually with him as producer and me as arranger/programmer. I'd had my first taste of producing with a solo artist called Nick Battle. What really got me started, though, was producing *Soul Train*, a Top 20 hit for Swans Way. I soon became quite busy, producing Kissing The Pink, Carmel and Pookiesnackenburger. I knew Hit & Run management. They had previously hired me to work on a few interesting jobs and introduced me to Twelfth Night; we met and found that we got on well. They were ambitious and keen to grasp this opportunity to make a good album on a major label. And I was ambitious, too, and saw this as a way to flex my production muscles.'

Andy Revell: 'When we arrived at Jacobs in November 1985, expectations were high.'

Pendragon closed out 1985 with a Christmas show at The Marquee on 18 December. Their encore of Slade's *Merry Xmas Everybody* included guest appearances from members of Solstice, IQ and LaHost, as well as some enthusiastic fans.

'About five of us mounted a stage invasion,' admits Jon Dunnington, 'to the dismay of Graham Bowden, their roadie, who got a roasting from Nick afterwards. Unsurprisingly, we'd all had a few beers but it was a good natured singalong, and I can now say that I have been on stage at The Marquee with Pendragon and the likes of Martin Orford from IQ.'

Twelfth Night remained resident at Jacobs until mid-January.

Clive Mitten: 'We were at Jacobs for New Year's Eve in December 1985. We bought a case of champagne and put it in the big freezer to let it chill. But we forgot about it and at some stage that evening it exploded. I'm sure there are more impressive tales of studio destruction, but you must agree that exploding champagne shows some class.'

1986:
Egos Check Cheques In Transit

> '*The Wedge* is intentionally different from *The Sentinel*. We hope that we have broken some new ground as a rock band and have been 'progressive' (oh that word!) in a TRUE sense.'
>
> Graeme Murray, *The Sentinel* newsletter, 1986

As 1985 turned into 1986, Twelfth Night were still recording their new album at Jacobs Studios. For them, a year that began with so much promise would end in disarray.

Andy Sears: 'At this time, I preferred late night recording sessions and, let's say, the 'rock and roll' lifestyle. I frequently socialised with Rick Parfitt and Francis Rossi, who were recording in the next studio. They invited me to sit in on their session for their song *In The Army Now* and it was great fun to watch them at work.'

Clive Mitten: 'Andy preferred to record his vocals late at night. But by this time the rest of us had been at work in the studio all day, so we weren't there. Unfortunately, this meant that the producers and engineers were working very long hours and were often overtired and stressed, which didn't help the atmosphere.'

Andy Sears: 'Recording the instruments would take up the daytime, leaving the wee hours for vocals. At times, we would go on until 3 or 4 in the morning, since I like to use a hell of a lot of multi-track harmonies and effects. Being the only singer in the band makes that a long process. So, while the rest of the boys were asleep, I would record. I would generally turn in just before the others awoke. It was hardly surprising that we often wouldn't see each other until dinner, unless there was something being recorded for which I particularly wanted to be present.'

The underlying tension of these sessions was getting to all of the band members and affected Andy Sears in the most dramatic way.

'By now,' Andy explains, 'with the pressure on maximum, and several personal crises to deal with, I had stopped eating anything other than lemons and diet coke for some time. I had in fact become anorexic. This was coupled with an ever increasing tendency to stay up all night. One day I apparently just didn't wake up. Nor did I wake up the next day. The first thing I remember is waking up with a needle in my arm and a doctor leaning over me with some nasty looking pink substance he wanted me to drink. All of this was most probably a result of the onset of depression, together with a sense of loss of control over my life. I had fought so hard to get somewhere with my music since I was 15 years old, and the pervading sense of disaster that was beginning to encircle the band was just too much to contemplate. It was time for a spot of denial.'

Clive Mitten: 'Andy went through a difficult time in 1986.'

By mid-January, with backing tracks complete, production moved to Rooster Studios in Shepherd's Bush, London, for overdubs, with a further session for strings at Jam Studios in Paddington.

Marillion and Pallas were on tour at this time, though not together. Marillion's tour started with three dates at Hammersmith Odeon, 8-10 January. These were recorded. The first was broadcast on BBC Radio 1 and the other two comprised a large part of the retrospective live album *The Thieving Magpie*. The rest of the tour included big theatre venues such as St David's Hall, Cardiff (recorded for King Biscuit Flower Hour), Edinburgh Playhouse,

Beltane Fire (Courtesy Clint Bradley)

BELTANE FiRE

Manchester Apollo and Sheffield City Hall.

Support was provided by British four piece band Beltane Fire, who were promoting their recent album *Different Breed*. Beltane Fire took the decision to maximise the opportunity afforded to them by Marillion and give away a free flexi disc to tour attendees.

'We sent our stuff to Marillion's management,' recalls singer/guitarist Clint Bradley. 'It was a big tour, completely sold out, so we were lucky to make it onto the bill. Before the tour began everybody kept telling us that Marillion's following hated support bands, and we got to hear all the stories about 'so and so' being bottled off. The tour kicked off at Brixton Academy and we walked on to an audience who were ready to give us some serious shit, especially as we didn't look like the standard rock band of the day… plus we had a double bass! As we plugged in our guitars a voice from the audience shouted, 'Fuck off, Elvis is dead!' Well, here we go, I thought, and we went straight into our opening song, *Night Fishing*. By the end of that first number, we had a portion of the audience on our side, and they really gave us the support we needed to play an excellent gig! It was one of those magical moments that I'll never forget. And that's how the rest of the tour went. By the end of it we'd built up a following within the following. We were so vastly different from Marillion, I think it made for an interesting support. I remember we played our own gig at the 100 Club a couple of weeks after the tour finished and a load of them came down on a coach to see us in our own right. It was really starting to happen. If only the record label had given us more time, we could have built something special.'

Clint recalls one story that reveals a different side to Fish's personality.

'In the lead-up to playing in Edinburgh we kept getting told, 'You're doing alright, but they're going to kill you in Scotland!' It was a sold out gig, absolutely rammed! And here we are, an English band, playing songs about life in the English shires, to a Scots audience who'd come to see their own boy, Fish, on his home turf. Well, the day of the gig arrived and I just lost my voice, whether it was nerves or just general strain I'll never know, but I woke up that morning like a frog. We soundchecked and I had a job to get through a number. I went up to our dressing room to try and figure out how the hell I was going to get through the gig when suddenly Fish appeared in the doorway. He had a jar of honey in one hand and a bottle of brandy in the other. He proceeded to pour the honey and the brandy into a pint glass and handed it to me with the words 'Drink that!' By the time we were due to go on I was totally wasted. Just as we were about to hit the stage, Fish appeared and said, 'I'm going to introduce you tonight' and he walked on with us. The crowd went wild, and he said, 'These are some friends of mine, make them welcome.' He made that gig so much easier for us that night. He really is a diamond geezer!'

The tour concluded with four further dates at Hammersmith Odeon: this took Marillion's tally to 17 shows in three years at the legendary venue. The last of these, 6 February 1986, was in aid of the Double 'O' charity, and featured sets from John Otway and Peter Hammill (who was uncharitably booed off the stage after two songs) as well as encores of *Shadow On The Wall* with Roger Chapman and Mike Oldfield, and *I Know What I Like (In Your Wardrobe)* with Steve Hackett. This concert raised £17,000 for the Double 'O' campaign and was written up, at length, by Mick Wall in *Kerrang!* A recording of Marillion's set (without the guests) was released in 2004 on *Curtain Call (A Live Archive 1983-1988)*.

HAMMERSMITH HEROES
MARILLION AND FRIENDS
Hammersmith Odeon, London

IT'S ALL about charity, kid. In this case, Pete Townshend's Double 'O' Charity, set up to raise money for non-government sponsored agencies, helping them lend a hand to the modern-day afflicted; battered housewives, Valium freaks, booze babies, junkies, all the people with all the anti-social problems nobody likes but nobody wants to do anything about. It's all about money to help people who really need it, but can't get that help on the National Health.

So, our cause is just. Now who in hell are the 'friends' part of this deal?

Suck it and see, said the chick. I drained her glass and mine and we went inside. Thousands of fools acting like loonies and thousands of loonies making fools of themselves. Me and the chick included. Then... darkness. In darkness I can hear ...MUSIC!

A classical piece I'll wager, I whispered in the chick's ear, having seen the show before (smirk).

And yeah, *The Thieving Magpie* fills the hall, the bomb finally drops at the end, the curtains swing back and ...here it comes! ...It's ... JOHN OTWAY!!

Blank looks and boorish boos. John Otway, accompanied no longer by Wild Willy Barrett, of course, but by guitarist Robin Boult. And then, just in time, John's all-time anthem to the simple pleasures of the born-again eccentric's life, *Really Free*, rescued everything and holy vibes were restored. When he topped that with his own highly personalised version of the old Bachman Turner Overdrive chestnut, *You Ain't Seen Nothing Yet*, replete with capricious guitar solo from Bad Billy Robin Boult and mad charismatic acrobatics off the drum-riser from the main man himself, then the audience were hooked. John Otway bounded offstage at the end with the vulgar sound of loud cheers following him every step of the way.

The same – and I mean this politely – cannot be said for poor Peter Hammill. Introduced personally by Fish, amidst horribly inappropriate cries for *Grendel* from the philistines in the audience (including the chick's mate, Babs), Peter Hammill went down like rain at a garden party, he died.

Accompanied by guitarist John Ellis, Hammill sang quite brilliantly – *The Happy Hour?* – I think that's what it was called – and performed, under the circumstances, with courage and astonishing verve.

He still died, though. Everybody ended up sitting down, and lots of wise-asses were yelling for Peter to F**K OFF! And then the slow hand-clapping started. Jesus, it was embarrassing!

Eventually, thank God, he left the stage, Peter

Hammill and John Ellis both. A more talented, admittedly dour, composer of modern music you could not find. He died tonight, though. Ah well, he's probably used to it by now.

There followed a brief intermission. Refreshments obtained, we settled ourselves for the evening's main entertainment.

To huge, huge applause, Marillion hit the stage: Fish as graceful as a matador, twirling his exotic cape around those broad high shoulders, the band fizzing mightily on the magic intro to *Emerald Lies*. Great arms extended, he inclines his head towards the ever-listening microphone, and begins again: 'So here I am once more…'

I've written that line half as many times as Fish has sung it at the Hammersmith Odeon, easy, and it still sends a cold chill down my crooked spine to hear him do it now.

From here on in, it's more or less the same set they've been playing all over Britain these past four weeks. The only exception is *Jigsaw*, omitted due to the strictures of time; this is to be a long show.

From where I'm positioned, the sound is all beautiful, strong like poison taken in heavy sips. Drink in hand, Fish signals drummer Ian Mosley into *Incubus* and the magic falls heavy into our waiting laps. Fish the red-light mystic cat-walking through the forbidden corners of his own heart, Steve Rothery (guitar) and Mark Kelly (keyboards) dosing the night with hidden colours.

The Web skips and hops and dances drunk and stout into its futuristic jig, the band meting out the climax, giving blood under the ghastly gaze of the jester, Fish away, lost in the wings, another jester's embrace repelled and remembered.

Marillion then perform *Misplaced Childhood* in its entirety, almost certainly for the last time ever before a British audience, and, of course, it's dedicated, as it has been almost every night of the tour, to Phil Lynott…

It's an emotional run through of the biggest deal Marillion have ever made with their God, whoever he is. Their masterpiece played before their people for the very last time. It was sad and brilliant, fitting and strange. As Fish prepares to vanish from the top of his ramp at the back of the stage at the climax of *White Feather*, a girl fan chases after him to no real avail. But she came mighty close there for a second.

'It's 13 years this month since the fall of Saigon,' says Fish into his hand-mike. 'And this next number is called…'

Fugazi ignites and flares and throws mad rushes of sparks and rainbows over everything in sight. The audience devours it all and spits it back at the band with loud, appreciative roars of animal delight.

Fish mumbles something about anything can happen in the next half-hour and out comes Mike Oldfield, his guitarist Joel, keyboard player Micky Simmons [sic], bass player Phil Spalding and singer Roger Chapman; all there to help the Marillion gang through a screaming blue murder version of *Shadow On The Wall*. The audience are alight, but when Steve Hackett saunters out all cool and convincing at the end of it all, Hammersmith has a heart attack, people writhing like f**king snakes on the floor.

It must be the number they've all started playing, Oldfield, Hackett and Marillion. Goes something like this:

'It's one o'clock and time for lunch…'

YES.

I Know What I Like and I like what I know, and what I know is this. It was a great something to see, and there we were, me and the chick, actually there when it happened: Marillion (with you know who) actually performing a G*n*s*s number!

HAHAHAHAHA! Up yours the rest of the dumb world. I'm just sorry you missed it. At the end of it all, Fish presented Pete Townshend with a giant-sized show-cheque for £17,000 and the band came back for *Garden Party*. It was funny seeing so many 'big names' getting up there onstage making monkeys out of themselves just because Marillion asked them nicely.

And, like I said, it's all about charity, kid. And Marillion are big enough these days to dish it out. Wonder when we'll see them at the Hammersmith Odeon again?

Pallas's album *The Wedge* would be released on 10 February 1986. *Dance Through The Fire* provides a loud, raucous opening, mixing spectacular drumming with a catchy chorus. *Throwing Stones At The Wind* features ZZ Top style guitar riffs alongside another catchy chorus and a prog breakdown. It's a great song, full of quirky moments. *Win Or Lose* had been part of the band's set for over a year now. It's a classy ballad giving Alan Reed a chance to spotlight his impressively soulful vocals. It also features a great solo from Niall. In contrast, the aggressive *The Executioner* is based on the story of Bernard Goetz, a vigilante who shot four young black men on a New York City subway train on 22 December 1984. This mixes loud guitars and drums with a questioning lyric. Side two kicks off with the cheery *Imagination*, which takes full advantage of the huge drum sound at the Townhouse. It sounds remarkably like Menel-era IQ. *Rat Racing* is the requisite 'epic'.

Graeme Murray: 'Alan wrote some great lyrics one sleepless morning whilst looking out his window across Aberdeen's rooftops and from that inspiration grew *Rat Racing*. This is a long song with four movements and lets the lads flex our collective musical muscles. Another of my favourites this, with some brilliant atmospheric keyboards from our Ron.'

The album ends with the wonderful *Just A Memory*, which sounds very 1986, with sequenced rhythm track, fretless bass and unusual samples. It has a floaty rhythmic feel and some soaring guitar at the conclusion.

The Wedge is a very different album to *The Sentinel*. But, then again, Alan Reed had brought energy and vision to Pallas. Reed was interviewed at length for *The Stairway* issue 2, published in April.

'A lot of the essence of the original Pallas is in *The Wedge*,' he said, 'but there was a lot of thought [that] went into what we did. We wanted to do something which was a little bit different from what one might have expected from a so-called 'progressive rock band'. Some of it is a lot more straight ahead and rocky… there's something very modern sounding. I think we've grown a lot as a band, we've become much more concise musically, and lyrically I think we've become a lot more human… basically the album's lyrics are about the experiences we've had over the past

A PLAYGROUND OF BROKEN HEARTS

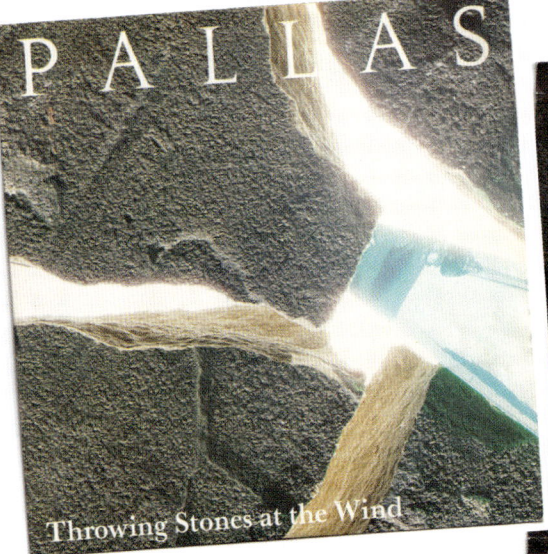

Throwing Stones At The Wind, front and back covers (EMI)

year and a half. It's very, very personal… some of it is very bitter… basically over the past year and a half, since I joined, a lot of people lost faith in us… the press wrote us off, the record company wrote us off, everyone almost went out of their way to make sure we ceased to function as a unit. We've been through a year of starting from scratch again and trying to prove that what we were doing was really worthwhile.'

Reed mused on the influences that colour the music on the new Pallas album.

'We sat down before we did the album,' he said, 'and as well as listening to the likes of Genesis, Yes, Rush, Purple, The Sabs and those people, we also listened to Tears For Fears, Simple Minds, U2, Peter Gabriel and The Cars. We listened to a lot of the major albums of the past couple of years… we wanted to make an album which in terms of production was going to be up there with the big boys… it's going to be as important an album in production terms as *90125* was for Yes, or *Heartbeat City*, or even Frankie Goes To Hollywood. I mean [*Welcome To The Pleasure Dome*] was an amazing album in terms of production, a lot of prog rock rip-offs there actually, and we wanted to come out with an album that was going to stand up alongside those.'

But will it be a success?

'It's really up to the punters in the street,' Reed said. 'People getting to hear about it, getting to listen to it, and making up their own minds. We can stand up and scream 'Hey, this album's wonderful', but there are a thousand other bands all doing the same thing, and we believe that it has to pay off in the end. I don't think this album, in terms of commercial success, is going to make us into superstars, but I think credibility wise it's restored a lot of faith to a lot of people, and it can only grow from here.'

The obvious single was the upbeat *Imagination*, but it was *Throwing Stones At The Wind* that would be selected as the band's next bid for chart success.

'We actually chose it as a single because it was the most unusual track,' said Alan Reed. 'It was just totally out of character for us. We thought we'd rattle a few cages if we stuck that one out, because everyone, even Pallas fans, would go 'what's that?'

It was a flop.

'...the hope was that people would latch onto it because it was a bit unusual, but it didn't quite work out that way. It's just that there's so many records being released every week. It's just a question of the chances that [a radio producer] happens to take a liking to it. I mean we had promises of a couple of Radio 1 daytime airplays, so we had a Top 75 chart position mid-week and EMI blew it. They didn't actually press up enough singles in the first week. Things just didn't come together. There's an awful lot of really good songs that are never on the radio. It's just one of those things.'

The B-side included a live performance featuring Reed singing the Pallas classic *Cut And Run* recorded at Ritzy's in Aberdeen on 22 October 1985. *Crown Of Thorns* from the same show was added to the 12" single.

'We needed some b-sides quickly,' he said, 'and we didn't have time to go into the studio and record some stuff. We just recorded one night at Aberdeen, warts 'n all. I think it's fairly good. It's also nice for me to have *Crown Of Thorns* with me singing on it. That was the song that got me into Pallas in the first place. When I went to see them for the first time I went down the road singing *Crown Of Thorns*.'

Pallas toured across the UK between 6 and 17 February promoting *The Wedge*. Their support act was Geoff Mann, performing solo. Gigs in Bradford, East Retford, Stoke, Hull, Lancaster, Burton-on-Trent and Leicester helped to raise Geoff's profile.

The release of *The Wedge* generated favourable reviews, with Alan Reed's voice helping the band to forge its new identity.

PALLAS *The Wedge* (EMI SHVL 850)
KKKKK

There can be few bands who have managed to assemble their musical influences and achieve an entirely revitalised identity after a major setback. Pallas have.

Watching Pallas change has been a genuine buzz for me. The first live shows featuring new vocalist Alan Reed prompted a previously unthinkable switch from overlong and complex 20 minute epics to more malleable altogether sharper statements devoid of awkward lyrical content and heralding far more human and thoroughly believable experiences. So what does *The Wedge* now tell us?

Whatever it is, and somehow I get the feeling there's a good deal of humour wrapped up here, the band certainly aren't afraid to gamble and risk what ground they've already gained. Initially, you'll notice that things are a lot harder – the guitars of Niall Mathewson are especially wild and peppered with all kinds of blistering extravaganzas.

Not only is the sound a lot heavier but there's not a moment wasted. No exceptions. *Throwing Stones At The Wind*, the current single, is a convenient example, featuring a monumental guitar riff and lyrics that capture real mystery, yet the instrumental complexity within the main framework gives surprising, sometimes amusing, results. Two spins and the effect is deadly. Play it again and you'll never get it off the turntable.

The Executioner and *A Million Miles Away* revolve around hard rock riffs (check out the guitar action in the latter), but are complex in construction and derive a lot of their success from

Ronnie Brown's deft keyboard touches (Styx, Kansas, Starcastle, Simple Minds, Go West... you know the score). *Dance Thru' The Fire* [sic] circumnavigates middle ground, entering on a mass of heavy rock pandemonium and slipping half way into a willing mid-pocket groove.

Lower down the volume scale there's the entirely fitting naivete of *Win Or Lose* to chew on or the obvious highpoint *Just A Memory*, constructed on an ethereal drum pattern and fully exploiting Alan's unique voice. This song is certainly a classic. *Rat Racing* is perhaps the nearest you'll come to material from *The Sentinel* = it's long, very complex and saved through the application of clever atmospheric twiddly bits (mostly screaming guitar).

Undoubtedly, a degree of *The Wedge*'s success is due to the production skills of Mick Glossop (the man responsible for the last Waterboys LP). Equating noise with emotion in a manner only previously exploited within Yes' *90125*, Glossop has led Pallas through the shadowy half-light of the last few months to an open platform where they can now claim to be in no particular category whatsoever. The Ace Place.

Derek Oliver, *Kerrang!*

PALLAS *The Wedge* **(EMI SHVL 850)** ****

PROGRESSIVE ROCK? The very words used to stick in the throat like two fingers and the music in question had the same stimulative effect. However, during comparatively blissful post *Topographic Oceans* years, 'prog rock' (gag) has undergone the once unthinkable. It's progressed. And into the '80s, too!

Pallas, although they're probably reluctant to accept the 'progressive' tag wholesale, typify the new, brighter and more intriguing face of this revitalised genre. At its best, *The Wedge* is marvellously atmospheric, the beautiful, frosted synth melodies of *Rat Racing* and *Just A Memory* being of particular note.

There are no overlong epics or twee lyrics, and pompous, meandering interludes have been cut to a bare minimum. In place of such leaden excess baggage come lighter, more tasteful keyboards, snappy rhythms (when needed) and stirringly good guitar work. Just occasionally a song winds up dead from exhaustive soloing, when every individual gets their oar in regardless of whether the track could best do without it, but that's a fairly rare occurrence and only a minor gripe.

This LP certainly isn't what I'd anticipated. Pallas brushed aside my natural aversion to their kind of music with remarkable ease, and *The Wedge* will doubtless melt a good many more icy receptions in the future. Try it out.

Paul Elliott, *Sounds*

These were bolstered by a lengthy feature in *Kerrang!* that same month.

'We've spent a year, almost,' Graeme [Murray] said, 'rebuilding everything that we have.'

'The way we look at it,' noted Alan Reed, 'the elfin-sized newish vocalist', 'is that we're a new band. We re-evaluated everything when I joined, and we felt that *The Sentinel* really wasn't a definitive Pallas album. We've always been a heavy band live, very powerful, and that didn't really come across on *The Sentinel*, which I think it does now. I think we're starting to find a harder sharper sound. Also, it's a good deal more modern. We were accused of being very dated with *The Sentinel*, so we decided we wanted to make something which I feel is lacking: modern rock. At the moment rock bands as a whole seem to be ashamed to use anything that comes from the post-punk era. They're frightened of it. It's like the world stopped in 1977 for most of them.'

For Pallas, then, the future still looked promising. The same could also be said for IQ who signed to Phonogram Records in February 1986. Their next album would be released on Squawk Records, distributed by Phonogram subsidiaries Vertigo in the UK and Mercury in the US. Squawk had been founded by Def Leppard's managers, Peter Mensch and Cliff Burnstein, with musician and producer Tony MacAlpine.

Martin Orford: 'Our management team of Tristan Rich and Geoff Banks had contacts with Peter Mensch and Cliff Burnstein. They liked our demos for songs such as *Promises (As The Years Go By)* and it was game on. I think we have been rather unfairly pilloried for *Nomzamo* and *Are You Sitting Comfortably?* in some quarters for taking a more commercial approach, but it was a necessary thing to do. We wanted to make records that would draw a mainstream audience into a more prog rock experience by containing pop/rock songs and prog epics alike. It didn't ultimately work, but it was a good objective that was worth pursuing. Any suggestion that Squawk were forcing IQ to stray from our prog roots into a more commercial direction is simply untrue.'

Orford is typically forthright about why commercial success was important to IQ.

'The fact is,' he says, 'we were getting pretty sick of the endless poverty and the never-ending vegetable stew. We wanted to try to improve our wretched lives and make some money. Prog roots could go to hell.'

'That Phonogram deal did a huge amount of good for us,' says Mike Holmes, 'and we were all really enjoying the benefits, but at the same time there was a kind of 'unspoken' pressure, at least that's what it felt like, to be more accessible and chart friendly. Nothing wrong with that of course, but it did feel a bit like there were certain pieces of music that didn't quite fit with that.'

Geoff Mann performed at The Marquee on 16 February 1986 with his new band The Bond. Support was provided by Niadem's Ghost, featuring his good friend Peter Nicholls. The five current members of Twelfth Night attended, and a 'slightly inebriated' Andy Sears spoke to Sean and Marina of the in-production fanzine *The Organ*.

Organ: Is it true that you're on Virgin?

Sears: Aaaahhhggg! I can't answer that! I can't say that!

Organ: Can you deny it?

Sears: I can't deny it either. To be honest, we have to be very careful what we say at the moment.

Organ: What have you been doing? It's been a long time.

Sears: We've been recording an album in Jacobs Studio in Farnham, Surrey… It's been very busy, very hectic… What we are going for is [a] very big album, and at the moment it sounds just as we want. We have six days left, then mixing. We have to have something out in April.

Organ: What about live plans?

Sears: Live… we hope to be back as soon as we finish the mixing. We were very concerned, it's been so long. We wanted to devote all our time to getting the album right… but we're also concerned about the fans, the enthusiasm, because we haven't played for so long, we hope they haven't forsaken the Twelfth Night camp. But I think, when they hear the new album, they will think the quality's good and the wait's been worth it.

Organ: What tracks are on the LP?

Sears: What can I tell you? There's a track called *Pressure*, we've got *Take A Look*, which should be our next 12".

Organ: With Disco Mix?

Sears: No, not quite – no Donna Summer tape-loop jobs… then we have *Blue Powder Monkey* which has changed a lot. We've got a new track called *Jungle*. It's generally a step away from the, quote, 'Progressive-Regressive' unquote scene, really more commercial in context without getting too throwaway – it is not throwaway. And *Take A Look* is the only long track, but hopefully it is sufficiently modern.

Organ: So you hope it will break you out of the progressive scene?

Sears: Yes, absolutely, yes. I feel that a lot of bands are wasting their time. When I joined the band we did an interview with *Sounds*. I said then – and I was very new to the situation, I wasn't really aware of some of these bands like IQ, Pallas, Marillion – I saw a lot of it like Genesis. I mean, Gabriel left Genesis and everyone in other bands felt a need to replace him in their band. It was as if they missed the guy so much you know, his whole image needed to survive, and when you look at all those bands, that is the era that these new bands seem to come from… what they should be saying is 'Look at 1986, we've got racial problems, we've got police problems, we've got all kinds of problems that are not sung about and they're the things that are happening.' It isn't anymore… I feel pressured, I feel I'm being oppressed, I feel I want to say things. I feel I'm an anarchist without being violent. I disagree with the system but I don't want to have to smash a telephone box to prove it. That's what is happening, and I feel that bands like IQ (even Marillion) – and I've got a lot of respect for these bands – I really feel that they are still back in that timewarp. You know, like they are trying to create an atmosphere on record, going for the atmosphere and not saying what is happening…

Organ: So when you reach mega-stardom, you're going to be bored and not want it?

Sears: No, we won't. I defy anybody who's in a band to come up to me and to say 'I don't want to be famous.' I wouldn't believe them for a second. Whoever is in showbiz, be it acting, singing, be it anything, they are there because they feel a need to be seen, to be recognised. Whoever is saying 'we're just a band for the people, we're just laid-back band' – it's crap, absolute bullshit! Anybody who's in the entertainment business is there because they want to be famous, they want to be somebody other than the ordinary Joe on the street… that the truth and there you go…

Final overdubs and mixing for Twelfth Night's new album were completed at Wessex Sound Studios in Highbury, London, in February and

Peter Gee, Fudge Smith and
Nick Barrett, 20 March 1986
(Photographs by Brian Cairns
and Peter Sims)

March 1986. On and off, the album had taken the best part of two years to write and record.

'John Walters just didn't get us,' says Andy Revell. 'I think Clive and, to a much lesser extent, Rick had quite a good time playing with sequencers and synths and stuff. But I think the rest of us didn't enjoy the sessions. Every ounce of emotion and life was produced out of that album.'

With a tour imminent and half a band short, Pendragon's drum stool was filled by Stephen 'Fudge' Smith formerly of the band LaHost.

'Nigel Harris had a unique style and feel that in my opinion really suited the band,' he says. 'On *The Jewel* and *Fly High, Fall Far* Nige's drumming just has his feel. I love it. I knew Keith Goodwin and he was supportive of all the up-and-coming prog bands. I had heard through him that [Harris' replacement] Mat Anderson was leaving Pendragon, so I called Nick Barrett… 'Hi Nick, it's Fudge. Is there any chance of an audition?' To which Nick said, 'I was going to call you anyway.' I drove up to Stroud, met Nick and went up to an attic room which had a drum kit in the corner. The attic roof sloped, so I played *Fly High, Fall Far* with my head bent forward. It worked and I got the job!'

Fudge would stay for the next 20 years.

Session keyboard player James Colah was drafted in to complete a series of UK dates, the *Moving Into Higher Circles* tour in February and March 1986.

'We had a tour booked and we were looking for a session player,' says Nick Barrett. 'James had the gear, perfect for the job. He could play a lot of soul stuff, but Prog really wasn't his thing. It wasn't a style that he was really used to playing.'

'I always had a regular advert in the *Melody Maker* making my services available,' Colah says. 'One day

'I got a call from Nick Barrett who had seen my advert. He told me that their keyboard player had left suddenly without giving any notice and asked me if I could take on the job to finish their tour. I decided to take on the challenge. I think I had just one week to learn the complete set for the tour.'

Fudge: 'We went to pick up James in the Pendragon tour van. It was an old Ford transit bread van. It had sliding doors only held on with rust. The cold wind used to blast in, so no one wanted the outside seats. It wasn't the best looking either. We all wondered that if James saw the van he might change his mind. We went at night and hid the van round the corner and loaded his gear into the van while Nick kept him talking, so when he got round the corner he couldn't say no! With a combined push on the shoulder, he was in.'

'Because the time was so short,' Colah says, 'Nick invited me to stay at his house for that week to learn the set. Learning all that music in such a short time was incredibly tough and stressful as most of the parts were very tricky. It was lucky that I had formal classical piano training. I remember writing all the keyboard parts down because it would have been impossible to memorise all the music in that time.'

The tour started in Coventry on 15 February and covered venues as far apart as Plymouth and Dundee.

The usual warm welcome from the Manchester crowd as The Dragons came onto the stage with a new intro tune (classical in origin). The set opened with *Pleasure of Hope* but before it was allowed to develop, a quick swap and straight into *Higher Circles*. The boys were well on form not a bad sound in sight except for Fudge (drums) as he seems to be a bit hard with his bashing. The new keyboard player James Colah (session man) seemed quite capable if a bit miserable. The set continued with usual flow, the newer tracks *Mark Of Time* and *The Mask* were early and were received with mixed reactions (a little in the *Higher Circles* vein but still with a touch of their own flavour). *The Haunting* was the third and last of the Newies. A guitar-less Nick Barrett took centre and what I think of theatrics was duly performed. His act could do with a bit of polish but passable considering this is not his style. The song is the best of the bunch and also the longest. It's all about the fear and loneliness of love and its failings, it works and it certainly sent chills down my spine. Finally the show closed with *Leviathan* one of my personal favourites, and an excellent closer. As for the encores, two in all *The Black Knight* and *Stan and Olly*. The former still a beautiful piece of modern writing and the latter, well what can I say but the real pair would love it! The Dragons certainly know how to entertain and tonight was further proof for their scrap-book...

Fan's review in *Rocking Horse* issue 1

'We all had a great tour,' Fudge recalls, 'probably the best one Pendragon ever did in the UK. All universities, it was fab. James always blew kisses to the audience at the end of the show, nice.'

'The shows throughout the tour were obviously incredible,' says James Colah. 'The fans were so enthusiastic and devoted. I remember signing so many autographs on that tour! The two Marquee shows were, of course, the pinnacle as far as prestige was concerned. I had always wanted to play there and was lucky enough to perform two nights in a row [29-30 March]. The fans went crazy at those two shows. I couldn't believe how small the venue was and wow was it hot and sticky in there. It certainly wasn't a luxury venue, but it sure had character.'

The previous year, Colah had toured the US and Canada with The Adventures, supporting Tears For Fears.

'We stayed in all the top five star hotels, touring in luxury,' he says. 'It was very different with Pendragon. After each show we would spend the night at the house of a friend of the band or with one of their fans. I don't remember once staying in a hotel, but I didn't mind the rough and ready tour conditions because we were made to feel so welcome.'

Pendragon's tour ended in the last week of March. Peter Gee was asked by *The Stairway* if he thought that Pendragon were closer to making it than they had been in the past.

'Well, I think we've always had a chance of making it,' Gee said. 'I mean the last year particularly we've been heading in that direction. We've got the material, and we feel we've got the live show, and the music, and the image…all we need now is the backing of a major record company.'

Between February and April, Marillion toured North American once more. Small club dates were topped and tailed by further support dates for Rush, performing parts of *Misplaced Childhood*, and sometimes *Incubus* and *Fugazi*.

Steve Rothery: 'Unlike the previous shows we'd done with Rush, these were fantastic. The audience loved us.'

The *Toronto Star* was forthright in their preview ahead of the band's show at the Concert Hall on 1 March.

Marillion is a strange case. Here is a successful English band ignoring rock 'n' roll trends by faithfully copying an art-rock phase that lost favor, and fans, a long time ago.

But that hasn't stopped Marillion at the Concert Hall tomorrow night from pursuing their complicated musical approach, which waffles between Genesis and Pink Floyd excess, borrowing heavily from both along the way.

Despite the cloning, the five member group has been ranked by UK critics as one of the best of the past few years, while Marillion albums sell well enough in Europe for them to be rated as a major concert attraction.

North America has been less kind, but the band has always found a welcome home in Toronto.

Capitol released the EP *Brief Encounter* to coincide with the tour. This odd compilation includes the B-sides *Lady Nina* and *Freaks*, a live version of *Kayleigh* from Hammersmith the previous February and live recordings of *Fugazi* and *Script For A Jester's Tear* from Leicester in March 1984. Although intended for the US market, the two B-sides and three unreleased live tracks generated significant demand in the UK and Europe. As a result, the EP was widely available as an import and reached number 42 in Germany.

Pallas also released a live album, recorded at Southampton University on 8 March 1986, the last gig of a two month tour to promote *The Wedge*. This

was sold via the fan club and at gigs and was available only on cassette.

IQ's demo of *Nomzamo* was pressed as a 500 copy limited edition 7" single for fan club members in April 1986. It was recorded on eight-track at the band's house in Harlesden. Paul Menel's vocals were recorded in the bathroom.

'Well, it's the comfiest place in the house,' Menel said. 'Not the upstairs one but the downstairs so we could shut the door. The idea is that the fan club members will get a free record every year that is totally exclusive, as our fans deserve the best deal we can give them.'

A UK tour visiting Stoke-on-Trent, Nottingham, Swansea, Dudley and London followed.

Twelfth Night, meanwhile, premiered their new album to Virgin staff and invited friends at The Marquee on 10 April 1986. All nine songs which would appear on the album were performed. The concert was recorded to multitrack via a mobile studio parked behind the venue. Master tapes reside in Virgin's vaults and were considered for release when the Virgin album was reissued in 2005. However, the band was not at its best and the audience seemed disinterested, so the recording has never seen the light of day.

IQ's biggest headline date so far took place at the Piccadilly Theatre in London on 20 April 1986. The set list mixed both old and new songs: *No Love Lost*, *It All Stops Here*, *Promises (As The Years Go By)*, *Nomzamo*, *The Wake*, *The Last Human Gateway* (end section), *Barbell Is In*, *Still Life*, *Widow's Peak*, *The Big Sleep State* (later renamed to *Screaming*), *The Thousand Days*, *Corners*, *Headlong* and *Awake And Nervous*.

In May, Twelfth Night were filmed in performance at the Town and Country Club in Kentish Town, London. This was scheduled for broadcast on BBC2's *Whistle Test*: a major event for the band. The band played their new single *Shame* several times,

1986: Egos Check Cheques In Transit

Graeme Murray and Alan Reed of Pallas
(Photograph by Mark Drake)

Ticket for 10 April 1986
(From the collection of
Peter Moltensen)

Below: Twelfth Night on
Whistle Test (Courtesy
Twelfth Night Archive)

followed by several 'back-up' run throughs of *Blue Powder Monkey*. It was a ragged version of this latter song that the programme's producers decided to include. Presenter Ro Newton introduces the song by remarking that 'perhaps it's now time for a progressive rock revival? Who knows?'

Andy Sears: 'I was living in a flat in Elephant & Castle at the time and I can remember buying a bottle of champagne ready to watch the show… we were ready to celebrate and pop the cork for our first decent TV show. They left our slot until last, and I remember looking at the time and thinking, 'If they don't cut to us soon there won't be any time left!' We were expecting them to focus on the new single, *Shame*. We had gone over it four or five times, and I remember we had a damn good version in the can with the whole audience doing the nutty vocal hook line. We also went over *Blue Powder Monkey* umpteen times 'for the benefit of the camera crew' apparently, by which time, after almost an hour of full-on performance under TV lights we were getting tired. Anyway, there we were, champagne glasses in hand, waiting, and then the presenter, Ro Newton, comes on and gives a derogatory introduction, and lo and behold they show the final take of *Blue Powder Monkey* with everyone knackered and sweating. It wasn't my TV, so I couldn't smash it! I just switched it off, got the champagne and put it back in the fridge.'

BBC Radio 1 also recorded the show but decided not to broadcast any of it. To add insult to injury, the band received a truly appalling review in *Kerrang!*

Pallas returned to The Marquee on 16 and 17 May supported by Geoff Mann, just as IQ released a picture disc of *It All Stops Here* and *Intelligence Quotient*. These were the re-recorded versions from *Seven Stories Into Eight*. That month Marillion returned to Barwell Court to commence writing sessions for their fourth album, without any tangible results.

The compilation album *Exposure* provided good publicity for some of the up and coming bands.

'The originally idea for this compilation LP came

from Stuart Martin of Coltsfoot,' write Guy Tkach and Peter Sieker, 'although Steven [Wilson] was responsible (with the help of Angel Romero who helped with the European bands) for contacting and compiling together various contemporary progressive rock bands including his own project No Man Is An Island Except The Isle Of Man, who contribute an instrumental track titled *From A Toyshop Window*. The title of the album *Exposure* is taken from the name of a Dutch progressive rock fanzine who helped Steven to compile this LP.'

It was reviewed in *Rocking Horse* later that year.

Compilation albums are a good thing, especially for the prog/rock world, for two simple reasons 1) They get bands onto vinyl (usually for the first time) and 2) They introduce the fans to new bands (which is never a bad thing to do). So now we have *Exposure* containing eight songs from eight highly different bands (including two from Spain), brought together for the sole purpose of entertaining YOU!

- Abel Ganz - *Unholy War* - Mainstream prog/rock, competent enough, likely to be most people's favourite yet has no real surprises anywhere.
- Coltsfoot - *Autumn* - This is a very gentle song and also thought provoking (even though it is not the best thing they have ever done). Just keyboards and vocals both used to their advantage.
- Pharoan - *Medianoche* - This is the first of the Spanish numbers and is terrible. If this is supposed to be an example of their music, then I feel sorry for them. The song just does not stir up any feelings within me. A very bland number with some awful rhythms.
- Borag Thungg - *Song of the Vineyard* - This song holds everything that Pharoan's did not. Emotion and a clarity in its delivery. A simple song yet comes across as one of the high points of the album.
- No Man Is An Island (except for the Isle Of Man) - *From a Toyshop Window* - There are some nice touches to this track but as a whole I found it disappointing, it never settles down and has too many breaks and changes of style.
- Twice Bitten - *End Play* - A befitting title, as this was to be the last track that they recorded as the duo. A fine song, very much in the style of the *No Third Man* cassette and so holds nothing really surprising or new.
- Comedy Of Errors - *Time There Was* - This for me is the best track on the album; everything modern progressive rock should be, emotional yet direct and to the point, with lyrics that dwell on the edge of the fantasy, and most of all, it must linger in the mind long after the song has ended.
- Aletsuida - *Living On Earth* - This is the other Spanish number and luckily it is far better than its companion. A subtle musical piece not too distant from the 1970s - Steve Hackett comes to mind for some strange reason.

Exposure is not a great album but is worthy of a place in any collection if only for its diversity of styles. It is available from all the featured artists for the laughable sum of £3.50 (plus 50p P&P).

1986: Egos Check Cheques In Transit

Adverts from *Sounds* and the *NME*
(From the collection of Guy Tkach)

During this period, Nick Barrett and Peter Gee made frequent trips to London, looking for a record deal. By now the band's arrangement with Elusive had lapsed.

'Basically they ran out of money,' Gee admitted. 'They put money into *Fly High, Fall Far* and *The Jewel* and they both sold as well as can be for an indie act who are not being given major publicity. But it was a mutual agreement really… it was exclusive to us… another thing was that we wanted to do singles as well as albums, so really if you're going to do singles, you need a big push behind it. We're looking for something new.'

'We're pressurising them very heavily,' Nick Barrett said. 'We're going in there and we're laying it on the line and they're buying it, which is a very nice situation to be in, you know? Who knows what's going to happen, but it will happen soon. We've got a lot of material… we've got almost all of side one and we've got enough ideas for the other side, but we can't really start recording until we get a deal.'

Whilst visiting record companies in London, Nick would often stay with his old friend Clive Nolan, who he had known since the age of four when they were at school together.

'I grew up in Gloucestershire,' Nolan says. 'We were a musical family. My father, Ron, was in an act called the Nolan Brothers. There were two of them, and they played accordions. Really fancy pieces of accordion playing. You know, in music hall when the curtains came down between acts someone would go out, a comedian or something, and then they'd open the curtain up again for the next performer? My dad and his partner used to do that. I have a feeling that they worked with Max Miller and Laurel & Hardy. He was often on the BBC Light Programme [the forerunner to Radio 2]. Later he dropped out of the whole entertainment thing and became a maths and music teacher. Both of my parents used to teach in a couple of rooms on the top of Stroud Music Centre. But occasionally my dad was invited to be an adjudicator at accordion festivals. I was amazed how big they were. I remember them going over to Ireland one time and they decided to take me with them. I met loads of people who'd been involved in light entertainment, the Mike Sammes Singers, all that sort of stuff, and they all knew my dad. It was only then that it started to leak out that he'd been so involved in all of this. I started realising little bits and pieces about him. And then, gradually, as I got more rock'n'roll, I realised that he had done it all before. So, when I wanted to go down that path myself, my father was surprisingly sympathetic. My mum still wanted me to be a classical composer or conductor.'

Nolan was a latecomer to rock music, only buying his first album aged 17.

'I had been going to Wycliffe College, the same school as Nick Barrett,' he says, 'but I moved to King's School, a cathedral school in Gloucester. I was there for three years, and it was probably the best time of my life. I'd been totally orientated towards classical music up until then. But I made some new friends and they were giving me rock music tapes to listen to, 'You have to listen to this.' And then one day I borrowed £20 and went down to WH Smiths, just to find an album. I needed to know what I was going to get into. I looked at all the records and one album really attracted my attention. It was *Seconds Out* by Genesis. I just loved the cover. I had no idea who Genesis were. It could just as easily have been the Sex Pistols. And I bought it and went home and started listening to it. I think probably the first time it kind of brushed past me rather, but little bits caught my attention. Three or four listens later I thought, 'Oh, this is great!' I went into school and I was having tea with some friends and I remember saying, 'Right, I think we should form a band.''

Nolan played in his band Sleepwalker in Gloucester before moving to London to attend the Royal Holloway College, part of the University of London, to study music. He was ultimately awarded both a BMus and MMus.

'My main studies were composition, orchestration and conducting,' he says. 'For the MMus, I had to write an orchestral piece, which was rehearsed and performed in front of a live audience. I developed a lot of skills, although when I first started finding myself in the world of rock music, I thought that I didn't need any of it. But, as time's gone on, I have made use of an awful lot of what I learned. I can see in my head how harmonies should work and therefore I can work parts out. I became very much involved in all the different layers of an arrangement, sorting out backing vocals, for example. The training paid off in the long run.'

Clive had a band in London called The Cast.

'When I left school to go to university I sort of went off the whole band thing,' Nolan says. 'One of the things you learn about working with rock bands is that it's 99% politics and 1% music. I didn't really have any interest in that, so I wasn't having anything to do with rock bands again. I formed a jazz rock trio with a couple of other guys, a percussionist and another keyboard player. That was called Danzante.

But I had sort of fallen in love with Kate Bush, so when the jazz rock thing fizzled out, I found a guitarist, Pete Holmes, and a singer, Rachel Schollar, and that's how The Cast began. I was very much inspired by the Kate Bush stuff I was listening to, at the time it would have been *Hounds Of Love*.'

It had never occurred to Nick Barrett to ask Clive to join Pendragon but, sitting up together late one night, Nick asked Clive if he knew any suitable keyboard players… 'I'll do it!' Clive said.

Fudge Smith: 'Clive's keys were great, we all gelled, it was easy.'

Nick Barrett: 'He was just an absolute breath of fresh air. And, you know, one of my oldest friends. We shared horrendously fatalistic senses of humour. We were awful with people and would clear a room because they couldn't bear us.'

Nolan joined Pendragon for a run of dates in late June and early July 1986. The Cast continued to operate in parallel and supported Pendragon at The Marquee a few times in 1986 and 1987.

Nolan agreed from the outset that he would not write for Pendragon.

'I told Clive that we didn't want any more songwriters in the band,' Nick Barrett says. 'Clive had his own projects for that. The arrangement was perfect.'

'The understanding was that I would have other projects and they would be my outlets to write,' Nolan agrees. 'I wouldn't step on his toes as far as Pendragon was concerned. If I'd been brought in as a writer I might say, 'Well, I'm not sure about that chord progression', or 'Why don't you do a diminished chord there?' I'd have been 100% sure that I was right. And Nick would have been 100% sure he was right. We knew that were both very strong minded and that it wouldn't have worked. We agreed that Nick would give me the music he had written, and I would take it up from there. That way there was never going to be an argument. And I suspect we wouldn't have lasted as long as we have if we'd done it differently.'

Indeed, almost 40 years later, Barrett and Nolan are still working together.

Twelfth Night's new album was released in June 1986. The vinyl version came with an expanding gatefold sleeve which illustrated some of the lyrical themes of the songs. There's a feeling amongst the band that the budget might have been better spent on promotion, especially as the album was released without a title. Over time it has become known as 'the Virgin album' and was later reissued on CD as *XII*.

TWELFTH NIGHT Twelfth Night (Virgin CASG 1174)

A healthy collection of brisk pop, heavy guitars, taut, punchy rhythms and absolutely lots and lots of polyphonic synths, digital oscillators and sequential farts 'n' parps. All in all, quite a stirring and pretty cool collection of ingenious noises, adding up to a rather dramatically different sound with Twelfth Night's eyes obviously set on a large scale slice of chart action. And let's face it, if those artful codgers Marillion can hoodwink the public using a technique as half as dynamic as displayed here, then why shouldn't Lucy Luck be on Twelfth Night's side, too? After all, with TN you don't have to sit, suffer and fidget through all those dreary impersonations of Phil Collins and Peter Gabriel.

This is the kind of intelligent pop that I like to

play during the afternoon after quenching my more vicious thirst with morning metal. Ideally suited to Radox baths, study periods or tea with the Vicar, Twelfth Night bursts with all kinds of hubble, bubble and far out, freaked out music. It's all here: mighty gung-ho power chording (limited in finesse I'll agree!), a dainty pot pourri of pop, highly innovative lyrics ... a gamut of styles with elements of Latin American, disco and jazz rock bouncing around. Can you spot the various similarities to Duran/Arcadia, Tears For Fears and, amazingly, sex kitten Kate Bush?!

The heavier tracks I like best. *Pressure* and *Theatre* are impressive, but it's the crunch of *Shame* that has the floorboards rattling and the landlady on the blower to the noise abatement society. Moreover, it's TN's dynamics that provide for the more addictive moments, highly demonstrated by the technical blowout of cuts like *Blue Powder Monkey* and *Take A Look*, both flowering with a considerable number of overdubs and quite memorable afterglows.

Yes, they can play very well (like a gang of old King Crimson members!) and, yes, they haven't wasted anyone's time in making this splendid record. I recommend, pundits, that you take a cotton swab to that blocked up lughole and invest your beer money in a highly pleasurable experience.

Derek Oliver, *Kerrang!*

Despite the positive review in *Kerrang!*, Twelfth Night was not generally well received. However, despite its poor reputation, the album features some strong material.

Last Song is a driving, dynamic full-on rock song. It doesn't pretend to be anything else. The chorus is catchy and it's a mystery why this (or *Theatre*) was not chosen as the lead single. The Duran Duran comparisons might be justified on *Pressure*. Revell's solo is treated with effects and there are Art Of Noise stabs which place the song firmly in 1986. Sears' chorus seems to be trying just a little bit too hard. The album gets back on track with the effervescent *Jungle*, although Andy Sears' vocal is mixed low in a too busy arrangement and it's easy to see how this song might have alienated an audience who had already waited four years for a full length follow-up to *Fact And Fiction*. We must not overlook the delightful *The Craft*, one of Andy Sears' very best songs, which benefitted from a more organic arrangement on the band's 2010 tour. The busy, bright production and inflexible drum machine simply don't suit the song. The strings and multi-tracked vocals are wonderful but are lost amidst the chatter. *Blue Powder Monkey* harks back to the band's prog roots – it was one of the first songs written with Sears, but all life has been pummelled from the arrangement. The earlier version available as a bonus track on later releases of *Art And Illusion* serves this song much better. *Theatre*, *Shame* and *This Is War* are short, spiky songs, each with a live feel and lots of guitar. *Theatre* might be the best short song on the album, with Sears on top form and a powerful production that feels less dated than others. *Shame* was the album's first single. It's a great song, with a simple hook, and sounds much better now than it did in 1986. But as a single? What were Virgin thinking? *This Is War* perhaps showcases Andy Revell's U2 influences too much, but is again a strong song without the baggage of the past. The

1986: Egos Check Cheques In Transit

Twelfth Night in 1986
(Photographs by Adrian Boot, courtesy Twelfth Night Archive)

album closes with *Take A Look*, the band's late period masterpiece. Sadly, this live powerhouse with its magnificent chorus is somehow reduced to a plod. Finally, we should also mention *Blondon Fair*, a brooding B-side of high quality: if only all of the album had been as good as this.

In 2010, a reunited Twelfth Night featured most of the album in live performance and the power and depth of much of the material was wholly evident. But the bright, 1980s production of the original album does the tracks no favours and the unavailability of the multi-tracks means that remixes from the sessions are impossible. Furthermore, there was growing bad blood between band members (and between the band and their record company) which ensured that, on release, the album was stillborn.

Between mid-June and late July Marillion continued to slog away on the concert circuit. Shows in Gothenburg, Stockholm, Munich, Vienna and Rotterdam were topped by 90 minute support slots for Queen at huge gigs in Vincennes (14 June), Mannheim (21 June) and Berlin (26 June). The second of these was broadcast on German radio station SWF3 and *Freaks* was later included on *The Thieving Magpie* and as a single in 1988.

A PLAYGROUND OF BROKEN HEARTS

Milton Keynes Bowl, 28 June 1986
(Photograph by Glenn Williams)

Marillion on stage at Milton Keynes Bowl,
28 June 1986 (Photograph by Glenn Williams)

Steve Rothery backstage at Milton Keynes Bowl, 28 June 1986 (Photograph by Glenn Williams)

'We were used to playing arenas and large venues,' concedes Pete Trewavas. 'But 80,000 is a lot of people. You couldn't really take it in unless you were in a helicopter or balloon. The main thing I remember was Queen's onstage sound... Just immense. They were so loud but it was clear as a bell.'

'Every night I'd stand by the stage and watch them,' says Ian Mosley.

Back in the UK, as EMI released an eight track VHS collection of the band's promo videos, Marillion closed a year of touring with a massive headline gig at the Milton Keynes Bowl on 28 June. This, billed as 'Welcome To The Garden Party', was their biggest headline concert to date with 35,000 to 40,000 in attendance. They topped a bill which included Jethro Tull, Gary Moore, Magnum and Mama's Boys.

Fan Glenn Williams attended, with his camera.

'It was a beautiful day,' he recalls. 'The kind of day that conjures up images of Miss Marple, cricket on the village green and strawberries and cream, that kind of thing. Rock photographer Tony Mottram had blagged me a backstage pass and we set off from his place early, arriving at the Bowl around 11 o'clock. Backstage, Tony goes off to shoot the day's events while I order a pint and park myself at one of the tables with sun umbrellas. Various musicians and music biz people are milling around; the delightful Marlboro girls are out in force handing out free packs of ciggies with a teasing smile. This is my base for the day as I wander back and forth into the arena to

1986: Egos Check Cheques In Transit

Milton Keynes Bowl backstage pass
(Courtesy Brian Devoil)

Fish and Freddie, Cologne, 19 July 1986
(Courtesy Piet Spaans' Archive and
Marko's Marillion Museum)

watch each band. Truth is though, as enjoyable as the other bands are, I'm really only there because of Marillion.'

Marillion's set comprised *Garden Party*, *Freaks*, *Assassing*, *Chelsea Monday* and *Script For A Jester's Tear*, then the whole of *Misplaced Childhood* and the main set closer *Forgotten Sons*.

'Opening with *Garden Party* was inspired and set the tone for the next couple of hours,' Glenn Williams says. 'Fish, after Steve's solo in *Chelsea Monday*, gesturing across the stage with a swoop of his arm as a string of rainbow lights lit up the two P.A. screens was delightful and the complete *Misplaced Childhood* – the last performance by this line-up as it turns out – was sublime. *Forgotten Sons* had been slowly being dropped from the set list over the past couple of years, but they topped off the end of the show with it; that would be the last time a UK audience saw that as well. There were rumours around the Bowl pre-show that the encore would include *The Web*, some fans were calling for it now, but it was not to be. Instead, we got *Incubus*, *Fugazi* and *Market Square Heroes*, a tasty trio to round out the day.'

On 19 July, Marillion supported Queen once again in Cologne before an audience of 80,000. Brian May, on his 39th birthday, guested with Marillion on *Market Square Heroes* and Fish returned the favour singing *Tutti Frutti* with Queen.

'We did earn a lot of money from those dates in Europe and at Milton Keynes, particularly the

ones with Queen, of course. But it was the first time we'd ever earned what you would call serious money since we'd been together,' said Fish. 'I tell you, I was fucking glad to get it! I didn't want to be an artist starving in an attic somewhere for the rest of my life. Who does, really? Anyway, I'd done all that. We all had. We'd paid our dues, whatever that means. It was great to finally see some kind of major return for all the work we'd put into the band all these years.'

'With the money we got from those shows we were all able to buy decent houses for ourselves, and a new car, maybe. But most of all, the money just bought us a bit of breathing space,' said Pete Trewavas. 'We did ten shows in all, over a period of about four

A PLAYGROUND OF BROKEN HEARTS

Pendragon soundcheck
(Courtesy Fudge Smith)

Flyer for Pendragon at The Marquee, 24-26 July 1986 (From the collection of Jon Dunnington)

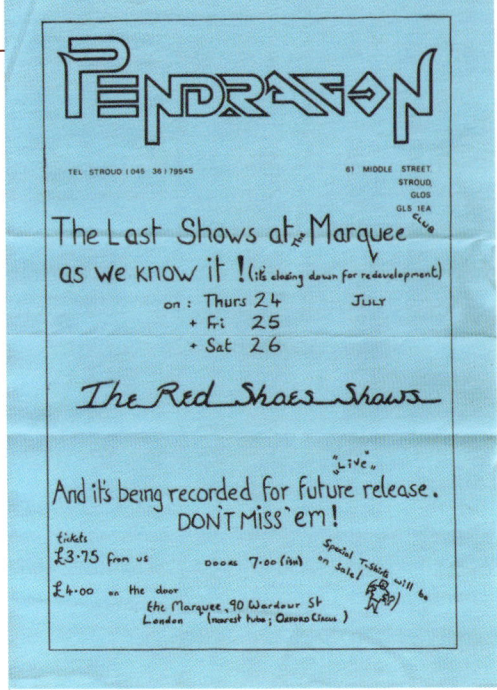

weeks… to bigger and more enthusiastic audiences than we'd ever known before, and because of that we ended up playing some of the best shows I think we've ever done. It was a very happy time for us, every gig was like a celebration.'

Pendragon, now with their longest lasting line-up of Nick Barrett, Peter Gee, Fudge Smith and Clive Nolan, performed again at The Marquee in late July. By now they could sell out three consecutive nights. These were recorded for a live album for release later in the year.

Marillion headlined a show called Soap Aid at the rugby league stadium in St Helens on 27 July. This bizarre event mixed the cast of *Grange Hill* singing *Just Say No* and *Coronation Street*'s Percy Sugden playing the ukulele with sets from Marillion and Icicle Works.

Mark Kelly: 'Soap Aid [was] a badly conceived follow up to Live Aid. Various soap stars took it in turns to embarrass themselves on stage until, as the headliners, we trooped on to play. During *Garden Party* a fight broke out which got so gallingly bad that Fish asked us to stop playing while he attempted to pour oil on troubled (not to mention soapy) waters.'

The band's robust performance of *Lavender* was broadcast on Channel 4 and sees the crowd singing with good-humoured gusto.

Their promo activity concluded with a short mid-afternoon set at the British Music Fair on 3 August with guitarist Robin Boult depping for an absent Steve Rothery, who was on his honeymoon.

'Tickets were handed out on a stall early in the day,' recalls Phil Macy, who attended the event, 'but most fans missed out as it wasn't widely publicised

164

1986: Egos Check Cheques In Transit

Pete and Fish at the British Music Fair, 3 August 1986 (Photographs by Glenn Williams)

where to get them from. Fifteen minutes before the band were due on there were a mass of ticketless hardcore fans wandering around outside the entrance to the stage, hassling anyone who looked like they had one. I managed to blag one off a bloke in a suit who admitted he had no real interest in the band at all and I think that was the case with most people. There were probably only 200 to 300 people there…'

After this Marillion would take an extended break from live concerts.

Solstice reunited for a charity concert at the Willen Lake Mini Bowl in Milton Keynes on Saturday 9 August 1986. They would share a bill with local bands the Mutants and Life Support and, for this one-off performance, comprised seven members: Andy Glass, Marc Elton, Mark Hawkins, Ken Bowley, Martin Wright, Sandy Leigh and Barbara Deason.

Andy Glass: 'Sandy had read a book called *The Magical Child* [by Joseph Chilton Pearce, published in 1977 and subtitled *Rediscovering Nature's Plan For Our Children*]. One of the rules in the book was that when a baby wakes up, the mother should be there, which meant that as soon as the baby fell asleep, she couldn't leave it. The deal was that the baby would be on the side of the stage! And if the baby fell asleep, she would have to abandon the show until the baby woke up. I mean, we were all hippies, you know? But please…'

And that was it for Solstice, for a while at least.

Andy Glass: 'Marc and I tried to get something going with Howard Rogers from Liaison on bass and vocals and a drummer called Grant Gilmour [later to join Pride Of Passion with former Marillion member Diz Minnitt]. But a couple of sessions led nowhere.'

1986: Egos Check Cheques In Transit

Solstice – a final gig (for now) in Milton Keynes (Photographs by Oz Hardwick)

Rogers: 'I don't remember that at all!'

Marc lived locally in his double-decker for a while and then moved to Swansea where he started a new life.

Glass: 'I fell into a cool covers band called Backstreet with some ace players including Craig Sunderland and Peter Hemsley, who would both join Solstice in the 1990s.'

Virgin released two singles from Twelfth Night's album: *Shame* (July 1986) and a heavily-edited *Take A Look* (August 1986). Both disappeared without a trace, suggesting that Virgin had no idea what to make of the band or its music.

Brian Devoil: 'I remember being told later that there were two marketing managers at Virgin at the time, one of whom was a fan, but the album was given to the other one to work. I'm not sure whether this is true, but it is symptomatic of the way we felt our relationship with them was going. I was always worried that Virgin's true interest was in re-signing Phil Collins, also managed by Hit & Run, and that we had somehow become pawns in a bigger game. We met Mike Rutherford and Tony Banks in the Hit & Run offices, but never Phil Collins. I did get to see one of his royalty statements though—ours was one page, his was a couple of inches thick. There was an awful lot of money being made at that time, though not by us, so perhaps we were rightly being seen as a 'minor outfit' by the people involved.'

'I didn't understand Virgin's decisions,' Andy Sears told the author. '*Theatre* was the obvious single, in my opinion. It was nice balance between the darker and fun sides of Twelfth Night… along commercial lines without throwing our integrity away. I'm still completely and utterly convinced that *Theatre* was the single. After all, *Calling All The Heroes* by It Bites was a Top 20 hit at exactly that time. *Shame* was a good, brave effort, but there are a lot of people who would turn their noses up at that because they maybe see it as stretching it too far. It's weird and we wanted to be weird. But is it hit single material? Patently not. Releasing *Take A Look* as a single was a disastrous idea. Nobody can understand that still. The caveat would be that we had signed to Virgin knowingly, and they were not exactly the symphonic rock label of the day. I was all too happy to get away from the archetypal 'prog' element and embrace the opportunity to take on a far more modern approach. After all, we were looking for singles material and we're not going to hide that… we wanted to get ahead too. The compromise that we tried to set out was perfectly dignified.'

'With the lack of commercial success of both the album and the two singles,' says Brian Devoil, 'it seemed that Virgin's interest in us cooled very quickly.'

Taking everything into account, the recordings had cost over £100,000 - money that Virgin was never going to recoup from the band.

IQ's show on 13 May 1985 was released as the live album *Living Proof* in August 1986, without the band's consent.

IQ would like to emphatically state to their fans, the music industry and media that there is currently an album on sale, available both through mail order and in selected record shops, they wish to be completely disassociated with.

It has been titled *Living Proof* and is available through Samurai Records cat no SAMR045 and distributed through Pinnacle.

This album is not the 'latest' album from IQ. It is the soundtrack to a live performance the band made for the new *From London* series of TV in May 85 prior to new singer Paul Menel joining the band. It has been manufactured without the consent of the performers or copyright owners. The company manufacturing and distributing this record, Samurai Records, have no licence granted to them for this purpose and they have also failed to notify the copyright owners under the 1956 copyright act of their intention to release this album.

None of the members of IQ endorse this release and consider it sub-standard as it has evidently been mastered from a rough monitor mix recording that is in Samurai Records' possession. In addition to this the album contains no material written since December 1984 and is being sold by mail order at the price of £7.50!

Details of the next official IQ album will be given early next year, as will details of a major UK and European tour.

Nervous with some very dodgy moments indeed. *Outer Limits* comes next and fortunately the sound has got itself together and things really start to pick up. *It All Stops Here* comes across in true brutal style as does *Just Changing Hands* which brings side one to an excellent close.

The Wake thrashingly opens side two which is nicely followed up by *The Magic Roundabout* and *Widow's Peak* (all three of which come across as memorable moments). What better way to finish off the album than with IQ's contributions to the world of pop - *The Thousand Days*, as lively as ever, and *Corners*.

All in all a really good live album (bootleg if you like!) and it is worth the asking price of £5.50 because it is well packaged and is a good clean recording despite being mastered from a rough monitor mix. The choice is now yours, whether to side with IQ or to add an excellent album to your collection…

Geoff Marland, *The Rocking Horse* issue 2
(January 1987)

Despite the poor sound quality, the release does offer the opportunity to hear most of the songs from *The Wake* in a concert setting.

This is the album that IQ are making a stink about and well they should, but we believe in letting people make up their own minds, so we will review it anyway.

The album is a live recording made at the Camden Palace in 1985 and features Pete Nicholls on vocals prior to his departure for more sheltered winds. Side one opens up with a rather shaky and disappointing rendition of *Awake And*

Living Proof was re-released in 2005 with improved sound quality on the band's own Giant Electric Pea label.

For reasons that still remain unclear, Twelfth Night's only live booking between May and October 1986 was at a club in Bideford, Devon, on 28 August. It seems that the promoter planned to send minibuses to the surrounding towns and pick up lots of Devonian Twelfth Night fans. In the end, the band played to a nearly empty venue.

'I don't think I actually said anything specific to the band at that gig,' says Andy Sears, 'but I

1986: Egos Check Cheques In Transit

Ticket for IQ, 26 September 1986
(From the collection of
Peter Moltensen)

remember thinking when I saw the flowery dance stage, the disco lights and Wheel-Tappers and Shunters glitter ball that Hit & Run had really lost it.'

'That summer was the most depressing time I can ever remember in the band,' recalls Brian Devoil, 'as we all felt so powerless. Our management and record companies seemed unwilling or unable to help.'

In between live engagements, Fish had recorded vocals for the song *Shortcut To Somewhere*, co-written with Tony Banks. Released as a single in September 1986, this song had been part of the soundtrack for the film *Quicksilver*, and was Fish's only commercial recording outside Marillion before his departure from the band in late 1988.

Pallas videoed their performance at The Marquee on 11 September (not August as commonly reported). The resultant *Live At The Marquee* VHS majors on tracks from *The Wedge*, and includes *Cut And Run*, *Throwing Stones At The Wind*, *Imagination*, *The Executioner*, *Rat Racing*, *March On Atlantis* and *Atlantis*.

Two days later Pallas and IQ performed a double-header together at the Paradiso in Amsterdam. This was the first time that IQ had played outside the UK.

As Marco de Niet recalls, 'Martin Orford and Paul Menel did a spontaneous open air performance in Leidse Square, Amsterdam in the afternoon, as a contribution to the Festival of Fools happening that day.'

On their return to the UK, IQ enjoyed a three night residency at The Marquee, 25-27 September 1986.

Friday, day two of the three night stay.

Opening with a hard rendition of *Outer Limits*, the fab boys seemed to be determined to play the whole set this way, as if they had something to prove. Actually, if this is how they were feeling, they certainly had me convinced of their abilities. The only slip up with the opening number was when Paul Menel forgot the lyrics at one point; nerves perhaps? However this can be overlooked for he certainly has improved and now seems well suited to the role of IQ frontman. His confidence and style have definitely developed and his personality is beginning to push through.

New songs peppered the whole set (some six in total), from the quiet *Still Life* to grander pieces like *Human Nature*. All show progression but are still in that unique IQ style. *Nomzamo* was also given an airing along with *Promises (As The Years Go By)* which first appeared on the Magnum support tour.

These songs were interspersed with older favourites such as *The Thousand Days*, *Widow's Peak* and even *It All Stops Here*. Ending the show with *Corners* gave everyone a chance to clap along or simply groove, whichever they preferred at the time.

One sad point I noticed was the lack of visible humour and fun which once abounded in IQ gigs. Their minds were probably on other things - like giving musical satisfaction for money. Also their lack of live dates this year may be a factor (out of practice you see!).

Encore of *The Wake* then straight into the grand finale of *The Last Human Gateway* giving a bouncy ending to a very enjoyable evening.

Mike Browne, *The Rocking Horse* issue 2
(January 1987)

During these dates, Mike Holmes undertook an illuminating interview with the *Rocking Horse* fanzine (appearing with the above review in issue 2).

Why have the band been keeping a low profile lately?

MH: We have been having huge hassles with our management company [Irate Management] from whom we have just split. There are lots of things I am not allowed to say as you can imagine, but suffice it to say that it took ages to sort out. Thankfully it is all sorted out now and we are hoping to avoid any legal hassles because at the moment there are threats all over the place. So that is basically why we have been rather silent on the public front.

So what was the reaction like from the fans at the departure of Pete Nicholls?

MH: Obviously there were people who were sorry to see him go because, to one or two, he was the best thing since sliced bread, but on the whole reaction has been favourable. Many who were sad to see him leave have told me that they're more than happy with Paul.

So do you think Paul Menel has been fully accepted?

MH: Yes I do, he is the best replacement we could get. As with any band which changes their vocalist, there are a few people who are not going to be satisfied no matter what. I think we have been very lucky with Paul.

Was anything special done to make him fit into his role easier?

MH: No. He was thrown in at the deep end. He joined us in late October [1985] and two weeks later we went out on tour supporting Magnum. Before then, he had never done anything more than 300 seaters, so it was a shock to his system but it is a good way to do it because you are out there on stage and you have to learn your trade, and that is what he did.

Will he be developing anything special on stage? Like make-up or theatrics in any form?

MH: I do not know. I do not think he is going to go heavily into the make-up side of things. That was a personal thing for Pete and I do not think it is a good idea for him to follow that, although I am sure that he has theatrical ideas. Also, as a band, we would like to put on a real show but we cannot do it yet due to the fact that we cannot afford it, things like slides and film shows which I have always wanted to do. Hopefully we can put it together some day.

'When we were approached by Irate with a management deal, we thought it was exactly what we needed,' Holmes says. 'It's true to say that they did a lot of good for us in terms of press, distribution and the Wishbone Ash support tour, but what we didn't know until later was that we were being ripped off with sales. As I understand it there was a lot of product pressed up and sold overseas that was never accounted for.'

'You may already have read in the music press

1986: Egos Check Cheques In Transit

IQ in 1986 (From the collection of Guy Tkach)

that we have parted company with our management,' Martin Orford wrote at the time, 'and many of the club members have contacted us and showed great concern about how the move will affect the future of the band. For this reason, on behalf of all of us in IQ, I'd like to explain something of the reason behind the split and our plans for the future. Since the success of the Piccadilly Theatre gig [20 April 1986], we were concerned at the way in which the band's business affairs were being handled. We felt that having successfully headlined a West End theatre we had done everything open to us as a band to prove our worth to the major record companies. When the long awaited deal was not forthcoming we began to wonder whether the reputation of Irate Management, the company to which we had been signed for nearly 3 years, was all it might be within the music business. A few enquiries revealed a long series of unpaid debts and a shaky reputation which was obviously beginning to rub off on IQ. At about the same time, we realised that, in the eyes of our loyal fans, we were beginning to acquire a reputation for ripping people off. We had allowed our record company to take control of the band's merchandising and we were dismayed when the T-Shirts for the last tour were to be sold for what we considered to be an excessive price. Various protests on our part brought little response and consequently very few shirts were sold. This, coupled with the high retail price of the IQ picture disc, meant that our standing with the fans, who have been the lifeblood of this band over the years, was at its lowest ebb. Although we realised something would have to be done we had hoped matters would improve, but as the summer wore on the band's destiny seemed more and more to be slipping from our grasp. The last straw came when Tristan Rich and Geoff Banks, who had worked tirelessly in the band's cause, suddenly left totally disillusioned with the way the company was being run. Both had become trusted friends of ours and without them our management contract was useless to us. Although much legal wrangling lies ahead, we now feel that IQ is in the hands of people who care about its destiny. We have approached Tristan and Geoff to manage our affairs and they will be setting up a new management company soon, and I'm happy to report that the record company interest is higher than ever and that negotiations for the next album have reached an advanced stage. I can't pretend we won't have a tough time ahead of us in the immediate future; we no longer have Irate Management's financial backing behind us but at least we've got our band back.'

Mike Holmes: 'Luckily for everyone, just after that, we were offered the deal with Squawk/Phonogram.'

Plans for Holmes to remix *Tales From the Lush Attic* ahead of a CD release did not work out.

'That was the last thing we were about to do when we left the management company,' he said. 'The studio was booked for me to go and remix it. I

Twelfth Night support The Enid (From the collection of Guy Tkach)

had three days, which is not much better than one day. We had a re-arranged version of *Fascination* for the extra track but now the whole thing has fallen through.'

After a few weeks' break over the summer, Marillion reconvened to write new music. They returned to Nomis, then Bray Studios, and finally Stanbridge Farm Studios at Haywards Heath to demo their latest songs.

'Stanbridge consisted of a Tudor style house with a smaller cottage nearby and a large barn', Mark Kelly recalled. 'There was enough space for the band and a few of the crew, who we paid to sit around for months on end just in case we needed someone to go to the shops. This casual and expensive idiocy was becoming more common with Marillion, primarily as John [Arnison] was controlling the purse strings and didn't really care how we spent our cash.'

Several songs are known to have been written. One of these, *Beaujolais Day*, was rewritten as *Seasons End* a few years later (the guitar solo was worked into *Warm Wet Circles*) and some of Fish's lyrics would appear in the song *Fortunes Of War* on 1994's *Suits*.

'There's been much speculation over the years about the 'lost' *Clutching At Straws* sessions,' writes Mark Kelly. 'The story, because that's what it is, goes that we wrote a whole concept piece that was rejected by the record company for sounding too much like *Misplaced Childhood*. Can you imagine EMI rejecting something that sounded like our biggest and most well-received album to date? Most people at record companies have so little imagination that repeating a previously successful formula is exactly what they want you to do.

'What actually happened was we wrote and arranged *Hotel Hobbies*, *Warm Wet Circles*, *That Time Of The Night* and some other bits and pieces into a proposed side one for the album. We didn't abandon it and start again, we just trimmed the excess fat.'

On 17 October 1986, Twelfth Night supported The Enid at Hammersmith Odeon, the second and final time they performed at this seminal venue.

Andy Sears: 'Our second Hammersmith Odeon concert should have been a glorious return to the venue. In reality, we were pretty much snubbed. We were afforded very few lights, the sound was practically sabotaged, and we were practically pushed off the stage by the backline. Perhaps somebody didn't want us to repeat the success of our first visit. I think we were all pretty pissed off about the affair. Ingenuity was called for. Our in-house artist, Greg Smith, managed to come up with a spotlight, which we secretly rigged up on the balcony, unbeknownst to the headline band. This certainly helped a fair bit. I certainly wasn't going to let it lie and resolved to make it a night to remember. We had already been advised that an encore was out of the question, so as the last choruses of our final song kicked in, I shouted out something like: 'Do you want to play the Hammersmith Odeon? Come on up!' I remember the look of sheer panic on the face of our manager, Patrick Williams, standing in the wings. To begin with, the audience were a little reticent, but once I had dragged a couple of them up on stage, the stampede followed. The stagehands tried in vain to get some of them off, but they were fighting a losing battle. In less than a minute the stage was heaving with Twelfth Night fans all chanting along to *Take A Look*. Sweet victory! I never got a medal, though. Gutted.'

Three weeks later, Peter Hammill, formerly of Van Der Graaf Generator and a huge inspiration to Fish, played three nights at the Bloomsbury Theatre in London, 6-8 November. Fish and Steve Rothery attended and were spotted by Sean Worrall, who was in the process of pulling together the first issue of his lively fanzine *The Organ*.

> On return from the bar I grabbed the chance to ask whether they had started recording yet.
> 'No, not yet,' said Fish. 'We don't want to fuck it up, we don't want *Misplaced Childhood* Part 2.'
> Steve was more revealing.
> 'We were meant to go into the studio last week, but we're still writing it…'

By now there was speculation about the future of The Marquee.

'I don't know what's going on!' Fish told Worrall. 'When is it going to close? Are we going to play there? Who's playing the last gig? Us, maybe. I don't know what's happening, I don't think it will close …'

Pendragon's *9:15 Live*, named after the time of the evening they went on stage each night, was released on 10 November by Awareness Records, an independent record label founded in 1985 which re-released most of Roy Harper's back catalogue in 1985-1986.

'Our records went out of stock with Elusive Records,' Nick Barrett said. 'John Arnison was not willing to press any more copies. People were writing to me, saying that they could not get hold of our records. Then we got a huge order from EMI France but we could not supply them with anything. So we worked out this plan to get our albums back, so that we could license them out to somebody else who was willing to get behind them. Elton Latter (EMI) told me that if we did get our albums back, try Andy Ware from Awareness Records. So I sent them down a couple of copies of our albums and he was really keen. The next step was to get back the ownership of our records from Elusive, which we did, and we got the deal with Awareness. So now we own all our albums and have licensed them out to Awareness for seven years. After [that] we can have them back and license them out to other people, if we wished.'

The Awareness deal allowed Barrett to continue to approach major record companies.

Barrett: '[The arrangement with Awareness] was initially viewed as a stop-gap… where we would release a live album and Andy would have three albums to tote and sell, because there still is a hell of a large market for our records and they have sold an awful lot. I did not realise that he would work this hard for us, getting the name of the band around and making sure that we are happy with things.'

Barrett outlined the reasons for releasing a live album.

'There are quite a lot of Pendragon bootlegs kicking around,' he said, 'I have even seen them on sale at a record fair for about £5 and as a rule they are totally crap! The quality of bootlegs is so appalling, so we wanted to release something which looked nice with a good cover. Also have

Awareness promo shot, 1986
Peter Gee, Nick Barrett, Clive Nolan, Fudge Smith
(From the collection of Darran Kellett)

Pendragon sign with Awareness
(Courtesy Fudge Smith)

some new tracks on it as well! The Marquee … is a very good place for audience reaction and to play. It is supposed to be closing down and so we decided to record our last gigs there because you cannot go away from The Marquee without recording it because it is a landmark.'

Released in November, the album includes *Victims Of Life*, *Higher Circles*, *Circus*, *Leviathan*, *Red Shoes*, *Alaska* and *The Black Knight* along with a new studio track called *Please*. Cassette buyers would get a bonus in the form of an in-concert recording of *Fly High, Fall Far*. A CD release in 1990 drops *Fly High, Fall Far* in favour of 1984 studio versions of *Dark Summer's Day* and *Excalibur* (from *Fly High, Fall Far*).

Live albums are a necessity in the music trade, due to the amount of horrible bootlegs floating around. Yet live albums need to be pretty good to live up to the standards of any studio album (*Seconds Out* is an example of a great live album). *9:15* unfortunately is not an album that stands out in any way, yet it is a competent and fairly good album. The main factor that spoils any live album is the fade between songs, ruining the whole effect that the album is trying to achieve, so *9:15* falls down on that point yet makes up for it by the amount of good material on the album. The likes of *Alaska* and *The Black Knight* resting next to each other should draw a smile of glee from anybody's lips, both played to the usual high level of competence. Plus the addition of *Please* (a studio track), a musical piece not too distant from *The Black Knight* and you have got a good side two. On side one we have *Victims Of Life* only half of it mind you for then it goes straight into *Higher Circles* and a very bouncy version at that. *Red Shoes* is a fun song, it is a shame that a lot of it has been edited (very cleverly done too) out due to copyright reasons.

This album will probably sell in vast amounts ('as it should' I hear you cry) but I cannot help feel that this album holds no surprises. It looks great, sounds great yet does not somehow feel great!

Mike Brown, *The Rocking Horse* issue 2 (January 1987)

Nick Barrett: 'I expected the music press to view this album as, 'okay, we've heard Pendragon, let's see what they're doing now.' I think a lot of them thought with a live album, quite wrongly, that it should break down new musical barriers, which is ridiculous… So yeah, I think people expected too much of it. I think however with the next album I

Below: Twelfth Night's 'last shows of '86', from *Sounds* (From the collection of Guy Tkach)

Ticket for 29 November 1986 (From the collection of Peter Moltensen)

I was given a signed and dedicated copy of *9:15 Live*, which sits proudly alongside *Fly High, Fall Far* and *The Jewel*.'

On 28-29 November 1986, Twelfth Night returned to The Marquee. These gigs would herald the end of their 1983-1986 line-up.

Clive Mitten: 'The band was falling apart on a social level throughout 1986. I had real doubts that Andy would even turn up for these two gigs at The Marquee. No one had heard from him for ages. We had Mark Spencer lined up to sing with us, just in case.'

Mark Spencer: 'It's true. I think I did a couple of tunes with them during soundcheck for the first night. No one seemed to be able to contact Andy (no mobiles in those days!) and no one had heard from him for ages in the run-up to the gig.'

Andy did, however, make it on stage for these concerts. But they would prove to be his last with

will expect some good reviews, and if we don't get them I think I'm going to be very annoyed.'

Awareness reissued *Fly High, Fall Far* and *The Jewel* on the same day as the release of *9:15 Live*. The new cassette version of *The Jewel* added the songs *Excalibur* and *Dark Summer's Day*.

In support of these newly available albums, Pendragon played a 13 date UK tour between 29 October and 26 November, mostly around the university and polytechnic circuit.

At one of these, they met up with their friend Jon Dunnington.

'Clive and Fudge had replaced Rik and Mat by now,' he recalls. 'They played at Huddersfield Polytechnic and there was a pretty scary trip across the hills to Huddersfield in the freezing fog, wondering if the ancient transit was going to last the distance. The venue was grim with catering hotplates stacked against the wall and a giant glitter ball. It was back to mine for beer and food and this time

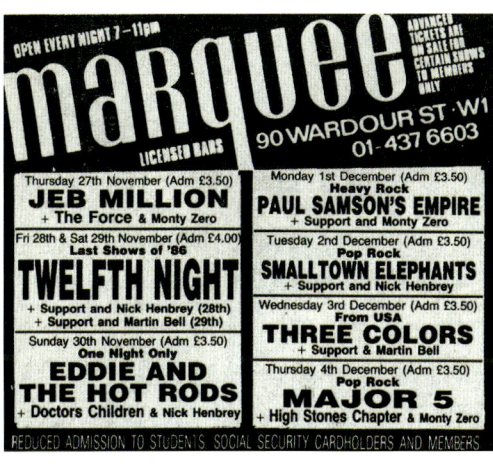

Twelfth Night for almost 22 years.

'I remember telling my partner that these would be the last ones', recalls Andy Sears today. 'I may have even mentioned something on stage, I really can't remember. But I do remember coming off stage and saying to [manager] Patrick Williams: 'That's it!' It was an immensely sad moment for me. I was angry too. After all, we had all worked so hard to break through, and whether through external forces or because of our own collective mistakes, it didn't really matter anymore: it simply wasn't to be.'

Andy Sears left Twelfth Night after these shows. It had been an eventful three years. He was replaced by Martyn Watson formerly of [The] Pookah Makes Three.

'I was writing music for films and art galleries having moved away from the pop world,' Watson told the author in 2009. 'I think I found out via Tony Visconti and Hit & Run that Twelfth Night was looking to find a new singer. So, I went along for a bit of a play.'

The new line-up wrote some songs together and rehearsed during December 1986.

'Writing music with Martyn was quite refreshing,' says Andy Revell. 'He was very collaborative and open-minded. I remember our first session together in my tiny music room in my flat in Chiswick. We wrote *Turning* in our first afternoon together. I had the riffs, chords and some words for what became the chorus. I started playing them to Martyn and he quickly came up with the bass line and words for a verse and we got the song into shape the same afternoon. We had a lot of fun. He was a really good, intuitive musician.'

Pendragon's 1986 Christmas show (From the collection of Jon Dunnington)

Pendragon's Christmas show took place on 12 December at The Astoria on Charing Cross Road in London, a short walk from The Marquee. They were supported by Pride Of Passion.

Marillion concluded 1986 with six dates between Christmas and the new year. New songs *White Russian* and *Incommunicado* were added to the set list. These dates included two fan club shows at Aylesbury Civic Centre on 27 and 28 December, supported by Pendragon.

'The whole Marillion thing was fab,' says Fudge Smith. 'Meeting Ian Mosley too was great and we became good friends. Pendragon had played many gigs with them before I came along.'

Bruce Dickinson of Iron Maiden guested with Marillion at the second of these shows.

There were two shows at the Royal Court in

Liverpool, again supported by Pendragon. At the second of these, Pendragon joined Marillion for their second encore, *Margaret*.

Nick Barrett: 'There was this girl who came on with whips, stockings, suspenders, the lot. We were on stage playing away and she started whipping everybody and of course Steve and Pete had these transmitters, so they just ran off round the back. Fish, on the other hand, decided to stay there for a short while and she started whipping and then started to take his clothes off. Well, I mean she just took his shirt off… That was enough, believe me. It was not a pretty sight! Not at all pleasant…'

Fudge Smith: 'I had to hit Ian's crash cymbals every time the dominating stripper got Fish with her whip…'

Marillion's year ended with another fan club show at Glasgow Barrowlands with ex-member John Marter in the audience. The journalist Mick Wall accompanied the band to Glasgow for a feature in *Kerrang!* Wall was writing the band's official biography, *Market Square Heroes*, which would be published the following summer.

The main point is this: to use up that week that stretches like old and torn pantihose between all the bothersome hoopla of Xmas and the near-hysterical invocation of a Scottish New Year, seven days that usually stumble blind like a cripple from one fat day of fearless feasting and maniacal merry-making to the next until night and day blur and collapse into an incoherent dark sludge of hideous waking dreams; to somehow avoid all that and give themselves the golden opportunity of breaking in some new material live before their fans, Marillion took to the road for the first time in five months. Five months that have been swallowed up with writing and re-writing material for the band's all-important new album, *Clutching At Straws*.

Writing, in fact, that is still not finished, though it should have been. And Fish tells me that the band are scheduled to begin recording the album in London the last week in January, but that he feels they're nowhere near finished writing the completed final versions of several key new compositions yet.

I ask Fish how much he thinks the writing this time around has been affected by the massive commercial success of *Misplaced Childhood*. Are they consciously looking over their shoulders, aiming perhaps for a fully-fledged and recognis-able follow-up, and all that that might imply?

'It's obviously been affected a lot, the writing side of things. Because we knew it would be so easy for us to go in and do another *Misplaced Childhood*. You know, *Part II - The Sequel* and all that s**t. String a whole lot of music together and put a dodgy concept on top of it and just go out and flog it! But people would be saying, 'Oh yeah, another concept album, how quaint, bye!' You know? And they would be right. What we have to do, what we've been trying to do all these months, just for our pride's sake even, is to put together and write an album that proves *Misplaced Childhood* wasn't the peak of our career. We want to say there are better things coming from this band; we're still breaking through, still going to come on strong… There's a hell of a lot of personal pride involved in this next one, a lot at stake in more ways than just the obvious one. We'll have to wait and see…'

1987:
Building Hope On Shifting Sand

> I don't think we'll make it in this country. I see our future in Europe... and possibly America. America actually is really picking up on some of the tracks from the new album. It's going well in Germany and Holland as well.
>
> Mike Holmes, *A Little Angry In A Very Nice Place*, 1987

Clive Mitten left Twelfth Night at the beginning of 1987. 'I would think we rehearsed five or six times as a five piece with Martyn Watson,' he says. 'I had lost interest by that time, so didn't contribute much.'

With Clive gone, Martyn Watson took over both bass playing and singing. Several new tracks were written during January and February and performed for Virgin at Westar Studios, Southall, on 13 February. At Virgin's request (and on their payroll) Martyn, Rick, Rev and Brian went to Strand Studios in Chiswick later in February and recorded demos of five songs. The sound and structure of these new tracks were very different from those performed by previous incarnations of the band, showing no hints of their progressive past. One of them, the remarkable *Zootime*, channels Killing Joke, no less.

'Initially, the A&R department were really excited about them,' remembers Andy Revell.

The tracks were strong and commercial. But were they Twelfth Night?

The same could be said for IQ, who filmed a promotional video for their first Squawk/Phonogram single, *Promises (As The Years Go By)* in February or March. The band mime to the song on the Beachy Head cliffs near Eastbourne. It's very cheesy, using reverse video effects. It can be seen on YouTube: at the time of writing it has had over one million views.

The video was shown on the Dutch TV show *Countdown*.

'The national media in the Netherlands, both TV and radio, paid attention frequently to the neo-prog bands, including Marillion, IQ and Pendragon,' notes Marco de Niet. 'For instance, Pendragon visited the radio show *Countdown Cafe* (our equivalent to the *Friday Rock Show*) a few times for live sessions.'

Pendragon's first single, *Red Shoes*, would be released on Awareness Records on 16 February 1987. This was a new Soundmill Studios recording of the track first released on *9:15 Live* and included new B-side *Searching*. Determined buyers could also obtain a 12" single with an extended *Red Shoes*, *Searching* and a third song, the oldie *Contact*.

'We were actually going to release it as a live single,' Nick Barrett said. 'But after playing it around a bit we thought maybe the production isn't quite good enough to be radio-playable, which is a very important thing for a band trying to get somewhere. I prefer the *9:15* version, but I said this when we were doing it. I said 'you're not going to get a better version, you're going to get a different version', and that's precisely what we've got. But having said that, I think if we'd have released the *9:15* version [as a single] I don't think it would have got any airplay. To most producers it probably sounds like Status Quo. Do you know what I mean? You've got this very heavy rock 'n' roll guitar thing on the live version, on the studio one it's a lot further back. It's more lushish, y'know, more songy. Perhaps more poppy I suppose. It's not a deliberate thing, you don't say, 'okay let's MAKE this poppy'.

1987: Building Hope On Shifting Sand

Fudge Smith and Nick Barrett, backstage at the Paradiso (Photograph by Martijn Kuiper)

Generally you just go into a studio and things just turn out some way and just end up like that.'

This release coincided with a radio session for Radio Veronica in Soest, Holland, and their first European headliner to 1,000 fans at the Paradiso in Amsterdam on 7 February.

'This was a defining moment for us,' says Clive Nolan. 'When I first joined in 1986, we were going up and down doing the pubs, clubs and universities. Some of that could be pretty demoralising. And we were sort of pounding away. I didn't join at a great time in the history of Pendragon. But then, out of the mist, came this offer to go out to Holland to perform at the Paradiso.'

'The Paradiso was amazing!' smiles Fudge Smith. 'It had that audience and atmosphere you got at The Marquee but on a much larger scale. That first Paradiso gig was absolutely electric. Great support too from a band called Oblique. I remember Clive was so overcome by the occasion he wouldn't come back on stage for the encore. I had to go back down those stairs backstage and talk him back into it.'

'That was the gig that kind of plugged us back in,' says Clive Nolan. 'We went over there and we could not believe the result. The reaction we were getting from hundreds of people… they were hanging off the rafters. It was just nothing like what we'd been doing at home, it was incredible. It's amazing how something like that can stoke your energy. You could be ready to give it all up and then something like that happens and you just think, 'We can do this.''

'All of those gigs at that time were really good fun,' Fudge Smith agrees. 'We hired a car and a transit van and just drove ourselves around the place. I was so tired after one gig that I nearly drove the car into the back of a lorry in Holland. Just remember everyone shouting 'FUUDDGGE!''

Suitably energised, Pendragon commenced demo sessions for a new album at Soundmill later that month.

Clive Nolan: 'David Munns at EMI put up a reasonable amount of budget for us to go and do what was supposed to be a decent demo of an album.'

Nick Barrett: 'EMI paid for us to go into the studio to record the entire album as a demo. We thought we'd put the short songs on one side of the album and have the long songs on the other side. I've always really liked pop music. It was perfectly normal for me to write pop songs. I've always liked soul music as well, great songs, short songs. So, doing shorter songs on *Kowtow* wasn't really alien to us at all. It was a very different beast from what we've done before but sometimes a dog leg change in what you do is what's needed.'

'Nick would always present the finished song to us, lyrics and arrangements in the bag,' Fudge says. 'Drums would be represented with the basic drum machine rhythms along with bass and keyboard outlines.'

A PLAYGROUND OF BROKEN HEARTS

Nomzamo period IQ patch
(From the collection of
Günter Schote)

The tracks were recorded at the Kitchen Studio in Norwich in April and May. However, when David Munns left EMI, his replacement was less than enthused with the recordings.

'We came out the studio,' Nick says, 'and within a few weeks David Munns had left EMI and gone to Polydor. The new guy at EMI was Nick Gatfield. He had been the saxophone player in Dexy's Midnight Runners. He rejected us in one sentence when he said, 'It's not my cup of tea.' All that hope and good work, building up to our big break… nobody's ever going to pay for a whole album and not sign you, right?'

Pendragon were in recording limbo, once again.

IQ's first album with Paul Menel, *Nomzamo* (April 1987), saw the band moving into the mainstream, with progressive rock tracks sitting somewhat uneasily with commercial songs such as *Promises (As The Years Go By)* and *Passing Strangers*.

No Love Lost is a beguiling mix of '80s pop and classic prog. It opens with wide open chords, pounding drums and a simple but gorgeous chorus. Menel's vocals are clear, if a little thin. So far, so good. The single, *Promises (As The Years Go By)*, is followed by the album's seven minute title track. Here we have something of a lost classic, with hypnotic, clattering drums under Menel's reflective vocals. This switches to what can only be described as bombast. It is wonderful.

Still Life is a slow ballad. Menel does a good job here, but at times it cries out for a fuller lead vocal performance. *Passing Strangers* is a pleasant AOR song which benefits from a rare Mike Holmes guitar solo. *Human Nature* is sophisticated and mature yet accessible, pulling together the best elements of the Menel era: symphonic keyboards, spiralling guitar, shifting rhythms. This is probably the best track on the two albums that Paul Menel made with IQ.

Screaming, in contrast, doesn't work. It's muddled and unfocussed.

Martin Orford: 'The only song I can't listen to from that era is *Screaming*, which somehow turned into an appalling stylistic mishmash from what had once looked like being a decent rock song. And the snare drum on those records is just too bloody loud, as was the fashion of the time.'

The last track on *Nomzamo* is the anti-war anthem, *Common Ground*. Musically, the song sounds as if it is influenced by *Cinema Show* and, for better or worse, the atmosphere of *Tales From The Lush Attic* and *The Wake* is recaptured, but with a much more direct set of lyrics than those in the Nicholls era.

The cassette version includes two bonus tracks: *Colourflow*, a very rare male/female duet featuring Jules O'Kine, and a stripped down piano and vocal version of *No Love Lost*. The single *Passing Strangers* b/w *Nomzamo* accompanied the album's release.

Marillion stayed close to home for formal recording sessions for *Clutching At Straws*, selecting Westside Studios in Holland Park, London. Westside was founded and owned by producers Clive Langer

1987: Building Hope On Shifting Sand

IQ promo photo, 1987
(From the collection of
Darran Kellet)

and Alan Winstanley and had recently been used by Depeche Mode, Duran Duran and Madness.

Mark Kelly: 'The whole album was about Fish's excessive drinking and drug taking and his feelings of isolation exacerbated by our success and his lifestyle choices. This was then compounded by the rest of the band closing ranks and shutting him out. It was dark territory we found ourselves in and its pervading gloom spread throughout the sessions.'

Steve Rothery: 'Certain people were taking too many stimulants. And again, it just all kicked off. I don't know if he threw a glass at me or something? Anyway, I walked out the studio and got the train home. And as far as I was concerned I was outwith the band. I just didn't want to deal with that anymore. Once he'd sobered up it was all OK, but it was confirmation of how far our relationship had moved away from that period around *Fugazi* and the early *Misplaced* period when we got on very well. It's sad when you have a great creative chemistry with someone but it gets blown apart.'

Coincidentally, Twelfth Night's *Art And Illusion* mini-album had been mixed at Westside in late summer 1984. The question of that band's immediate future was answered in May 1987 when their contract with Virgin was terminated. This was the final nail in the coffin for Twelfth Night as a professional band.

Andy Revell: 'Although our Virgin contract was for 10 albums, there were sales targets attached to each. We didn't meet the sales target for the first album, so they had the right to terminate. We lost the deal and had had enough.'

Brian Devoil: 'We weren't having much fun - and weren't making a living either. You can cope with having only one of these, but not both!'

And so Twelfth Night just fizzled out.

Pallas, too, were considering their options. To bring in some cash, they (minus Alan Reed) toured as the backing band to British chanteuse Kiki Dee between 5 and 11 May. These were the band's only live shows in 1987.

'It was probably our manager, talking to Kiki's manager,' suggests Niall Mathewson, 'and a deal was done.'

'Harry Maloney arranged this,' Graeme Murray confirms. 'We were a professional band and we were in the middle of a dry period for gigs of our own. Harry was friendly with Kiki's manager and set up for us to be her band for a tour.'

Niall: 'It was good fun and the band played well, but we did have to dress up like a pop band. We probably gave her music a slightly heavier edge than Kiki was used to, but she was well received wherever we played, so I guess we did a decent job.'

Graeme: 'She was brilliant, with an awesome voice, and a really nice person as well. We enjoyed it immensely and it gave us chance to try something different.'

The tour finished at the Town and Country Club in London. There was a rumour that Elton John was going to make an appearance.

'We were all excited about that,' Murray admits. 'But, sadly, he didn't turn up as he'd just been outed by the press.'

So, we need to picture Pallas backing Kiki Dee whilst Graeme Murray duetted with her on *Don't Go Breaking My Heart*.

'It was a buzz!' he admits.

Kiki Dee, for her part, has no recollection of the musicians on her tour.

'That's not surprising really,' suggests a pragmatic Ronnie Brown. 'We were only in her company for two weeks in total. For her, that would be like trying to remember people you met on holiday 30 years ago.'

Changes were afoot though, as Brown chose to leave the band after six and a half years.

'We usually say that Ronnie went out for a pint of milk one day and never came back!' laughs Alan Reed. 'In truth the lack of regular money took its toll. He had a young family and eventually had to make a choice. That was a really hard thing to do. We all understood.'

'I stepped down due to family commitments,' Ronnie explains. 'I got married in 1984 and our daughter was born in 1985. We'd been managing, only just, to stay afloat financially, but the bills were mounting up and I needed to get some order and stability into our lives. So, after a lot of soul searching, I took the decision to step away. In my opinion, no one ever really leaves Pallas.'

Pallas went back into their past and re-recruited Mike Stobbie, who had been with the band from 1976 to 1979.

'Graeme called me on the phone in London and said, 'Better the devil you know… Ronnie has left Pallas and we can't think of anyone better than you to replace him. What do you think?' I went up to Aberdeen to meet them at the farm.'

Alan Reed: 'Mike was undeniably the best keyboard player available to us. He was also very enthused about the band and brought a fresh impetus that the rest of us were lacking. We'd been ground down by the vicissitudes of touring and the record company politics. Mike brought back a bit of sunlight that we badly needed.'

'Alan had an amazing voice,' Stobbie says. 'He was young and dynamic, and I when I re-joined he said, 'Well at least I'm not the newbie in the band anymore!'… To which Graeme said, 'That's not strictly true…''

Ronnie Brown: 'I met Mike shortly after joining Pallas in 1979. We became, and remain, good friends. Mike and I have this fun thing between us about signing in and out – a little like handling the day and night shift between us, only each shift tends to run on a little – normally about a decade. So I clocked in in 1979, then out again in 1987 – leaving Mike to do the back shift through the early to mid-1990s. I clocked back in in 1997. Since then, Mike's been very busy with his own writing and production, but he's never been far from the Pallas establishment.'

Meanwhile, Marillion released their new single, *Incommunicado* on 11 May. This powerful, anthemic song returned Marillion to the Top 10. The Genesis influence is very strong, think *In The Cage* with pop hooks: not that far from Genesis's then current album *Invisible Touch*.

'We didn't expect it to be a hit single,' admitted Mark Kelly. 'It was totally different from anything we had released before apart from maybe *Market Square Heroes*. We had started to get a bit of a name as a ballad band going a bit soft… and we were getting a bit concerned about it! Once you get in the charts people tend to think you have gone 'pop' so we decided to release the rockiest number we had as the first single. We never expected it to do really well, never expected to get any radio play. It's not the kind of song you could expect to go to number one at any stretch of the imagination! But we were surprised by the amount of radio play it got and the fact that it went straight in at number six proved that there were a lot of people waiting for it!'

The B-side *Going Under* was included in a variant mix on the CD version of the parent album, *Clutching At Straws*. Collectors could also enjoy a different mix of *Incommunicado* on the 12" single and, a first, the CD single. The album followed on 22 June, entering the charts at number 2 at the head of a 13 week run.

IQ's UK tour started on 12 May. They were supported by south coast prog rockers Jadis. After a single date in Folkestone, IQ flew to Switzerland for two showcase shows at the Montreux Rock Festival, 13-14 May 1987.

Martin Orford: 'We weren't on at the main event in the casino, but there were various fringe events in the town put on by various record companies as showcases. We appeared at one of those, I think with the Georgia Satellites.'

Five songs from the 13 May show were broadcast on FM radio: *No Love Lost*, *Promises (As The Years Go By)*, *Nomzamo*, *Passing Strangers* and *Human Nature*. The band returned to the UK for another 12 dates across the country. Their usual encore was an unlikely but loud and tight cover of Deep Purple's *Burn*: some 'mindless boogie', as Paul Menel would say in his introduction. The tour ended in Bradford on 29 May. June saw the release of a second fan club single, *Fascination*, with *Bold Grenadier* on the B-side.

The band's first concerts in Germany (in Stuttgart, Munich, Dusseldorf, Hannover, Bruchhausen, Hamburg and Frankfurt) took place between 2 and 8 June. Three tracks recorded on this tour, *The Last Human Gateway*, *Passing Strangers* and *Common Ground*, would be included on the Germany-only EP *Here, There & Everywhere* in September. These Germans shows were followed by back to back dates at the Paradiso in Amsterdam and at Noorderligt in Tilburg, 19-20 June. This was a band working hard towards success.

Promises (As The Years Go By) was released as a single in France and Germany.

'It was being played on the radio hundreds of times per day in Europe,' Paul Menel says. 'The record company was caught completely unawares and didn't have enough product in the record shops. It was a tragedy and could have been avoided. I knew it was a hit, but hearing it on the radio and then hearing the bullshit excuses from the record company was a hard pill to swallow. Had that been a hit, I think you would have been talking about us in the same company as Coldplay or U2.'

Menel is undoubtedly protesting a little too much here. Radio play for *Promises (As The Years Go By)* peaked ahead of the single's release in April and May following the song's appearance on *Nomzamo*. By the time copies were pressed for a late June single, the momentum had been lost.

Sessions for Marillion's *Clutching At Straws*, released on 22 June, had been tense.

'I'm still not sure how or why, but coke and booze certainly played their part,' according to Mark Kelly. 'Steve and Fish had a blazing row, which ended with

Fish pinning Steve up against the studio wall and threatening to punch his lights out, while accusing him of saving his best ideas for his solo album. Not only ugly and unnecessary, but manifestly untrue as Steve had written most of the music for our latest album. I'm not sure what Fish thought Steve might be hiding.'

'I'd had enough of the egos and temper tantrums,' Steve Rothery recalled. 'The thing I'd wanted to do more than anything else in my life had become something I hated. As far as I was concerned, that was it – I'd left the band. Fish hadn't realised how much he'd upset me. I'd made the decision that he'd never get to me in that way again.'

Mark Kelly: 'Understandably, Steve was done with Fish and by association with the band too. He decided to quit and was only talked out of it some days later by the ever pragmatic Ian. But the die was cast; things between Fish and Steve were never quite the same again after that.'

Clutching At Straws starts moodily with *Hotel Hobbies*, which builds to an energetic conclusion. *Warm Wet Circles* is an accessible and highly personal ballad. It has a seductive ebb and flow, gentle guitar fills, a great Fish vocal and a classy guitar solo, the first of many impressive turns from Steve Rothery. *That Time Of The Night (The Short Straw)* exudes Floydian mellowness, as Rothery pulls off a decent David Gilmour impression (and there's nothing wrong with that). Fish's vocal is fragile and reflective initially, but he lets loose in the last couple of minutes. The intense conclusion includes the female backing vocals of esteemed session singer Tessa Niles. It's a very good song. *Going Under* is a dark intermezzo, all throbbing synthesisers and reserved singing. *Going Under* was not included on the vinyl or cassette versions of *Clutching At Straws* whilst *Just For The Record* is pure Genesis. In a neat songwriting quirk, the 4/4 choruses are much quieter than the 7/8 verses. The lyrics are excellent.

Just another gesture with an empty glass.
Just another comic actor, behind a tragic mask.

There are some *Garden Party* style rhythms and keyboards sounds, as well as some abrupt changes of mood. The edgy *White Russian* is classic Marillion, with a nod to the shifting rhythms and dynamics of *Forgotten Sons* and a short, fluid guitar solo. Its anger mixed with melancholy is infectious. The lead single, *Incommunicado*, follows. Its liveliness sits uneasily two thirds of the way through this album, even when the rhythm section unexpectedly drops out in the bridge. *Torch Song* is a slow piece with a great 'burn a little brighter now' refrain. This leads straight into the melodic *Slàinte Mhath* (Scots Gaelic for 'good health', or 'cheers'), which could be from *Misplaced Childhood*, or even one of the quieter numbers by The Who. Rothery's chugging guitar underpins a very good song.

Despite its very downbeat, sentimental tone and very sad lyrics, *Sugar Mice* is simply beautiful, possibly the best song that Fish recorded with Marillion. It's a melancholic pop ballad with a folk feel and a simple but perfect hook.

For when it comes right down to it
There's no use trying to pretend
For when it gets right down to it
There's no one really left to blame
Blame it on me, oh you can blame it on me
We're just sugar mice in the rain

And Steve Rothery's guitar solo is glorious; it bursts like the sun through the rain clouds. Fish's singing in the last half of the song is also magnificent.

Mark Kelly: 'I love the music and lyrics, especially the lush chords that Steve wrote for the guitar solo section.'

The album ends with the tight, wholly progressive *The Last Straw*. The tension breaks as the key changes and Steve Rothery plays another devastating guitar solo. The final two minutes are aggressive. Tessa Niles' vocal spotlight is outstanding, as her 'we're still drowning' refrain takes the song, and the album, to a satisfying conclusion.

The album had been promoted with an interview in *Sounds* dated 20 June 1987 and headlined *The Marillion Dollar Bash*.

'Musically, *Clutching* offers few surprises,' wrote Paul Elliot. 'It's a further refinement of the band's flowing and somewhat introspective melodrama - the old gibbering, stilted awkwardness now all but vanished. Lyrically, it's more complex. Slightly wordy and cryptic, it at first appears to be a one dimensional, Fish-eye view of the world seen through the bottom of a glass and blurred by the highs and lows of whisky and cocaine. Alcohol is the constant: a view, a leveller, a mother comfort and a release.'

> Torch is the writer who's trying to come up with a new novel and trying to dry out at the same time. And he's suffering from writer's block. So he goes out to some of his old haunts to try and regain some of the inspiration, and as he goes back he starts to recognise himself. In *Warm Wet Circles* he goes back to his adolescence, and by *Sugar Mice* he's got to the point of self-loathing where he recognises drunks in the bar as potentially him. In *The Last Straw* he actually starts writing again and goes back to the booze. It's saying that escapism isn't illegal, but that it's wrong to escape all the time and face responsibilities, y'know?
>
> Fish, interviewed in *Sounds*, 20 June 1987

After three days of production rehearsals in Warsaw, Marillion's European tour commenced in Gdansk on 22 June.

To assist with Pete's backing vocals and cover the notes that Fish was having trouble reaching, the band agreed to add a female singer for the tour. Originally noted session singer Linda Taylor was engaged. But, before the tour began, Taylor was replaced by American born, London domiciled singer Cori Josias.

'I was about to do a tour with Go West,' she says, 'when they deemed I wasn't funky enough. Linda Taylor wasn't right for Marillion, so we swapped gigs!'

Josias only knew of the band through their recent hit singles. On tour she was particularly effective singing high harmonies on one of these, *Lavender*, adding an echoing female voice which fits the song perfectly. She would really belt out the 'still drowning' refrain in *The Last Straw*.

'She added something new and different to the live set,' said Mark Kelly. 'Mainly due to things like *The Last Straw* we thought that it would be a good experiment to get someone in to sing them.'

The tour started with six dates in Poland.

'We were treated like kings,' Mark Kelly remembered. 'It was if the Beatles had reunited and

A PLAYGROUND OF BROKEN HEARTS

Cori Josias
(Photographer unknown)

decided to kick things off in Krakow. The fans went crazy everywhere we went. I'm not sure I liked it; there's something scary about your bus being surrounded by a mob, any mob, even the amiable kind. … The tour was promoted by the Polish government who paid us in hard currency, US$100,000 for the six shows. They also gave each of us a daily spending allowance in zlotys.

'We were told that we couldn't take zlotys out of the country, so we had to spend them before we left. That was hard because there was very little to buy in the shops. We all came home with chess sets and miniature leather-bound wooden chests. The rest of the considerable pile of banknotes we amassed during our stay were collected together by Fish at the airport and handed to some unsuspecting old woman pushing a broom around. She took them almost without stopping, before stuffing them inside her apron and resumed cleaning as if it was the third time this had happened to her that day.'

'I remember that Poland was still a Soviet Bloc country,' says Cori Josias, 'and it was somewhat shocking to learn that when I bought a round of drinks in the bar, a Polish friend of mine told me that it was the equivalent of one month's salary in Poland to pay for it. It was surreal. Crystal vases for £2, and groups of students talking about how much they longed for capitalism. This was in stark contrast to the students at that time in the UK. But I loved it on so many levels. Marillion were incredibly fun to tour with, they were like a family. The music was challenging enough to be interesting. Fish is a great lyricist and performer too. If I'm honest, it wasn't the kind of music I would have chosen to listen to, but once I was immersed, I really enjoyed it.'

The tour moved through mostly outdoor shows in Italy, Switzerland and France before arriving in West Germany.

The Out On The Green festivals would take place across different venues in Germany and Switzerland. Marillion headlined the Friday night at the Pferderennbahn in Frauenfeld, near Zurich, on 10 July 1987, topping a bill with Magnum and Katrina and the Waves. The following night, they took part in another Swiss outdoor festival in Leysin, close to the French border, the only British act on a bill dominated by French singers and musicians, Bernard Lavilliers, Catherine Lara and Viktor Lazlo.

This leg ended at the impressive open air Loreley amphitheatre, high above the Rhine near Frankfurt, on 18 July 1987. Three other bands were on the bill: Magnum, It Bites and Fate. The Cult were also due to perform but pulled out at a late stage.

'We walked on to a huge roar and directly into the assault of *Slàinte Mhath*,' Fish wrote later. 'The place erupted like a volcano and all I could see were upraised hands in perfect rhythm moving to Steve's hypnotic riff. We fired into *Assassing* as the second number. The place went wild and the waves descended on the barriers throughout. We navigated through a set peppered with a 'best of' element. *White Russian* and *Incubus* were perfect in the open air theatre of Loreley, *Russian* even more poignant than usual as it resonated with history. *Fugazi* had the terraces on fire and the choral work by the crowd was stunning in its ferocity. As a band we were in full attack mode and kept pushing the envelope and reaching ever higher. We had decided to play only one side of the *Misplaced* album and it was obvious we had to go for the one containing the 'hits'. It was a mesmerising performance and when we hit the peak in *Heart Of Lothian* the voice of the crowd blew me away. Pete was bouncing around the stage like Tigger. The last encore was the by now traditional duo of *Garden Party* and *Market Square Heroes* and the night was most definitely ours.'

Marillion's performance was filmed, and much of it was released later in the year as the VHS *Live From Loreley*. The video footage would be re-released on DVD in 2004. After various dribs and drabs over the years, the audio of the full concert followed in 2009.

> It had been a tough tour with a mish-mash of indoor and outdoor shows which had taken their toll. My relationship with the band and the management wasn't going well, and only a week before, I'd been up to the early hours of the morning in a Parisian hotel going through my troubles with Tony Smith, the Genesis manager, who as our publisher had flown in for the show at the Zenith. For me the fun was going out of it all. There was too much powder around, too much alcohol and not enough control, especially from the management. There was a lot of money being generated by the Marillion machine, but it didn't seem to be filtering down to the band that was on an endless rolling road. We were selling millions of records and playing to thousands of people, but the talk in the back of the tour bus was about struggling to pay mortgages on less than extravagant homes.
>
> Fish, *Live From Loreley* sleeve notes, 2009

One of the songs performed throughout the tour, *Sugar Mice*, comprised Marillion's second single from *Clutching At Straws*, released a few days ahead of the Loreley concert. The B-side, *Tux On*, tells the story of a rock star who gradually loses touch with reality. It reached number 22, Marillion's eighth consecutive Top 30 hit.

IQ's single *Promises (As The Years Go By)* backed with an edit of *Human Nature* would see release on 27 July. Fans could also buy a 12" version containing a 'specially re-recorded, re-mixed extended version of *Promises (As The Years Go By)* subtly subtitled 'The Shocked And Stunned Though Incredibly Together Beaver Mix'. This was promoted by appearances at the British Music Fair in Olympia on 31 July (6pm), 1 August (3pm) and 2 August (4.30pm). The single, inexplicably, was a flop. Perhaps the silly video filmed earlier in the year was the downfall of what should have been a major commercial success for the band.

Pendragon, meanwhile, performed an afternoon festival at Gloucester Park on Sunday 9 August. Two weeks later Nick Barrett was interviewed by Clive Aspinall for the fanzine *A Little Angry In A Very Nice Place*.

Aspinall: So you reckon this LP [the unreleased *Kowtow*] will give you big time success!

Barrett: Yeah. This LP should – if it's promoted properly and [with] the right push. I mean there [are] singles on there without a doubt, things like *The Mask*, *Time For A Change*, *Solid Heart* - it's all very much still Pendragon. We've always written short songs, something like *Dark Summer's Day*, but this is a kind of natural progression. The writing space between *The Jewel*

A PLAYGROUND OF BROKEN HEARTS

Pendragon in 1987 (Photographs by Brian Cairns)

and this one has been about four years and there have been lots of times when we haven't been allowed to progress fast enough due to not having a deal.

Aspinall: What's the lyrical subject matter on this LP?

Barrett: There is a lot. There's the first love song we have ever written [*I Walk The Rope*] which is a very strong song. There is a lot of my own feelings towards things coming out. Like *The Mask* which is about the mystery girl, the one you always fall in love with on planes or platforms (laughs), well I do anyway. *Time For A Change* was written when Rik and Mat left the band and is based on that whole era. *Solid Heart* is just a triumphant kind of thing you know. Then there is a track called *2am* which is about desperation and *Total Recall* which is about the opposite of desperation. It's all a lot stronger and more direct and the lyrics are a lot more straightforward and a lot more personal.

1987: Building Hope On Shifting Sand

Twelfth Night's last concert, supporting 'Jeoff' Mann (From the collection of Russell Morgan)

Martyn Watson singing at The Marquee with the final 1980s iteration of Twelfth Night (Courtesy Twelfth Night Archive)

Marillion's touring schedule continued in mid-September with 22 dates across four weeks in North America, starting at the 400 capacity Coach House in San Juan Capistrano on the California coast an hour south of Los Angeles. One of these, at The Chance in Poughkeepsie, NY, was broadcast by local station 101.5 WPDH. This proves that, with a receptive crowd, Marillion could take the roof these smaller venues. But it was a long way from Loreley, just four weeks before.

'Everything was going so well,' John Arnison said in a 2021 interview, 'but behind the scenes there was some issues. Fish did come to me with his thoughts about the future of the band, which, without going into detail, I did not agree with. He wanted to make changes there and then. I suggested that we finish the tour, have a break and then [he should] discuss his thoughts with the rest of the band [later]. Lots of things were going wrong on that leg. I was kept up to date and went over for a few days to speak with Fish. I then got a call from the band, saying they had had a letter from Fish telling them what he wanted to change. One of those was a change of manager. I was then told by the band members of the personal issues that they'd had with Fish over the last couple of years. I was asked if I felt they could continue without Fish.'

These issues continued to build over the next several months.

Since leaving Twelfth Night in 1983, their singer Geoff Mann had followed an idiosyncratic career. He had released three solo albums, performed in two gospel musicals, written a play that was performed in London and Edinburgh, and started ordination training with a view to becoming a vicar.

He also formed a new band, The Bond, in November 1985. The Bond continued to gig as Geoff's studies allowed and were booked at The Marquee on 11 October 1987. The support act was Andy Revell, Brian Devoil, Rick Battersby and Martyn Watson, the musicians once known as Twelfth Night but now concluding their career with a final show to support their old friend. Six new songs formed their 30 minute set list. After this, Geoff Mann came onto the stage to sing *Creepshow*, complete with his white coat and trademark mic lead

IQ in Wiesbaden, 1 December 1987
(From the collection of Günter Schote)

Marillion promo shots from the *Clutching At Straws* tour programme (EMI)

strangulation routine. As the final encore and swan song, a second singer joined the band: Andy Sears duetted with Geoff Mann on the band's signature ballad *Love Song*.

This would be the last Twelfth Night concert for 20 years.

A remix of *Warm Wet Circles* was released as Marillion's eleventh single on 26 October, featuring a live version of *White Russian*, recorded at Loreley, as the B-side. The 12" includes *Incommunicado* from the same source.

The band appeared on German TV programme ZDF *Na siehste!* [*Now, You See!*], lip-syncing their new single. The presenter announces the song as *Wild Wet Circles*. Backing vocals on the studio version had been performed by experienced session singer Tessa Niles. Here, the band's wardrobe assistant, Victoria 'Toots' Hurry, gamely steps in.

After a warm-up gig back at The Marquee, 23 October, with guest Julian Siegel on saxophone, Pendragon toured extensively again between late October and mid-December. There were several dates in the Netherlands and Germany, including a return trip to the Paradiso and concerts in Tilburg, The Hague, Arnhem, Bad Segeberg and Kaiserslautern. This activity coincided with the formation of an official fan club. For £3.00 you'd get copies of *Contact*, a badge, a signed photograph and some posters.

A few days later, Marillion headed out on a lengthy

European tour, opening with three nights at the 10,000 capacity Wembley Arena, 3-5 November. These were their first home country gigs for almost a year. The last of these was a charity concert in aid of muscular dystrophy charities. Prince Edward was in attendance. His response has not been recorded. Sixty minutes of the show was broadcast by BBC Radio and would be released on *Early Stages: The Official Bootlegs 1982-1987* in 2008. The attendance across those three concerts was the equivalent of 60 shows at The Marquee.

IQ also undertook a short European tour in November and December 1987 visiting the Netherlands, Germany and France, then two further dates at The Marquee on 8-9 December.

Marillion returned to the UK for dates in Edinburgh and Birmingham to close out the year. Their entire 19 December show can be heard as part of the 2018 re-release of *Clutching At Straws*. Pendragon's Christmas show at The Marquee took place on 21 December 1987.

'The Christmas shows were fun,' says Fudge Smith, 'with the traditional spray string and playing *that* Slade song...'

The album of demos they had recorded the previous spring gathered dust.

'Nick and I would meet and discuss our plans at a cafeteria in Maidenhead,' Clive Nolan says. 'We used to talk a lot, you know. 'What the hell are we going to do?'... We came to the same conclusion in the end. If you want to get something done, you do it yourself.'

1988:
Indifferently Ticking In Cold Deserted Mansion Halls

> The progressive movement really dug its own grave. A lot of the bands really were to blame, us included. Too many of the bands were recycling old clichés. Some of them got very successful recycling old clichés but others didn't.
>
> Alan Reed, *The Organ*, 1988

If 1985 was the year that everything started to change, then 1988 was, in many ways, a definitive full stop. It started with discontent amongst the members of the most successful of the new prog bands.

'There was a lot of friction,' says Marillion's drummer Ian Mosley. 'We were on the road for ever, it seems. We should have had a break, taken a year off.'

Keen to make as much money as possible, EMI's compilation album *B'Sides Themselves*, released on 4 January 1988, would collect together nine of Marillion's various B-sides. This includes many of the band's adjunct tracks on CD for the first time, although with some notable omissions: the live versions of *Chelsea Monday*, *White Russian* and *Incommunicado* from 1985 and 1987 were not included, nor was the B-side mix of *Going Under*. Different versions of *Cinderella Search* were used on the CD and vinyl editions.

Marillion continued their *Clutching At Straws* tour in Aberdeen on 7 January, although now without backing singer Cori Josias. This tour took in the UK and Europe (late January – mid-February) and included rare gigs in the Channel Islands and Luxembourg (in late March). The band's concert in Palatrussardi, an indoor arena in Milan, on 26 January 1988, was later released in full on *Curtain Call (A Live Archive 1983-1988)*. Fish was still having trouble with his voice. Three of the UK shows were pushed back by a month, and two in Europe were cancelled.

Marillion (EMI)

1988: Indifferently Ticking In Cold Deserted Mansion Halls

**Pallas in Amsterdam, February 1988
(Photograph by Mike Bentley)**

The band performed at Hammersmith Odeon on 16, 17 and 18 January, supported by Jadis, a band from Southampton who had been creeping around the edge of the scene for several years.

Jadis' keyboard player at that time, Pete Salmon, is Steve Rothery's brother-in-law.

'But the rest of the band didn't know that for a long time,' says fan and friend Stephanie Bradley. 'They always wondered why Pete turned up with loads of guitar strings. He'd been given them by Rothers. Pete eventually confessed. I followed Jadis around all over the place, meeting up with friends. Pete and I wrote to each other for a long time. Wasn't it lovely in those days when you used to write to people?'

Stephanie now works for Marillion, but initially was resistant to their music.

'Being a die-hard fan, to me they were a Genesis rip-off,' she admits. 'I was going to have nothing to do with them at all. I just wouldn't listen to them. I saw them for the first time in December 1983, and it kind of got the better of me, you know? And I thought, 'Actually, they're alright, really. I'm being far too prissy about this.' And then I really got into them. So when Jadis supported Marillion at Hammersmith in 1988, I was invited to the after-show, and then we all went back to the Hilton afterwards. The champagne was flowing, and I have this memory of being really hungry. It was about three o'clock in the morning by then, and I was wondering how I'd get back to Sussex to go to work. All of a sudden this plate of cucumber sandwiches arrived.

Rothers had ordered it. I got to know him and Jo a bit because they went to lots of Jadis gigs.'

This connection led, eventually, to Stephanie joining Marillion's backroom team in 2005.

'To think that I work for Marillion and my old friend Jerry is the editor of *Prog*,' she says. 'Neither of us would have predicted that when we first met at The Marquee as teenagers in 1983. Dreams can come true!'

Back in 1988, Pallas performed a short UK tour, visiting Bristol, Nottingham and Birmingham, then travelled to Amsterdam for their second booking at the Paradiso on 6 February.

They had written their next album, *Voices In The Dark*, and had started to record some of the tracks. Alan Reed was interviewed for *The Organ* ahead of a booking at The Marquee on 8 February. Reed discusses with candour how it's difficult to achieve commercial success without 'selling out'. His frustration with this dichotomy is never too far from the surface…

Organ: So, what have Pallas been doing?

Reed: Musically as Pallas not as much as we would like. We've been writing new material, contacting record companies and doing other things to basically survive, a bit of this and that…

Organ: Have you got a deal at the moment?

Reed: What we've actually got is a production deal. Someone, we can't say who, has put up some money so that we can actually record the album. We had a lot of material actually down on eight-track. People liked it but the eight-track recording didn't really do it justice. People were asking us to go away and record it again on twenty-four track but we had no money. We've had some interest, some near misses and now this production company have put up the money and we're recording on twenty-four track digital. We've got it all written, some of it's been about for some time. We've finished recording the first three tracks and they are being mixed now. We've been in the studio for a month and we have a record company on first refusal. The idea is this will be a major release at the right time.

Organ: What about musical direction?

Reed: It's certainly not as much of a departure as *The Wedge* was. It's very much a crystallisation, a clarification of what we are. We've achieved a band identity.

Organ: Has there been a conscious change and an attempt at commerciality having lost your EMI deal?

Reed: Well we have two or three tracks that would by some be considered as commercial in direction. We are hoping that we will have a commercial single from this album. I do think that the only way that we are going to break through in this country without going abroad and trying somewhere else is to have a single that gets airplay on Radio 1. If we can't get on Radio 1 then there is not much point in us having a single, and without a successful single now I don't think there's much hope for us in this country.

Organ: Are you consciously trying to write a single then? We were a talking to a band the other day who told us they had given up writing songs and were writing product!

Reed: We did go through a stage where we did try and write a single but we couldn't do it, we were never happy with the results. We have now

Ticket for IQ's last gig at the Wardour Street Marquee (From the collection of Peter Moltensen)

got one or two things that have come about naturally, they aren't totally representative of the band, but they are of a standard to be under the Pallas name and also they will hopefully get us airplay. We're certainly not ashamed to give it a bash.

Organ: Can I just say that having heard the soundcheck it was nice to hear that you haven't 'sold out'.

Reed: Oh no, I don't think anyone could accuse us of selling out.

Organ: No that was made clear from the soundcheck, and it comes as a relief after the activities recently of some bands.

Reed: As I said before there are one or two things on the album that could be considered commercial, but we are still very much an album band. There are two long tracks on the album. The reaction we have had so far having played the tracks to some reliable people in the fan club… has been good. In fact I was far more worried about *The Wedge* and I didn't hear too many complaints.

Organ: A lot of the bands that were part of the so called 'progressive rock revival' have completely changed and instead of playing prog music they are now playing some sort of ok-ish pop.

Reed: I think 'progressive' was really a bit of a misnomer for a lot of us. We've become a progressive band in the fact that we have progressed… we've taken our influences and taken them a lot further. We're a rock band, we don't think of ourselves as 'progressive'. After our fiasco with EMI we've had enough of all that, we don't give a damn anymore.

IQ's last show at the Wardour Street Marquee, their 35th in just over five years, took place on 28 February 1988. They included a cover of an old Curved Air song, as Paul Menel told the audience, 'A few surprises tonight, I think… bring a grin to people's faces. We're going to do a song right now which I think the old hippies in the audience may remember [from] when they were in the students' union bar when they should have been doing their essays. This is a song called *Back Street Luv…*'

The band also revisited their old cover of The Tubes' *White Punks On Dope*.

Pendragon started to show the size of their international audience when they played to a 2,500 strong crowd at La Locomotive, a club in Paris.

'France was absolutely incredible for us,' says Nick Barrett. 'And then everywhere else – Holland and Germany, then Poland a few years later. Eventually we got to South America, that was incredible. Argentina, Chile, Brazil. The doors just opened in all these places.'

Pendragon chalked up two more dates at The Marquee, 1-2 April, and released a special cassette to fan club members called *Beginers Guide To Pendragon As Beginirz* [sic]. This included 11 old recordings not generally available elsewhere. Volume two would follow in 1989.

The first *The Web* UK fan club convention was held at The Marquee on 24 April 1988. Music was provided by Jadis, joined by Steve Rothery, Ian Mosley and Pete Trewavas for *Market Square Heroes*.

Pendragon's Fudge Smith and can of Carling Black Label at The Marquee (Courtesy Fudge Smith)

On 11 June 1988 Mark Kelly appeared in the house band as part of a tribute concert to Nelson Mandela, an event noted for launching the career of Tracy Chapman.

'I got a phone call from Midge Ure asking me if I would take part,' he says. 'It was just out of the blue. I don't know how he got my number, probably from the office, but he phoned me at home, said he was organising to play at this Nelson Mandela gig and would I be in his band? Of course, I'm not going to say no.'

Midge Ure: 'By 1988 I had a track record as a musical director who could be trusted to put the band together, and make sure everyone was happy, which is why I got the call for Nelson Mandela's 70th Birthday Tribute at Wembley Stadium. There was this gaggle of loose artists - Fish and Joan Armatrading, Curt Smith from Tears For Fears, Paul Carrack, Paul Young, the Bee Gees - who didn't have a backing band. I called up some of the guys who had worked with me on Prince's Trust concerts and soon had a pretty good band.'

The house band comprised Ure and Kelly with organist Paul Carrack, bassist Mick Karn, a horn section led by David Sanborn, and drummers Mark Brzezicki and, inevitably, Phil Collins.

'It was supposed to be Curt Smith playing bass,' Kelly says, 'but he bottled it and Midge brought in Mick Karn. We rehearsed as a band for two days somewhere in London, then brought in the different singers during a day's production rehearsals at Brixton Academy or somewhere like that.'

Mark Kelly and Fish did not attend, as they were on holiday. Marillion reconvened to write new material ahead of a couple of festival bookings in June and July. A handful of demos would be recorded in this period in Pete Trewavas' garage: the tracks *Sunset Hill*, *Story From A Thin Wall*, *Shadows On The Barley* and *Tic-Tac-Toe* would be released as bonus tracks on EMI's 1999 and 2019 re-releases of *Clutching At Straws*.

Twelfth Night reunited, briefly, in 1988 when Brian Devoil and Andy Revell were determined to close out the band's history with a 'best of' album.

Andy Revell: 'We wanted to put together a compilation of what we felt was some of our best material across the years and different line-ups, as well as get a version of *The Collector* released, a piece in which we had great pride.'

Clive Mitten and Mark Spencer had opened a recording studio called Animal House in Bloomsbury, London. Twelfth Night's 1981-1983 line-up duly assembled to record *The Collector* in May 1988. While they were at it, they also re-recorded *Love Song*.

'The sessions were smooth and relaxed,' adds Andy Revell. 'Nothing like as fraught as when we were trying to 'make it', whatever 'it' is!'

'On the day of the show,' Ure recalled, 'I was standing backstage, when I got a tap on the

1988: Indifferently Ticking In Cold Deserted Mansion Halls

Melody Maker ad for Alan Reed's last gig with Pallas
(From the collection of Guy Tkach)

shoulder. I turned around and I'm staring straight into this beautiful blonde's breasts. It was Daryl Hannah, the Hollywood superstar, who was going to introduce us on stage. Nobody had warned me and there I was drooling out of the side of my mouth. Daryl went on stage and did the whole 'Ladies and gentlemen, please welcome Midge Ure's All Star Band' thing. There was huge applause. Unfortunately she announced it ten minutes before I was meant to be on, so I was still floating around backstage. Nobody had given us any warning and there was something of a gap before we all toddled on.'

The final running order was Tony Hadley, Joan Armatrading, Midge Ure, Paul Carrack, Fish, Paul Young, Curt Smith, Bryan Adams and the Bee Gees. Fish sang an upbeat rendition of *Kayleigh*. The band cooked up a storm in the last chorus and Ure pulled off a fluently brilliant copy of Steve Rothery's guitar solo.

'He did a pretty good job,' Rothery concedes. 'And having Phil Collins drumming on a version of *Kayleigh* was a bizarre twist of events!'

'I was well out of my depth,' Mark Kelly says, 'but it was fun.'

A week later, 18 June 1988, Marillion played their biggest ever headline show to over 90,000 people at the Radrennbahn Weißensee cycling track in East Berlin. Support came from a recently reformed Fischer Z, East German band Rockhaus and Polish hopefuls Voo Voo. The entire show was broadcast on DDR, the East German state broadcaster. Cracks were starting to show.

'It was a big gig,' says Ian Mosley. 'And as we were coming off stage I said to Fish, 'That was amazing!' and he said, 'I really didn't enjoy it…'' That was a red flag for me. We were in trouble.'

Pallas performed again at The Marquee on 23 June 1988. This was Alan Reed's last gig with Pallas for five years, although it would be some time before any public announcement.

IQ, meanwhile, pushed on with Paul Menel, developing a stadium friendly sound that owed a great deal to Simple Minds. Mullets, synth guitars and rain are on show at three Out In The Green festival bookings, at Volkspark Dutzendteich in Nuremberg on 9 July, in Frauenfeld, Switzerland on 10 July and at Verein für Ballsport Waldstadion, Gießen near Frankfurt, on 16 July. A fourth show planned for 17 July at Walsrode near Hamburg was later moved to a new venue in Oldenburg but cancelled at very short notice.

They opened a long and varied bill, the same at all three shows, with a 40 minute set. The Frankfurt show was officially recorded and broadcast by Hessischer Rundfunk. As the rain poured, IQ tried to liven up the crowd with *No Love Lost*, *Nomzamo*, *Sold On You*, *Nothing At All*, *Human Nature* and a

A PLAYGROUND OF BROKEN HEARTS

The programme for Out In The Green at Nuremberg on 9 July 1988 (From the collection of Günter Schote)

medley of *The Wake*, *Headlong* and the closing section of *The Last Human Gateway*.

IQ were followed on stage by T'Pau, Ten Years After (reuniting their original line-up), Starship, Foreigner, Jethro Tull and an odd coupling of Ron Wood and Bo Diddley. The Frankfurt show was filmed from a single onstage camera. The footage still exists. The band were, by now, mid-way through recording their fourth album, *Are You Sitting Comfortably?*, at Jacobs Studios in Farnham with former Rush producer Terry Brown.

On 23 July Marillion headlined the first night of an ill-fated two day Festival For The Future at the Craigtoun Country Park near St. Andrews in Scotland. Poor weather badly affected attendances and, with a planned TV broadcast also falling through, the organisers were seriously out of pocket. So-called 'Fife Aid' marked Fish's last concert with Marillion.

Under pressure to start recording, the band hired producer Bob Ezrin for a series of sessions due to begin in September. Mark Kelly: 'We returned from Scotland feeling demoralised, but we still felt we had enough music to make it worthwhile recording some demos. We went to a studio in Wallingford, Oxfordshire, the aptly named Tone Deaf, to put down what we had so far. … [Bob Ezrin] came to visit one afternoon and was not impressed by what he heard at all. He said the music just went backwards and forwards … there were no songs and we should go away and finish writing the album before approaching him again.'

Two weeks later, Fish left Marillion. Mark Kelly is typically forthright on the reasons for Fish's departure: 'Somehow, between us, we had poisoned the well we drank from… I received a letter addressed to the four of us from Fish…

Imagine the last and final argument you had with a partner when all the other bad feelings and buried hurt comes bubbling back to the surface, that one time you get to tell them what you think of them and make it count. Think about that and then multiply it by a hundred. Then maybe write it down, seal it in an envelope and send it… Here, in this letter, was talk of Fish versus the rest of band, Machiavellian subplots, lines drawn grandly in the sand. Hurt and stories of subterfuge creeping through the pages in Fish's scrawly hand… Though, as Fish's letter made clear, there was something closer to the dark heart of all this. We weren't even able to make music like we once did, he said… He finished up his plaintive pages of passive/aggressive prose with one final shot across our bow. The message was clear: I'll make music with or without you and this monstrous band… He asked or demanded (depending on your point of view) for change. But for change to come, it has to come from both parties. At this point we were a million miles apart. I don't know if a break from each other would have helped, some time to contextualise it all, but we were done with the other; tired, fractured and spent. It was how we as a band felt and, judging by Fish's letter, it was how he felt too. It was about the only thing we had left in common… The four of us and John [Arnison] made a number of calls over the weekend and unanimously agreed that we should accept Fish's resignation. We didn't have a plan or any idea what we would do next, but we had reached the end of the road with Fish.'

Pete Trewavas: 'The sad reality is that although we had achieved so much together and come so far, we had spent too much time touring and going through the music business mill. In the end it was hard for us and Fish to work together. We tried for about a year going to various places to try and write and get that camaraderie back, but it wasn't to be.

It was a relief in the end when it finally happened.'

Fish submitted his resignation letter on 9 September 1988.

EMI's press release, dated 15 September 1988, reads:

It is with regret that Marillion announce a change in their line-up. It has been mutually agreed by all five members that Fish leave the band. During the process of writing the new album it became apparent that differences, both musically and lyrically, between Fish and the rest of the band were irreconcilable.

Says keyboard player Mark Kelly, 'Marillion have always worked as a democratic unit and will continue to do so. We're currently working on our new studio album, and, as soon as we find a suitable vocalist, we'll be recording and planning live dates. Fish's contribution to Marillion has been invaluable but we all knew it was time for a change. Steve, Pete, Ian and myself all wish him the best of luck with his solo career.'

Fish commented, 'I've had a brilliant seven years with Marillion, however, recently the musical directions of the band have diversified to such an extent I realised the time had come to embark on a solo career. I'm very excited by this move and I'm looking forward to continuing writing and performing music and getting involved in a number of alternative projects that I never had the freedom to pursue within the framework of the band. I still hold a great deal of respect for Marillion and I want to thank them for giving me the opportunity of having reached this point in my career.'

Final words from Steve Rothery, 'As a gesture and a big thank you to our fans who've given us such incredible support so far, we're planning a live double album encapsulating Marillion's 7 year career to date and we're hoping to see this released during November.'

Fish: 'Marillion became a really big band. And I wasn't enjoying it, you know? It became too complicated. The demands on my personal life, the demands on my private life, it was detrimental to my health. Marillion were under a lot of pressure after *Clutching At Straws* and EMI wanted another *Kayleigh*, another *Incommunicado*, another *Lavender*. There was so many people that were making a lot of money off that band and we were still going back home at the end of a tour going, 'How do we pay the mortgage?' The other four guys… we were strangers to each other. I left Marillion after making what I thought was our best album.'

'Throughout the *Clutching At Straws* tour there had been a terrible atmosphere, both on stage and off,' Steve Rothery says. 'It was about ego and somebody wanting control. It just couldn't have continued. At the very most we would have made one more album with Fish before things imploded.'

The music written that year as a follow-up to *Clutching At Straws* would not go to waste. *Story From A Thin Wall* would morph into *Berlin* in 1989, and *Sunset Hill* was reworked as *The King Of Sunset Town*, both tracks on *Seasons End*, Marillion's first album with Steve Hogarth.

Steve Rothery: 'We'd written a lot of music before Fish left. He wasn't thrilled with it but we felt it was some of our strongest material. So when we had the parting of the ways, creative differences, however you want to describe it, I personally felt that we still had something to offer musically. We just had to find the right person. Not a Fish clone, because we had quite a few of those out of the hundreds of auditions we did, but somebody that could add something else, something different and special to what we did. I was blindly optimistic.'

Fish's last gig with Marillion was matched by a more symbolic event a week later: the closure of The Marquee Club in Wardour Street. The building had literally been shaken to pieces after almost 25 years and several thousand gigs.

A survey in 1987 had determined that the facade of the building at 90 Wardour Street had started to move and demolition was therefore scheduled for 1988. The Marquee quietly closed on Sunday, 31 July 1988, after a show by the British rock singer Lisa Dominique, with Lemmy guesting.

'He got up to do a jam with Lisa Dominique,' recalls Bush Telfer. 'Some fella went to grab her by the knockers and Lemmy took his microphone and bonked this fella on the head with it. And a big 'oooh' went round the room.'

The building where the main room of the club was located was dismantled, but not before Fish claimed one of the handpumps from behind the bar. A restaurant has taken its place. The archway where the entrance of the club used to be still remains, and is now the entrance to the Soho Lofts apartments.

In summer 1988, the club was relocated to 105-107 Charing Cross Road. This version of The Marquee remained an important venue, opening on 16 August with a concert by Kiss. 'We brought the West End to a standstill,' recalls Bush Telfer.

But for Gregory Spawton: 'When The Marquee moved, it felt like the end of an era. Wardour Street was our home ground.'

The two remaining looking-for-success prog bands of the 1980s continued to play dates at the new Marquee venue: Pendragon in November and December 1988 and again in November and December 1989; IQ in December 1988 and four times in 1989.

'We played the Charing Cross venue several times,' says Fudge Smith, 'but it was never as good as the old Marquee in Soho we had played so often.'

'The Wardour Street Marquee was a completely different animal to the Charing Cross venue,' Mike Holmes says. 'The Wardour Street venue felt more like a club – the atmosphere was always great no matter who played there, and we got to know the staff and the DJs really well. It was definitely a home crowd for us, and I'm sure hundreds of other bands, and it just felt great to play there. By the time it moved to Charing Cross it felt a bit different… it just kind of missed that spark that Wardour Street had.'

The IQ gig on 18 December 1988 was notable for the unavailability of Paul Menel. Martin Orford tells the story of how he accidentally sang lead vocals for IQ.

'I was living back in Hampshire by then and I'd often break the journey by staying in the flat in Reigate owned by Tristan Rich who was still our manager then. Tristan wasn't in the country and he'd left the key out for me the night before The Marquee show, so I was settling down for a quiet night in watching the telly.

In the way of best laid plans, a knock came on the door and it was a chap called Ferg from the neighbouring flat who was having a bit of a party and asked if I wanted to join them. I believe Ferg and his friends were bikers and may well have been Hells Angels for all I know, but they were certainly marvellous hosts and the conversation, tequila and flaming sambucas flowed for many hours. When I did finally figure out how to get the key into the lock to collapse on Tristan's living room floor, I was predictably quite the worse for wear. I don't think I'd have woken up at all that morning had it not been for a most unwelcome call from Paul Menel to let me know he had flu and wouldn't be singing that night. A series of other phone calls ensued in which the band decided I would have to sing instead, as it was too late to cancel the show.

The problem was that after that degree of alcohol intake, I couldn't really speak, let alone sing. Throughout the day things really didn't improve and I could barely muster a whisper. The soundcheck was most unpromising and it was time for drastic measures, so I headed for the chemist just down the road and loaded up with Night Nurse. I'm pretty sure this stuff isn't meant to be drunk two bottles at a time, but unbelievably it worked and armed with a pile of lyric cheat sheets it was showtime. Somehow, we got away with it, though of course there was lots of audience participation for the bits I couldn't remember (which was quite a lot of it).'

The set consisted of *Nostalgia*, *Outer Limits*, *No Love Lost*, *Passing Strangers*, a TV adverts medley, *Still Life*, *Sold On You*, *Widow's Peak*, *Promises (As The Years Go By)*, *Common Ground* and a Glenn Miller medley. From the band's usual set of the time, the songs *Drive On*, *Wurensh*, *Through My Fingers*, *Nothing At All*, *The Magic Roundabout*, *Human Nature*, *The Wake* and *Headlong* were dropped with those two time-filling medleys added.

Pendragon, meanwhile, were still hopeful that their EMI demos would manifest into a recording contract.

Fudge Smith: 'I don't believe that the record company had actually heard the band demos of *Kowtow* before we presented the finished album to them. I think what happened was the relationship between Awareness and EMI broke down, effectively ending our contract and distribution. EMI paid for the studio time in advance, so Nick at least wound up with an album for free.'

'I just thought nothing could get any worse,' Barrett said. 'We'd just lost our management, attendances at The Marquee were starting to dip, I was doing a bread round that started at three in the morning. To add to that, the press hated us.'

Nick Barrett's response was to negotiate ownership of the EMI demos, form his own record company and release the album himself.

Peter Gee: 'It is all because of Nick's business acumen, and him taking a step of faith at just the right time, that mapped out a long-term way forward for Pendragon. Out of the top six new progressive bands of the 1980s, Pendragon and Solstice were the only bands to have never had a major record deal. This, coupled with the recording costs of the *Kowtow* demo album already paid for, turned out to be a big long-term blessing for Pendragon. We have Andy Latimer's partner and Camel manager, Susan Hoover, to thank for the idea of Toff Records, as she said to Nick, 'If you can't get a record deal then why don't you set up your own record label?' Nick asked EMI whether they

Kowtow era promo shot
(Courtesy Fudge Smith)

would let us keep the *Kowtow* tapes plus the rights to the music. Amazingly, EMI said, 'Yes'… Nick made an appointment with his bank manager and applied for a loan of £5,000 to start a new small business. This paid for the manufacture of the album. Incredibly all of the copies of the *Kowtow* album sold, paying off the band's debts in one stroke. It was Nick's faith and business abilities that propelled Pendragon into a whole new exciting era, just at the right time, when things had previously seemed fairly hopeless for us all.'

'Without a doubt it was Nick's formation of Toff Records and his drive to self-management that was the key to Pendragon's survival as the 1980s turned into the '90s,' says Fudge Smith. 'Hats off to Nick for single-handedly saving and propagating Pendragon. That guy used to be in the office till 2am sorting out tour logistics after rehearsing with us during the day. I admire him very much for all of that.'

Kowtow (pronounced 'Cow-toe'), with distribution by Pinnacle, comprised the EMI demos plus

A Little Angry In A Very Nice Place, 'Anima Mundi' issue, 1988 (From the collection of Darran Kellett)

Solid Heart from the earlier Soundmill sessions.

Nick Barrett: 'It was then that we decided to start our own record label. That was the best thing we ever did. I went with the *Kowtow* tape to Pinnacle, the distributors. I walked in thinking I was gonna get the same kind of vibe as the record companies. They asked for proof of sales, and I had some royalty statements and they said 'yes' straight away. It's the most positive reaction we've ever had. Suddenly, there was none of this, 'Well, you haven't got a frontman who dresses up in a fox's head', or 'You haven't got a hit single…' We had a following and we had record sales, and that's a business. *Kowtow* was the first album on Toff Records. It was all ours.'

Kowtow is an album of two halves. Side one includes the shorter tracks and ballads. *The Mask* opens *Kowtow* and is a bright pop song, commercial and charming. *Time For A Change* sounds almost nothing like Pendragon, coming off like an A-ha / Yes hybrid and firmly rooted in the mid-1980s. *I Walk The Rope* is a gorgeous ballad with an emotive saxophone break. It is surprising that EMI did not see potential in songs like this.

'I thought that *I Walk The Rope* was one of my best ever songs,' Nick Barrett says. 'I love it.'

Solid Heart has a strong pop-rock feel, but one could argue that Barrett's voice is not suited to this type of music, which perhaps needs a Bono or Mike Scott to pull it off. *Solid Heart* was much more effective as a set closer as each band member left in turn just leaving Fudge's pounding drums. The gentle *2 AM* starts with smooth saxophone and is a calm, peaceful and slightly sad ballad with an abrupt ending, quite unlike anything else on this album or on any other Pendragon release.

Side two comprises three long prog songs, *Total Recall*, *The Haunting* and *Kowtow*. *Total Recall* features Clive Nolan's fluid piano playing, some quite beautiful guitar lines and a simple but effective chord structure. One can hear how later Pendragon compositions would develop. Likewise, *The Haunting* points towards Pendragon's future direction. It includes a long and truly outstanding guitar solo. The closing *Kowtow* is intricately arranged and perhaps influenced by the feel and rhythm of Marillion's song *Fugazi*. The album is a stepping stone from the band's early songs to the stylistic shift of *The World*. It's not the place to start if you're learning about the band's music, but side two, in particular, shows a developing maturity and confidence. It's no coincidence that the band that recorded *Kowtow* would stay together for another 18 years.

The 7 November release of *Kowtow* was promoted by a date at the new Marquee, 19 November, and a post-Christmas show at the same venue.

Fish's valedictory live album with Marillion, *The Thieving Magpie*, would be released on 28 November 1988. The album's title is taken from the snippet of Rossini's opera *La Gazza Ladra*, first performed in Milan in 1817, used as the band took to the stage. The album release was preceded by a single, a live version of *Freaks* with an in-concert take of *Kayleigh* as the B-side.

'Maybe it was the same sort of blind optimism I had when I gave up everything and moved down in 1979,' says Steve Rothery, 'but we didn't doubt that we could continue because we had written a lot of great new music, a lot of *Seasons End* and parts of *Holidays In Eden*.'

1988: Indifferently Ticking In Cold Deserted Mansion Halls

========= 1988 - A RETROSPECTIVE LOOK =========

1988 was a strange sort of year, was it not? A lot of things happened on the music scene, and most of those were in their way surprising.

Okay, remember about the things that hit the national music press. Not being satisfied with Belinda Carlisle's approximation to his idol, Rick Nowels came to England to find someone else to do Stevie Nicks. Found one in Bristol, he did,,but we all know about that one.

This piece of information leads us on the way to the fact that a certain fanzine editor got a job with Kerrang! reviewing albums and gigs. It is rumoured that he only got the job because of his, er, friendship with the aforesaid Rick Nowels protege. Anyway, Harris stuck his job for two weeks before suffering a nervous breakdown due to his being forced to listen continuously to albums by Kreator, Destruktor, Sabbat, Krismax, Predatur, Viktim, and hundreds more obscurer thrfrash bands. He immediately went off to turn his fanzine into a semi-professional organ with nationwide distribution, call "Absolutely livid in the worst pit I've ever seen". During this sojourn in one of the better sanatoriums, his gifted co-editors managed to publish without much problem.

New prog-rock abounded; Haze split and reformed with several members of Twelfth Night to form a band called Evening Mist, soul/disco combo with instant chart appeal. Pendragon released two more albums, on different labels, produced by Dave Gilmour and Kate Bush respectively, both consisting of a mix of live and studio work. Rumours that they were offering a prize to anyone who could tell which were which are unfounded.

Kate Bush, indeed, took to visiting various folk clubs up and down the country incognito, there to stand up and perform a cappella renditions of some of her self-penned folk style songs. At the last minute she turned down a gig with Fairport Convention, on the grounds that there was no room for her to bring her Fairlight on stage with her.

Down in Bracknell things were popping. Prog-rock gigs every weekend down at the Bridge House all through the Spring and early Summer. Unfortunately all this ended when I went off on holiday for a few days to find that the place had been burnt to the ground by the local Soul Boy Protest Movement branch. Hordes of hells angels then had trashed the entire housing estate from which the Movement was rumoured to have emerged. Things got back to normal when I returned, of course...

Pink Floyd did a secret gig down at the Marquee, at which both Roger Waters and Syd Barrett guested, the latter during a limp rendition of Shine on You Crazy Diamond, during which he stood with his head on one side, continually playing one guitar chord over and over again... Waters and Gilmour almost came to blows on what song to perform as the encore; in the end they compromised with "On the tide is turning away".

A sorry end to the year came about when Rick Astley joined Marillion for a Christmas single...

As for 1989... who could possibly guess what might happen in the Music Scene?

1989:
Watch The Old World Melt Away

> His voice struck me straight away. There was a picture of him with the tape, and he was a good looking boy. I thought it was too much to ask that he'd be a nice bloke as well.
>
> Ian Mosley, in conversation with the author, 3 October 2023

As 1988 ended, Marillion had already started looking for a new singer with adverts placed in *Melody Maker* and elsewhere. Alan Reed of Pallas and Stuart Nicholson of Galahad are two of a number of singers who are known to have auditioned, along with Tracy Hitchings, then with Quasar.

'It was spontaneous and not planned by them!' recalls her bandmate Dave Wagstaffe. 'Quasar were rehearsing at Nomis Studios in west London at the same time as Marillion were auditioning singers there, and when Tracy discovered this, she decided to gatecrash their proceedings and insisted on singing something. I think the band, after getting over the initial surprise, humoured her cheek. They were quite clear that they wanted a male singer to replace Fish!'

By early 1989 Marillion were rehearsing with Steve Hogarth.

'I joined Marillion in January 1989,' Hogarth said. 'It was a kind of an accident, really. I went into the office of my publishers at the time, Rondor Music, in Parsons Green in London. They had a studio in the basement. I used to go there sometimes and make demos and there was always a really nice atmosphere in the building. When [Hogarth's band] How We Live finally hit the wall, and I was trying to decide what to do with my life, I thought I could work in the office at Rondor, to tide me over. I went in one day and said, 'Can anyone think of anything for me to do?' What I meant was, I dunno, ordering Tippex for secretaries, or grooving around making tea. That was misinterpreted. They thought I was asking them if they could find a band for me to be in. The general manager, Alan Jones, was lying face down on a sofa – they were all hungover as it was Christmas and they'd been to lots of parties. He lifted his head and opened a bleary eye and said, 'Did you know that Marillion are looking for a singer?' And I told him that I just wanted to work in the office!'

Hogarth agreed to send a tape to Marillion's management, with some of his How We Live songs. *Games In Germany* from their 1987 album *Dry Land* was one of them.

'I didn't prevent them doing it,' he said, 'but I didn't give it any thought either. I was considering getting out of the music business to live a quiet life as a milkman. And then, in January 1989, I got a call from [The The's] Matt Johnson who wanted to know if I wanted to play piano on his *Mind Bomb* tour [later in 1989]. I really wanted to do that: maybe I should put the milk float on hold. I went to see Matt, we had a chat about it. I told him to count me in.'

'Pete had converted his garage in Aylesbury into a rehearsal studio,' notes Ian Mosley. 'I was living in Gerrards Cross, about 40 minutes' drive away. I'd use the time to listen to the cassettes we were sent of prospective singers. I'd listen to them as I drove along, then say 'No!' and throw them over my shoulder onto the back seat. One morning I put a cassette in the player and Steve's voice came out singing *Games In Germany*. I stopped the car and just listened to it all. I arrived at Pete's house and got the others to listen to the tape. Straight away they all said it was brilliant.'

Mosley realised that he and Hogarth had a mutual friend, the former Curved Air violinist Darryl Way.

'I rang Darryl and told him that we wanted to meet Steve,' Mosley says.

Mark Kelly: 'I heard his voice on *Games In Germany*. It sounded like the right voice for us. He had a bit of a Gabriel-esque quality to his voice, which I really liked. He clearly could sing. And the lyric was quite interesting. It wasn't your usual pop rubbish. We were all quite excited when we heard there was a few other songs on that tape. Our expectations were quite high.'

Hogarth's phone rang again a couple of days later. Marillion wanted to meet him. But Hogarth remained uncommitted. Shortly afterwards he had a conversation with Darryl Way.

'I just happened to mention to him that Marillion had called me up. And he said, 'They're really nice people, you should check them out, go and see them.' So it was really Darryl giving me a nudge. I went to Pete's house.'

Mark Kelly: 'And, you know, he was a bit tardy with his, with showing up a day late and all that. But, you know, it was a shape of things to come.'

Hogarth: '[Pete] had got cats so I couldn't go in the house, so we all sat outside in the garden. In January. They said that they'd heard the tape, and liked it, 'and we've got some equipment set up in the garage… would you like to sing while we play?' They gave me these words, *King Of Sunset Town*, and said 'just sing those!' Ten minutes later we had the verse and chorus. It was obvious from that point that we had a chemistry. It was the last thing on earth I would have wanted to do, but the four personalities in this band made the role easy for me.'

'We asked him to join,' reveals Ian Mosley, 'and he told us he'd think about it. He'd been offered a gig with The The. He'd been through grief with several record companies and was in a dilemma about joining a band. I went back to Darryl. We told him that we thought Steve had a great voice and wanted him to join. I wondered if I should send flowers to his wife, or something. But Steve got back to us eventually and said he would give it a go. We got on very well with him, straight away.'

There was some discussion about changing the band's name, but it was decided that a change of singer was not a major change in the Marillion sound or music.

'I think we made the right choice,' says Mark Kelly. 'Obviously there's some baggage with keeping the name, but we've been around long enough now that we don't have to worry about it.'

With Marillion's new vocalist in place, it was time for Pallas to come clean about their change in personnel. Graeme Murray sent a newsletter to the band's mailing list in the early weeks of 1989.

'Several weeks ago,' he wrote, 'Alan decided that it was time for him to leave the band, having spent the last twelve months predicting doom and gloom and generally depressing all of us. Perhaps the combination of our running out of money and the prospect of filling his hero Fish's boots in Marillion proved too irresistible, given the very difficult path that lies ahead for ourselves.'

Plans for their incomplete *Voices In The Dark* album, recorded with producer Mick Glossop at Great Linford Manor Studios, were abandoned.

'There was quite a lot of good music on it,' says Niall Mathewson. 'But when push came to shove, we decided it wasn't really where we, as a band, wanted to be musically.'

The cassette *Sketches*, which collected eight splendid demos sung by Alan Reed during pre-production for *Voices In The Dark*, helped to raise some much needed capital. The possibility of working with Nigel 'Axe' Atkins, who had been one of the three final candidates to replace Geoff Mann in Twelfth Night, did not develop into anything concrete. Atkins was, in his words, 'too poppy'. Despite hoping to continue with Graeme Murray as vocalist, it seemed that, after 14 years, Pallas had ground to a halt.

Return visits to Tilburg and Amsterdam for IQ on 13-14 January preceded their latest single, *Sold On You*. This was released on 6 February 1989 (with *Through My Fingers* on the B-side, and the nine-minute *Wurensh* added to the 12"). *Sold On You* is perhaps IQ's most obviously commercial song and deserved to be a huge hit. It's a terrific track but sounds nothing at all like the band's first two albums, nor anything they have done since.

Are You Sitting Comfortably? followed on 20 February. It is arguably their most simple, accessible and pop oriented album. It is impeccably produced.

It opens with *War Heroes*. Paul Menel sings particularly well here, as the track builds dramatically until Paul Cook's brightly mixed drums kick off a loud and uplifting chorus, which sails in direct contrast to the gritty lyrics. Even at 6:29, this song seems to be far too short.

The single-to-be *Drive On* is very commercial and catchy. It's songs like this which failed to satisfy either their traditional fanbase, or those who might prefer their altered direction. The clever songwriting doesn't hide a rather tired and uninspired performance.

Nostalgia is a return to full on prog rock, a short and spacey instrumental, which acts as a lead in to the magnificent eight minute *Falling Apart At The Seams*, during which the band exhibit impressive prog chops. This is a definite throwback to the IQ's earlier preference for epic, symphonic songs, even if the chorus is more It Bites than Genesis. It also points to their future, as this was one of a handful of Menel era songs that Peter Nicholls would sing after

1989: Watch The Old World Melt Away

IQ in 1989 (From the collection of Guy Tkach)

IQ supporting Mike + the Mechanics, Mainz, 10 March 1989 (From the collection of Günter Schote)

he returned to IQ.

Sold On You had preceded the album as a single. Its B-side, *Through My Fingers*, is a mainstream rock ballad with fretless bass and fluent keyboard and guitar solos. It's pure 1989 and a bold attempt at something new. Despite some clichéd lyrics, *Through My Fingers* is tremendous and a typical example of an attractive, commercial song that somehow sits right outside what you'd expect from IQ.

Wurensh is long and complex, a traditional IQ song with hints of Yes. The closing *Nothing At All*, beautiful and dramatic, is surely Paul Menel's finest moment in IQ. Huge chords, an epic production, a tight guitar solo and a simple message close out the album with a flourish.

'I agree,' Menel says, '*Nothing At All* is probably my finest moment in the band. But there was more fuel in the tank, and I think, if that album had been promoted better, the follow-up one would have been our magnum opus.'

Listeners are split over the merits of *Are You Sitting Comfortably?* As with *Nomzamo*, *Twelfth Night* and *The Wedge*, here we have a band trying hard to move on after the loss of a hugely charismatic and theatrical frontman. The more commercial journey that these bands embarked on provided some great musical moments but split their audiences. In each case, IQ, Twelfth Night and Pallas were (or had been) unable to continue in their current format.

Are You Sitting Comfortably? was released just ahead of a five week, 20 date tour of the UK and Europe with Mike + the Mechanics. These included their first shows in Denmark, Sweden and Belgium. Their set typically comprised *No Love Lost*, *Wurensh*, *Passing Strangers*, *Nothing At All*, *Sold On You*, *Widow's Peak* and *Common Ground*.

'The Mechanics tour was a bit different,' says Paul Cook. 'Europe was a much better territory to gig in for prog bands. One gig somewhere had a large IQ banner hanging over the balcony, which was nice. The tour seemed very long with lots of lengthy drives between concerts. We were now using tour buses to sleep on where the rule was drink until you drop! Or was that just me?'

'That tour really felt like a bit of a disappointment to be honest,' admits Tim Esau. 'I was really delighted that we got on to that tour as Mike Rutherford was one of my favourite bass players at the time and, of course, there was the Genesis connection. But it wasn't as huge and career boosting as I'd hoped and really signalled the end of that period of my time in IQ. Despite us going down really well at most of the shows and probably picking up lots of new fans, I basically got too impatient and too frustrated… not the best time for me at all.'

Later that spring, for IQ's own headline dates in June, support was provided by Birmingham based Ark. Ark's bassist John Jowitt would join IQ a couple of years down the line: this was the first time he met the band, but he was familiar with their work.

'I remember Mike Holmes coming up to us

A PLAYGROUND OF BROKEN HEARTS

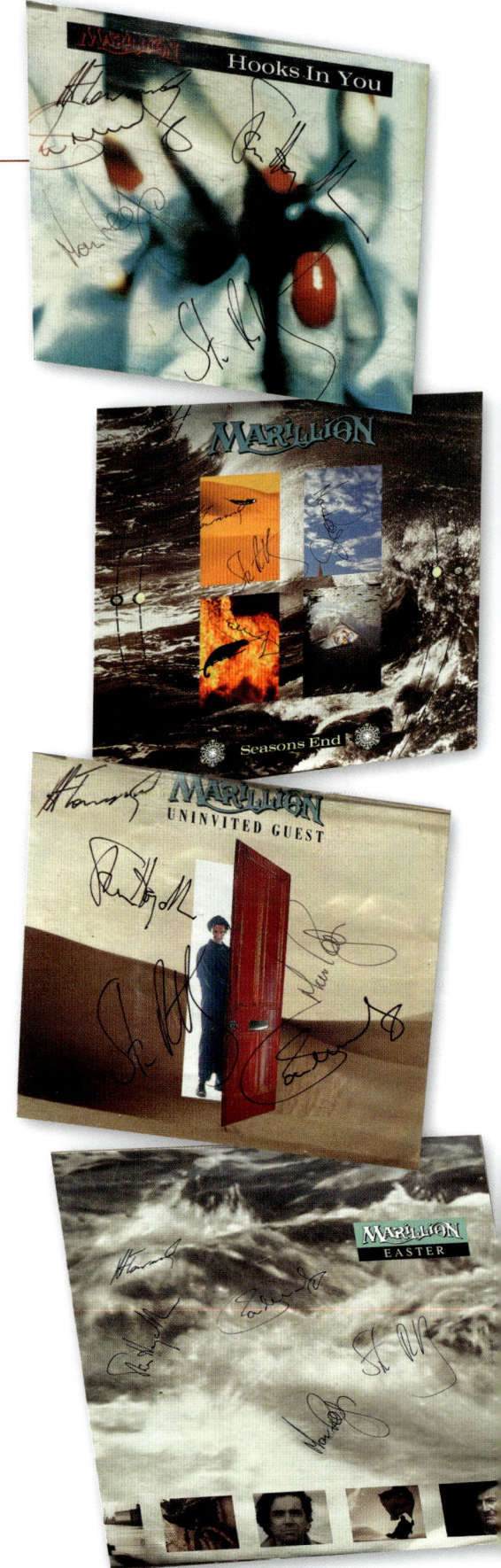

Marillion's first releases with Steve Hogarth: the album *Seasons End* and singles *Hooks In You*, *The Uninvited Guest* and *Easter* (From the collection of Gordon Graham)

at our first gig together in Birmingham [6 June],' Jowitt recalls. 'He was the first person in the band I talked to. They were kind enough to sort us out some beers. Apparently they'd been told they should make more effort talking to people! We played football against them before the Manchester gig; they rescued a 6-6 draw when they brought in some tactical substitutes, including Tim's pointy shoes… It's funny because I was regularly being told 'You remind me of IQ' by audience members at Ark gigs. Someone recommended *The Wake*, so I bought it – and fell in love with it. I used to work in Warwick at the time, so travelled to work in my Austin Metro listening to tapes. They got me from the start of *Outer Limits*.'

Jowitt also enjoyed both *Nomzamo* and *Are You Sitting Comfortably?* and agrees that Paul Menel had a great voice. But Menel didn't really engage with Ark on the tour.

'I remember wishing it was Pete up there,' Jowitt says, 'because he had a real presence on the first two albums. Paul's live versions and on *Nine In A Pond* didn't do it for me. I got talking at each gig to Anne Fox [Mike Holmes' sister], who did their merch even then. We kept in touch, and she used to come along to some Ark gigs. I remember telling her how much I loved IQ, and would love to play for them.'

Jowitt would need to be patient.

IQ's next single, *Drive On*, came out on 19 June. For the first time, this was released as a CD. There were three extra tracks: *War Heroes*, *Passing Strangers* and *Sera Sera*. A second booking at the relocated Marquee followed on 20 July.

Marillion's single *Hooks In You*, released in August 1989 and the twelfth Top 30 single for the band, would be followed by *Seasons End* that September, which entered the UK album charts at number 7.

Seasons End heralded a new period of success for the band.

Pendragon's shiny, bouncy, commercial and very appealing single *Saved By You* was released in September 1989. It was included on later reissues of *Kowtow*.

Paul Menel and Tim Esau left IQ in September 1989.

'We lost the deal with Phonogram,' explains Mike Holmes. 'At that point it seemed that Paul and Tim had a shared vision of what they wanted to do in the world of music and it didn't really fit with the rest of us. Shortly after that we all had a meeting to discuss the future of the band and it seemed that Tim and Paul had already made their minds up to go their separate ways (only together…).'

'Despite what has been written in some quarters,' says Martin Orford today, 'this was all perfectly amicable. We had lost our record deal by then and Paul and Tim wanted to pursue a more commercial direction as a duo to try to get another deal. This was absolutely fair enough.'

Orford wrote, at length, in the band's newsletter number 11.

In view of recent events, many people have been very concerned about the future of IQ, and rumours and hearsay are rife, so I'll try to explain exactly what's been happening.

One of the most frustrating features of IQ's career has been the continued apathy of Phonogram Records towards the band. Whilst Squawk Records have financed the last two albums, that record company only really existed as a provider of financial backing; the marketing, promotion and general administration of our records was left up to Phonogram, and here lay the root of the problem. With a few notable exceptions, the employees of Phonogram Records have never really liked IQ. Whether it was our type of music, or the fact that they had to work with us although they didn't want to sign the band themselves, I don't know.

One thing I do know for sure is that when we arrived back in the UK from the Mike + the Mechanics tour, the *Are You Sitting Comfortably?* album was dead as a doornail already as far as Phonogram UK were concerned. It had only been out for about two weeks, and it was abundantly clear that only the bare minimum of promotion had been done. A few press releases, and a one week advert in a couple of music papers. An office junior must have spent quite a leisurely afternoon getting that lot together.

Internationally, things had admittedly been much better. With the German and Dutch divisions of Phonogram working particularly hard on the band, but, even in these territories, album sales were relatively disappointing, despite the enthusiastic support we had received from the IQ fans in Europe.

Knowing that we needed a hit record somewhere to justify keeping our record deal, our last chance seemed to lie in the US market. Here, *Drive On* had been selected as a single, and Squawk Records had parted with a great deal of money for us to make an excellent video for this song. Then came the news that only two out of the many FM radio stations had playlisted the single, neither of whom ever played it. The video, despite being accepted by MTV, never saw the light of day either, and, by now, we were getting seriously worried about the future of our deal with Squawk. However, when news came, it was not quite as we feared; rather than simply dropping IQ, Peter Mensch informed us that he was closing down Squawk Records completely to concentrate solely on his management company. Considering the fact that Squawk had always maintained a policy of signing acts on their musical and songwriting ability rather than instant commerciality or image, its demise is a rather sad reflection on the current state of the music industry.

From our point of view, Squawk were always willing to finance every project we chose to pursue, and they must have lost hundreds of thousands of pounds on IQ alone. I can't help thinking that if they had had the time and the inclination to become directly concerned with the way their records were being marketed, rather than just sitting back and handing over the money, it could have been a very different story.

So where did all this leave IQ? By the time we heard of Squawk's demise, the UK tour had already been booked for early June, so despite the fact that we were no longer receiving any financial support the five members decided that the tour must still go ahead.

Fortunately for us, the band has many valued friends who were able to pitch in and help us to make the tour a success. With the tour out of the way, the problem still remained that the band really was in a dreadful mess. Whilst the initial intention of some band members was to try to find another record deal, there is no getting away from the fact that this is extremely unlikely. Back in 1987, when we were looking for a deal every one of the major (and pretty much most of the minor) record companies turned us down, so two years on, with two fine but unsuccessful (and also very expensive) albums behind us, there seems to be even less reason for a company to sign the band now. The material which has been emerging in rehearsals this year is far from being commercial and, short of abandoning the band's principles and opting for a completely commercial direction, it would seem that our time in the big bed (dead end) music industry has inevitably come to an end.

Having been the main writer in the band for the last couple of years, and written the music for *Promises (As The Years Go By)* and *Drive On* (neither of them commercial enough for Phonogram's liking) I know that those songs are about as commercial as we want to get, and, to be honest, if we continued in that vein, we would lose the real essence of IQ. However reviewing the situation with the members of the band present, we finally realised that IQ was becoming separated by two musical ideologies, both of which would become increasingly frustrated if things were to continue in the present format.

So what for the future? PL and Tim are planning together soon to do some song writing, perhaps with the ultimate intention of getting a new band together. They are both intent on staying in the music business if possible, and they have the good wishes of myself and everyone connected with IQ.

As far as I am concerned the established music industry can go screw itself. I'm sick to death of this band being regarded as some kind of joke because we play progressive rock, and as a result being sneered at, if not downright sabotaged. Progressive rock is Britain's finest musical export, as anyone who grew up in the seventies will testify, but Britain has shunned its own music as willingly as it has accepted music from other cultures with the result that today's stars are the stars of the 1970s, and Britain's producing no lasting acts at all.

I've a sneaking suspicion that when the likes of Paul McCartney, Phil Collins, Tina Turner, Bruce Springsteen, Mark Knopfler and those other people that are always turning up and playing at each other's gigs decide they've made enough money and want to retire, the record companies are going to be left with no artists on their rosters, and no semi-pro music scene from which to sign any more. Perhaps then they'll regret not investing for the future whilst the raw materials were available.

As for IQ, we are planning to play a 'farewell to Tim and Paul' gig at the Marquee on 1 September, after which Mike, Paul Cook and myself are intending to stay together, adding new members as soon as possible and hopefully returning to the Marquee in the Autumn (with or without the new members). We then intend to start recording the next album as soon as possible. We would hope that all future IQ records will reflect the progressive rock tradition of the band, which will mean that we may have to start our own independent record company to achieve this.

If our music has brought you enjoyment and excitement in the past, I hope, under happier circumstances, we may be able to continue to enjoy your support in the future, coz we think you're a gaggle of groovy geese for being so gorgeous. (truth).

'We lost belief in ourselves,' Menel explains. 'The whole thing imploded. But I'll always be proud of those two albums.'

'Paul was certainly a big part of that period,' agrees Tim Esau. 'But we all were. Even I wrote some of the main bits of the really unpopular songs – *Sold On You*, *Through My Fingers*, *Passing Strangers*. On reflection, I think that something similar would have happened with whoever we chose to replace Pete and history would probably still show it to be our least appreciated period by the wider IQ fanbase. I actually really quite enjoyed the earlier times of being signed to Phonogram myself – until it all fell to bits!'

IQ's last gig with Paul Menel and Tim Esau, 1 September 1989, featured *Promises (As The Years Go By)*, *Wurensh*, *No Love Lost*, *Nomzamo*, *Through My Fingers*, *Still Life*, *Nostalgia*, *Falling Apart At The Seams*, *Passing Strangers*, *War Heroes*, *Sold On You*, *Human Nature*, *Nothing At All*, *Common Ground*, *Sweet Transvestite* and *Colourflow*.

'Thank you very much,' Paul said as he left the stage. 'You've been fabulous. Thank you for four great years.'

IQ subsequently recruited Les Marshall, formerly of The Lens and more recently of Jadis, on bass.

'The band then went into something of a hiatus,' says Martin Orford, 'though we did start writing some material with Les Marshall.'

'I really thought it was the end at the time,' recalls Paul Cook.

Going Underground:
The 1990s And Beyond

Out of the blue IQ were offered a show in Paris on 22 February 1990.

Martin Orford: 'As I recall, they were prepared to pay us quite a lot of money. The problem was that it had to be with Peter Nicholls. I didn't much like the idea, as I thought we would be raking over old ground, but Pete seemed happy to do it, so things gradually swung round to that way of thinking. We did a bit of a trial show at The Marquee, 6 January 1990, where having miraculously managed to avoid going to another Hells Angels' party, I did the vocals for most of the set with Pete coming on for the encore to a rapturous reception… hardly surprising after an hour or more of my singing.'

'Mike had phoned me a few weeks before,' Peter says, 'asking if I'd like to join IQ on stage for the encore. Of course, I said yes. We decided to do *The Enemy Smacks* in all its theatrical glory, and *Awake And Nervous*. It was a great moment. We all really enjoyed it, and the audience went nuts. I don't know how but a French promoter had heard about this, before the gig happened, and he offered us a slot on the bill in Paris, supporting Magma, but on the condition that I was in the line-up. The rest of the band were initially unsure as the Marquee encore was just a one-off thing, it certainly wasn't me rejoining the band. Eventually, we decided to do the Paris show, and I believed this would mark the end of my musical career. I hadn't been asked to rejoin IQ, in fact the plan was for them to recruit a new singer. My band Niadem's Ghost had folded in 1987, and I had no intention of starting another one, so this was the end of the road for me, and a nice way to go out.'

Orford: 'We did the Paris show and after that it became pretty obvious that Pete was rejoining and that seemed the natural direction of travel. On the way back from Paris, we got stuck in traffic for hours and eventually tried to get home by attempting to steal a cross-channel hovercraft, but that's another story.'

The Paris concert, where they supported Magma, was the only show by this iteration of IQ. The band were badly shaken when Les Marshall committed suicide later that year.

'That really came out of left field,' Mike Holmes suggests, 'and for a while I think we all had some kind of 'survivor's guilt', and it felt almost disloyal to think about the band. It was a shock and it took a long time to get past it, but that kind of thing makes you appreciate the things and the people that you still have in your life. There was a general feeling of 'We need to start looking after each other', so in a way we managed to take the awful tragedy of Ledge's death and turn it into some kind of positive outcome. Still miss him today.'

'It was after Les died and we all met at his funeral that the idea of reuniting, as friends more than anything, started to present itself,' says Peter Nicholls.

In the meantime Martin Orford moonlighted with Jadis and Mike Holmes set up a new record label, Giant Electric Pea, releasing an IQ rarities collection, *J'ai Pollette D'arnu*, in June 1991.

And John Jowitt saw an opportunity.

'After Les died,' says John Jowitt, 'I reminded Mike's sister Anne that I'd told her I'd love to play with IQ. She said, 'You'd leave Ark?' I said I already had!'

Peter Nicholls: 'We started up again with John. It was basically a group of friends doing this. It wasn't that big a thing about me rejoining the band or anything. I certainly didn't see it that way. I was just happy to be with friends again. Since then, the band seems stronger than ever. The relationships have been a lot easier and more relaxed, and I think that now we have a lot more space within the band to do what we do best.'

'I could see it was a difficult time for them,' John Jowitt observes. 'They'd lost the major label deal and were setting up Giant Electric Pea. Pete was back, which the fans welcomed. And then there was me, so all in all a big change for the band.'

Paul Menel and Tim Esau subsequently wrote songs together for their own project, Raising Cain.

'Spurred on by our enthusiasm for the poppier, more commercial sound, Paul and I worked on a few songs after we left IQ,' Esau explains. 'We had a little home studio set up in a shared flat and did some stuff at Orinoco Studios with Gerard Johnson, who had engineered for the mix of *Nomzamo*. We even made a video. We touted a few of these songs around the usual labels but received a complete lack of interest. Outside pressures to actually earn some money, and life in general, though, eventually saw us spend more time painting and decorating and landscape gardening than making music. Things finally ground to a halt when I started spending some time in the USA with my then girlfriend and I saw less and less of Paul.'

'We recorded a few tracks,' Menel says, 'but it was never going to work out.'

'I got so fed up with nothing happening that I started working on another project with someone else,' Tim contends.

'So we called it a day,' concedes Menel.

Peter Nicholls' first full show back with IQ was at The Marquee on 6 July 1991.

John Jowitt: 'I remember that a review of our first gig at The Marquee said something along the lines of 'John Jowitt clearly doesn't get IQ, he moves around too much…' Then there were deaths of close friends and family members around the band at the time, including a little later, Geoff Mann, who we played a couple of shows with when I was there, and who the band knew well. So, a difficult time.'

Consistency was important. Through sheer hard work and bloody-mindedness IQ, now with day jobs, would retain their Nicholls / Holmes / Orford / Jowitt / Cook line-up for the next 14 years. They released the much admired *Ever* in 1993.

'*Ever* was a culmination of everything we'd done and learned up to that point,' explains Mike Holmes. 'We were able to write and play anything we wanted, and we'd learnt a lot from the two producers we'd worked with. It was great to write something in 13/8 and feel the freedom to develop it in a way that best suited the track. Working with Terry Brown on *Are You Sitting Comfortably?* was a great masterclass in production for me. I was able to take that approach and apply it to the recording and mixing of *Ever*, and I think it really stepped up our game of self-producing. And, of course, it was the first proper IQ album on GEP, so there was an added impetus and a sense that this was finally all ours.'

'It was a great album,' says John Jowitt, 'and one that has a real atmosphere about it, for me, reflecting all that was going on. It showed we could do this. And have fun.'

Several other albums of new material would follow: *Subterranea* (released in 1997 and 'where the 1990s IQ really hits its stride', according to Martin Orford), *Seven Stories Into 98* (1998), *The Seventh*

House (2000) and *Dark Matter* (2004), featuring the magnificent *Harvest Of Souls*.

Paul Cook took a four year sabbatical from 2005 to 2009. Martin Orford would leave the band he co-founded in 2007.

'I've never had any regrets about leaving IQ,' he says, 'and had I stayed, I think the band would have quickly self-destructed. The fact that it still exists today is justification enough that I made the right decision.'

John Jowitt, after 19 years with IQ, stepped down in 2010. Tim Esau returned on bass, and, with Neil Durant on keyboards, IQ have retained a stable line-up since then, perform regularly and release new albums every five years or so. *The Road Of Bones*, the band's astounding 11th album, would reach the lower reaches of the German albums chart in mid-2014. Both *Resistance* (2019) and *Dominion* (2025) evidence a band with plenty more left to say.

Peter Nicholls: 'IQ has been a constant for most of our adult lives. In over 40 years, we've survived more than our fair share of challenges and struggles, but this is a unique family which extends to our crew and audience, and there's great strength in that. We're proud of our achievements and our longevity, and crucially we still enjoy what we do together. There are no ego clashes and arguments, we support each other and we're not done yet. We'll keep going as long as we're able to and as long as people still want to hear what we create.'

Paul Menel formed The Great Outdoors in the mid-1990s, the first of several musical projects over the years.

'I'm more proud of the work I did with them than with any other band I've ever worked with,' he says. 'That album, *Carpenter From Nazareth Seeks Joiners*, is still my favourite. It's timeless and still sounds fresh. I shone brightly but briefly in the IQ night sky and left a legacy of sorts. My era is long gone.'

After five years of inactivity, during which time Alan Reed moved to London to work for the BBC, Pallas reunited in 1993.

'Mike [Stobbie] kept in touch as we both lived in London, and eventually persuaded me to re-join,' Reed recalls. 'We did the odd gig, and worked on various demos that became *Beat The Drum*. Everyone had a day job, and it was hard to find the time to make it work. I think it was Graeme bumping into Ronnie at the supermarket which became the catalyst for him re-joining the band [in 1996] and *Beat The Drum* finally taking shape. Mike was by far the flashier keys player, but Graeme and Niall had more of a rapport with Ronnie.'

'Ronnie was in Aberdeen,' Mike notes, 'whereas I would have to drive 1,100 miles with all my keyboards from London to write, record, rehearse and play with them. This could only be for two days, once a week or fortnight. So Ronnie it was.'

'Between 1986 and 1997, I had some of the best fun you could imagine, playing with local Aberdeen musicians in various covers bands,' Ronnie admits. 'And by the time I clocked back into Pallas in 1997, I was ready for a huge helping and more of progressive rock! For me, 1997 to the present day has been the most enjoyable period of involvement. We may have played bigger gigs in the earlier years, but there was an underlying security in the latter years where I felt that we were more in control of what we were doing, and exactly how we wanted to connect with the industry. In the former years, it felt like we were always being swept along by events, never quite fully in control.'

Pallas' comeback album, *Beat The Drum*, was released in 1999, with Colin Fraser replacing long-time drummer Derek Forman, who had left after the sessions, necessitating re-recording of all of the drum parts. By now the band was purely a spare time activity, but they released new albums in 2001 and 2005 and carried out some short tours.

Alan Reed: 'We ran it as a small business, doing an album and tour every four or five years. It was as much as we could manage, and any money we made was reinvested into equipment and studio time. None of us have ever made much from Pallas!'

The Cross & The Crucible (2001) and *The Dreams Of Men* (2005) would both be followed by reunion gigs with Euan Lowson, with each singer fronting the band for different songs.

Alan Reed's last gig with Pallas was at The Peel in Kingston on Thames on 5 December 2009.

'I received a call from Graeme saying I was out of the band,' he recalls, 'and there was an email in my inbox explaining why.'

'Alan was genuinely bereft by this,' suggests Mike Bentley. 'He was shaken to the core and felt betrayed, I think. But at that stage the band justifiably believed that he'd lost interest. It was a bad set of circumstances.'

Reed was replaced by Paul Mackie, who had been fronting drummer Colin Fraser's side-project Blues Deluxe. Mackie recorded two new albums with Pallas: *XXV* (2011) and *Wearewhoweare* (2014). Reed, to everyone's surprise, not least his own, rejoined Graeme Murray, Niall Mathewson and Ronnie Brown to reform Pallas in 2022. A new album, the dark, dense and wholly worthwhile *The Messenger*, followed in 2023.

The 1984-1986 version of Twelfth Night reunited for the final time in 1993 to pay tribute to Geoff Mann, who had died of cancer in February 1993.

'After Geoff passed away, and it was decided to make the tribute album, *Mannerisms*, it seemed obvious that Twelfth Night should get together again for a contribution,' says co-producer Clive Nolan. 'I think only such a tragic loss could have brought those boys back together then. There seemed to be a lot of… tension there! I had already worked with Brian Devoil on the *Casino* album, and he suggested recording at Thin Ice. We did actually get the whole band in one room for a whole two minutes at one point.'

Mannerisms was released on SI Music in September 1994, with profits split between cancer research charities and Geoff's family. Peter Nicholls appears on three very different songs, including a magnificent new version of *Apathetic And Here, I…* with IQ. Prog contemporaries Jadis, who at the time also had amongst their members IQ's keyboard player Martin Orford and bassist John Jowitt, provided a fine rendition of *Never Mind*. Pendragon reworked *Human Being* and Clive Nolan arranged and orchestrated a gorgeous version of *Love Song*, with vocals by Pallas' Alan Reed.

The mid-1990s saw progressive music at its lowest commercial ebb: Marillion's EMI contract was terminated in 1995 after their eighth studio album, *Afraid Of Sunlight*, had peaked at number 16, their lowest chart placing to date.

John Arnison: 'It's funny that they were dropped by EMI because an album only sold 250,000! Today that would be number 1 all over the world, but that's what happened. EMI decided they would rather invest in a new artist rather than pay Marillion the advance due.'

Marillion signed with Castle Communications who released *This Strange Engine* (1997), *Radiation* (1998) and *marillion.com* (1999).

Independent record companies including SI Music, Giant Electric Pea and Inside Out Music would commence re-releasing classic prog albums, as well as supporting new releases. SI Music released new albums by Geoff Mann, Citizen Cain and Landmarq, and developed a close working relationship with Clive Nolan. Giant Electric Pea released IQ's *Ever* – the band's first full album since it had parted with Mercury Records – and subsequently music by Big Big Train, Threshold, John Wetton, Spock's Beard and others, as well as IQ's back catalogue and new releases.

The Classic Rock Society was formed in 1991 and did much to support progressive music for the next 28 years. They promoted gigs by IQ, Pallas, Pendragon and Twelfth Night, as well as older bands such as Camel, Caravan, Steve Hackett, Rick Wakeman and the Strawbs, and newer groups such as Magenta, Mostly Autumn, Spock's Beard, The Tangent, Threshold and Touchstone.

'In 1991 we were absolutely on our knees,' Pendragon's Nick Barrett admits. 'We had tons of debt. There was no way forward. I was doing a bread round job, renting a room, had a crappy car. And it was awful. But we managed to raise enough money to make one more album, which I thought will pay off all the bills, and then we'll see where we go – we'll just make an album we like. And that was *The World*. Within two weeks of its release everything changed. Eventually, as a result of that, I bought a house and got a studio and life improved.'

Pendragon would reach a new peak with their fifth album *The Masquerade Overture* (1996), which sold 60,000 copies. They were also finding that there was a huge demand for prog music in Poland.

'It turns out that since the communist era, a guy called Piotr Kaczkowski had been smuggling records into the country under lorries and playing them on [pirate radio station] Warsaw 3,' Nick Barrett said. 'So we [went] over, and the first gig we do there's over a thousand people. It was unbelievable, almost like a religious experience. I've never seen such joy on people's faces. Kids just got on the stage, the security guards got completely overrun, and we played the whole set again because they wouldn't let us leave.'

This was a huge boost for a band which had never signed a major recording deal.

'I was able to buy quite a nice house in Ascot,' Barrett recalled. 'I remember looking out of the window, thinking: 'All the years of struggling, it's finally paid off.' Then within a couple of months I got divorced. I lost the house, lost my marriage and I was in bits. It was the biggest fuck-up I've ever had in my life.'

This period of personal chaos led to the emotional album *Not Of This World* in 2001, which, with Barrett nearing 40, emphasised a growing maturity in his songwriting. The familiar West Country burr and distinctive guitar playing is still in place, surrounded by Clive Nolan's keyboard arrangements, which can only be described as 'lush'.

Long-term drummer Fudge Smith left in 2006 after a disagreement over band finances, but Nick Barrett, Peter Gee and Clive Nolan continue to perform and record as Pendragon.

Going Underground: The 1990s And Beyond

'Things happen in waves,' Nick Barrett suggests. 'I was pissed off about illegal downloading for a period of time. But you've got to pick yourself up, brush yourself off and find some other way of making it work for you. We've done that for 45 years with no management and no record company.'

Barrett's drive is still strong. Now based in Cornwall, he's not slowing down yet.

'Nick was born to do music,' says Peter Gee. 'Pendragon certainly intend to carry on recording and touring for as long as we can. Nick and Clive often joke about carrying on just to spite people, but the reality is that we all love doing it. And I guess the day when Nick no longer loves it will be the day that Nick stops. But at present I can't see that day coming in any way. And whilst the pandemic initially threatened to end touring and left Nick without any new income for nearly three years, it made us all fall in love with music all over again, and realise just how much we missed it. I personally owe Nick so much for giving me the opportunity to become a part of this wonderful band that is Pendragon.'

Clive Nolan, too, is as busy as ever, as he manages multiple projects from his rambling Victorian pile in Herefordshire. He has built his own, in his words, 'Viking mead hall' for events on site.

Marillion have released 15 studio albums without a line-up change since 1989. With their contract with Castle Communications fulfilled, Marillion asked their fans if they would help to fund the recording of their next album by pre-ordering ahead of recording sessions. The result was astonishing: an impressive 12,674 pre-orders raised enough money to record and release *Anoraknophobia* at the beginning of May 2001. A year later, Marillion held their first weekend event at Pontins Holiday Park, Brean Sands, in the West Country. Fans attended from all over the world for three days of Marillion, including three full concerts. A second weekend followed in March 2003 at Butlin's in Minehead. Many more have followed, both in the UK and further afield.

The success of the *Anoraknophobia* pre-order would establish a business model that has sustained the band ever since. 2004's *Marbles* was offered for pre-order mid-production and 18,000 fans responded. They unexpectedly returned to the singles chart in 2004 when *You're Gone*, the lead single from *Marbles*, gave them their first Top 10 hit since 1987. 2016's *FEAR* would make the Top 5 in the UK, and the following October they performed for the first time at the prestigious Royal Albert Hall playing *FEAR* in full.

'That was one night where it felt that everything was working perfectly,' Mark Kelly said. 'The band were on fire.'

Reflecting on more than 40 years of success, founding member Steve Rothery remains thankful.

'To get a record deal is like winning the lottery,' he says. 'To have a successful album is like winning the lottery twice. To be still doing it 40 odd years later, then you've been winning the lottery every few years. But then again, hopefully you have to have something special that puts you there in the first place, some ability, talent or individuality.'

2022's *An Hour Before It's Dark* would give Marillion their second highest album chart placing ever, reaching number 2 in the UK (and in Germany and the Netherlands).

'Being in a band is like walking a tightrope,' says Ian Mosley. 'But we've been together such a long time and the older we get, the mellower and more forgiving we've become. We all get on very well.'

Marillion founder member Mick Pointer joined Clive Nolan in Arena in 1995, with 10 studio albums to their name so far.

'Mick was sucked back to the dark side,' Nolan suggests.

From 2008 Pointer toured with Nick Barrett and others as Mick Pointer's Script, performing material from his time with Marillion.

Against all expectations, Twelfth Night reunited in 2007, with Mark Spencer replacing Rick Battersby. Well received gigs in Kingston upon Thames and Deptford were followed by three more in 2008, including the Tiana Festival in Spain. Further gigs in 2010 resulted in a new live album, *MMX*. 2018 saw a first ever studio version of *Sequences*, recorded by the remaining Twelfth Night trio of Andy Revell, Brian Devoil and Mark Spencer. Geoff Mann makes an appearance using vocal tracks from unused 1983 live recordings. All royalties from the sale of this album were donated in Geoff's memory to The Royal British Legion.

Andy Glass and Marc Elton relaunched Solstice in 1992 with the album *New Life*, which comprised new recordings of older songs such as *Morning Light*, *The Sea*, *Pathways*, and *Guardian*. They were joined by vocalist Heidi Kemp, drummer Peter Hemsley and bassist Craig Sunderland.

Martin Wright: 'I had kept in touch with Andy, and when he and Marc were recording *New Life* I voiced my interest in helping with the drum parts. I had joined a popular local band called Togmor and with my focus on them the *New Life* thing never happened. Perhaps I should have been more proactive…'

Glass toured as the guitar player for American soul legends Bill Withers and Geno Washington during this period, as well as undertaking session work. *Circles* (1997) features a completely new set of Solstice songs. The album introduced singer Emma Brown and fiddle player Jenny Newman. Clive Bunker, of the classic Jethro Tull line-up, played drums on *Circles* and on the tour that followed.

'I recorded the *Circles* album in the downtime between session work,' Andy Glass says. 'I was engineering at Audiolab in Buckingham where I produced an album for Mick Abrahams [*One*]. Ian Anderson came in to record some flute and blues harp and we got on well. A few days later I got the call from Tull's production manager saying Ian would like a musician on 'front of house' sound. An audition was arranged for me in Ian's studio at his Wiltshire pile, where I was given three hours to mix a track from *Roots To Branches*… that's when I discovered Ian likes a chat… with the conversation over, I was left with no more than an hour. It forced me to be very straightforward with the mix, keep it simple and avoid all but the most essential processing. It turned out he was doing me a favour. Several of the cream of FOH engineers, whose 'auditions' had preceded mine had, in Ian's opinion, over-processed the mixes. This was a pet hate of his. I was offered the job and would spend the next couple of years touring extensively with the band. I met Emma through singer and studio client John Maguire, who would later add vocals to *Sacred Run* from *Circles* and *Warriors* from *Prophecy*. Emma was just out of her music degree at the time and looking for gigs. I was already working with Jenny Newman when we recorded *Circles*, but she was touring Canada with Rock Salt and Nails during the recording sessions, so Marc came back one last time. He was focusing on his own studio and playing semi-acoustic gigs down in Swansea. His problems with tinnitus stemming from a decade earlier meant touring with us wasn't an option.'

Martin Wright moved to Calgary, Canada, in 2006 and currently plays with The Prairie Dogz, who signed a five year agreement with Emanant Music/Blues Vox Records in 2022.

A second and more permanent Solstice reunion took place in 2007, with Emma Brown singing once again and Pete Hemsley from the mid-1990s iteration returning on drums. Playing bass was Robin Phillips, whose mother, Margaret, played piano on Solstice's debut album. Two albums followed, *Spirit* (2010) and *Prophecy* (2013). Three of the band's members, Andy Glass, Jenny Newman and Pete Hemsley, perform and record as 3 Sticks. Andy also teaches guitar.

Solstice's current line-up, together since 2020, features singer Jess Holland and has generated some of the best reviews of their career. The album *Sia* – released on Giant Electric Pea – saw a band back at full strength and, as a lovely bonus, includes a tremendous reworking of their 1980s' song *Cheyenne*. The follow up, *Light Up* (2023), is simply magnificent. Their most recent, *Clann*, was released in April 2025. As Gregory Spawton says, 'I was lucky enough to hear an advance copy of *Clann*. It may well be a career high for Solstice.'

Andy Glass: 'For years Solstice was almost like a vanity project, really. I didn't see it like that, but it was - we'd do an album occasionally and a few gigs each year. I'd missed the kind of creative partnership I had with Marc Elton but like a gift from the gods, suddenly it's there again with Jess. It's been life changing, I think for both of us. You know, this is 'it', and I'm so grateful for that at this point in my life. Belatedly, I feel ambitious and driven. As ever, not for commercial success or money but to make the best music we can and play it to as many people as possible. I can see how all the hard work of the last few years has had a profound impact and that's so motivating and fulfilling for me. It feels like we're just getting started.'

Calling All The Heroes

The six bands which are the main focus of this book weren't the only players of note in the Marquee based progressive rock scene of the 1980s. Other talented and ambitious groups of musicians from across the country were gigging and recording, including Cardiacs from London, The Enid from Kent, Chesterfield's Dagaband, Airbridge from Norwich, Essex's Tamarisk, Middlesex band Liaison, Multi-Story from South Wales, Sheffield's Haze, Trilogy from Essex, Cumbria's It Bites and London's Quasar.

The Enid were founded in 1973 by the enigmatic (perhaps eccentric would be a better adjective) Robert John Godfrey. They first appeared at The Marquee as early as February 1976 and were particularly prominent in the key years of our story, 1983 to 1986. It was their fifth album, their first with vocals, 1983's *Something Wicked This Way Comes*, that placed them squarely within the 1980s' prog scene. They appeared at the Reading Festival that year on a bill that included Pallas, Solstice, Pendragon, Marillion and Twelfth Night.

The Enid provided support opportunities for Dagaband, Solstice, Pendragon, IQ and Twelfth Night between 1983 and 1986, so will have been very familiar to fans of these bands.

Their *Friday Rock Show* session, broadcast 25 February 1983, and seemingly permanent booking at the Reading Festival (1976, 1981, 1983, 1984, 1986, 1987) ensured a regular gig schedule despite a lack of commercial success. Whilst gigs have become less frequent in recent years, The Enid performed six shows in 2024.

*

Dagaband had also started in 1973, formed by brothers Greg and Phil Boynton. They originated in Chesterfield, Derbyshire, and first appeared at The Marquee in 1975 supporting a long forgotten band called The One. Headline slots followed in June and September 1975, a support slot in June 1982 (with Budgie headlining) and they shared the bill with Marillion in December 1982. This led to a booking with Solstice, Pallas and Twelfth Night at the venue three weeks later.

Dagaband released only one single and two EPs

Greg Boynton of Dagaband
(Photograph by
Mark Drake)

Cardiacs' compilation cassette from 1989 (courtesy Mark Guenther)

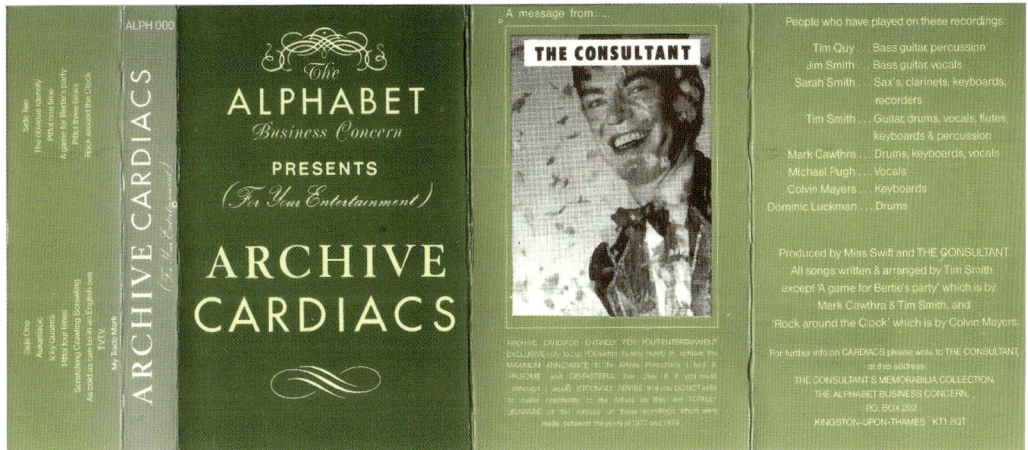

before splitting in 1987. They later reformed for occasional gigs. Both Greg and Phil Boynton have now sadly passed away.

Sean Worrall: 'Dagaband were by far the biggest prog band in the north. Dagaband were playing the big stage at Bangor University while Marillion were still playing the bar.'

*

Cardiacs were formed in 1977 in Kingston upon Thames by brothers Tim and Jim Smith, initially using the name Cardiac Arrest.

Their debut single *A Bus For A Bus On The Bus* in 1979 was followed by a self-released cassette only album called *The Obvious Identity* in June 1980. They shortened their name to Cardiacs the following spring and, after many line-up changes, and two more cassette albums, settled as a six piece in autumn 1984. Whilst not strictly a prog band – Cardiacs fused many musical influences into their own idiosyncratic and unique sound – there are enough progressive rock elements to intrigue and satisfy prog fans with open minds. They appeared at The Marquee over 30 times, starting in August 1983.

Their first major breakthrough was supporting Marillion on their *Real To Reel* tour in late 1984, apparently at the personal invitation of Marillion's vocalist, Fish, presumably after he saw one of their performances at The Marquee.

'Unfortunately,' writes Mr Spencer on the Louder Than War music blog, 'the headliners' audiences took an extreme dislike to the strange opening act and, as word spread, fans travelled to venues fully prepared to make merry with missiles. When a typically hostile reception was dished out at London's Hammersmith Odeon, Marillion's frontman Fish launched an angry onstage rant at his own narrow-minded fans. 'If you don't like it,' he told them, 'fuck off to the bar and let them get on with their set.' However, the well meaning singer's cause was lost a few days later in Manchester when his fans attempted to set fire to the safety curtain during Cardiacs' set…'

The band dropped out of the last three dates of the tour.

Cardiacs played the Reading Festival on 24 August 1986. The following April the video for *Tarred And Feathered* (from the *Big Ship* mini-album) was broadcast on Channel 4's music show *The Tube*. This was Cardiacs' first exposure on national television. A radio session on Janice Long's BBC show, broadcast in December 1987, preceded their first proper albums, *A Little Man And A House And The Whole World Window* (1988) and *On Land And In The Sea* (1989). *Is This The Life?*, a single lifted from the

A PLAYGROUND OF BROKEN HEARTS

Paul McMahon, Arthur Deas and Chris McMahon in Sheffield, ca. 1982 (Courtesy Chris McMahon)

former, crept into the lower end of the UK singles chart: their only chart entry of any kind in their home country.

Sean Worrall: 'Cardiacs have been described as: fairground music; punk rock; prog rock; beautiful; frightening; deadly serious; total euphoria; ugly; sexy; avant garde; pop genius; totally genuine; disturbing; uplifting… Let's cut this attempt short, let's just say that they really are all things to all people. Just remember that a ridiculous number of their fans loathed them on first hearing, then (by some mysterious process that we're still unable to fathom) suddenly had to run to a record shop five years later to buy all their albums.'

Cardiacs continue to record and tour, despite the premature death of Tim Smith in 2020.

*

Haze, one of the hardest-working bands on the circuit, was formed by the McMahon brothers, Paul (guitar and vocals) and Chris (bass, keyboards and vocals) in Sheffield in May 1978.

'We started playing in the mid-'70s, when I was 15 and Paul was 13,' says Chris McMahon. 'We were brought up on music. I have memories of hearing Holst and Tchaikovsky when I was young and we liked the classic British bands of the '60s - The Beatles, The Rolling Stones, The Animals. I think you have the roots of prog rock there: the power of British Beat mixed with the polyrhythms and polytonality of classical music. I learned to play keyboards on my mum's piano at home. We had an old acoustic guitar and Paul learned to play really quickly. I'd play bass lines on that old acoustic as well, and eventually our parents bought us electric instruments for Christmas. A little later we started in school bands, and we were writing original songs even then. I was a huge fan of Slade, Deep Purple, Uriah Heep… then I discovered Pink Floyd, Genesis, King Crimson, Yes… We wrote *The Exile Song* and *Seven Stones* in the very early days.'

They picked up a cheap drum kit ('second hand for 30 quid') and recorded some demos onto a two track reel to reel.

'I'd play drums and Paul would play rhythm guitar onto one track,' Chris remembers. 'Then I'd overdub bass at the time same that Paul added lead guitar onto the second track. We'd then copy it onto a cassette machine, and I'd add organ and Paul would sing. We weren't great musicians, but we were sufficiently good to look down on disco and punk. We were already snobs by then!'

Chris was still only 17 when he formed Haze with his brother and friends from school. Initially a four piece, Haze slimmed down to a trio in 1979 and, with Chris at university in Salford and Paul still at school in Sheffield, they went through a series of drummers before settling on Paul Chisnell in July 1983.

Haze had a do it yourself ethic. They worked as their own managers, booking agents, engineers, producers, manufacturers and distributors.

'It's not any kind of elitism on our part,' says Chris McMahon. 'We simply never found anyone we wanted to work with.'

They spread the word by almost constant touring. Initially gigging almost exclusively in South Yorkshire, when they went full-time in 1983 Haze

Haze's self-released single, 1981
(Courtesy Mark Guenther)

started booking themselves across the UK: 123 gigs in 1983, 134 in 1984, 160 in 1985. They bought and kitted out an old ambulance, hired a trailer for their gear and PA and drove themselves everywhere.

'I would spend hours scouring the back pages of *Sounds*,' Chris says, 'going through the gig adverts, looking for venues, then run up huge phone bills calling them asking for gigs. Nine times out of ten they'd tell you to get lost. But our persistence paid off. Eventually we had a list of places that we knew would take us. We started to draw crowds at our regular venues in Sheffield, York, Nottingham and Northampton. We often did little runs of four or five gigs together. We might play Nottingham on a Wednesday night, Birmingham the next night, then on to, say, Bristol and Cardiff and back via London for a couple of nights at home before doing it all again. But we played everywhere, sleeping in the van in lay-bys if it was too far to come home.'

'Touring with Haze, while perpetually hilarious, wasn't exactly glamorous,' says Twice Bitten's Rog Patterson. 'Budgets were zero, hotels were unheard of. Nothing makes one question one's career choice as much as waking up at 4am, freezing cold, lying across the front seats of a decommissioned ambulance, in February, in a snowy car park in Motherwell.'

When not away from home, Haze would also often provide local support for visiting prog bands, including IQ (Sheffield University, 19 October 1983), Solstice (The Leadmill, 2 October 1983; Sheffield University, 20 March 1985), Pallas (The Leadmill, 14 August 1984) and Pendragon (Sheffield University, 11 November 1987).

Haze fans were entertained by the band's idiosyncratic but professional looking newsletter *The Hum*. Fan club members were sent exclusive cassette releases recorded in their own studio called The Cellar in the family home in Fir Street, Sheffield. *The Cellar Tapes* (March 1983) was the first of a long series of self-produced cassettes.

Haze performed at The Marquee eight times in two and a half years. The first occasion was supporting Solstice on 7 January 1984.

'We had supported Solstice in Sheffield, and they invited us to play at The Marquee with them,' says Chris McMahon. 'That was our first big break, actually. The guys in Pendragon were also very helpful.'

'My main memory of our first Marquee gig was the noise and sheer enthusiasm of 400 prog fans,'

Chris McMahon at The Marquee, 11 August 1984 (Photograph by Dave Jones)

enthuses guitarist Paul McMahon. 'We were used to the hard slog of provincial pub gigs where we had to win over reluctant punters who weren't necessarily fans of us, or prog in general. It was a very new experience to play to such a large audience of committed fans, and to sell bucketloads of cassettes, albums and T-shirts. I believe we still have fans today who first saw us at that gig.'

Haze supported Pendragon at The Marquee on 11 August 1984, 20 October 1984, 18 May 1985 and 1 June 1985, as well as performing around the country with Pendragon, IQ, Pallas, Solstice, LaHost and Dagaband.

Paul McMahon: 'Pendragon gigs were excellent. We were definitely building a following there, usually bolstered by a 53 seater coach full of Haze fans from York, Nottingham and Sheffield.'

Haze were due to be supported by 16 year old Steven Wilson's band Karma at the Royal in Guildford, 13 December 1984, but parents intervened and stopped Wilson and the other youngsters from appearing.

Haze were never offered a deal with a major record company. Even the idea went against the band's policy of self-sufficiency.

'I like having the image that we would have turned a deal down,' muses Chris McMahon. 'In practice, we'd probably have bitten their hand off.'

A distribution deal with Pinnacle and the formation of their own Gabadon Records (named after the family Land Rover) resulted in *C'est La Vie* being released in April 1984 on cassette and vinyl.

Actually, it has to be said that the most interesting thing about this record is the cover - a kind of cobalt plastic affair with the floor plan of a studio and the title embossed onto the front. It also smells kinda funny! Intriguing!

Ok, interest piqued, what we have inside this indie release proves very pleasant listening: well played, well executed music best appreciated in the small hours of the morning or, conversely, on drifting summer afternoons. It's not especially demanding stuff and it isn't going to have you rocking in the aisles (despite guitarist Paul McMahon's claims to guitar hero-dom at the close of *Don't Leave Me Here*, which, together with *Fallen Leaves*, are the album's best cuts).

What *C'est La Vie* does have, however, is an all-pervading atmosphere of 'to hell with it'. It sounds like an album that's arisen out of the sheer enjoyment of playing. I doubt if it's going to shift in huge quantities, but then the band probably don't care much about that. They've succeeded in making a good LP that doesn't reek of commercialism or hype or any of the usual bulls**t - it's just there to be enjoyed.

So who is going to enjoy it? Well this isn't what I would term a 'prog rock album' and I'm loath to place it in a pigeonhole, but it's that type of thing, OK? It's an album to be enjoyed by people who're into that easy listening trip, who like to hear instruments played with clarity and precision,

Chris and Paul McMahon of Haze
(Photographs by Mark Drake)

and if the band occasionally delve into deep stuff in their lyrics, well so what, it's their album.

I like this, and as an independent product it should be commended.

Dave Dickson, Kerrang! issue 73
(26 July – 8 August 1984)

Cellar Replay (April 1985) included re-recordings of older songs, or those 'which we felt deserved adequate recordings before being put out to grass' as the sleeve notes would have it. The 12" single *The Ember* followed.

Haze paid for their own recordings and also for their albums to be pressed, then delivered boxes of finished product to Pinnacle's warehouse in Orpington. Pinnacle would then distribute the albums to record shops.

Haze were also included on the important *Fire In Harmony* compilation. This, along with a feature in *Sounds* in March 1985 and generous coverage in various fanzines, led to their sole Marquee headliner on 26 August 1985, with support from Twice Bitten.

'It could just be our Yorkshire psychology,' Chris says, 'but we always felt like outsiders. Perhaps because we're northerners, or perhaps because we never bought into the

whole media bullshit game. It might sound naive if I said that we were only ever interested in the music, but we really were. We had no idea about which people in the industry you had to be nice to or all the people you had to pretend to be interested in to get noticed. So I hassled The Marquee management team, trying to get a headline and eventually they booked us. I think they must have had a cancellation as it was quite short notice. We took a coach load of fans down from Sheffield and we just about sold it out.'

That was most likely the biggest headline gig that Haze ever did.

'The headline gig was, for us, the culmination of all the long years of slog,' Paul recalls, 'although we only got the headline as a last minute cancellation, and I don't think the management expected a near sell out! Sadly, by that time, I think the management of The Marquee were losing interest in prog - they told us that they saw Pendragon as a pop/rock band—so no further headline gig was forthcoming. It's a great pity, the Wardour Street site was a hell of a venue.'

This is the gig Haze have deserved for ages, after a few support gigs at The Marquee their first headliner there. I travelled up on a coach specially laid on by Haze at a cost of £7.50 which included admission (not bad as the coach came from Sheffield through Nottingham and Northampton). Haze didn't let the crowd down and vice versa. Twice Bitten supported them, as on many occasions and as usual Haze came on at the end of the set to join them for Barclay James Harvest's *Hymn*. Haze already showing the great sense of occasion, yet humour by their various guises as they came onstage one by one. The near capacity crowd may have been slightly biased as most, if not all, were already Haze fanatics, but a reception Haze got. All the songs off their forthcoming 12" single plus all the old favourites such as *Gabadon* and *The Hum*. Haze were even bouncier than usual (if that's possible) with Chris' Medusa like hair filling the stage, his feet playing the bass pedals like Elton John on the keys. Musicianship was superb all round and it is tragic that Haze can't get another gig at The Marquee before the big change and are unfortunately unlikely to get a headliner there after. Haze will never play in front of large audiences, but it is a shame that somewhere like The Marquee should be denied them. If you haven't seen Haze for a while go again, if you've never seen them, find out what you've been missing.

Brian Hoskin, *Signals* issue 19

Two further visits to The Marquee saw Haze supporting Dumpy's Rusty Nuts (18 July 1986) and Pendragon (25 July 1986). But a nasty road traffic accident near Oxford on 1 October 1986 took the band off the road for a while.

Chris McMahon: 'We'd taken a few weeks away from touring in August and September to record a new album, which we called *Stoat And Bottle*. We got *Tunnel Vision*, our choice of single, ready for release to coincide with the tour.'

But, on the way from Sheffield to Southampton, passing Abingdon on the A34, the band wrote off their ambulance.

'That was our darkest hour,' recalls Chris, who still reels from the memories after almost 40 years.

Tunnel Vision
(From the collection of Piersandro Pallavicini)

'There were roadworks, so the road was one lane, rather than the usual dual carriageway. I remember there were two lorries heading north and one of the lorries pulled out to overtake the other, cutting off a woman in a Volvo, who was trying to overtake them both. She slammed on her brakes and lost control. I remember that Paul Chisnell was driving and he said, 'Shit, look at that car – it's going to hit some—'.'

The band's ambulance was hit head on, was tipped onto its side and slid along the road for some distance. The trailer sheared off.

Chris McMahon: 'Paul [Chisnell] broke a few ribs when he collided with the steering wheel and also broke his wrist and ankle. He needed metal plates fitting to hold them together. I lost a front tooth and couldn't walk properly for about two months. The others weren't quite so injured and most of our gear was OK, luckily, but we were badly shaken up.'

It took three months for the band to recover enough to recommence playing gigs. They used the down time to re-work *Stoat And Bottle*, which would be released in April 1987. About this time, Pinnacle, who distributed Gabadon's releases, had a change of management.

'We weren't big business to them,' Chris notes. 'They heard *Stoat And Bottle* and declined to get involved. We released it independently.'

This was a big disappointment to the band, especially as the album received a cautiously positive review in *Kerrang!*

Despite my avowed aversion to most progressive rock, I rather like this record. As a rule I would go to great lengths to avoid the likes of Marillion (bleurgh) and Yes (double bleurgh); I mean, it just ain't rock 'n' roll is it?

However Haze, whilst being unmistakably 'progressive' (now there's a misnomer) in sound, bring a refreshingly down to earth approach to an overly pretentious genre. They sing about quaint English pastimes like going to the pub, although they can't resist going on about girls called 'Ophelia' as well!

The production is surprisingly clear, considering the low budget the band must have been labouring under and vocalist/producer/guitarist Paul McMahon's gentle, melodic guitar work suits Haze's mellow tone just fine. I particularly enjoyed the instrumental *Humbug* which reminded me of Canuck superstars Saga, being almost jazzy in places.

An essential purchase for anyone still wearing bell-bottoms.

Maura Sutton

'That review is absolutely typical of the music journalism of the time,' suggests Paul McMahon. 'Reading the review, you would know exactly what the writer thought of prog in general, but you wouldn't have a clue what Haze sound like, or what sort of songs are on the album! We once had a full interview in *Sounds* with photos, and again, the interviewer (Mary Ann Hobbs) just wanted to talk to

A PLAYGROUND OF BROKEN HEARTS

Susan Robinson
(Photograph by Mark Drake)

us in the ambulance, surrounded by cooking equipment and smelly socks, and never really said a word about the music. I think she called it 'emphatically prog' whatever that means!'

The band pressed on and completed another 88 gigs in 1987, including a self-booked, self-driven two week tour of the Netherlands in September 1987.

'We did a classic Haze move,' says Chris McMahon. 'We were offered a gig at the Paradiso in Amsterdam. But they wanted us only to play there, and nowhere else in the country. We were so focussed on playing every toilet in every country, and we'd already confirmed nine dates by then, that we let it go. Maybe we'd have earned more prestige from that one gig at the Paradiso, who knows?'

Later that year their track *In The End* was included on Steven Wilson's *Double Exposure* album.

A loss of confidence after the accident, the loss of their distribution deal, the constant lack of money and a general weariness after 10 years on the road - in December 1987, for example, they played 10 consecutive nights in York, Southampton, Birmingham, Sheffield, Gravesend, Bristol, Northampton, Nottingham and Sheffield (again) - contributed to Paul Chisnell's decision to leave the band after a 10th anniversary gig at Sheffield University on 29 May 1988. Haze reconstituted as a four piece with bassist Alen Shaw and drummer Andy Feeney for 10 gigs between October and December 1988 before the band finally threw in the towel.

'We thought we'd given it our best shot,' admits Chris McMahon.

Paul, Chris and Alen recorded some demos and performed a number of gigs as, variously, Alen Shaw Quartet, World Turtle and Alien Shore in 1989 and 1991 (borrowing Fudge from Pendragon). Chris also joined the Pendragon roadcrew for a while.

The classic Haze line-up of McMahon, McMahon and Chisnell reformed in 1998. These same musicians also formed an acoustic spin-off called Treebeard later that same year. Chisnell retired in 2013 to be replaced by Paul McMahon's son Danny. At the time of writing, Haze are still performing and recording. They released their latest album (*The Water's Edge*) in July 2024. Chris McMahon, for his part, has played well over 3,000 gigs since 1978, most of them with his brother Paul.

*

Quasar was formed in 1979 by founder writer/bassist Keith Turner. Turner had been in other bands previously but wanted to write his own material and formed Quasar to perform it.

'I wrote the songs *Mission 14*, *Logic* and *UFO* first,' he says, 'thinking those three would be enough to start working with a band.'

The original members of Quasar were Turner with Steve Clarke (drums), John Clark (guitar), Geoff Banks (keyboards), Sylvan Valet (keyboards) and Mike Kenwright (vocals). Kenwright was replaced by Paul Vigrass and, after many line-up changes with only Turner remaining from the original band, Quasar released their debut album *Fire In The Sky* in 1981.

'Paul sang on the first album,' Turner recalls, 'but when we started gigging he was unhappy to perform much. We parted ways as the rest of the band wanted a more active front person. We had gigs lined up and needed a singer urgently. Someone recommended Susan Robinson as she had left Solstice. She fit right into what we wanted.'

A PLAYGROUND OF BROKEN HEARTS

Quasar at The Marquee in July 1984: Cyrus Khajavi, Dillon Tonkin, Susan Robinson, Keith Turner (Courtesy Keith Turner)

They were interviewed by *Court Jester* for issue 5 in early 1984.

Court Jester: Why did you start the band?

Keith: The band started when I got the desire to write for myself and not play other people's music. I wrote *Mission 14* and got some people together and started. Since then there's been continuing problems with people leaving. I think it's because of the type of music, you need some courage to stick at it as it's not fashionable. It seems a lot of musicians don't have the guts to play it and stick at it because it's not safe. Anyway, now we're all set, and have been going strong for the last eighteen months.

Court Jester: Who are your influences?

Keith: My influences have always been the likes of Genesis, Mike Oldfield and Gentle Giant. I also like assorted classical music, especially with a powerful sound. People's performances impress me also, and I think it's a vital aspect to the music. Of course the band is a unit and incorporates other musical tastes, but mainly we are in agreement on what we all want and like.

Court Jester: In your first three line-ups you've had male vocalists. Was the change to a female singer a conscious one?

Quasar: Is she female? Oh yes. We didn't even think about male or female singers. Sue was very professional and experienced, being from Solstice. And she liked the challenge. That was it really. The previous singer was good, but not live. He couldn't get the show together, and Sue got stuck in immediately. Basically she's damn good at it, and that's what counts.

Calling All The Heroes

Quasar's live tape, 1985
(Courtesy Mark Guenther)

With keyboard player Dillon Tonkin now on board, Quasar played hundreds of shows over the next few years.

Turner: 'We gigged up and down the country. We got supports with Solstice, IQ and Trilogy and then The Marquee's manager, Nigel Hutchings, said we should move up to headlining.'

They duly headlined The Marquee in March and November 1984.

Turner: 'We sold out every show from the start, which was extremely encouraging.'

In early 1985 drummer David Cairns and guitarist Cyrus Khajavi were replaced by Dave Wagstaffe and Kevin Fitzgerald respectively.

'I saw an advert in *Melody Maker* for a drummer,' Wagstaffe says. 'I don't recall the wording, apart from mentioning they had just finished a 40 odd date tour, but I liked the description given of the band. I went down to the auditions in a studio in London's docklands, and watched several drummers in the queue before me struggling to play this 15/8 rhythm in one of the songs, and thought "Let me at 'em!" I absolutely loved what they were doing, and afterwards they seemed keen to get me back, but there was quite a bit of dithering going on and a second bash before I was asked to join. Keith gave me a copy of the *Fire In The Sky* album to listen to and I thought, and still think, it's something of a classic, despite the limits of the recording budget. The first important gig I did with them was at The Marquee, which I remember was on the same night as the Tottenham riots in Broadwater Farm a few miles away [6 October 1985].'

This line-up – Keith Turner, Dave Wagstaffe, Kevin Fitzgerald, Dillon Tonkin and Susan Robinson – recorded a new version of *Fire In The Sky* for the EMI compilation album *Fire In Harmony*.

'That was one of the first things on the agenda just after I joined,' says Dave Wagstaffe. 'The studio was called the Sound Mill and somewhere in Berkshire, I believe. The producer Pete Hinton wanted to give the song a heavier sound and when he played it back at full blast I thought it sounded great. I didn't understand the kind of feel and the subtleties that Keith was after, and Pete was not overjoyed at Keith's response! So he let us have some studio time for Keith and Dillon to make some adjustments.'

Further line-up changes brought in vocalist Nick Williams and keyboard player Steve Leigh. An album's worth of material was recorded in their own eight track studio by this iteration of Quasar, but these remain unreleased. They were later reworked as the album *The Loreli*, by which time Williams had left and Tracy Hitchings took his place. Hitchings was Quasar's fifth lead vocalist.

Dave Wagstaffe: 'Tracy brought a lot more power and dynamism to the vocal department, having just come from the heavy metal band Panic. But she also liked and adjusted to the more subtle side of the music.'

Leigh left in mid-1988. 'I started to struggle mentally again and felt I had something more to give elsewhere, which eventually resulted in forming Landmarq.'

Guitarist Toshi Tsuchiya was on board for the recording of *The Loreli*, the band's second album. Released in 1989, this had the line-up of Tracy Hitchings, Toshi Tsuchiya, Keith Turner and Dave Wagstaffe.

'The recording of that album was probably my least enjoyable recording experience,' says Dave Wagstaffe, 'not due to the people or the songs but for budgetary reasons, as it was done on a shoestring without any label backing. We recorded on 'down time' at a friend's studio on the 'graveyard shift' during the early hours and Keith, who was doing the recording, was surviving on a diet of coffee and cigarettes!'

The biggest gigs the band did would probably have been as part of a Dutch tour where they played the Paradiso in Amsterdam and the Noorderligt in Tilburg, both with Pendragon.

'We played in Tracy's hometown in Cornwall,' recalls Dave Wagstaffe. 'There was a thunderstorm and the power kept cutting out midway through various songs, which we then had to start again. In one case, we started again twice in one song and we're not talking three minute pop songs! Eventually some locals went and got a generator and we finished the set. Being in front of her home crowd, Tracy was devastated!'

But changes were afoot once more when Quasar lost another vocalist.

'We climbed from nothing to The Marquee,' Keith Turner says, 'replacing a singer and drummer, then back touring, more of The Marquee and the Paradiso… but Tracy quit, so I was left to pick up the pieces again for the third time.'

Quasar still record and perform. *Fire In The Sky* was remixed and re-released in 2021 with vocal tracks by Susan Robinson recorded in 1984-85. A new album, *Memories Of Times Yet To Be*, followed two years later.

Some years later Tracy Hitchings went on to join Landmarq with Steve Leigh. She died of cancer in 2022, at 60 years old. Steve Leigh: 'Tracy was a real discovery and a wonderful singer. She was a beautiful soul, whom I miss dearly, and she brought fun and laughter to the band. She was quite literally a breath of fresh air.'

*

Abel Ganz came together in Glasgow in 1980 and became a regular feature on the local concert circuit. They comprised Hew Montgomery (keyboards), Malcolm McNiven (guitar), Hugh Carter (bass) and Kenny Weir (drums). Montgomery and Carter also sang and played 12-string guitar.

Hew Montgomery: 'Abel Ganz had formed when Hugh and I began chucking some song ideas round at our respective homes in a suburb of Glasgow called Bearsden. Bearsden and neighbouring

Milngavie had a thriving musical scene, including bands like Orange Juice and Lloyd Cole and the Commotions amongst others. The very first gig we ever played as Abel Ganz was in Milngavie Town Hall in – I think – 1982 with support coming from Del Amitri. They went on to better things, if memory serves me rightly! We then moved the sessions from our parents' homes to the music shop that Hugh jointly owned with Steve Caban in Park Road in Glasgow – the well-known CC Music, which is still thriving today at another location nearby. Park Road was mostly rented tenement properties with shops at street level, and the locals must have loved their evenings being ruined by our weird, proggy sounding creations! Nobody actually ever complained though… It was a great place with a handy chip shop, so fish suppers and fizzy juice were an essential accompaniment to the music. It also helped that there was a shopful of instruments on hand as well – we were very respectful with the merchandise! Hugh and I were joined by Malcolm McNiven on guitars and Ken Weir on drums, and the band began to take a serious shape. As for the band's name, I'm claiming that one just because I liked the name! Abel Gance (different spelling) was a French film maker who in the 1920s had made a six hour epic film about the life of Napoleon.'

They were one of only a small number of prog bands in Scotland at the time.

'Comedy of Errors were kicking around at the same time as us if I remember correctly,' recalls Hugh Carter, 'and there was a local band called Chaser doing Rush covers, but nothing else. I knew of Pallas as they would come down to Glasgow on occasion.'

Abel Ganz were heavily influenced by Genesis – *Cinema Show* was an in-concert favourite – and also wrote their own music. They released a three track demo in 1983.

'We had a degree of local success at first,' says Hew Montgomery, 'but mostly in the well known Glasgow rock pubs such as the Burns Howff. We were treated as a bit of an unfashionable joke by the 'cool' Glasgow bands. They were, however, mostly tolerant of us because our bass player co-owned one of Glasgow's increasingly well known music shops. One of the local small newspapers was particularly derisory about our style – it was, after all, a time when prog was pretty unfashionable – and he inspired me to write the song *Gratuitous Flash* which was about him and became the title of the first album. The actual title was something that Malcolm had said during a rehearsal one night when we'd all gone wildly over the top with individual solo-ing self-indulgence. We stopped on a huge crash and, in the few seconds' silence after that, Malcolm turned to me and said somewhat disgustedly, 'What a load of gratuitous flash that was!''

Later that year, they added a singer.

Hugh Carter: 'Hew and I shared the vocals in the early days of our first few gigs. We needed a better singer, and there was that thing of a prog band needing a frontman as a focal point. I don't necessarily agree with that, but that was the way the band thought we should go. We advertised in the *Melody Maker* for a singer, if memory serves me.'

'I saw an ad in a music paper for a band in Glasgow looking for a 'Phil Collins type singer', Alan Reed recalls. 'I knew I could do that, so I responded. It turned out to be Abel Ganz.'

Hew Montgomery: 'We had outgrown the music shop and moved to a number of Glasgow's more

Three of Abel Ganz's cassettes from the 1980s (Courtesy Mark Guenther)

salubrious studios for rehearsals. It also became clear that we needed a singer. Hugh and I had at various times tried to fill this role with varying degrees of success. We advertised in the local music shops for a vocalist and held auditions on a horrible, torrentially wet night in a studio known as The Arches in the west end of Glasgow – run by a lovely guy who was simply known as Archie. We never did find out his real name! The water was literally running down the walls, but it was a bit of a Glasgow music institution and much beloved by all local musos. Alan was one of the guys who had contacted us, and he actually turned up early – he was a bedraggled, diminutive figure whom we actually sent away because he was too early… we didn't think he would come back but he did, even more drowned and bedraggled! We agreed to try a run through of *Squonk* as a song well known to us all, and when he opened his mouth to sing the first line of the song, we literally just watched and listened in total amazement – we had found our man. Alan seemed to enjoy his evening and joined up on the spot.'

'I don't remember who else we auditioned,' says Hugh Carter, 'but once we heard Alan that was it, he was the man!'

Reed: 'They had an album written and needed a singer to complete the line-up. The album was *Gratuitous Flash*.'

Gratuitous Flash was released, on cassette only, in the first half of 1984.

'It was my first time in a studio, and, listening back, my pitching wasn't great,' Reed admits. 'But the rest of the band gave me room to experiment, and I learnt a lot. I'm still proud of it.'

Abel Ganz played a handful of gigs locally but had a champion in DJ Tom Russell of Radio Clyde, who had a very successful rock show, broadcast on a Friday immediately after Radio 1's *Friday Rock Show*.

'Tom played us a fair bit on Radio Clyde,' says Hugh Carter, 'and got us onto the bill at the prestigious Kelvingrove Festival, which we stormed to an enthusiastic audience of around 7,000.'

'It was a beautiful summer's day,' says Hew Montgomery, 'and we got the first encore of the day. We were entirely unprepared for this and scrambled through a version of *Squonk*, which we used to jam in the rehearsal studio on occasions. We then sold out the batch of *Gratuitous Flash* cassette tapes we had brought along. I will never forget looking down from the stage at the rush of people coming forward to buy an album from us.'

Carter: 'It was that gig that alerted Pallas to Alan's fine vocals, and it proved to be his penultimate gig with us.'

Reed left in 1984 to join Pallas.

'We were pretty miffed when Pallas poached him just as we seemed to be getting some recognition,' notes Hugh Carter. 'Not surprised, as he was and is a great singer, just sad to see him go.'

Montgomery: 'It's fair to say that we all recognised Alan's fantastic frontman and singing abilities and had a feeling he would move on to bigger and better things eventually. Pallas were looking around for a new singer not long after Alan had joined us, and they turned up at one of our gigs in a venue called the Paris Rock Club at Paisley. It seemed the obvious move and we were delighted for him, although sorry to lose his talents of course.'

Malcolm McNiven also chose to leave. Abel Ganz regrouped with new guitarist Paul Kelly to release

Gullibles Travels in 1985 and *The Dangers Of Strangers* three years later. In between they had tracks on Steven Wilson's *Exposure* and *Double Exposure* compilation albums: *The Unholy War* and *Dangers Of Strangers*.

They split in the mid-1990s after a fourth album (*The Deafening Silence*) but reformed in 2001. By the time of the release of 2020's *The Life Of The Honeybee & Other Moments Of Clarity*, none of the original members remained.

*

Janysium were formed in London in 1980 by two school friends, guitarist/vocalist Peter Matuchniak and drummer Simon Strevens. The band were so named after Matuchniak overheard a conversation about the singer Janis Ian, and interpreted this as Janysium. By 1981 they had expanded to a four piece with Martin Polley on bass and his friend Sean Lewis on piano. Polley also played in another school band called Mach One. Mach One had been founded by the Sprackling brothers: Tim (keyboards) and Geoff (guitar). Simon Strevens became their drummer in February 1981. By that November they needed a second guitarist, and Peter Matuchniak would join the band.

'So, for that period,' Matuchniak recalls, 'the three of us played in both bands. We had enough original Janysium material to go into a recording studio, and from this came our first cassette album in January 1982. Our average age was 16 years old.'

A PLAYGROUND OF BROKEN HEARTS

Janysium in 1981: Simon Strevens, Sean Lewis, Peter Matuchniak, Martin Polley (Photograph by Jeremy Christey)

The joint Janysium / Mach One cassette from 1983 (Courtesy Mark Guenther)

Sean Lewis left school to pursue his studies in music, therefore Janysium was put on hold allowing Matuchniak and Strevens to focus on Mach One. And then they met Phil Collins' mum.

'We met her by chance at a Genesis concert at Hammersmith Odeon in 1982,' Matuchniak says. 'We bumped into her as we were all taking our respective seats before Genesis took the stage. I recognised her from Armando Gallo's Genesis book and said, with a bit too much familiarity perhaps, a warm hello. She must have mistaken us for somebody else, as she started mentioning that she had meant to give our tape to Phil, but she had forgotten to put it into her purse. I was about to inform her that she had us confused with another band, when Simon took out a copy of our tape from his pocket and said, 'Here you go, take this one!' Genius. A week or so later, we get a phone call from Mrs Collins. Apparently Phil had the tape and really liked it. They were going to forward it to Jeff Chegwin, who was looking for up and coming bands for a new record label he was running. As part of that same phone call, she invited us all to the Barbara Speake Stage School in Ealing for tea and biscuits - which is exactly what we did, quite unbelievably. She gave each of us a photo of Phil, personally signed by Phil to each of us. We were on cloud nine! A few weeks later we received a letter from Jeff saying that he received the tapes and basically wrote a nice rejection letter. Had we been signed, this would have been quite the story. As it is, we still have a remarkable series of events that, even as I tell people, sounds like maybe it never really happened.'

By now, Matuchniak had met famed public relations guru Keith Goodwin.

'Geoff Parkyn reviewed our Janysium recording in 1982 and gave it a short but glowing review in one of the Genesis Information fan club supplements,' Matuchniak says. 'Suddenly our cassette album sales took off, with some European sales

Calling All The Heroes

```
            JANYSIUM
1. PEACEFUL ACQUAINTANCE (Simon, Sean)........7:16
2. MORPHEUS (Simon, Peter)....................6:42
3. HONEST POLICIES (Peter, Simon).............18:42
4. HIPPY IN THE RAIN (Peter, Simon)...........4:08
5. ROLL-A-JOINT (Peter).......................2:40
6. A BIT OF NOTHING, REALLY (Sean)............2:30
            MACH ONE
7. CENTRE OF THE UNIVERSE (Tim, Geoff)........5:35
8. CHOCOLATE ECLAIR (Peter)...................5:55
9. NO TIME TO SLEEP (Peter, Simon)............3:14
10. INTO THE PIT (Tim, Geoff, Peter, *Iain)....8:26
11. IRON LUNG OVERTURE: 1st Movement (Geoff)...3:10
12. THE REINCARNATION (Martin,Geoff,Simon,John)5:27
13. URBAN JUNGLE (Steve).......................3:30
14. DON'T LET THEM GET YOU DOWN (Steve)........3:30
15. ESSENCE OF LIFE (Tim, Martin)..............4:43

© Copyright exists                    MAK3  1983
```

JANYSIUM	MACH ONE
Sean Lewis	Peter Matuchniak
Peter Matuchniak	Martin Polley
Martin Polley	Geoff Sprackling
Simon Strevens	Tim Sprackling
	Simon Strevens

Mach One in 1985 (Courtesy Peter Matuchniak)

ordering them by the hundreds. A guy called Alan Pask started to write great reviews about us in *Afterglow* fanzine, and began to focus his attention on both of our bands. This is where I first became aware of the other new prog rock bands like Marillion, IQ, Twelfth Night and Pendragon. We were, I felt, a bit younger than our counterparts, who were beginning to gig regularly, especially in my hometown, London. At this time we were still doing the odd high school gig and studying for our O Levels and A Levels.'

Keith Goodwin contacted the band and he invited them to his office in Ealing Broadway.

'Keith was always very inviting and encouraging,' says Matuchniak. 'He showed us the ropes and told us what we needed to do to step up, in the same manner that he had done so for all those other bands. We put together a few dozen gigs around London clubs and universities around the country in the summer of 1983. I was 18-19 and stuck in the void between high school and university, although at the time I only ever saw myself as a full-time musician. I envied the focus and diligence of the other bands, particularly Fish, who Keith always spoke very highly of, not just about talent but even more so about his drive and willingness to learn. We grew a lot as a band from 1983 to '84 but deep

down I knew that, as a collective, we lacked some of that drive and maturity. I did eventually go to university in late 1983 but dropped out in 1984 to make a real go of it.'

Mach One released *Six Of One* in spring 1984. Janysium's *Half A Dozen Of The Other* cassette album dates from mid-1984. Mach One's sole vinyl album, *Lost For Words*, followed in late 1984, having established a residency at the Cafe Emil in Kensington, London.

'Keith arranged a distribution deal through Pinnacle Records,' says Peter Matuchniak, 'and we started selling most of our 1,000 pressings through them. Then Pinnacle went bankrupt and we lost all of our potential income. The band broke up due to a lack of maturity and raw dedication, and I crawled back to university to complete my maths degree.'

*

Liaison headlined The Marquee eight times between January 1984 and July 1985. They formed at the end of 1980 and, in their final, best known line-up, comprised Howard Rogers (vocals), Keith Young (guitar), Frank Keepfer (bass, keyboards) and Barry Connell (drums). Musically, Liaison were highly regarded with a very tight rhythm section, a talented and charismatic singer and, in Keith Young, a simply phenomenal guitarist.

Andy Glass: 'We thought Liaison were the dog's bollocks. As a guitarist, I always felt seriously inadequate next to Keith Young… lovely guy.'

Liaison, who were based in and around Harrow and Wembley in north London, evolved from Rogers' earlier four piece band, Spring Fever, for which Rogers was bassist alongside singer Chris Benson, guitarist Andy Sutcliffe and drummer Dave Hall. Having met drummer Barry Connell at a mobile burger and pie stand in Harrow, Hall was shortly to be replaced. With Connell on board, the band changed its name to Liaison, but soon altered membership again with the departure of their guitarist Andy Sutcliffe, to be replaced by Keith Young. Connell worked at Harrow Music Centre, a shop more commonly known as 'Sid's' and a popular meeting place for local musicians, including Young.

'I used to go and see them before I joined,' Young says.

The first Liaison line-up - Rogers, Young, Connell and Benson - played a number of gigs in late 1980 and early 1981 and recorded a demo.

'Chris Benson had a new wave sound, a bit Tony Hadley / Simon Le Bon,' says Keith Young.

'And he used to play a monophonic keyboard on some songs,' notes Howard Rogers.

'We played local pub gigs,' Young says, 'Southall, Wembley, Feltham, Hayes, Putney, Amersham… but also places uptown like the Starlight Rooms and the Kensington Ad Lib.'

It was probably at the Ad Lib in mid-1981 where Liaison hooked up with a manager.

'A manager, of sorts, called Brian Whitfield,' says Howard Rogers. 'He had his own PA company called Catweazle.'

This gave Liaison access to a top class PA system, 'a huge sound' as Howard describes it.

Singer Chris Benson's departure from Liaison was later forced by circumstances.

'Chris broke his leg in a skiing accident,' says Howard Rogers, 'and we had an important gig coming up at the Headstone in North Harrow. As I was singing backing vocals and had written all the lyrics, it was an easy decision to play that show as a three piece. We also used to do a cover of King Crimson's *Epitaph*, which I used to sing and people would tell us that they preferred my singing to Chris… and that was the beginning of the trio.'

Having previously padded the set with some well chosen covers, their first 'all original' gig as a three piece was at the bottom of the bill of a three band show at Borehamwood Civic Hall on 5 September 1981, headlined by As Above So Below.

'We were a three piece band with a four man road crew!' says Keith Young.

A series of dates across the UK supporting dogged blues rockers Stray in September and October 1981 tightened the band's sound, and gave them a cache of on the road stories.

'We went all around the country with them in a transit van,' Howard Rogers says. 'We learned our chops by playing every night for 10 days straight.'

The tour included the band's first support gig at The Marquee on 14 October 1981, six days ahead of Marillion's first show at the venue. This opened opportunities for several more support shows at The Marquee in the coming months: Liaison were local, based only 15 miles from Soho, and were simple to set up with just drums, bass and guitar.

'We supported loads of bands that were totally unsuitable for us,' says Keith Young, 'horrible heavy metal bands.'

The 1982 single *Play It With Passion* combined the drive of new wave with a smattering of prog influences à la Rush. Rogers displays some impressive vocal gymnastics.

The four track self-released cassette *Turn The Gun Around* was recorded at Fastbuck Studios in Chiswick, London, on 2-3 May 1982.

'This was funded by Brian Whitfield,' says Young.

'And we all chipped in to pay for the sessions.'

As 1982 turned into 1983, changes were afoot.

'I was an avid reader of the music press at the time,' says Keith Young. 'I used to get *Sounds* and *Melody Maker*, sometimes *NME*. I'd read about the emergence of these new prog rock bands and went to see a show by a few of them.'

Young and Rogers attended the four band concert at The Venue in London on 20 January 1983. Sets by Pendragon, Dagaband, Twelfth Night and Solstice convinced them that, with a few tweaks, Liaison's music could be aligned to this new wave of music.

'I knew that we would go down really well with this audience,' Young says. 'Our music already had elements of prog in it - some clever bits, touches of Rush and Camel.'

Subsequently Liaison supported Pendragon at The Marquee on 23 March, Twelfth Night at New Merlin's Cave in London on 22 April, and travelled with both Pendragon and Solstice to Cardiff University on 30 April 1983. They appeared again at The Marquee supporting Pendragon on 12 June and Solstice on 15 July.

By the time of their second cassette, *Only Heaven Knows*, recorded at Fastbuck on 21 August, bassist Frank Keepfer had been added to the band.

'We had interest from a record company,' Rogers explains. 'We were friendly with a chap called Richard Bron. He was the son of Gerry Bron of Bronze Records. Richard's job was to find new acts for the record label. He was interested in us, but he wanted to put his stamp on everything. He had a hang-up with Barry and wanted us to replace him, but we couldn't do that. In the end we thought that if he thinks there's a problem with the rhythm

A PLAYGROUND OF BROKEN HEARTS

Liaison at the time of *Only Heaven Knows*, 1983
Frank Keepfer, Howard Rogers, Barry Connell, Keith Young
(Courtesy Howard Rogers)

section, then perhaps we should get a bass player, and free me up to concentrate on singing.'

Frank Keepfer came to the band though an unusual route.

'My dad worked at Kodak in Harrow,' Rogers says, 'and he knew Frank's dad, who was quite a well known jazz musician locally. My dad told me that he'd seen Frank playing with his dad's band at a Kodak social club event. Said he was quite good! We had auditioned a few bass players, none of whom we felt excited about. Frank came along to play with us and musically he was an instant fit.'

'Frank could play anything,' says Keith Young. 'Jazz changes, slap bass, piano, bass pedals… he could rock out as well.'

'And he could sing!' says Howard Rogers. 'He had the lot.'

Liaison's musicianship was significantly enhanced by Frank Keepfer's instant musical lock-in with Keith Young and Barry Connell. *Only Heaven Knows* includes the magnificent title track, unquestionably one of the finest songs from this era of prog music.

'It's a blues in 3/4,' says Keith Young, 'with a few extra chords. Of all the songs that Howard and I did together, that was one of the quickest we wrote.'

'It's the classic story of 'We wrote the whole song in two minutes'…', Howard says. 'Everything just fell into place instantly.'

The song features an exceptional vocal performance from Rogers and a wonderful guitar solo.

Keith Young: 'There's some Andy Latimer in that solo, some Steve Lukather, bits of Larry Carlton. I'm not the fastest guitar player in the world but I like to make everything tuneful. If you can hum a solo and remember it, that counts for everything.'

High profile support bookings at The Marquee supporting Solstice on 10 September, 11 September and 28 December 1983 led to the first of their headline bookings on 3 January 1984.

'It was a Wednesday night, straight after Christmas,' laughs Howard Rogers. 'There were probably three men and a dog in the room that night.'

A few weeks later, they would perform their biggest gig at the Southampton Gaumont supporting Marillion.

'Somebody rang me up,' says Howard Rogers. 'It might have been Keith Goodwin. We had really short notice, perhaps no more than a day. I had to take a day off sick from work!'

Only Heaven Knows was released as a single at around this time. Further headliners took place throughout 1984. They were also booked to play the cancelled 1984 Reading Festival.

The superb and incandescent *A Tale Of You* can be found on the *Fire In Harmony* compilation. But, by the time the album came out in March 1985, gigs were drying up and Liaison's time was almost spent.

Howard Rogers: 'We'd missed out on the Reading

Liaison at the Red Lion in Brentford, 14 July 1984
(Courtesy Howard Rogers)

Festival, interest from Bronze Records had died on the vine, we had loads of letters from record companies telling us that we weren't quite what they were looking for… I was 27 and felt that we'd hit a glass ceiling. We'd given it our best shot. It was time to try something new.'

Keith Young: 'Creatively we'd come to a bit of a full stop. Frank told us that he wanted to leave. We wanted to finish on a high with a final gig at The Marquee.'

Their last show on 5 July 1985 was a sell out, with support from Pride Of Passion. Liaison played an immense 16 song, 85 minute set. The crowd sings along with every word of *Only Heaven Knows*. They encored with classy versions of songs by writers as diverse as George Gershwin and Chuck Berry.

'It wasn't an easy decision,' says Barry Connell, 'but there was an element of realism in it. I didn't want it to end, I loved playing in that band. I'm not ashamed to say that I wept when we came off stage.'

Connell played sessions and guested with Pride Of Passion. Young and Rogers went on to perform and write together including support slots at The Marquee with Twelfth Night and Solstice.

Liaison's unique mix of complex songs, supreme musicianship and powerful performances might have made them huge in 1971 – by the mid-1980s they were, unfortunately, out of time.

The original trio reformed for shows in 2018 and 2019, and, expanded to a five piece, shared the bill with Trilogy in October 2023 as part of Trilogy's commemorative *Fire In Harmony* reunion tour.

*

Tasburgh Village Hall is about 10 miles from the stately East Anglian city of Norwich. Local band Airbridge performed their first gig there on 7 January 1981. They comprised Sean Godfrey (vocals), Lorenzo Bedini (guitar), Paul Austin (guitar), Graham Chilvers (bass) and Dave Beckett (drums).

Bedini describes himself as 'a rather nerdy little boy from the wilds of Norfolk with an obscure Italian name.'

'I grew up listening to bands like Genesis and King Crimson,' he says. 'By the late 1970s, I was living in London where it was morally wrong to even mention these bands in public. If you weren't punk you were nobody. So I escaped that extraordinarily conformist moment in music fashion by

going back to Norwich and I got an audition with a band called No Parallax. That band had Graham Chilvers on bass, Dave Beckett on drums and Sean Godfrey on vocals. And me possibly, if I passed the audition. And when I arrived, they said, 'Well, we're not just looking for a guitarist, we're looking for somebody who can write some songs.' So I played them a few songs and they more or less said, 'Right then, you're in.' I promptly said, 'Well, look, does anybody else want to write songs as well?'… I didn't want to be writing and arranging everything. But they all looked at me and said, 'No, no, we don't write songs…' So I took Graham, Dave and Sean and a guy called Paul Austin, who had a twin-necked Gibson, and started Airbridge.'

Shortly after, Airbridge decided to lose Paul Austin ('much too loud' according to Lorenzo). Bass player Graham Chilvers then departed. After trying one or two possible replacements, Sean Godfrey was persuaded to move to bass.

Bedini: 'I said to Sean, 'You've got a vague idea of how to play guitar chords, right?' And he said, 'Yes.' 'Right then, here's a bass. I'll tell you how it works!'

He took to it like a duck to water for someone who quite literally had a bass guitar chucked into his arms.'

After rehearsing as a three piece, they eventually replaced Chilvers with vocalist/guitarist Ed Percival.

'I'd been to Bristol University, and played in a student production of *Tommy*,' Percival notes. 'I came back to Norwich where an old school friend of mine was organising jam sessions. This was at a pub up on the north side of the city. I met Lorenzo at the second of these. I remember that he was trying to direct people to play one of his songs. But he hadn't written it down. We were shouting the chords back and forth to people as we worked through this piece. I was deeply impressed by the cheap synthesiser that Lorenzo had. I gave him a lift home that night. We chatted on the journey. He told me he'd got this band and would I like to audition?'

Bedini: 'I said, 'Would you like to join Airbridge, because we're short of a pair of hands, really?' I just took it for granted that he could write songs.'

Percival got the job in July 1981.

Rogers and Young with guest Martin Orford, supporting Twelfth Night at The Marquee, 22 August 1985. (Photograph by Andy Inman)

'I had never sung in public,' Percival admits, 'but for me it was manna from heaven. I loved Genesis and Pink Floyd and I thought, 'You mean I can play in the band like that?' So that was my great joy. However, I had already booked a trip to Italy to hitchhike for a month so we rehearsed a bit and I attempted to write some songs before drifting around Italy. One was a very nasty Pink Floyd rip-off that had people throwing themselves off tower blocks. The other was about falling in love in haystacks. We rehearsed in a huge double caravan, which was parked at Lorenzo's family estate. We rehearsed endlessly, possibly four or five nights a week. We were miles from anywhere so we could make a lot of noise. Dave Beckett was a proper proggy drummer. He had a fantastic Premier kit with loads of drums around the place and cymbals and things. It took up about half the caravan. It was brilliant because we could go in there and play for hours and hours.'

Percival's first gig with Airbridge was at Whites on 10 October 1981. Three months later, they recorded an album which they called *Paradise Moves*.

'We had this bunch of songs,' says Ed Percival. 'Lots of Lorenzo's songs, some that I'd written, another based on a set of Sean's lyrics which was called *Paradise Moves (A Bridge In The Air)*. We went into a studio in Carnaby Street in London, which was owned by Mike Hugg, formerly of Manfred Mann. We recorded the backing tracks – guitar, bass, drums and some keyboards – for every song on the album in pretty much one take, and mixed it down to two track in one eight hour session. That was our £150 budget blown in one day. After that all we could do was overdub, which tended to mean that we lost much of the solid foundations.'

The plan was for Lorenzo to transfer the two track master to a reel to reel for subsequent overdubbing 'at a little flat in West Hampstead'.

'Talk about a triumph of optimism over reality,' he says. 'I had a little bit more experience than the others, but when it came to recording I knew where the stop and start buttons were on a recording machine. And I could count up to eight in terms of tracks. But I made an absolute mess of the whole thing. I didn't know what I was doing, and I wasn't pretending that I did. The reel to reel had a speed control knob and at some point that had been adjusted. It had sped up slightly and was therefore recording a shade too fast. All the overdubs we did were recorded at the wrong speed. So we mixed it down and sent it off to be pressed, not realising what we'd done. Several months later we got this box of records. But when I stuck it on an actual record player, we realised that all of the music was slowed down. There was this great song that Edward wrote called *Round Dance* that was a poppy, catchy tune. It came out slightly funereal, like a very early King Crimson demo.'

Ed Percival: 'We would rehearse four times a week and gig every fortnight, usually at Whites. I was churning out songs as rapidly as I could think of them. By the time the album was released, we'd moved on from those tracks almost completely.'

Airbridge supported West Midlands heavy rock band Diamond Head in April 1982, in the West Runton Pavilion. This rural outpost on the north Norfolk coast was a regular venue on tour schedules in the 1970s and 1980s: Motörhead played there eight times between 1977 and 1983, after which the venue closed (presumably coincidentally).

'We spent all bloody day with their drummer

checking his snare drum sound,' remembers Ed Percival. 'We didn't get a soundcheck at all. It was packed, hundreds of heavy metal fans, probably the biggest audience we ever played to. Every time we started something vaguely fast they all started headbanging. It was a rickety old place, and the wiring was so dodgy that, at one point, Lorenzo leaned forward and I saw this huge arc of electricity come out at the end of his microphone onto his forehead. So, from that point, I was singing from three yards behind the microphone…'

'Their roadie was basically the size of a planet and spherical,' Lorenzo says. 'I saw a spark jump from my guitar strings to my little finger. The spherical roadie grabbed the mic with one hand and my guitar with the other and said, 'Ah yeah, hang on…' He disappeared with a screwdriver, fiddled about, then came back, grabbed the mic and guitar again and said, 'OK, you're fine now…'.

Gradually, Airbridge built up an audience in East Anglia before they accidently tapped into the London music scene.

'In mid-1982, I was hitchhiking to London to see my girlfriend,' Ed Percival says. 'On one occasion I got a lift all the way from near Cambridge to London with the guy who happened to run the Rock Garden. He started to give us support slots, and we ended up playing with a whole bunch of people like The Go-Betweens, The Members, The Lurkers and Any Trouble in this very swanky venue in Covent Garden. We did a support in Hampstead to a band called The Red And The Black that next week changed its name to The Waterboys. In October that year, we did our only ever continental gig, two nights in Amsterdam at a venue called the Last Waterhole, a strange place run by hippies. We were trying to take the message out into the world.'

Paradise Moves was finally released in spring 1983, 15 months after it was recorded.

'The record company sat on it,' says Ed Percival. 'And rather than leading the way, we were labelled as jumping on the bandwagon.'

Nevertheless, the album did receive some positive reviews:

> Alternates early psychedelic numbers featuring misty keyboards with a more straight ahead 70's style.
>
> **Record Business**

> No synthesisers or trendy haircuts, they play honest to goodness mainstream rock.
>
> **Music Week**

Stephen Bennett joined Airbridge in March 1983 at around the time of the release of the *Paradise Moves* album.

'I'd met Stephen even before I knew Lorenzo,' Ed Percival reveals. 'It was at one of the jam sessions in Norwich. I was very impressed by Steve. He clearly knew what he was doing. We had decided that visually, it wasn't really working, so we'd to try and find a fifth member. Sean and Dave were sort of nudging me forward to be more of a frontman and, as I'm not that great a singer or guitarist, it made more sense to me not to be playing an instrument while I was attempting to sing. Stephen turned us down.'

'I'd come down to Norwich from the North West

Words And Pictures
(From the collection of
Piersandro Pallavicini)

sometime in 1979,' Bennett says, 'and then permanently in 1981. The city had a pretty good music scene then and was blessed with quite a few brilliant bands who were playing then unfashionable progressive rock - but Airbridge were the ones that stood out.'

'We continued to court him,' Percival admits. 'We'd started to put on gigs at a room in the Theatre Royal in Norwich. We did two or three there. Then we supported Liaison at the Ad Lib in Kensington, and we brought them up to support us at the Theatre Royal. And one of those gigs we had Steve's band at the time, The Space Between.'

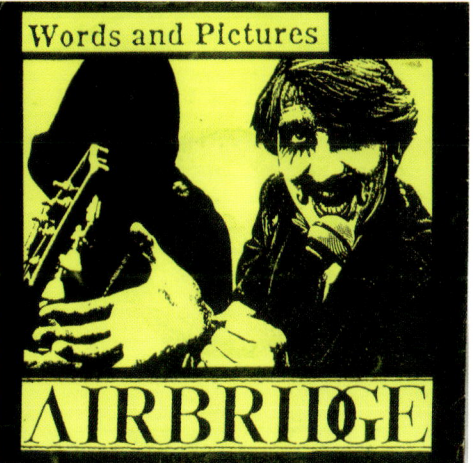

'Airbridge were brilliant live,' Bennett says. 'It was clear that they needed a keyboard player.'

Ed Percival: 'So we've finally got the five piece band that we should always have been. Lorenzo took to the stage in a monk's habit, I painted my face with a big moustache. A reviewer described our stage appearance as a five piece as looking like a cross between Duran Duran and Hawkwind. Cruel but fair. But now we've got this fantastic wall of keyboards and somebody who knows how to use them. Lorenzo was able to concentrate on playing the guitar and I started writing songs that would use huge chords. One called *Stage Struck* became our opening number, and the very first time we played that was at The Marquee. We'd finally bashed down the door and got a gig there, on a Sunday night supporting Trilogy.'

This was on 15 May 1983.

'Playing at The Marquee was a dream come true for me,' Stephen Bennett says, 'as I had seen so many of my favourite bands there. We played a lot of gigs and soon decamped to Hillside Studios in Ipswich to record a single, *Words And Pictures*. Malcolm Bradbury played the single on Radio 4's *Desert Island Discs* [broadcast 26 August 1983], as his son was a friend of the band.'

Ed Percival: 'We bashed it down, recorded and mixed it in a day, and it escaped rather than was released. I think my brother still has about 800 copies of it in his attic. But I've written a Desert Island Disc. There you go.'

Kerrang! reviewed *Words And Pictures*: 'Very Domesque. In other words, rather silly prog rock, though that doesn't stop this being an appealing single. Quite clever arrangements, coupled with some interesting synth work from Stephen Bennett, and let's not forget the guitar from Count Lorenzo. A must for early Yes and ELP fans.'

Airbridge did just 11 gigs as a five piece before Lorenzo Bedini decided to move on.

Percival: 'We decided that we needed to go to London if we were gonna make this thing happen. Lorenzo was really reluctant to do that and decided

Count Lorenzo's super rare EP released in 1984 (Courtesy Mark Guenther)

Airbridge, Marquee 26.11.83.

Airbridge decided to call it a day after this gig supporting IQ and split up. I'm not sure if this has been expected for some time, Airbridge's history has been rather unstable, with different members and different line-ups. One of the reasons for the split stems from an argument between bassist Sean Godfrey and lead singer Ed Percival. Apparently Ed auditioned with Twelfth Night for the vacated lead singer position left by Geoff Mann, and he didn't consult Airbridge about it. Well anyway the band has gone its separate ways, Ed and lead guitarist Geoff Chamberlain are forming another band. Drummer Dave Beckett has got himself involved with session work and Sean is forming another prog rock band (it has been mentioned another re-incarnation of Airbridge, but not definitely!).

Airbridge sneaked on stage, rather smartly dressed, with focus point Ed in his familiar black and white face make-up, looking rather like a dapper Ben Turpin. *Stage Struck* was the opening song, a heavy-ish outing with Ed and Geoff both on guitars chugging away. Geoff's riffs sounding Rush-like, gad! he looks a bit like Alex Lifeson?

Next was a heavier rendition (no keyboards in this band) of the desert island disc *Words And Pictures*. After *Words* was another single orientated song *Travelling Salesman* dedicated to former keyboard player 'Shirley Bennett'. A good song with modern sounding guitar work, more like U2 here rather than Rush. Ed then explained about the band splitting up after three years (of torture!) continuing the set with *Reflections*, another rocky number with heavy guitars and thudding bass. More for the heavy metallists with

to leave. We did a farewell gig for him at Whites and soon afterwards we found Geoff Chamberlain, a fantastic guitar player from a band called Dreamweaver.'

This new line-up had one rehearsal in the caravan still in the grounds of Lorenzo's house.

'And then, almost instantly,' Percival notes, 'Steve said to me, 'I don't want to do prog rock any more. I'm leaving the band.''

'Though I loved playing with Airbridge,' Bennett says, 'Sean, Ed and Lorenzo were all brilliant songwriters, so there wasn't much opportunity for me to contribute. I left the band to pursue some other creative avenues.'

Ed Percival: 'We invested in an expensive PA system and signed up with Keith Goodwin, so the money was pouring out of our bank accounts. I think the entire royalties that I received for our album were about £200. And I then had to pay £300 for my share of the PA…'

Airbridge recorded an album's worth of new material and played two further support dates at The Marquee, with Trilogy on 2 November 1983 and IQ on the 26 November.

Calling All The Heroes

Ed Percival fronting Airbridge in 1983 (Photographs by Mark Drake)

the rock and roll, announced by Ed in heart-shaped glasses with Geoff leading the way with a *Xanadu*-ish guitar riff, Dave making more of an impact with a drum solo.

More theatrics from Ed when he had returned to the stage wearing a night shirt and night cap clutching his Teddy (aah!). *Beyond The Veil* was then played, again another solid number. Moving into insanities with Ed being strangled by Ted, then screamed, collapsed, smeared (his make-up in case you were wondering). This met with a loud and thunderous applause, a lot of long-time fans here tonight, paying their respects.

Airbridge returned for an encore, with a song dedicated to the band and all the previous members. Unexpectedly it was a cover version of *Putting On The Ritz*, well played and rather humorous, ending with custard pies being exchanged between the band members. A fitting end? Possibly. It was good to see the band bow out in high spirits.

Russell Morgan, *Afterglow* issue 13

Monopoly the next song, Ed particularly outstanding with his maniacal singing.

Oskar followed *Monopoly*. 'A song for old time fans' announced Ed. *Oskar* is in fact based on the book and film *The Tin Drum*. The music is reminiscent of XTC, making plans for Oskar? *The Hunter*, an energetic instrumental continued

'I'd auditioned to replace Geoff Mann in Twelfth Night by then,' Ed says, 'so we knew that the end was nigh. We decided that the Marquee show with IQ would be our last gig. And we had a great time, we all parted as friends. It was all over and Airbridge was finished.'

Except, not quite.

'Lo and behold,' Ed Percival smiles, 'a few weeks

Airbridge bow out at The Marquee, November 1983 (Courtesy Ed Percival)

later, I went to an Airbridge gig!'

This was a contractual booking at Whites on 30 December 1983.

'When Airbridge finally folded,' notes Stephen Bennett, 'Sean Godfrey contacted me and asked me whether I'd like to form a new band with him. I'd always loved his bass playing, so I eagerly agreed, and we soon recruited David Valentine-Hagart on guitar.'

'Every weekend,' Valentine-Hagart recalls, 'Norwich musicians would go to Whites. There was a big room in the back, and they always had quality live music on. Airbridge were one of the regular bands. I liked Airbridge, and particularly the playing of Geoff Chamberlain, and after a few gigs had worked out some of the songs. I had a three piece college band that did '70s rock covers and a bit of Rush. We used to jam/rehearse in a college room, and I began to introduce the guys to some of the Airbridge I had worked out. Meanwhile Geoff Chamberlain left Airbridge. By some majick in the universe or unexpected mutual musician connections the Airbridge guys, Sean and Stephen I think, had heard about 'a guitarist that could play some of their stuff'. One day they turned up at one of the college sessions. Shortly after I was asked if I'd like to join the 'project that would come after Airbridge' and which became The Host and then LaHost.'

The line-up of The Host was completed by a drummer, Dave Beckett, and a roadie called Crazy Steve who was clearly unsuited as a singer and was dismissed after a single pseudo-Airbridge concert at Whites. Bennett: 'We were still looking for the right people to join the band.'

They placed an advert in *Sounds* for a drummer and vocalist. This came to the attention of 17 year old Mark Spencer.

'We lived in Norfolk at the time,' Spencer says, 'and, if I recall correctly, my sister Angela had been to see Marillion up in Norwich [19 November 1982] and seen Airbridge as the support act. [Airbridge did not support Marillion but the members of the band did attend the show.] At the time, I was a drum roadie for a Norfolk covers band, Axia.'

Axia's drummer was Steve 'Fudge' Smith.

'The first time I remember meeting Mark was at an Axia rehearsal at Scoulton Rectory, about halfway between Norwich and Thetford. The rectory was an original commune from the 1960s established by artist and poet Cressida Lindsay. A band called Junior's Eyes used to live and rehearse there: their guitarist Tim Renwick later played with Pink Floyd and many others. The rectory still maintained that vibe when we all arrived to rehearse and live there in 1982. Steve Sayer, Axia's keyboard player, painted the entire *Lord Of The Rings* map on his ceiling. I remember *Dungeons & Dragons* played with dice, and the radio series of *The Hitchhiker's Guide To The Galaxy*… there were great personalities at parties, held in the guise of the Norfolk Tree fairs with Pete and Cressida Lindsay holding court. Mark was just there at rehearsal. He hung out and watched us play and later attached himself as our roadie.'

Axia comprised Fudge with Dave Heighington (guitar), Nick Prendergast (bass) and Steve Sayer (keyboards). They played a handful of gigs; the most notable were supporting Tygers Of Pan Tang at the Assembly Rooms in Swaffham and Budgie at the Breckland Sports Centre in Thetford.

'We got the name Axia from Vent-Axia. Me and Dave were having a pee after a gig and looked up and said that would make a good name!' Fudge recalls.

One of the punters at the Thetford gig was a young guitarist called Mark Trayton.

'I played bass in a band called Millstream from Thetford,' he recalls. 'One night, I went out with my friend and bandmate Steve to see an interesting local band called Axia, whose drummer was Fudge Smith. They played at Thetford Sports Centre. I remember thinking that he was a pretty good drummer and went to chat with him after the gig. He offered me a spliff. After a while, my band split up, and I moved to a flat above a shop in Watton, near Swaffham in Norfolk. I used to practise guitar and work on song ideas in my flat. One day, I had a knock on the door. 'Hi, my name's Fudge. I'm a drummer and I work just up the road. Every time I walk past your flat, I can hear you playing some pretty amazing guitar, so I thought I'd come and say hello!' That was where my friendship with Fudge began.'

Trayton and Fudge would write and jam together at Scoulton Rectory, apropos of nothing much, until Mark Spencer's sister spotted an ad in *Sounds* stating that Airbridge were looking for a singer and a drummer.

Fudge: 'Mark Spencer saw the *Sounds* ad and asked me to take him into Norwich for an audition with Airbridge. He was still too young to drive. Off we both went one evening. I pulled up outside a house in Norwich. Mark went in while I waited. Mark came down and said they were looking for a drummer too.'

'I remember we went to a remote and muddy part of Norfolk called Watton,' says David Valentine-Hagart. 'There we were introduced to Fudge and his compadre Mark. Mark was a keen young dude that liked to hang out with the band. Stephen and Sean, seeing the obvious potential, asked Mark to have a go on vocals.'

Stephen Bennett: 'We had quite a few auditions, the most memorable of which was a bloke with an enormously loud North kit with flared toms. But most of them could not make the complex time signatures we required sound natural and funky. Until Fudge came along that is. Up until that point I'd played with some brilliant drummers, but Fudge was something special. Mark Spencer was still a teenager, but he had the look of a young Mick Jagger about him, and I thought he'd make a fine frontman. Like Fudge, he took everything I threw at him in his stride.'

Mark Spencer: 'I'd never sung in front of anyone before, but wanted it very badly. Sean and Stephen had sent me a copy of their single *Words And Pictures* for me to learn. I sang my heart out and got the gig. Luckily, so did Fudge. Sean and Steve decided that the Airbridge name was finished, so we went out as The Host.'

'Fudge came up to the flat one day with Mark

The Host's Marquee debut, 5 July 1984
(Photographs by Mark Drake)

The Host supporting Pendragon, 10 August 1984
(Photograph by Andy Inman)

Spencer, who I think had just left school,' Mark Trayton says. 'They told me they had auditioned for a band in Norwich called The Host and were doing Marquee gigs. They also needed a guitarist and put my name forward. Unfortunately, I was leaving the area to do a short course in computer programming in Ipswich.'

The band was rounded out by a percussionist friend of Mark and Fudge's called Jaff.

'Jaff was a great drummer playing additional percussion alongside Fudge,' says Valentine-Hagart. 'He really brought something to the band, and I missed him when he left.'

They performed their first gig at Whites in Norwich on 18 February 1984.

'While Mark's musical inexperience was clear initially,' notes Valentine-Hagart, 'he was already a natural frontman.'

The Host recorded a cassette EP called *Thoughts Out Of The Window* and had their first big break supporting Pendragon at Norwich Theatre Royal on 16 June 1984. They then performed at The Marquee on 5 July 1984 supporting IQ.

'What an amazing baptism of fire for a 19 year old musician with only local live band experience,' says David Valentine-Hagart. 'I remember arriving and Jinx, our 'road manager', driving in the big old grey van, squeezing it down the side entrance with inches to spare, unloading, setting up on that iconic stage. The gig itself was terrifying, and tremendous. We'd had the first cassette EP out and that had found a good audience. A lot of them seemed to be there at The Marquee. The scene had a great supportive community vibe to it.'

Further Marquee bookings would follow supporting Pendragon, 10 August, and Solstice, 1 November.

Stephen Bennett: 'We began playing gigs at most of the places familiar to fans of the day including The Marquee. When we weren't playing at The Marquee, we were often in the audience there and got to know the other bands. It was a brilliant time, and we really felt that a community of musicians was building up that was distinct from the other genres prevalent at the time. Most of the bands, including LaHost, took elements from pop, rock, new wave, new romantic and punk as well as prog. Many of the most successful non-prog bands at the time were scathing about 'classic' progressive rock, though it was obvious many were influenced by it and, of course, have now come out as fans of bands like Yes and Genesis. I was never embarrassed about any of the music I loved and the songs I wrote reflected this.'

The Host newsletter issue 3 (Courtesy Mark Guenther)

The Host's second demo tape (From the collection of Russell Morgan)

Around this time, David Valentine-Hagart chose to leave.

'I left because of tensions between myself and Fudge,' Valentine-Hagart admits. 'He's a great drummer, had all the complex chops we needed. He had a fast/slow awareness but absolutely no loud/soft. It was all loud. To me at any rate. Eventually it came down to 'live with it and maybe go deaf' or leave. It was quite a wrench though. I'd been there from the start and felt there were better things to come. But hey ho.'

Valentine-Hagart would be replaced by Fudge's pal Mark Trayton, or Spindle as some people call him.

'I auditioned for them in Norwich,' Trayton says. 'I learned the material fast, and the gigs started coming in, among them a couple of Marquee gigs, one supporting Solstice and another supporting, I think, Quasar. We also did gigs with Haze and some of the others on the circuit. I remember the first rehearsal I went to. It was the first time I played with progressive rock timings, and some of Steve Bennett's tracks had a few timing changes. I found them intriguing, and he had some pretty long pieces of music, which made it easy to forget where you were, if it wasn't for the musical triggers of the other musicians. What I particularly liked was when Steve did keyboard solos. They sounded like guitar solos but silky smooth and sounding as though he was playing them on a flamethrower. He's a very talented musician and introduced me to a style of music I never imagined that I'd be playing, but I absolutely loved it!'

By the time the band supported Solstice at The Marquee on 24 and 25 March 1985 they had changed their name to LaHost.

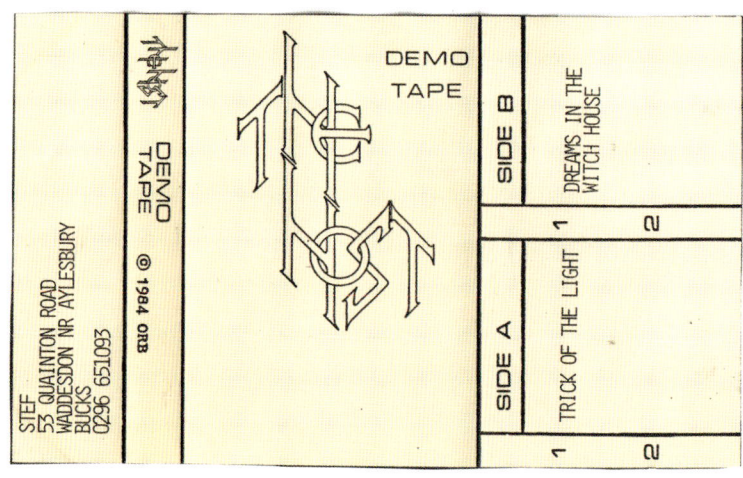

Calling All The Heroes

LaHost outside the Sainsbury Centre, UEA: Fudge Smith, Mark Spencer, Sean Godfrey, Mark Wyatt, Stephen Bennett, Jaff (Courtesy Fudge Smith)

'Stephen Bennett was contacted by an Irish folk band with the same name,' Fudge says. 'They had pipped us at the post.'

The Bennett composed song *Blood And Roses* was included on the *Fire In Harmony* compilation album in March 1985.

'We couldn't use a live track,' says Mark Trayton, 'which was really a shame for us as we had a few excellent, well recorded tracks. So we went about putting something together very quickly and went to Hillside Studios in Ipswich. We had a tight deadline, with only a day to go, and I think Mark got the master to London the next day.'

Further support gigs followed at The Marquee with Liaison, 6 April, and Pendragon, 17 May 1985.

A memorable booking was at the Fleece and Firkin in Bristol.

'It was a pretty big spit 'n' sawdust kind of place,' Mark Trayton says. 'At the end of the gig, we were packing up and taking our gear outside when I spotted a local tea leaf trying to take off with some of our stuff. I called the other lads out to help me, and we ran after them, only to be confronted by several more jumping out of a car. It ended as a huge punch up. Fudge was knocked down, and as I tried to save him, I just about avoided a couple of huge punches myself. Mark had his pretty face bashed up I think, and we had to take him to A&E. He lived to sing another day. And at some point we got friendly with Stef Jeffrey, the manager of Marillion's fan club, The Web. Stef became our kind of manager, and we stayed at her place while running around gigging. One night, Stef had gone over to Fish's place. Mark

LaHost at The Pennyfarthing, Oxford (Photograph by Mark Drake)

LaHost headline The Marquee
(From the collection of Phil Macy)

called her up and got us all an invite over. We needed to take some alcohol and looked all over Stef's place for anything she had, which wasn't a lot, like half a bottle of brandy or something. We eventually turned up at Fish's house in Aylesbury and gate crashed his sister's birthday gathering. As we walked in, I admit I was blown away by the gold discs he had propped up against the wall. By now, I'm thinking, we could be definitely hitting the big time, we're definitely mixing with the right people. At some point, while still staying at Stef's place, we arranged for Steve Rothery, Marillion's guitarist, and his wife to have dinner with us. He turned up in his sports car, looking every bit the rock star.'

But Trayton's time in LaHost was coming to an end.

'I did some recording in a basement studio in Norwich with Fudge and my old bandmate Steve O'Neill, who became a very successful producer for radio, TV and film. We played the recording to other members of LaHost, and I had a feeling it didn't go down well. I felt they thought I was trying to set up a new band with Fudge, though I could be wrong.'

Fudge Smith would also leave LaHost around this time.

Stephen Bennett: 'I remember being really upset about Fudge being forced out. I can't recall the reasons now, but I know that these things happen in a band.'

'Back when Live Aid was happening in mid-1985,' Fudge says, 'many cities were doing their own little concerts. Norwich wasn't missing out. I had been recording with a local singer/songwriter Stash Kirkbride. He had been chosen to close the show which was televised locally on the BBC. As I'd recorded the track, I was asked to play live on the night, on the telly! Because of this LaHost probably had to cancel a gig or turn one down. Anyway, the unwritten rule is your band always comes first. I've only broken that rule twice. I was summoned to a band meeting at the Free Wheel, a Norwich bookshop which was a popular rehearsal place. The vote went against me and Airbridge drummer Dave Beckett was back in. I'm still great friends with Mark, Sean and Stephen.'

Fudge would join Pendragon the following year.

With Mark Wyatt on guitar, LaHost played their first headline show at The Marquee on 29 September 1985.

Looking something like a cross between Sigue Sigue Sputnik and Mötley Crüe, LaHost hardly look like a typical progressive rock band, but that's probably because they don't sound like one either. Although they bear more than a passing musical resemblance to Twelfth Night, they have, for the most part, a pretty individual sound, which hinges on their use of two drummers, one on a standard acoustic kit, the other on a Simmons. The vocalist (yes that was a pink Mohican) is very energetic, and very visual, and the rest of the band share the limelight pretty equally.

Musically their songs are varied, and there is some nice keyboard and guitar interplay, but from what I could hear of them, the lyrics sounded a jot naff.

They finished with a cover of *Ghostbusters*, hardly a very original choice, but the crowd seemed to like it.

Before I make any real decision about LaHost, I feel I should check out some of their recorded stuff, and maybe see them again. They seem to have quite a strong following, and they definitely have some original ideas.

The Stairway, **issue 1, November 1985**

Former Airbridge frontman Ed Percival was in the audience.

'They were full of energy,' he recalls, 'and I was surprised to find out that they were using my song *Words And Pictures* as their encore.'

A single, *Just Breaking Away* b/w *The Big Sleep*, was recorded at The Enid's studio in Clare, Suffolk.

Bennett: 'As we were laying down some lovely synthesiser pads, Robert John Godfrey came in and simply said 'lush!'. We stupidly released this with no proper A-side, so when *Kerrang!* reviewed the single, they chose the drum machine and synth ballad *The Big Sleep* rather than the upbeat rock song *Just Breaking Away*. I believe the review said, simply, "nuff said'…'

The single was also reviewed in the first issue of the fanzine *Rocking Horse*.

[*Just Breaking Away*] is a very pop orientated single, up-tempo and very up-market for La Host. Multi-layer drum beats with guitar playing in between (great sound, not too distant from Big Country)…

Vocal-wise I like Mark Spencer on this one (I know people who don't) and I think that he's improving with each new product, as are all the band as a whole. My only disappointment with this track is for such a short one, it has far too many changes, some seem totally out of place and very disjointed, while others are suited.

That said I like it but not as much as the other side, *The Big Sleep*, very dreamy and so lovely for the summer daze. This the total opposite from side A, laid back and as gentle as they come. But Mark seems out of place on this one, his voice is just too rough. The backing vocals are great (female in origin) and DO fit in. This one again is not long enough, just as the guitar solo (?) gets started it's time to end (this is a fault I've found with most of the La Host tracks.) But this is probably the problem with crossing prog and modern pop?

Anyway you can make up your own minds. It's £2.00 (expensive for seven inch) but worth adding to the collection. Available from: La Host, 17 St. Germans Rd, Forest Hill. London SE23 1RH.

A PLAYGROUND OF BROKEN HEARTS

Multi-Story with Paul Ford
(Courtesy Rob Wilsher)

LaHost's final gig was to a large audience at the Rock Garden in London on 18 February 1986. It was just over five years and, at best guess, around 10 different line-ups of the two bands since Sean Godfrey had formed Airbridge with Lorenzo Bedini.

The *Erotic Antiques* compilation collects all of LaHost's recordings. Bedini and Godfrey reformed Airbridge in 2012. Godfrey left the following year, after the release of a new EP *Return*. *Memories Of Water* followed in 2021, *Openings* in 2023. There are plans to remaster and re-release Airbridge's 1980s' back catalogue.

*

Multi-Story were formed in South Wales in 1981 by singer/guitarist Paul Ford and keyboard player Rob Wilsher. The band's line-up was completed by Roger Nasey (bass) and Steve Byrne (drums). Although the band were influenced by the likes of Genesis, Pink Floyd and Yes, their music would always have a commercial, hard rocking edge. With the addition of Andy Carney on lead guitars, the band recorded a seven track cassette *Chimes* and the self-financed single *Cutting Close* at the rural Loco Studios near Usk in Monmouthshire.

Paul Ford: 'Loco Studios was a competent 16 track studio located in the beautiful Welsh countryside not so far from the more famous Rockfield. This was an important learning curve for Multi-Story. It's where we got to grips understanding the recording process and became our choice of studio for demos. *Cutting Close* was an inexpensive memento to be sold at live gigs.'

'Loco Studio was gaining a good reputation,' agrees Rob Wilsher. 'We had recorded our first set of original songs there as a four piece band with a guest sax player and two Polish female backing singers. *Cutting Close* was recorded and released as a single so we had something credible to sell at gigs.'

At around the same time, in the first half of 1984, Ford met Pendragon with a view to becoming their lead singer, and also auditioned to replace Euan Lowson in Pallas.

'Paul was spotted by Nick Barrett and he had auditioned with my blessing,' says Rob Wisher. 'Four of us had full-time jobs that we were reluctant to chuck in to 'go professional', which naturally frustrated Paul and hence his ambition to secure a band at a higher level. I always supported Paul in his musical endeavours, even though he would have been difficult to replace.'

That autumn, the band were invited to BBC Maida Vale Studios in London to record a session for Tommy Vance's *Into The Music* radio series.

'Unknown to us,' Rob Wilsher says, 'one of our fans sent in a cassette to Tommy Vance. You can imagine my surprise when Tommy's sultry tones came down my telephone one day inviting us to a session at Maida Vale Studios produced by the late Dale Griffin, drummer with Mott The Hoople.'

The session was recorded on 13 October and broadcast 12 days later. Multi-Story performed three of the longer tracks from *Chimes*, namely *Ahead Of Your Time*, *I, Marcus!* and *Willow And The Sun*. This attracted the interest of FM Records, who had just signed veteran Birmingham rockers Magnum, and no doubt heard some similarities.

'We were already in discussion with FM prior to the broadcast,' says Paul Ford, 'but the performance session certainly solidified the deal.'

Multi-Story's debut album *East/West*, recorded at Rockfield, includes new versions of several songs from *Chimes*. It would be released in late 1985. *East/West* pairs melodic guitars, atmospheric keyboards with Ford's tenor vocals and tight songwriting. Without the long instrumental breaks of their peers, and with actual choruses in their songs, Multi-Story were a more commercial prospect than other prog-leaning bands of the time, even if the 1985 singles *Carrie* and *Breaking New Ground* in 1985 failed to make any impact.

Multi-Story's *Carrie* single, 1985 (Courtesy Mark Guenther)

MULTI-STORY: *Carrie* (FM)

HMMM, TASTY stuff indeed. Multi-Story sound like a very classy outfit indeed, lots of well placed atmospheric keyboards and equal amounts of exuberant guitar attack, wearing a broad smile all the while. Very up, very good. The B-side is rather like Shy without the shrieking harmonies and somehow ends up feeling not unlike Starcastle with balls. Strange.

Kerrang! **issue 93**

As well as headlining The Marquee on 4 June 1985, the band toured extensively with label mates Magnum to promote *East/West*.

'It was an amazing experience,' agrees Rob Wisher. 'I was teaching full time and each day I met up with our bassist, Roger, and we drove to the gig and home again… St Austell, Manchester, Nottingham, Sheffield, London… luckily the Scottish gigs were during my half-term holiday, so I flew up to Glasgow and travelled in the van with the band. It was an old Luton transit and on top of the gear were some old doors that we slept on as we travelled through the night to the next gig… the things you do, eh?'

'There may be some stories to tell from this tour,' Paul Ford says, 'but I'm not, because they are naughty!'

The band also appeared on local Welsh TV station HTV in September 1985 performing *Carrie*. A second album for FM, *Through Your Eyes*, would follow, by

A PLAYGROUND OF BROKEN HEARTS

Multi-Story with Grant Nicholas
(Courtesy Rob Wilsher)

which time Paul Ford had left the band.

'After the tour with Magnum we were now a really tight unit,' Ford says. 'We did lots and lots of gigs. Rob and I had written enough new material for a second album. We liked the quality of production on Magnum's *On A Storyteller's Night*. It had been produced by Kit Woolven, so we asked FM, our record company, if we could have him for *Through Your Eyes*. Kit agreed, so it was on. Kit stayed with me at my home for a week, and we carefully listened to our latest demos getting a feel for what we wanted to achieve, and what he could do to make that happen. He wanted to go to Loco Studios, where we'd recorded the demos, to see the set-up. By now it was a fully functional 24 track pro studio. We were six weeks into the recording sessions and working under the instruction of Kit when we had a visit from FM. They were displeased at the pace of expected progress and halted the recording. And that was that. I'd had enough and left the band.'

'We had a budget from FM for six weeks,' explains Rob Wilsher. 'Kit Woolven didn't make enough headway and the record company pulled the plug. Paul left. Shortly after that we had a load of gear stolen from our rehearsal place, including my brand new Yamaha DX7, for which I had to carry on paying HP at £50 a week for the following 2 years! The record company took away the incomplete multi-track tapes and we were basically stuffed.'

Wilsher persuaded a young musician called Grant Nicholas, who he knew and lived locally, to join the band to complete the album. Nicholas, then 19 years old and now internationally famous with the band Feeder, re-wrote some of Ford's lyrics and recorded new vocals.

'A Bristol businessman stumped up the additional recording costs,' Rob Wilsher explains. 'I had to sign my life away to get the multi-tracks back from FM and continue the project a year later. We did get it finished and FM released it in 1987, but it didn't turn out as we had hoped.'

Unsurprisingly, *Through Your Eyes* exhibits a strong Magnum influence. The proggier elements from *East/West* are mostly absent: these are short, tight, commercial tracks. *Through Your Eyes* is impeccably performed and produced. But, by the time of its release, Multi-Story were close to falling apart.

They played three gigs supporting Pallas at the Bristol Bierkeller (2 February 1988), the Paradiso in Amsterdam (6 February 1988) and The Marquee (8 February 1988) before Grant Nicholas left to move to London to start a recording/production course and subsequently form Feeder.

Ford and Wisher reformed the band, its name now hyphen-free, in 2014 and continue to record and tour, with new studio albums released in 2016 and 2020.

*

Trilogy burned brightly, but for a very short time. They were formed in East London in November 1981 by guitarist/keyboard player Paul Dennis, bassist John Garnett and drummer Keith Thompson. Dennis had previously been the frontman for Minas Tirith. This is not the same band that Euan Lowson worked with after Pallas, but an East London outfit which later morphed into Lone Wolf and then Di'Anno (fronted by the original Iron Maiden singer). Dennis and Garnett were also in a band with the unlikely name of Aubergine.

Paul says: 'My first set of bass pedals was a Roland SH101 synth which sat on the floor. Obviously, my feet were too big to play the keys, so Keith made me a sandal with a toothbrush sticking out of the front to press the keys. Worked perfectly!'

This line-up did not perform any gigs, as Keith Thompson left to join the experimental band The Legendary Pink Dots, with whom he recorded several albums.

'So John and I were looking around for a drummer,' says Paul Dennis, 'and saw Nik Szymanek playing with [local heavy metal band] Dragonfly at the Ruskin Arms. Ignoring the fact that he looked like a praying mantis having a fit, we decided then and there that he would be ideal.'

Szymanek: 'Dragonfly were a NWOBHM band inspired by the likes of Judas Priest, Van Halen, Scorpions and Black Sabbath. This was great, but I was happy to join Trilogy as the band was going more in the direction of heavy prog and hugely influenced by the 'classic' era of Rush. Whereas Dragonfly featured dual guitars, the new Trilogy incarnation experimented heavily with multiple keyboards, bass pedals and complex time signatures, which allowed a lot of creative development.'

Trilogy's first gig was at the Ruskin Arms pub in East London, famous as the 'home' of Iron Maiden and owned by boxer Joe Lucy, who offered Trilogy an unpaid Monday night try-out in November 1981. The Ruskin Arms was a regular venue for other bands of this genre. The 'heavier' prog bands - Haze in particular - also frequently performed there.

Trilogy recorded a demo cassette at Golddust Studios in Bromley in March 1982. This included one of their best known songs, *Arctic Life*. They secured a residency at the Bridge House pub in Canning Town and played dates all around the East London area. At the end of that year, Garnett was replaced by Mark Bloxsidge.

'I'd seen Dragonfly at the Ruskin and loved them,' he says. 'One of the guitar players, Steve Heath, worked in a record shop in Ilford called Penny Farthing Sounds and you could buy the Dragonfly EP there, from one of the musicians who recorded it. They were a big band in the area, and I'd go and see them as often as I could during 1979 and 1980, getting to know them quite well. A couple of years after that, I ran into guitarist and lead singer Rudi Riviere, who was playing in Sapphire by that point. We had a chat, and I asked about the other guys in Dragonfly and what they were doing. He told me that Nik had joined a three piece band called Trilogy, so I went to see them. And there was Paul Dennis, playing guitar and keyboards, who I also knew from Minas Tirith and an earlier band called Government Property. So I already knew both Paul and Nik… and then the original bass player decided to leave, so they advertised for a new bass player in *Melody Maker*. I gave them a call, auditioned and was in.'

'Due to a number of personal issues,' notes Paul

A PLAYGROUND OF BROKEN HEARTS

Trilogy, 15 May 1983
(Courtesy Mark Bloxsidge)

Trilogy, New Merlin's Cave, 1 January 1983
(Courtesy Mark Bloxsidge)

Dennis, 'Nik and I very reluctantly felt that we couldn't carry on with John as we needed 100% commitment. Mark took the trouble to learn the whole set in time for an upcoming gig and fitted in perfectly.'

Bloxsidge's first gig with Trilogy was New Year's Day 1983, at New Merlin's Cave in King's Cross, London, followed by his Ruskin Arms debut on Friday 7 January.

'Trilogy were treading a prog path,' he says, 'but we had more of a rock and metal background than maybe some of the other bands on the scene.'

In short order, Trilogy were booked to play at The Marquee supporting Twelfth Night on 16 January, although, due to both bands being locked out until the early evening, Trilogy were unable to perform. They were compensated by a repeat booking on 26 January when they supported Pendragon at the Gloucestershire band's first headline show. Pendragon were promoted to headliner following a cancellation by Solstice.

In an amazing week for Trilogy, just five days before their Marquee debut they recorded a *Friday Rock Show* session at Maida Vale Studios, returning there for the mixdown on 28 January.

'A friend of ours knew Tony Wilson, the producer of the *Friday Rock Show*,' says Mark Bloxsidge, 'and he had sent him one of our demos. We didn't even know he'd done that until we got a phone call from Tony asking us if we wanted a session. It was quite short notice. I think they'd had someone lined up for session and they dropped out and our tape was on his desk. It was just one of those happy coincidences. I'd done just two gigs with the band and was going to Maida Vale to record the *Friday Rock Show*!'

The broadcast followed a couple of weeks later, 11 February, with Richard Skinner sitting in for Tommy Vance. The songs performed were *A Legion In Morocco*, *Necrosleep* (all six and a half minutes of it), *Arctic Life* and *Dark Humour*.

They supported Twelfth Night at The Marquee on 20 February, promoting a new four track cassette called *Turn The Gun Around*. As with many other bands of the time, Trilogy signed on with Keith Goodwin.

'Keith told us that EMI were putting together a compilation album and there might be a chance of

262

getting us a track on it,' Mark Bloxsidge recalls. 'He said, 'Do you wanna come up to my office and talk about it?' So we travelled the full length of the Circle Line to Ealing Broadway to meet him. We got in there and said, 'How about this album?', and he says, 'Oh, that's probably not gonna happen, but I'm a publicity agent and do you want to sign up with me?' It was the same tactic that he used with everyone! And, of course, we had no idea at the time that he had a track record of working with Yes and other huge names in the 1970s.'

A third Marquee support, this time with Southend's punk-goth band Le Mat, took place on 27 February.

Mark Bloxsidge: 'We had very dubious fashion sense and used to take the stage in Rush inspired kimonos, but at least it made a change from jeans and tee shirts, I guess. Paul had a pair of black leather trousers and a genuine heavyweight silk top which got very hot under the lights. One sweaty night at The Marquee I remember hearing the same synth chord sustaining for a great deal longer than it should have and looked across to see Paul hanging onto his keys to stop himself falling over. Apparently he got so hot he nearly passed out on stage.'

It was still only three months since Mark Bloxsidge had joined. The Marquee bookings, the association with Goodwin and the publicity garnered by the *Friday Rock Show* session attracted the attention of Pallas' manager Harry Maloney.

'We were being managed by a local guy out in east London called John Aspey,' Bloxsidge says. 'He worked quite hard on our behalf and was sending out tapes to all and sundry and trying to get us gigs, but ultimately he just didn't have the experience or the connections. We were approached by Harry. He helped us get out of our contract with John and signed us up.'

Trilogy recorded two demos for Phonogram in late April 1983, who passed and signed pop singer Marilyn instead. A repeat broadcast of the *Friday Rock Show* session on 22 April included a plug for the band's headline booking at The Marquee on 15 May 1983, supported by Airbridge.

Bloxsidge: 'It was a fabulous, fabulous gig and a real achievement for us because The Marquee was the Holy Grail. That was the place that all of our favourite bands had played at some point.'

A further Marquee headliner on 24 June 1983 followed, supported by Tamarisk. A demo session for EMI at Manchester Square in London on 17-18 July resulted in two more songs, but again no record deal was forthcoming, so the band released a new version of their *Arctic Life* cassette instead, including a re-recording of the title track and regular set closer, along with *Buddha*, *Messages* and *Seance*.

'EMI was concentrating on Marillion,' Mark Bloxsidge says, 'and were looking to sign Pallas as well, so had already used up their prog budget for the year, I guess!'

Later that year Trilogy were back at The Marquee on 2 November, supported by Airbridge, then were part of the Brave New World tour with Pallas and Solstice in November/December 1983. After a warm-up gig at North East London Polytechnic in Barking, 11 November, the three band bill was due to complete 19 shows at large venues across the UK. But the tour was abruptly cancelled with several dates remaining. Trilogy subsequently supported Pallas on some dates of their tour to promote *The Sentinel*, appearing at Birmingham Odeon (26 March), Sheffield Polytechnic (3 April), Queensway Hall, Wellingborough (7 April), Queensway Hall, Dunstable (8 April), and Golddiggers, Chippenham (9 April).

Trilogy were booked for further headline dates at The Marquee on 11 July (supported by Quasar) and 16 September 1984, their last, when they were supported by Spider.

They recorded the track *Hidden Mysteries* at Abbeydale in September 1984. This was included on the *Fire In Harmony* compilation released in spring 1985.

'Each band was offered a sum of money,' recalls Mark Bloxsidge. 'I think the choice was that you could either have it as a day in the studio with their engineer and producer to record the track, or if you had a suitable track already, they would buy the rights off you for £200. We desperately needed the money, so we said, 'Well, we've got this song already. We'll give you a copy of that and you can stick that on the album…' We took the money to repair the van, or something.'

Fire In Harmony, their only official release on vinyl, came out in March 1985.

But Trilogy were unable to maintain momentum and split up later that year after a private booking in Lincoln on 5 August.

'All three of us wanted to have success,' recalls Mark Bloxsidge. 'We wanted to record an album and back then the only way you could do that, unless you had some finance behind you and paid for your

**Trilogy, 11 July 1984
(Photograph by Dave Jones)**

Citizen Cain:
Tim Taylor, Cyrus, Gordon Feenie
(Courtesy Citizen Cain archive)

own studio time, was to get signed up by a record company. Sadly, we'd been round them all and they all passed, not necessarily because they didn't like we what we're doing, but they just didn't think it was commercially right for them at the time. Harry told us that he'd tried everyone. 'You can't really go round them again,' he told us, 'because they've seen you and they've made their decision.' You were so reliant on someone agreeing to sign you and then putting the power of that record company behind you for the publicity, the access to a recording studio and everything else. Things are different now. It was the power of social media that brought us back together.'

Trilogy reformed in 2022 and played gigs with Haze and Solstice in 2023.

*

Citizen Cain originally formed in London in 1982 with Gordon Feenie (drums, flute) and George 'Cyrus' Scott (bass, vocals). They had earlier played together in Scotland, in a band called Not Quite Red Fox, for whom Fish unsuccessfully auditioned. As the story goes, when Marillion were looking to replace Doug Irvine in late 1980 Cyrus was offered the job of lead singer and bassist after a gig in Luton when Not Quite Red Fox and Marillion shared the bill. Both sides forgot to exchange contact details…

Feenie and Scott were joined in Citizen Cain by Tim Taylor on guitar.

'My main prog influences at the time were Yes, King Crimson and a bit of Rush,' Taylor says. 'There was also a bit of U2 and Led Zeppelin in there. George was into Gentle Giant and Jethro Tull. Gordon liked Zappa and Wall Of Voodoo, stuff like that. There were lots of other things in the mixing bowl too, but we weren't seeking to emulate anyone else. We wanted to be unique. We practised hard – you had to, with the complex stuff we did – so I guess we were quite a tight unit at that time.'

Their track *Unspoken Words* was included on the *Fire In Harmony* album.

A PLAYGROUND OF BROKEN HEARTS

Citizen Cain, Portsmouth Polytechnic, 21 November 1985 (Courtesy Citizen Cain archive)

'The record company paid for us to do a recording at a nice studio out in the sticks,' Taylor says. 'I can't remember the name of it. We recorded a few tracks, including *Ghost Dance*. *Unspoken Words* got the nod in the end.'

Citizen Cain played at The Marquee twice, supporting Cardiacs and IQ, as well as at Walthamstow Assembly Hall supporting The Enid.

'We played most of the main club venues in London at one time or another,' Taylor says. 'The 100 Club, Ronnie Scott's, Dingwalls. Though I loved the music, I was starting to wonder whether the band would ever achieve enough commercial success to make a living from it. A point came when I had to either pack my job in or leave the band, and after some soul searching I did leave, by mutual agreement. It was an amicable split, and I remember going round to Gordon's to teach guitar parts to my replacement. I remained in touch with Cyrus for a while after that and got the impression the band wasn't really working out.'

Taylor was replaced by guitarist Frank Kennedy, but the band did not last much longer. Kennedy hooked up with teenage drummer Stewart Bell.

'After a few months of jamming and playing cover versions of some of our favourite Genesis songs,' Bell recalls, 'Frank received a call from an old bandmate who was eager to return to his love of playing and writing music. That was Cyrus looking to reform Citizen Cain.'

Initially calling themselves The Kleptomaniacs, Stewart brought in his keyboard, which had a few of his song ideas programmed into it. Cyrus suggested he move from drums to keys and take the main role of composer for the band, which was renamed Citizen Cain once again in 1989. They released their debut album *Serpents In Camouflage* on SI Music in 1993.

Cyrus and Bell still work together as Citizen Cain and have released several well regarded albums.

*

Jadis, who formed in 1982, are led by Gary Chandler (vocals, guitar), and originally included Trevor Dawkins (bass) and Mark Ridout (drums).

'I started playing music in my last year of school,' Chandler says. 'This was in the late 1970s, so I was about 15 years old. I had met up with two friends, Mark and Trev, who were into the same sort of music as me: Genesis, Pink Floyd, Yes, Camel and Supertramp. The rather starchy music teachers did not really show any enthusiasm for our style of music, which comprised a drum kit, Vox amplifiers and some very cheap guitars that we would buy from 'Rip-off Des'. This was a second hand music shop in Southampton. It was actually called Music City, but many of the aspiring musicians at that time were not getting the best deals and, being naive, were sold some dodgy looking and sounding guitars with unpronounceable names… We managed to secure

Jadis badge (From the collection of Günter Schote)

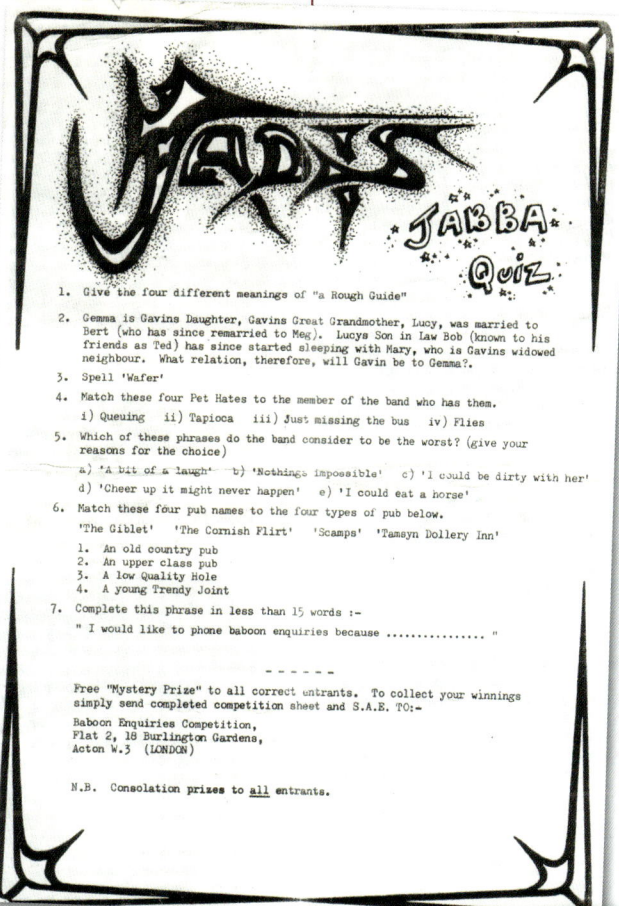

Jadis quiz sheet, ca. 1984 (Courtesy Mark Guenther)

the drama room for rehearsing after school as rock and roll was way out of the comfort zone of our music teachers. Playing by ear and not reading music was frowned upon and not encouraged.'

The band went by a number of names, including Icarus and Saruman Grass. They became friendly with members of another local band, The Lens, which would later morph into IQ.

'I met both Mike Holmes and Martin Orford while queueing overnight for Steve Hackett tickets for his gig at the Gaumont in Southampton on his *Spectral Mornings* tour [27 June 1979],' Chandler recalls. 'We were the first five or six people in the queue. Someone was playing a cassette of The Lens' first demo *No TV Tonite* and from there we chatted about progressive music and our respective bands. Mike Holmes did play the first few Jadis gigs with us mainly in and around Southampton, because at the time we did not have a keyboard player and needed another instrument to fill the space. We actually had a second guitar player but every time a gig was offered he would make an excuse as to why he couldn't make it, citing a fear of heights or having fallen victim to a wasp sting… though I think he just had stage fright. Mike would

A PLAYGROUND OF BROKEN HEARTS 💔

Gary Chandler and Les Marshall, 19 August 1984
(Photographs by Dave Jones)

step in. He's a talented guitarist so he didn't need to rehearse too much to learn the parts.'

The band moved to London in 1982. 'At that point we were a four piece with guitarist Les Marshall, who was a very close friend of both Mike Holmes and Martin Orford.'

Their first demo tape, *Hot Beans*, was released in spring 1983. This was followed by the eight song *Baboon Enquiries* the next year.

'*Hot Beans* and *Baboon Enquiries* were very crudely recorded using an old Tascam portastudio which belonged to [IQ's bass player] Tim Esau,' Chandler explains. 'He was kind enough to lend it to us for what was quite a long time. We didn't have any recording experience, so it was all guess work and trial and error. The drums were recorded in an old, converted barn in the grounds of a huge convent in Fair Oak, a village about eight miles north-east of Southampton. I have vivid memories of going outside the barn to see nuns collecting vegetables and tending their allotment. They never told us to shut up or even turn it down… very tolerant nuns indeed.'

Jadis supported IQ on many occasions, including at The Marquee in August 1984.

'The Marquee was, at that time, hallowed ground,' says Gary Chandler. 'It was a big deal to play there. Just having photographs taken with the iconic logo was a big lift for us, and it made all four of us living together in a tiny flat in London seem almost worthwhile.'

Jadis supported IQ on the *Nomzamo* tour in 1986.

'Again, this was through our connection with Mike and Martin,' Gary Chandler admits. 'We all knew each other, so that helped, and they had a 7.5 ton truck which we followed in our mate's red transit. I think we built some seats in the back for added comfort, although that description is a bit of a stretch as the seats moved independently from the van. Later that year we supported IQ for some dates in the Netherlands and by that point we had bought ourselves a much bigger Iveco van. It was freezing, so we bungee-tied a domestic Calor gas heater to the corner of the van to gain a few degrees in warmth. Health and safety weren't invited to look around and I am sure it wasn't 100% legal… These were great shows, we met lots of great people who would, from that point, help us considerably and we picked up a really good following from those gigs.'

With the personnel shifting again—Paul Alwin now on drums and new keyboard player Pete Salmon—the self-released cassette *Jadis* (1987) was produced by Marillion's Steve Rothery.

Chandler: 'Our involvement with Steve was a case of 'right place, right time'. We were auditioning for a keyboard player and one of the guys who auditioned was Steve's brother-in-law, Pete Salmon. Steve heard one of our four track portastudio recordings. He thought we had some very good tunes and very kindly offered to re-record and

Jadis promo shot, late 1986
Rear: Paul Alwin, Pete Salmon,
Gary Chandler. Front: Trev Dawkins
(From the collection of Günter Schote)

produce them at his home studio. As a result of meeting and working with Steve, he was able to get us onto the *Clutching At Straws* UK tour. We learned lots from Steve during that time and have always been grateful for his help with pushing Jadis forward.'

The cassette was reviewed in the second issue of *Cosmic Crystal* fanzine in early 1988.

The unusual but catchy guitar opening marks the beginning of the first track on this two track demo from this Buckinghamshire based quartet. *G-13*'s instrumental introduction helps to familiarise us with the style of the players. The guitar is definitely the main instrument, while keyboards provide backing to outline the melodic/pomp feel of the music.

Gary Chandler is clearly the frontman, doing lead vocals, playing guitar, and introducing songs in the live situation, but the other members have an equally important role: the fresh drum sound of Paul Alwin, Pete Salmon on keyboards and the subtle sound of Trev Dawkins on bass. The track explores commercial flavourings, while not lowering standards of musicianship or writing.

The B-side, *Out Of Reach*, doesn't really match

G-13, but nevertheless is a sound song.

Chandler's not a great vocalist, but he is adequate, and his sound complements the music.

The cassette was produced by Steve Rothery (Marillion) and is available for £2.00.

This release was followed by a second two track cassette featuring *Don't Keep Me Wondering* and *In The Dark*, recorded at Woodcray in September 1987 and again produced by Steve Rothery.

Jadis played large venues such as the Manchester Apollo and Hammersmith Odeon supporting Marillion.

Chandler: 'This was a really big deal for us… playing in these amazing provincial theatres up and down the country. It was such a great experience watching how the big Marillion shows were put together… the staging, organisation, sound equipment, lighting, road crews and catering. I was fascinated by how it all went together from the huge trucks arriving to the moment that the stage was ready for a soundcheck. I was very proud to see 'Marillion plus Jadis' on the billboard at the Hammersmith Odeon when we played there for three nights [16-18 January 1988]. These were great times.'

Three months later, on 24 April, Jadis performed at the first Marillion Fan Club convention at The Marquee. Mark Kelly and Fish did not attend.

'We played some Jadis songs,' says Gary Chandler, 'and Steve got up and played *G-13* with us. We finished with *Market Square Heroes*, and a guy from the audience jumped up to sing.'

A period of extensive touring in pubs and clubs throughout the UK built up a strong following and led to Jadis' first Marquee headline at the Charing Cross Road venue on 18 February 1989. Later members included drummer Steve Christey and both Martin Orford and John Jowitt (moonlighting from IQ for the debut album *More Than Meets The Eye* in 1992).

Jadis continue to record and perform with Chandler, Orford and Christey and were joined by bassist Andy Marlow in 2007. Their most recent album is called *More Questions Than Answers* (2024).

*

Twice Bitten supported Twelfth Night, Pendragon, Solstice and Haze and were unusual in that they were a two guitar duo, often playing with two 12-string guitars in the style of early and mid-period Genesis. Twice Bitten were formed at Nottingham University in 1982 by Rog Patterson and Greg Smith.

'I was 21,' Patterson says. 'I'd taken three gap years to drink beer, eat curry and play bass in an unknown heavy metal band. Greg was 18. We both studied philosophy. On our first day I spotted him as a musical soulmate via the *Trick Of The Tail* paintings on his jeans. We hit it off instantly on discovering that we were both huge fans of Anthony Phillips.'

Their self-funded cassette *Dialogue* was released in 1984.

Patterson: 'If memory serves – and, quite frankly, usually it doesn't – I played football at university with someone who knew a studio sound engineer [Robin Prior, who worked with Twelfth Night] who was willing to help us record. The result was *Dialogue*. Robin somehow helped us to blag onto a Marquee gig supporting Twelfth Night. I don't remember exactly how we attached ourselves to Pendragon, but everyone knew everyone else and

Calling All The Heroes

Twice Bitten, 5 May 1984
(Photographs by Robin Willcocks)

Twice Bitten information sheet
(Courtesy Mark Guenther)

> **TWICE BITTEN....**
>
> Once upon a time, there was a Brummie bassist called Rog. Years of heavy metal had left him bored, balding and broke. Then one day he encountered a large hairy being, brandishing an out-of-tune 12-string and claiming to come from Billericay. His name was Greg (which in ancient Brum-speak means "my round,") and the two discovered a mutual interest in Anthony Phillips, chocolate biscuits and tuning difficulties. Aware of the social stigma involved in being 12-string guitarists, they tried to keep such tendencies hidden by masquerading as perfectly normal, socially acceptable bassists. But in their secret Nottingham hideaway, they could give vent to their true feelings, indulging in many feverish nights of chord variations and early Genesis cover-versions, tuning and re-tuning until their strings could take no more. For a whole summer they remained in their barely-amplified den, writing things with names like "Crocus Point" and "Blue Sky Century," emerging only to play cricket and feed the squirrels. Then one day tragedy struck: the beer ran out. Impoverished and guilt-ridden, they realised they must "come out," hoping the world would take pity on them despite their obsession with minor chords and broken G-strings. They took the name Twice Bitten - a reference, perhaps, to the pavement which removed their trusted chronicler's front teeth, in a fearful incident involving a bicycle and 10 pints of Abbot Ale. So now they perform unashamed, using their instruments as they wish, unfettered by social norms - they no longer sit in dark corners of folk clubs, fiddling with their tuning heads. They are no longer embarrassed about having too many strings (not to mention too many necks) or writing songs with big words in them! Who knows where all this will end? Legalization of the dulcimer?! God, we live in enlightened times.
>
> GREG SMITH is 19; he plays various twangy things, and has been known to sing. Too tall.
>
> ROG PATTERSON is as old as the hills; he plays 12-string, has a bit of a sing and tends to write a lot. Don't mention dinosaurs.

we somehow, quite accidentally, became part of the scene. We met Haze through our group of friends in Nottingham and immediately gelled with their intrinsic silliness.'

Their two guitars, no drums or keyboards line-up helped secure many support bookings, including at least four at The Marquee with Solstice (4-5 May 1984), Pendragon (17 June 1984) and Haze (26 August 1985).

'We didn't get in the way too much,' Patterson says, 'and offered very little musical threat! Audiences seemed to enjoy the ad-libbed comedy, and my insistence on gently taking the piss out of the headliners became a surprisingly positive USP. And I think people just liked having Greg around – he's the nicest chap one could hope to meet. The

Tamarisk, *Lost Properties* cassette, 1983
(Courtesy Mark Guenther)

other bargaining chip was that I used to promote gigs in Nottingham – I'd put on a Pendragon show in return for a Marquee support, or a few university gigs, or whatever. That's how we met Solstice, I think.'

Dialogue would be followed by the well regarded *No Third Man* (1985). The last track they recorded before splitting in 1986 was suitably titled *End Play*. This was included on the *Exposure* compilation album compiled by a very young Steve[n] Wilson with whom Patterson co-produced the 1987 cassette *Action At A Distance* for Coltsfoot.

Rog Patterson continued as Pendragon's tour manager as well as a solo artist – *Party Piece* can be found on *Double Exposure* (1987) – before joining Coltsfoot in 1988. He released some solo cassettes followed by the vinyl album *Flightless* in 1989. Twice Bitten perform from time to time, most often as support act to their old friends in Pendragon for whom Rog is a regular member of the live line-up.

*

Tamarisk, from Essex, were formed in 1982 by Andy Grant (vocals) and Steve Leigh (keyboards), both previously members of Chemical Alice - the band that gifted Mark Kelly to Marillion.

Chemical Alice had been formed by guitarist Dave Weston.

'Dave had a plan to form a band in the vein of Hawkwind, Gong, Steve Hillage and Here & Now,' Mark Kelly wrote. 'He wanted it to be a 'jam band', a style of creating music made popular in the US by the Grateful Dead, but it was a concept that had yet to reach the UK. Dave wanted to call the band Chemical Alice. The name was plucked from the pages of a Michael Moorcock fantasy novel.'

The original singer, Tim Kelly, was replaced by Andy Grant in early 1981.

'I had never heard of them until Dave Weston contacted me to invite me along to see the band play with a view to see if we could all work together,' Grant recalls. 'At that time, they didn't have a frontman/singer. Dave and Mark Kelly were handling the vocals. They had a really enthusiastic following. They were good players and they definitely needed someone up front. I met them after the show, along with Jack Grigor the bass player. We all hit it off and they offered me the gig there and then. I quit the band I was in the next day and that was that.'

Six months later, Mark Kelly was poached by Marillion. He was replaced by Steve Leigh.

'My name was passed on to Dave Weston,' Leigh says. 'He called me out of the blue and asked if I would be interested in coming in as a replacement for their keyboard player, who was leaving to join another band. I went to the audition and pretty much got on with everybody. I took on the job and that's really how I met everyone in the band, who were already an established line-up.'

'I'm not sure Dave and Jack were ever really happy with Steve,' Andy Grant recalls. 'Losing Mark really seemed to affect them. Both Steve and I wanted different things to Dave and Jack. They wanted improvisation and a more abstract feel to the lyrics, more made-up stories. We wanted structure and songs rooted in the real world. It was never going to work. We started to fall out and it wasn't long before we parted ways, about nine months I think.'

Leigh and Grant immediately formed a new band, Tamarisk.

Leigh: 'Andy and myself wanted to continue musically and we tried a few get-togethers with various musicians before coming together as Tamarisk.'

Grant: 'Tamarisk was meant to be about fully formed songs with ideas about politics, relationships and our real life experiences.'

The line-up was completed by Richard Harris (drums), Peter Munday (guitar) and Mark Orbell (bass). They released two cassette EPs, *Tamarisk* in 1982 and *Lost Properties* in the early part of 1983.

The track *Ascension* from the former was broadcast on the *Friday Rock Show* on 20 May 1983.

'Tommy Vance actually contacted me directly to find out a bit more about us before he played it!' says Andy Grant. 'That was pretty surprising. We felt something might be about to break for us. There was even talk of us going in for a session at one point, but it never happened. Once again we failed to capitalise on the good things happening to us.'

Tamarisk played at The Marquee supporting Trilogy on 24 June 1983, but never broke through to headlining status.

'We had a good press agent in Keith Goodwin,' Steve Leigh says, 'but I guess it's all about the numbers. If Andy, Pete or I had had the money at the time, I'm sure we would have personally guaranteed every ticket and bussed in family and friends wholesale. Would that have made a difference? Who knows?'

Grant: 'We had some good nights there. The DJ really liked us and pushed for us. But, no, we never did headline.'

A line-up change brought in a new rhythm section of Nick May and Brian Roberts. But Andy Grant was unhappy.

'I tried to leave the band in early 1984,' he says, 'but Steve convinced me to give it one more go. By October I just couldn't do it any more. My personal situation was not good, we had no one working on the business side, it was slowly fading away. So Steve and I split it up and went our separate ways.'

'I think that was my fault as far as I can recall,' Steve Leigh admits. 'I was struggling a bit mentally and left. Ultimately you get a feeling that some things have run their course and it's time to put it to bed or allow others to take a project forward or in a direction that "freshens it up". I think, subconsciously, I had a rule of thumb that if you haven't released a full album of some description within three years as part of a cohesive unit, then it's time to knock it on the head and do something elsewhere. This appears to have been a common theme throughout my musical endeavours.'

Steve Leigh joined Quasar for a time before forming Landmarq in 1990. May joined Dagaband, Jadis and The Enid.

Grant and Leigh reformed Tamarisk in 2012. Their most recent album, *Suspended Animation* (2021), consists of six songs written and performed in 1983-84 but not previously recorded.

*

A PLAYGROUND OF BROKEN HEARTS

Tamarisk at the Ad Lib, Kensington (Courtesy Keith Turner)

Gothique were a five piece band from Hertfordshire and played mostly around the Home Counties, supporting The Enid and Solstice at a number of gigs and appearing at The Marquee with IQ in June 1983.

'They were one of my favourite bands from the early '80s era,' remembers David Futter. 'I first saw them at Melbourn Rock Club in Cambridgeshire. They delivered a fantastic set that night and the band allowed my friend to record the set on a tape recorder placed on a table in front of the stage. I had a copy of the live recording at Melbourn for years on cassette until it got lost in a house move about 10 years ago!'

Gothique released a self-produced demo tape in 1982 called *Face Of Ages*, and a professionally recorded four song cassette, *Kristiana*, in 1983. Their line-up was Colin Molloy (guitar, vocals), Simon Lee (lead vocals, guitar), Ken Gascoigne (keyboards) and Andy Scarlini (drums) with, at various times, Chris Blackman, Stuart Dear and Andy Day on (bass). They supported IQ at The Marquee on 15 September 1983.

'Their early material was inspired by Tolkien,' says Sam Smyth, 'but they ran into issues with the Tolkien Society, so some song names were changed. They never quite had the success of the other, bigger bands, but they were our friends so we followed them everywhere.'

'They were a much more traditional

prog band with fantasy lyrics but could really rock when they got going,' suggests David Futter. 'Gothique had the songs and, as musicians, could match the other bands but it never happened for them. I guess it probably came down to management and commitment.'

For a short while, Gothique featured a young singer called Tim Bowness. Bowness had previously sung in a local band called Always The Stranger, later regrouped as After The Stranger, who played in and around Manchester including a couple of dates with Peter Nicholls' mid-IQ band Niadem's Ghost.

'I'd put an advert in *Melody Maker* and various shops,' Bowness says, 'along the lines of, 'Distinctive vocalist seeks ambitious band. Influences include Scott Walker, Peter Hammill, Peter Gabriel, David Sylvian, Durutti Column, Virginia Astley, Eric Satie, Kate Bush and Nico,' and received quite a number of incredibly varied replies. I passed a couple of auditions to join two very different bands. One was an atmospheric rock band from Manchester with strong U2 and Simple Minds influences and the other was Gothique. I decided on the latter as they were really nice people, talented musicians, and had decent connections with record labels. However, I only ended up being in the band for about five weeks. I felt very uncomfortable singing the band's epics – it wasn't music I'd have chosen to make – and I refused to dress up in the elaborate stage costumes they wanted me to. Additionally, I was selfishly foisting my music on them. There was a massive creative incompatibility, and I was naive for thinking a compromise was possible. I did one gig with them supporting The Enid (who were great) at the Letchworth Town Hall. I came on for the 12 minute encore, which was intended to act as a means of introducing me gently to its audience. As was my way of the time, I barked like a loon throughout the piece. I have no doubt that I was absolutely dreadful, but somewhere in the audience was a young Steven Wilson who apparently thought I was alright.'

'We saw Gothique one final time,' says David Futter, 'again in Hitchin supporting Solstice who, by this time, had Barbara Deason on vocals [1985]. By now they had changed their name to Mothers Pride, and then, I guess realising that this was a brand of bread at the time, just Pride. They aimed for a simpler, straightforward, more contemporary style, which for me and my friends didn't work. I still believe they were the lost act of that prog era. I would have loved to have heard a proper studio album from them.'

*

It Bites were formed in Egremont, a small market town in Cumbria, in 1982 by guitarist/vocalist Francis Dunnery, bassist Dick Nolan and drummer Bob Dalton. Keyboard player John Beck, from nearby Whitehaven, joined later that year.

'I met Bob on my first day of school, when I was five years old,' Dunnery says today. 'Dick was a year younger than us. I remember at 10 or 11 years old, when I was at Saint Bridget's Catholic School, taking a guitar to school and wanting to be in a band then.'

Dunnery played in a cabaret band in Egremont, with a friend of his playing organ. Like so many others, he was guided by his brother's record collection.

'My brother, Baz, was a fantastic musician, a very bright light,' Dunnery recalls. 'Everybody wanted to hang out with him, he was one of the most popular people in the town. He was the biggest influence on me personally and I think he was the biggest influence on everybody. We would sit round and listen to his record collection: Mahavishnu Orchestra, Chick Corea, Soft Machine, Larry Coryell, Weather Report. I liked Genesis, Bob liked Led Zeppelin, Dick liked Jethro Tull…'

As pals they also enjoyed the BBC's *Sight And Sound In Concert* series, which started in January 1977 and was broadcast each week, usually in the gaps between series of *The Old Grey Whistle Test*.

'I remember watching Gentle Giant and Colosseum II with Gary Moore and Jon Hiseman,' Dunnery says. 'That was our life, we didn't really do anything else. We'd watch these bands and we just thought, 'Wow, these are like proper people, proper bands.' And we didn't know anything about colleges. Nobody's expecting you to go to college. You were expected to get a fucking job digging roads or something like that. If you were lucky. But we didn't do that. I left school at 15. I was a fucking lunatic.'

'We started up in 1982 playing gigs at working men's clubs and nightclubs,' Bob Dalton said, 'but we were young lads at the time and fairly irresponsible. We ended up getting banned from nearly everywhere because we got so drunk and rowdy. One time we were playing a two night gig at Carlisle nightclub Talk Of The Border. The first night went great but by the second I was so drunk I thought it'd be a good idea to pull Dick's shorts down. Then we all decided to do it. Naturally we had nothing on underneath. Some sneak decided to sell the story to the *Sunday Sun*. They headlined us 'Bottom Of The Pops'. We never lived that one down.'

The band split up in 1983, but reunited the following year when they all moved to a squat in Peckham, London, to write original material.

Dunnery: 'You know, there's something liberating to me about delving into the 60% of your potential that is untapped. And so I went to London by myself. I got on the M6, hitched down to London and slept in Euston Station for about three or four nights. I used to go to Dingwalls – it was the only place I'd heard of – and wait outside and look for musicians. I had this phone number from a guy called Keith Thomas, a saxophonist who I'd met when he played in Whitehaven with the singer Forrest [who scored a Top 5 single, *Rock The Boat*, in March 1983]. I ended up in a R&B band with him. And we did some recording at Odyssey Studios. And then somebody told me about squats. They said, 'If you put your own lock on, then it's yours and they can't kick you out for a year.' I went to Peckham 'cause that's where they said the best squats were. I kicked the door in. I put the lock on. I waited for the police, and they didn't come. I called the guys back home and they came down and they got a squat two doors away.'

'The flat had nothing in it apart from equipment and us,' Dalton recalled. 'We slept on camp beds that we put away during the day. But it was actually the perfect situation because all we could afford to do was write songs 24/7. All that time was the making of us. We became strong writers and strong players.'

'We just started writing songs,' Dunnery says. 'We were on the dole and fucking starving. We used to steal milk off people's doorsteps. I was as skinny as a rake. But we would record every night onto a cassette player and send these tapes off to all the record companies. And then Paul Morley from ZTT sent us a message and he said, 'Listen, I just want to give you guys a heads up here. You're never gonna get a fucking deal with these tapes. You gotta do proper demos.' So we saved up our money and went to an 8 track studio. We did three demos. One was called *Danger Money*, one was *Let My Heart Decide*, and the other was maybe *All In Red*. We got turned down about six times. I got sick of this, and I said, 'I'm going to go into the record companies and just give them my tape.' I went to Warner Brothers and the fucking security guards wouldn't let me in. I don't know whether I was arguing with them, but they basically said, 'If you don't get out of it, I'm gonna kick your fucking teeth down the road.' And then this guy called Martin Mayhead walked past. He worked for a company called Modern Media, which was a media company who promoted Simply Red. So we gave him the tape and he loved it.'

Bob Dalton: 'He agreed to pay for rehearsal time [at Clink Street Studios in London], polish us up and get us a record label.'

Dunnery: 'And then one thing led to another, and we got all the record companies down. They didn't think we could do it live, but it was dead easy. We had great melodies and good songs, we had the new romantic clothes on. We're only like 21 or something. The Virgin guys really liked us. We were a pretty marketable package at that point, there's no doubt about it.'

A support slot with Faith Brothers at The Marquee on 16 August 1985 preceded a recording contract with Virgin. They signed at around the same time as Twelfth Night.

It Bites' first single *All In Red* (released 18 March 1986) failed to chart. But the follow-up, the irresistible *Calling All The Heroes* (June 1986), was a big hit, reaching number 6 in the UK.

TV appearances followed, including *Wogan* and *The Old Grey Whistle Test*.

'An unknown four piece from Cumbria,' writes Paul Stump, '[It Bites] had fame somewhat thrust upon them in 1986 when they appeared live on national UK TV, in the prime-time *Wogan* chat-show slot, while still living in a South London squat. Virgin Records had signed them on the strength of a demo tape, placed them on a national tour as support for period piece 1980s' popsters Go West and wangled the TV slot to promote the quartet's first [sic] single, *Calling All The Heroes*. After a brace of wanly unimpressive power-pop verses and choruses there was an abrupt accelerando and they broke into a galloping instrumental middle eight of sheer progressive virtuosity without missing a pop trick - heavens, you could dance to this stuff. As unashamed of their pop sensibility as their sedulous study of the virtuosity of Yes and Led Zeppelin, It Bites consciously broke through into a postmodern flux with an exalted and puppyish enthusiasm.'

Gregory Spawton: 'It Bites came along at a time when the prog scene had fallen apart again. I was at university by then and I'd more or less given up on going to see the '80s prog bands. Then my old school friends mentioned It Bites and, suddenly, there they were, an exciting new talent. They had nailed a sort of pop/prog rock hybrid. I watched them on *Top Of The Pops* [14 August 1986] and I thought, 'Wow, this is incredible!' The level of musicianship in that band was extraordinary. And they could write too.'

It Bites' debut album *The Big Lad In The Windmill* (July 1986), charted at number 35. The band toured

A PLAYGROUND OF BROKEN HEARTS

It Bites at Nottingham Trent University, 19 February 1988 (Photograph by Gregory Spawton)

with Marillion (five dates in December 1987) and Robert Plant, and headlined The Marquee once more, on 23 February 1988.

Sessions with producer Steve Hillage resulted in the singles *Kiss Like Judas* (February 1988) and *Midnight* (April 1988). Marillion must have been listening. Their first single with Steve Hogarth, *Hooks In You*, has a distinct It Bites feel.

Dunnery: 'We were poppy at our essence. I loved The Beach Boys, 10cc… Paul McCartney's one of my favourites. I have a real big poppy element to my writing.'

'It Bites' songs *are* pop songs,' suggests Paul Stump. 'The harmony tonal and recognisable, save for some well chosen moments of extra colourful symphonic melodrama. Indeed, the band's trump was their almost innocent willingness to use as elements of a progressive alloy an array of musical styles most progressive fans found vulgar and commercialised. These were pop, punk, dance music and metal.'

Once Around The World (March 1988) showcased their more progressive musical influences, especially the 15 minute title track and the complex *The Old Man And The Angel*.

Dunnery: 'It was really on *Once Around The World* where we became ourselves. That's really the essence of the band.'

Paul Stump: '*Once Around The World* locates the band in … rockist pastures, but the fact that this subtle shift still throws up some sublime music is worthy of any band's epitaph. In a previous era, the LP would have been the breakthrough of coming superstars. Instead, in 1988, its reception was less than thrilling. A single that caught the public ear, like *Calling All The Heroes* was absent, although *Midnight* opens the album with a martial flourish and pounding chromatic progressions that would grace any Top Ten. At least Dunnery's boys never fail in their triple targeting of mind, heart and body.'

The band toured to promote the album. Their Liverpool gig was reviewed in *Kerrang!* issue 189 (28 May 1988).

What do you think of these lads? Are they the band that's going to drag progressive rock into the 1990s? After all, many people hail them as the new Yes. Or are they merely popsters with a penchant for complexity?

Hmmmmm.

It Bites play very complicated music. Perhaps it's too complex at times with songs like *Yellow*

Christian and *Plastic Dreamer* flitting across time signatures and melody lines to the point of distraction. And there's a fair amount of sampling going down here too I'll wager, so much so that at times you begin to believe that this has got more to do with currents on circuit boards than fingers on frets.

If there is a human side to this band then it's Francis Dunnary (sic). He's a consummate frontman, oozing charisma from every pore and drenching the crowd with it. They can rock a bit too, without confusing the issue by overt intricacy, *Black December* reminding me very much of Alex Harvey's *Faith Healer*.

That they were going to play *Screaming On The Beaches* and *Calling All The Heroes* as the finalé pieces was predictable l suppose, but sliding Ol' Blue Eyes' *New York, New York* into the encore left me amused and bewildered.

Are they the new Yes or merely a progression of Duran Duran? Well, to be honest, they're neither in my opinion. It Bites didn't bite me all that hard but, by the same token, they didn't suck either.

'By the time we did *Eat Me In St Louis* [1989] we had an American record company,' Francis Dunnery says. 'They wanted Mike Stone to produce us [Stone had produced albums for Journey, Asia and Whitesnake]. But then we listened to Mike Stone, and we didn't want to do that.'

Eat Me In St Louis was recorded at Musicland Studios in Munich with producer Reinhold Mack, best known for work with ELO, Queen and the Rolling Stones. The album received great reviews in *Kerrang!* and elsewhere.

'People say to me that there's more guitar on this album,' Francis Dunnery said, 'but there isn't really. It's just that instead of flying around at 9,000 miles an hour, I've been playing tunes that people can remember.'

Despite *Eat Me In St Louis* giving the band their third Top 50 album, and a headline booking at the Hammersmith Odeon in April 1990, Dunnery left the band to focus on a solo career.

It Bites tried, with considerable success, to assimilate their prog rock and fusion influences into a pop setting but still couldn't meet their label's demands for hit singles and albums.

'We were not able to cross over at all,' Francis Dunnery agrees. 'The whole concept of being in the music business just didn't suit us. We were a West Cumbrian band who messed around, drank beer and weren't cut out for this clinical Jon Bon Jovi kind of success.'

'Part of the problem was the friction between us and Virgin bosses,' Bob Dalton said. 'They were predominantly a pop label so they wanted us all poppy but we were determined to stay prog rock. In the end we were a curious mix between the two, which was good in a way because nobody had that sound apart from Genesis. But we resented it and Virgin found it hard to market us.'

Not only that, but the media hostility towards prog music that had dogged It Bites' immediate forebears was still in place.

The original band's final release, a live album called *Thankyou And Goodnight*, would follow in August 1991. Dunnery auditioned for the lead singer role in Genesis in 1996.

'I wanted to sing *In The Cage* with Tony Banks and Mike Rutherford. That's all I wanted to do,' he says

Francis Dunnery at the It Bites fan convention, Rock Garden, Covent Garden, 17 December 1989 (Photograph by Gregory Spawton)

today. 'They were asking me to do all these Phil Collins songs. I can't do that!'

A 2003 plan to reunite fell through, but a version of It Bites, without Dunnery, was launched in 2006. Dunnery's role as guitarist, vocalist and frontman was taken on by John Mitchell. This version of It Bites seemingly came to an end in 2018. Dunnery now tours as It Bites FD (with a changing band line-up) and has recently released new albums *Live From The Black Country* (2023) and *Return To Natural* (2024).

Doubters are directed to the astounding videos of the band's October 1989 concert in Tokyo: It Bites were energetic, tight, supremely skilled and one of the great hopes of the tail end of the 1980s. For a while, Francis Dunnery was a bona fide rock star.

'I was just a bit more frightened than I am now,' he says. 'I'm not frightened anymore. I'm actually a very gentle person. But back then I didn't know that about myself. Maybe it was false arrogance, maybe it's all just fear. I'd get recognised (by girls) in the street, sure. Yeah. And then I slept with them.' [laughs]

*

Although not strictly a progressive band, Pride Of Passion included, at various times, several musicians who were part, or on the fringes, of the progressive scene.

'When I left Marillion [in spring 1982],' notes bass player Diz Minnitt, 'I initially played in a Northants band called The World Service.'

The band was short-lived, despite some memorable gigs, including one at the RAF base at Upper Heyford where, according to Diz, 'The front of stage had a metal grid, floor to ceiling, and it became clear why as we exited stage left, and the base itself fairly rapidly thereafter, with the sound of smashing bottles still ringing in our ears…'

Diz joined a band from Harrow called Benzene Jag, later truncated to Benzene, in November 1982. The band included vocalist and songwriter Jenneth Venture (real name: Colin Parry) and two future members of Pride Of Passion, drummer Barry Talbot and guitar player Nigel Spennewyn.

'The original line-up was Colin, me, my cousin Michael on bass, a guy called George (rhythm guitar) and a drummer whose name escapes me,' Spennewyn recalls.

That first line-up was short-lived.

'Colin and I recorded a few demos in the shed at his parents' house in Hayes,' Spennewyn says. 'We added Joe Rumsey on guitar and keyboards and Barry on drums. Our first recording session was at a studio in Rayners Lane with Vincent Crane, formerly of Atomic Rooster. Colin and I went to his large house in Maida Vale to talk and watch him and his wife smoke dope a few times. I honestly don't know why! We recorded the songs *Doppelgängers* and *Jag Snap*, I think. It sounded pretty good. I can't recall who else was on that session. I don't think Vince dug it, and that was that. He was a weird guy.'

They recruited Diz Minnitt on bass.

'Rehearsals went well,' Diz recalls. 'At the same time, we were busy building a fully functional soundproofed eight track studio in Colin's garage. The band had a good vibe and I thought would benefit from the inclusion of a proper keyboard player and so I enlisted Brian Jelleyman. We started to gig sporadically. I spoke to Andy Glass of Solstice, who generously included us as support at one of their Marquee gigs [22 April 1983], which was well received by the Solstice audience.'

Gigs, however, were sparse.

'There just wasn't the same level of impetus, hunger and drive I had been used to with Marillion,' Diz admits. 'Colin monopolised the songwriting and was actively resistant to allow the space for others to contribute to songs or ideas for arrangement. I enjoyed the songs, but I felt creatively stifled having come from Marillion where mine and Brian's contributions had been crucial in the creation and evolution of many songs, including *Market Square Heroes*, *He Knows You Know*, *Garden Party*, *Three Boats Down From The Candy* and *Grendel*. I was becoming progressively frustrated - pun intended - in being someone else's bass player, with a creative itch I couldn't scratch. It was very much Colin's band and I didn't want to push him out.'

Diz's solution was to leave, and take most of the band with him.

'Myself, Nigel, Brian and Barry left and began rehearsing and writing new material while searching for a vocalist and a permanent name. We found the former with a heavy rock style vocalist called Adey Gibbs who joined for a few weeks. One Sunday we were rehearsing when Deborah Hopper turned up for an audition.'

Hopper had grown up in Grimsby, about as far from the beating heart of the music business as it's possible to get.

'It all started with me answering an ad in the *Grimsby Evening Telegraph*,' Hopper recalls. 'Vocalist for acoustic band required. I was 15, and it was my

A PLAYGROUND OF BROKEN HEARTS

Pride Of Passion at The Marquee, mid-1985
(Photograph by Andy Inman)

**Deb Hopper at The Marquee
(Photograph by Andy Inman)**

very first audition. I can't remember what I sang, but I got the gig. It was two guys in their mid-20s. I think I must've been the only applicant.'

The band was called Bordello.

'I went along with it because I had no idea what it meant,' she admits.

After several line-up changes, the band was renamed to Mr E, and settled as Deborah Hopper (vocals), Dave Burman (bass), Paul Lindemann (guitar), David Rhodes (guitar, *not* the Peter Gabriel sideman) and Tom Watson (drums).

'Both the Daves had gone to the same school as me,' Deb says, 'but they were both a couple of years older than me, so we hadn't really known each other at school. The songs came together well, with Dave Burman writing most of the music, and either myself or Paul writing the lyrics. We recorded a few songs in a local studio, and the producer was putting together an album of local original bands, and we agreed for a couple of our songs to be included.'

They entered the first Humberside Star Group Contest in 1981, which they won.

'At that time I was being very theatrical, kind of dramatising every song, and had a rainbow painted onto my face which merged into a gold star painted on my neck. I was, and still am, a massive Kate Bush fan, so I think there was definitely an influence! We decided to venture further afield, and got a first gig in London, at the Rock Garden. We'd changed our name at this point, to Silhouette. I remember we got a coachload of supporters to come to the gig with us. We decided to uproot ourselves and move to London in a bid to be discovered. We played a few gigs here and there and supported Liaison at the Ad Lib club one night. I thought they were brilliant, but not sure what they thought of us! We were all living together in one house, so it lasted about six months and fizzled out. The boys all moved back to Grimsby, a little bit disillusioned I think. I decided to stay. I was determined to try and make a success by joining another band. I went for a few auditions, and turned up for one in Aston Clinton. They had clearly forgotten that I was coming along…'

'I had arranged the audition,' Diz says, 'and completely forgotten to cancel it when we took on Adey. We then had a classic British farce scenario of keeping Deb talking outside whilst convincing Adey to pretend he was just a friend listening to us rehearse. We invited Deb in to 'audition'. I noticed that she kept looking over at Adey with this curious expression, but I was so keen on maintaining the socially awkward tension at a manageable level that

I didn't dare ask what she was thinking. We politely bade her farewell. I called her later to gently let her down, but complimented her on her singing, which was, awkwardly, much better than Adey's. About a week later Adey decided that the band wasn't really his style and apologised for his decision to leave. My reaction, somewhat unfortunate, was at exactly the wrong end of the 'tragically disappointed' / 'positively elated' continuum. This guaranteed my permanent removal from any future Christmas card list he may have been contemplating. I drove home and called Deb at close to midnight, explained the somewhat bizarre scenario of her 'audition' and invited her to join.'

'I liked the guys,' Deb confirms, 'and really liked their music. They had a couple of instrumental tracks that they had been working on and gave me a cassette recording to take away with me. Diz called and confessed about forgetting that I was coming along for an audition, and that they did already have a singer. I'd figured that out, as he had been mouthing words along to the songs as they were playing them in the audition. But I told Diz that I liked what they were doing. About a month later, Diz rang me again, as things hadn't worked out with their singer. He asked if I was still interested. I worked on some lyrics and melody lines for my next meeting with them. These turned into the songs Legions and Moments And Lines.'

'So, by 1984,' Diz says, 'we had the first line-up of Pride Of Passion.'

This was Deborah Hopper (vocals), Nigel Spennewyn (using the name Nigel Child - guitar and vocals), Diz Minnitt (bass and bass pedals), Brian Jelleyman (keyboards) and Barry Talbot (drums). Brian and Barry left before the band's debut show at The Wheatsheaf in Dunstable on 10 April 1985. They supported Solstice at The Marquee on 25 and 26 April and Liaison, their final show, at the same venue on 5 July. That summer they would have three different drummers—John Sullivan (5 gigs), Graham Collins (3 gigs) and Barry Connell (ex-Liaison, 6 gigs).

With Connell the band recorded a self-titled demo tape in 1985.

Finally, they recruited a more permanent

drummer, Grant Gilmour, formerly of Craft with ex-members of The Enid. The mini-album *Favourite Pleasures* was released in 1986 with some tracks produced by long-time Gerry Rafferty associate Hugh Murphy. This line-up also recorded a single, *All My Life / And You Hurt* and played at The Marquee in January, April, June and September 1986.

In a curious twist, Pride Of Passion added a young musician called Steven Wilson on keyboards in spring 1987.

Wilson wrote, in his book *Limited Edition of One*, 'In 1987, acknowledging to myself that I'm probably never going to be a great guitar player anyway, I use my job income to buy a Korg DSS-1 sampler and an Ensoniq ESQ-1 synthesiser, and decide I'm going to be a keyboard player instead. I start going for auditions and end up playing in a female-fronted band called Pride Of Passion. The band is definitely aspiring to play the big arena pop of the day, albeit with a more muso aspect. By my previous standards it was a professional band with regular gigs at legendary venues like the Marquee Club in Soho, and twice weekly rehearsals and writing sessions. The band were self-styled to look like the offspring of Kajagoogoo: big hair, hats, jewellery and cross-dressing. I didn't feel comfortable with any of this, but it wasn't my band and so I went along with it for the sake of experience. Plus there was once again a Marillion connection. On bass was a guy called Diz Minnitt, who had been the bass player in the band. There were a few more months of gigs and trying to get a record deal before the band dissolved. For me it was the only time I ever joined someone else's band. But everything was a learning experience. It was an important stepping stone and I really enjoyed the discipline of being in a motivated semi-professional band with regular rehearsals and gigs.'

Wilson was with Pride Of Passion for around nine months and played a number of concerts with them including the Bull And Gate in Kentish Town, the

Pride Of Passion at The Marquee:
Deb Hopper, Nigel Child and Diz Minnitt
(Photographs by Andy Inman)

Comedy Of Errors information sheet
(Courtesy Mark Guenther)

Mean Fiddler in Harlesden, the 100 Club in London, the Royal Standard in Walthamstow and The Wheatsheaf in Dunstable.

Minnitt's time in Pride Of Passion, however, was coming to an end: he withdrew due to ongoing complications with his time in Marillion, which he felt was holding back his current band.

'The Marquee, at the time, had been our main fanbase in London,' he says. 'Initially we couldn't understand why suddenly we weren't getting new gigs there as we had always sold out; however, I had suspicions which were later confirmed. The impact was huge and we had to start again building a following based around another venue, the Mean Fiddler. We had also been getting some record company interest at The Marquee and that also went quiet. The impact was increased friction and ultimately, my departure and a change of name. My history, that had once been an asset, had become a liability.'

Pride Of Passion's final gig was in Banbury on 16 May 1987. They would shortly regroup as Blazing Apostles but without Minnitt, who was replaced by Frank Keepfer formerly of Liaison.

'Nigel thought of the name,' says Deborah Hopper. 'It was a Be Bop Deluxe song title.'

'I think we demoed one song,' Wilson recalls. 'It was awful, a terrible song called *Boxing Clever*. I remember it was an attempt to write a hit single, which is always a terrible premise to start writing music, trying to contrive something that's going to appeal to record companies; it's a death knell for anyone creative. I hope it's lost forever. It's a shame because the rest of the material we came up with was excellent and very creative, but none of it was ever recorded properly.'

Blazing Apostles split shortly after.

Hopper, Spennewyn and Minnitt reformed Pride Of Passion in November 2023 to record some of their songs from the mid-1980s. Grant Gilmour rejoined the following year, reuniting the 1985-1987 line-up.

*

Comedy Of Errors were formed in Glasgow in 1984 by Joe Cairney (vocals), Jim Johnston (keyboards), John MacPhee (drums), Mike Barnard (guitars) and Steve Stewart (bass). Stewart was quickly replaced by Mark Spalding.

'My influences were very much classical,' says Jim Johnston. 'I was very much attracted to prog rock in its symphonic forms. I was self-taught in music and composition. There was never a big prog scene in the '80s in Scotland. However, there was always a hardcore group of fans who were passionate as their numbers were few.'

Their first recording, a demo called *Ever Be The*

A PLAYGROUND OF BROKEN HEARTS

Comedy Of Errors at the Paradiso, Amsterdam, 12 September 1987 (Photographs by Marco de Niet)

Prize was recorded at a studio in Blanefield in Stirlingshire in 1985.

'Recording was expensive,' Johnston recalls. 'We went to Blanefield because at the time it was the only way of getting at least a half decent sound, even if the music was pretty basic then. Travel was difficult and we were far away from the English scene. We suffered from being extremely remote from London. We knew Pallas had a studio, so we recorded our mini-album there, where we could take control and not have record companies constraining us to release singles.'

This self-titled five track mini-album would be recorded at Pallas' Ice Station studio at their farmhouse retreat with the assistance of Graeme Murray, Niall Mathewson and Mike Bentley This was released in 1986. The production, unsurprisingly, is strongly influenced by Pallas. The track *Time There Was* from this album was included by Steven Wilson on the first *Exposure* compilation album, alongside music by Abel Ganz, No Man Is An Island Except The Isle Of Man, Twice Bitten and others.

When guitarist Mike Barnard left the band, Barry Henderson joined on bass while Mark Spalding switched to guitar. This line-up recorded the demo tape called *24 Hours* in November 1987 at Evenload Studios in East Kilbride. This was later combined with the mini album to form the band's only CD release on the French MSI label.

Hold On (from the collection of Mark Guenther)

Singer Joe Cairney left in 1989, due to the pressure of work commitments. New lead vocalist John Cowden heralded a more standard rock approach. The demo tape *Hold On* was recorded at Evenload Studios in May '89 but Comedy Of Errors were starting to wind down.

'We decided to go on hiatus until the invention of the internet and social media,' Johnston says. 'I continued to write music and lyrics and study the intricacies and form of classical music – from the Renaissance onwards. I amassed a lot of material which I felt was good enough to see the light of day. Eventually with the advent of decent software I could record music to a high quality of production. Around 2010 I got Mark Spalding and Joe Cairney back, added Bruce Levick to the line-up, then later John Fitzgerald. Social media allowed us to spread our music wider than we had ever before. Six albums later we're still going. Upwards and onwards!'

The highly regarded *Threnody For A Dead Queen* was released in 2023. Cairney and Spalding are also members of Grand Tour with ex-Abel Ganz keyboardist Huw Montgomery.

*

Galahad were formed in Bournemouth in 1985 by guitarist Roy Keyworth and singer Stuart Nicholson.

'The music scene at the time was dreadful,' Keyworth says. 'I couldn't find anything I liked and I could no longer buy any quality new prog rock: Yes had turned into an AOR band and Genesis had sold out. So I thought I'd make my own. And then I went to see Twelfth Night at the Marquee Club in London. They were astounding. The venue was packed, and I realised that you could play prog and find an audience. I went home and started to form Galahad straight away.'

Galahad in 1986 and 1988
(Courtesy Stuart Nicholson)

Their first live show, as a top heavy seven piece, was in August 1985. Their set comprised covers of the 1970s and 1980s prog bands, with just the occasional original song. Drummer Spencer Luckman joined in early 1987, and incessant gigging led to local support slots, with Pendragon at the Regent Centre, Christchurch, on 21 November 1987 and with IQ at the same venue on 4 March 1988. They also supported Ark, Jadis and Haze in their early days.

Singer Stuart Nicholson auditioned to replace Fish in Marillion in December 1988.

'I travelled up to London on the morning of Monday, 12 December 1988,' Nicholson says. 'My recollection of the studio itself is pretty sketchy. The NOMIS studio complex in West London was owned by Simon Napier-Bell, a well respected industry mogul and band manager. The studio room was quite dark but full of expensive musical and audio equipment. There was a large mixing/recording desk at one end, complete with sound engineer, and Mark Kelly's keyboard rig at the other. The other guys were set up in between. First of all, we ran through a few Marillion staples, some of which I'd tried to learn hurriedly in the few preceding days. I can't remember the exact order but the songs we ran through were *Forgotten Sons*, *Slàinte Mhath*, *Kayleigh*, *Lavender* and *Heart Of Lothian*. They asked me if I had any lyrical ideas, so I grabbed a few pages from my trusty red folder and we jammed for a while. It was actually great fun, and I didn't feel nervous at all. They were all really friendly and encouraging.'

Pete Trewavas offered to give Stu a lift home but wasn't so keen when Stu told him he lived in Dorset and not London.

Galahad's first cassette album, *In A Moment Of Madness*, saw the band leaning heavily on their influences. The subsequent *Nothing Is Written* (1992) and the highly regarded *Sleepers* (1995) saw an

Ark badge (From the collection of Günter Schote)

identity starting to emerge.

It was the recruitment of keyboardist Dean Baker in 1999 which gave the band new impetus. The diverse *Following Ghosts* introduced an electronic sound alongside the more traditional prog structures. After over 20 years of graft, the 2007 album *Empires Never Last* introduced a new muscular sound courtesy of engineer and co-producer Karl Groom. Their subsequent five albums are uniformly excellent. Roy Keyworth retired in 2017, but Nicholson, Luckman and Baker, with renowned guitarist Lee Abraham and bassist Mark Spencer (ex-LaHost, Twelfth Night) celebrated the band's fortieth anniversary in 2025.

*

Ark came into existence in Birmingham in 1986, following incarnations as Damascus and Kite. Their first line-up consisted of Tony Short (aka Ant) on vocals and flute, Pete Wheatley on guitar, Steve Harris on guitar synth, Steve's brother Andy Harris on bass and drummer Dave Robbins. Their first gig was supporting Roy Harper.

By the time they played at The Marquee, supporting the Lloyd Langton Group, on 17 January 1988, Ark had a new bass player, a certain John Jowitt.

'My first musical love was jazz,' Jowitt says, 'together with Gilbert and Sullivan. I was influenced by my dad. My first instrument therefore was the trumpet, and I loved playing in the school orchestra. As for bass, I just kind of fell in love with it. I particularly remember the breakdown to the bass in The Walker Brothers' *You've Lost That Loving Feeling*. Friends at school had older brothers and sisters who were into prog where I heard all kinds of stuff. At my school it was either Genesis and Pink Floyd, or Yes and ELP. I played bass for Angie Bowie in 1985-86, and she was happy to rehearse in Birmingham at the studio I knew, Rich Bitch in Bournbrook. After that, I joined a band called The First, very Killing Joke, with Mark Gemini Thwaite, later of The Mission and others. When that stopped, I did too. But Rob and Lynne, who owned Rich Bitch, remembered me, and put me in touch with Ark in 1988 when their bass player left. I saw them live before my audition and thought they were great. We entered the Brumbeat Battle of the Bands to try to build our profile, and get into gigs in Birmingham, where it was all metal, and won it. That got us profile, a bigger audience, and a better class of gigs, The Marquee and all.'

The band were booked into Rich Bitch to record the mini-album *The Dreams Of Mr. Jones*.

John Jowitt: 'Part of the prize from the competition was recording time. I'd played in the studio before with my first gigging band Revolver, with None But The Brave, and also The First.'

Sean Worrall reviewed the album in *The Organ* issue 10.

First impressions first... First, a notable, wonderful, colourful cover. The work of Birmingham artist Pete Worrall (Uncle Peter? no not I think) I'd like a great big version of this cover hanging in *Organ* land. I shall tell you now that I have little time to get with this six track mini album. The record arrived today and we print tomorrow. However here goes.

The album opens with *Gaia*, a harsher version

than the one we are familiar with from the previous demo, it has a feeling of Tull and features the flute of vocalist Anthony Short. *Through The Night* is more AOR than I remember live and perhaps does not show Ark in their best light. *Kaleidoscope* is the cry of a very English band. *Power Of The Gun* opens up side two in the style of latter day Pallas and features some good bass work, a good tasty, lengthy outing of a prog nature. Anthony Short's vocals seem a little harder than live, so far it's good, but it's not the best Ark work. *Mabeline* on first listening is not the best Ark song ever, but I must stress the haste of this review. The rockier end of Ark does not come over as well as it does live. *Nowhere's Ark* skirts along the realms of metal and then takes us through a jam of prog, folk and a great jig and is a song that lays out the many sides of Ark, a track of Celtic delight. Celtic and yet English is what Ark are. The mini album is good but Ark are at their best live. They, on this first listen, have not caught their best side. It is good but Ark have set their standards high on stage.

A good album, which tells you a bit about Ark but does not tell all. £3.00 is the cost plus 75p P&P from Ark, PO Box 1198, Halesowen, West Midlands.

Richard Deane replaced Dave Robbins, who quit early in 1989, arriving in time for the band to enter TVM Studios in Birmingham to record the *New Scientist* EP. This led to a support slot on IQ's *Are You Sitting Comfortably?* tour during June 1989. Ark played a headline date in Paris and support to It Bites for a one-off date in Tilburg, Holland.

'I was with them for three years before I left,' says John Jowitt. 'The band were great live, good sense of humour and a wonderful frontman in Tony Short. We played about 70 gigs a year – Wednesday night in Hull to 13 people, anything we could get. It was pretty full on, and I loved it.'

Jowitt would be invited to join IQ in 1990.

'I left Ark about a year or 18 months before I joined IQ,' he says. 'My reason was that they decided they should be more Guns N' Roses, which I found really boring. It lost us our USP and our audience. It's been my mantra: I'm never going to make much money in it, I'm doing it because it's fun, so when it stops being fun, I'm off.'

*

In July 1987, towards the end of our story, Timothy J Bowness met Steven J Wilson.

Wilson, you might recall, had seen Marillion's first ever gig, aged 12. He formed a duo, Altamont, and a band, Karma, recording a number of cassettes. Always busy, Wilson produced a compilation album called *Exposure* in 1986. One of Wilson's many projects was called No Man Is An Island Except The Isle Of Man. The No Man track *From A Toyshop Window* is included along with contributions from Abel Ganz and Twice Bitten amongst others.

He joined the band Pride Of Passion as keyboard player in March 1987. Later that year, a follow-up to *Exposure* included tracks from Anthony Phillips, Haze, Rog Patterson and Geoff Mann's then current band The Bond.

'Tim had a band called Plenty, who were interested in contributing to the second compilation,' Wilson wrote.

'I was obsessed with films and film soundtracks

from a very early age,' Bowness says, 'so the first music that I loved was by the likes of John Barry, Bernard Herrmann and Ennio Morricone. After that came Beatles, Wings, 10cc and Sparks, and then, as I reached my teens, I got interested in anything and everything from Bowie and Roxy Music to progressive rock (particularly Pink Floyd, King Crimson, Genesis, VDGG and Yes) to jazz, new wave, post-punk, classical minimalism, soul, funk, singer-songwriters, classic rock and the emerging electronic and music of the early 1980s – Associates, Teardrop Explodes and Japan were favourites. When I first started singing in the early 1980s, my biggest inspirations were David Bowie, Peter Hammill, Scott Walker, Julian Cope, Billy Mackenzie, David Sylvian, Kate Bush and Peter Gabriel. Plenty was formed in 1986. It was a heavily electronic orientated art pop band, for want of a better term! At that time, my feeling was that Kate Bush, Peter Gabriel and King Crimson were the ones taking 'the progressive spirit' into genuinely innovative 1980s territories. As such, the new prog bands were not a big thing for me. However, as a fan of the 'old school' progressive bands and a regular music paper reader, I was certainly aware of it. I bought and liked some albums, and I thought that Marillion, Twelfth Night and IQ, in particular, had an intensity that fused prog ambition with new wave grittiness and NWOBHM power that made for something new.'

Bowness had previously sung in a local band called After The Stranger, who played in and around Manchester, including a couple of dates with Peter Nicholls' mid-IQ band Niadem's Ghost.

Bowness: 'In 1986, partly to get out of the demo/local gig/demo/local gig loop, I put out a self-financed vinyl album with After The Stranger. I'd been supported by local radio stations and media in the North West for years but the album generated wider national and international attention. I got 'demo of the month' in a couple of big UK publications and the LP was reviewed in several European magazines. In the mid-1980s, they used to print home addresses, so you could buy the music direct from the artist. Steven Wilson encountered one of these reviews, liked the sound of the music from the description, and sent me a letter [in April or May 1987] asking if I'd be interested in appearing on a compilation album he was putting together. That was the first time we were in touch.'

Bowness and Wilson immediately exchanged cassette tapes of their own self-recorded music.

'The material Tim sent seemed closer to the world of David Sylvian or The Blue Nile,' Wilson wrote. 'His voice was distinctive and had an emotionally rich gravitas to it, while his lyrics were more like those of a poet or a short story writer.'

'We started off talking on the phone and sending each other tapes of music we found exciting,' Bowness says. 'Nothing was off limits, so the tapes would include Associates, Slab!, Stockhausen, Miles Davis, Yes, Nick Drake, James Brown, A Certain Ratio, Dead Can Dance, Steve Reich, Wire, Eberhard Weber, Jane Siberry, Marvin Gaye, Gentle Giant and lots, lots more. I'm not sure how, but I managed to talk Steven into accepting two Plenty tracks and allowing me to design the album cover. I must have been persuasive! Steven had written a track for *Double Exposure*, but he wasn't confident about his singing on it. It was called *Give Me The Needle* and had a brooding Pink Floyd quality about it. He

No-Man promo shot for One Little Indian – Steven Wilson, Tim Bowness and Ben Coleman (Photograph by Colin Bell)

asked me to sing on it and I agreed. I learnt the song and travelled to Steven's NoMansLand studio in Hemel Hempstead in July or August 1987. By the time I got there, he'd changed his mind and wanted to drop the piece. We talked for about four hours non-stop on my arrival at the studio and then started writing and recording. Within a couple of hours of turning the equipment on, we'd come up with the basis of Faith's Last Doubt and the entirety of a piece called Screaming Head Eternal. One was a lush and epic ballad, the other a short sharp alt punk funk piece. It felt great that we could effortlessly operate in such diverse musical areas. The possibilities seemed vast, and Steven was the first musician I'd worked with who, like me, had an interest in many different areas of music, not just one or two specific genres.'

Wilson: 'We ended up talking for hours. He was articulate and talked endlessly and knowledgeably about music and books that I'd never heard of, or if I did know them I had believed until then I was the only person that did. In a short period of time he introduced me to things like Scott Walker, Prefab Sprout, the industrial funk group Slab!, Nico's The Marble Index and Momus, all of which became reference points for our collaboration to come.'

Bowness' first contribution to No-Man was on Faith's Last Doubt.

Steven Wilson describes it as 'a kind of weird halfway house between sensitive ambient pop and progressive rock, with a bombastic Gilmour-esque solo in the middle played by Nigel from Pride of Passion / Blazing Apostles.'

'I found someone who had the same curiosity and drive as me to just splurge out music on to tape,' Wilson wrote. 'Our musical influences went all over the place, and if we were ever stuck for ideas Tim would often just play me some amazing song or record I'd never heard before, and we'd be off again. These were the beginnings of No-Man (as No Man Is An Island became), although it took another three years of developing our sound before we had any kind of professional breakthrough.'

Violinist Ben Coleman joined in late 1988 and the band added guitarist Stuart Blagden for a time. Blagden had previously played with Bowness in a band called Still and had also worked with ex-Twelfth Night singer Geoff Mann.

'We managed to build up an audience,' Bowness explains. 'Our second gig was at the Hemel Hempstead Battle Of The Bands 1989 and we won, mainly due to the 'celebrity judge' and future King Crimson member Jakko Jakszyk. After that, we were playing headlines at the Eurobeat 2000 nights at a venue called The Flag in Wembley and this led us to playing Eurobeat 2000 nights at The Marquee. We were also playing the likes of the 100 Club and the Rock Garden and getting decent responses. At one point, we had a tiny deal with Plastic Head Records and released an awful EP, *The Girl From Missouri*. So, we had a small following, but we were going nowhere and we were feeling very disillusioned.'

But in a big change of fortunes, their next single *Colours* was *Melody Maker*'s single of the week in 1990.

'The single emerged out of a joke,' Bowness says. 'I'd read that the Happy Mondays were about to record a version of Donovan's *Colours*. Along with Nick Drake, Sandy Denny and John Martyn, Donovan was one of our biggest singer-songwriter inspirations, so we decided we'd beat Shaun Ryder and the boys to it. We quickly recorded a very stripped down ambient, classical, hip-hop version of the song and released it within a month or so of the idea being discussed. We only sent about five copies of the single out, but amazingly we ended up with *Melody Maker* 'Single Of The Week'. At the next gig, we had A&R people galore attending. We eventually signed to One Little Indian in the UK, Epic 550/Sony in the US, Nippon Columbia in Japan and Genesis's publishing company Hit & Run. With the latter, we were signed alongside Kula Shaker, Space and Right Said Fred as the company's attempt to bring in fresh talent. As a big fan of Genesis and Peter Gabriel, I was delighted of course. The Happy Mondays never released their cover of *Colours*.'

This led, in 1993, to the first of many albums.

Ever productive, Wilson created, in parallel, a 'pretend' band called Porcupine Tree, dreamt up in cahoots with his friend Malcolm Stocks and inspired by XTC's fake psychedelic band The Dukes of Stratosphere.

Wilson: 'The rest of my 'band' included… absurdist figures like Sir Tarquin Underspoon, Mr Jelly, The Expanding Flan, Timothy Tadpole-Jones and Sebastian Tweetle-Blampton III. There was clearly a Bonzo Dog Band influence creeping in there too. It was all very silly and self-indulgent, but it kept us amused on those rainy afternoons while we listened to Peter Hammill and Daevid Allen records.'

Eventually, recordings that Wilson made under the Porcupine Tree name gained enough momentum to merit the formation of an actual band in 1993, a band which went on to achieve four Top 40 albums in the UK. Porcupine Tree and Steven Wilson have, arguably, the highest profiles of any artists who work within the genre of progressive rock and who have emerged since Marillion.

Closure:
Impressions Lost And Overstepped

There will always be a type of young (and not so young) music fan who equates long, meandering instrumental passages and tricksy time signatures with profundity, and I guess I was one of them. We were the ones who wanted content in our music, but were too intimidated by post punk's overcoat brigade and not cool enough for the Rough Trade bands. We were the self-consciously clever kids in our rubbish camouflage jackets and Marks & Spencer jeans, scared to dance but always ready to discuss our favourite Michael Moorcock novels. I think that pretty much summed up most of the bands too, certainly judging by their names, with references to fantasy and myth (Marillion, Pallas, Pendragon), allusions to high culture (Twelfth Night), and show-off braininess (IQ). These people clearly weren't interested in being 'cool' (at least not yet), but they weren't stupid – while characterised as just slavishly reproducing the sounds of their prog forebears, a fairly small gene pool of bands at that, it took some guts (and just a touch of self-importance) to be unashamedly making this type of music in the era of leg warmers, bubble perms and Gary Davies.

Joe Banks, The Quietus, 27 October 2015

One should not view the music business of the 1980s with rose tinted spectacles. In the era of Charles and Di, *Dallas*, those Giant Swatch Watch wall clocks and the radio friendly dial-a-tunes of Stock Aitken Waterman, the record industry was interested in only one thing: cold hard cash.

In words which have been attributed to Hunter S Thompson, 'The music business is a cruel and shallow money trench, a long plastic hallway where thieves and pimps run free, and good men die like dogs. There's also a negative side.'

Thompson didn't actually say that, but many professional musicians will nod, sagely.

And here is the challenge: how can the artist, who has a vision that he does not want to compromise (and with very rare exceptions, the musicians here were all men) stay true to himself when the labels want commercial success almost at any cost?

Add to that the reality that the music these bands played was seriously out of fashion. The days of number 1 albums by the likes of ELP (*Tarkus*), Pink Floyd (*Atom Heart Mother*) and Yes (*Tales From Topographic Oceans*) were seemingly long gone, ended by the upheaval of punk.

There's an argument that punk killed prog. There's another that prog had simply run its course: just another entry in a long list of briefly popular genres that sparked, burned brightly and fizzled out. The truth, as always, is more complex.

Dave Everley of *Loudersound*: 'As the 80s dawned, prog was on the ropes. The myth that punk had 'killed' it has been overstated – prog was doing a good job of killing itself. Its founding fathers had either imploded (Yes, ELP), streamlined their sound so much as to be virtually unrecognisable (Genesis, Rush) or faded into commercial irrelevance (Caravan, Camel). But there were pockets of people who still loved it.'

Joy Division / New Order drummer Steven Morris, who enjoyed and saw concerts by the likes of Hawkwind, Genesis and Amon Düül in the early 1970s, writes: 'Yes to me symbolised everything that was wrong with music. Concept albums that went on and on – *Tales From Topographic Oceans* – do me a favour! Even the most elevated of consciousnesses would have struggled to see anything but old farts blabbering… I did my best to love the Mahavishnu Orchestra but just got a headache. If you were pretentious enough you could say, 'I could almost feel the contractions of punk waiting to be born."

'Punk signalled a huge shift in attitudes as to what rock music was for,' writes prog historian Mike Barnes, 'particularly in the relationship between the musicians and their audience. It was fundamentally opposed, not just to progressive rock, but to all big, established rock acts who had lost touch with their audience.'

One of the biggest of these established rock acts, Pink Floyd, toured France in June 1974. Their hour long first set consisted of just three songs, illustrated by light shows and specially commissioned projections and delivered with quadrophonic sound; their second set featured the whole of their most recent album, an expensively produced treatise on madness, death and money.

Three months earlier, a young band played their first gig in their rehearsal space on Manhattan's East 20th Street. They blasted through seven songs in about the time it took David Gilmour to tune his guitar. Their songs bore self-examining titles such as *I Don't Wanna Go Down To The Basement*, *I Don't Like Nobody That Don't Like Me* and *Now I Wanna Sniff Some Glue*.

The Ramones had arrived. That August they made their debut at New York's legendary music club CBGB, sharing bills with the likes of the Patti Smith Group and Television, bands which included phenomenally talented musicians such as Lenny Kaye, Richard Sohl and Tom Verlaine.

The Ramones, however, revelled in their lack of musical skill. Their sets remained nasty, brutish and short.

London born Malcolm McLaren, wayward boutique owner and aspirant impresario, worked with the fading glam rockers the New York Dolls in this period and witnessed the CBGB scene for himself. Returning to the UK in May 1975, his King's Road clothing store, Sex, was frequented by some of the young musicians who would be brought together as the Sex Pistols. They first performed together on 6 November 1975 at Saint Martin's School of Art. The world would never quite be the same again.

The Ramones' first album was issued in the US on 23 April 1976. Six weeks later the Sex Pistols played Manchester's Lesser Free Trade Hall. Future members of Buzzcocks, Joy Division, The Fall and The Smiths were in attendance. The support act was a short-lived Bolton based prog rock group called… Solstice.

Anarchy In The UK followed in November and *God Save The Queen* the next spring, by which time punk had become a major cultural phenomenon.

The Sex Pistols' Glen Matlock: 'The glam rock thing was over. Bands like Yes and Barclay James Harvest didn't really touch the kids in the street around my way. Punk was something that kids could identify with and get their teeth into.'

Howard Devoto of Buzzcocks: 'I was not totally loath to a little bit of prog rock. I do remember going along to the college gigs every Saturday night, but really getting very fed up with it and feeling, I wish I could go and see The Stooges or something like that, something that's really going to be confrontational and aggressive and exciting and a bit dangerous.'

'The weird thing is,' writes Steven Morris, 'that back in the mid-1970s all the teenage kids who went on to love punk would have been listening to heavy rock, bits of Bowie, Iggy and Lou Reed and of course a fair bit of prog – but that was all swept under the carpet after 1976 for fear of mockery and persecution by the musical cognoscenti. These days, it's nearly OK to admit to owning *The Snow Goose* by Camel, but in 1976 it was a real no-no, a musical faux pas.'

'Prog rock didn't fit into the backdrop really,' suggested Buzzcocks' Steve Diggle, 'because it was coming up to a million people on the dole. I think our generation was questioning their lives, rather than wanting to be entertained.'

Prog was several years old and, by now, increasingly passé. In response, many bands were either moving towards a new sound, were not active, or were embracing commerciality. However, some of the most successful prog rock bands of the '70s were still at the top of their game.

A Trick Of The Tail (February 1976) and *Wind & Wuthering* (December 1976) saw Phil Collins step up as Genesis's frontman. *A Trick Of The Tail* opens with the mighty *Dance On A Volcano,* a dyed in the wool progressive rock track. Collins also shines on the gorgeous prog rock ballad, *Ripples*, whilst the hummable title track is perhaps an early sign of the band's more commercial sound that developed over the next few albums. *A Trick Of The Tail* rose to number 3: Genesis's third of 11 consecutive Top 10 albums in the UK. Significantly, its placing at 31 in the US was their highest to date there. *Wind & Wuthering* includes Mike Rutherford's plaintive, accessible *Your Own Special Way*. It was the band's first charting single in the US, 'the start of a tickle', as Rutherford described it. The same year's *Spot The Pigeon* EP, with its lead track *Match Of The Day*, would give Genesis their first UK Top 20 single. The powerful, energetic and massively influential double live album *Seconds Out*, recorded in June 1977, was the last Genesis album to feature Steve Hackett. It is perhaps the definitive statement from this short-lived iteration of Genesis and reclaims the Gabriel era back catalogue for the new line-up. With Hackett gone, Collins, Banks and Rutherford continued as a trio and began to move away from their progressive rock roots. Whilst longer, more complex songs would always form part of the Genesis catalogue, their albums now adopted a more radio friendly pop rock sound in their shorter songs. This strategy was immediately successful when the uplifting pop ballad *Follow You Follow Me* – released in February 1978 and taken from *…And Then There Were Three…* – became their first UK Top 10 and US Top 40 single.

Pink Floyd's *Animals*, released in January 1977, was much more assertive that the preceding *Wish You Were Here*. *Animals* was ominous, dark and bitter. It lays claim to be the band's best album. ELP regrouped for *Works Volume 1* (March 1977), which spawned the massive hit *Fanfare For The Common Man*. Yes's *Going For The One* (July 1977) features shorter, more commercial songs, including the major hit single *Wonderous Stories*, alongside longer pieces such as the glorious *Awaken*. They continued this success with *Tormato,* featuring the single *Don't Kill The Whale* in 1978.

Rush, meanwhile, achieved their first UK chart entry with *A Farewell To Kings* (September 1977), a prelude to six Top 10 albums in the 1980s.

'While punk had crystallised many writers' hatred for the genre,' writes Joe Banks, 'and had made toxic the very term 'progressive', most of the big names were relatively unaffected by the supposed Year Zero of 1977. And while much of prog's dead brush had indeed been burnt away, its roots were still intact, with many of the neo-prog bands having their origins in the late 70s.'

By January 1978, the Sex Pistols had disintegrated, having given pop music (and British culture) a right royal kick up the arse.

Andy Glass of Solstice: 'I was very aware of the punk thing. I was living in Aylesbury. The pub there, the Green Man, was full of hippies, bikers and punks. And we were all doing the same shit. It was great. Now I thought punk was just fucking terrible, complete and utter rubbish. It was an insult to musicians and great music. These guys can't even play… Of course, the good ones could, you know? But in the media world it was fully embraced, and it pushed aside everything else and 'destroyed the dinosaurs'. The media loved that. But people didn't suddenly say, 'Well, I'm not gonna listen to Yes any more… I wanna listen to Johnny Rotten now.' It's part of the rich tapestry of the musical world, isn't it? But I don't blame it for destroying prog.'

'Progressive rock is an easy pigeon-hole,' Euan Lowson told *Kerrang!* in 1983. 'Progressive rock does not exist anymore. Progressive, or what was once called progressive, was the music that some of the band grew up with in the '70s. There are no ready-made labels for this group.'

'None of the bands that you and I know we are talking about,' commented Ronnie Brown, 'would honestly admit to being part of the progressive movement. They're embarrassed about the misconception that immediately springs to mind when folk mention 'progressive'. Bands haven't been given the chance to be heard as individuals.'

'A lot of people seem to think that we are restricted by a lack of image,' said Lowson, 'but music should not be a fashion or a movement. We don't want to go and get Woody Woodpecker haircuts to sell records – that's why the press doesn't like us, those people slamming us for being 'progressive' are the ones worried about showing their real age! I don't see why people who don't like us can't just turn around and go and listen to something else instead of lumping us all together and saying we're all shit. This is music that people can go and watch if they want to watch. No one's forcing them.'

The punk attitude certainly influenced the DIY approach of the prog bands of this period.

Mike Barnes: 'While the bigger progressive rock and other more mainstream rock groups and artists were engaged in an arms race for more and more equipment, bigger staging and more special effects, the emergence of punk showed that all that was essentially showbiz, and not actually necessary. In January 1977, Manchester band the Buzzcocks even did without a record company, rustling up £500 to record, press and distribute their debut EP *Spiral Scratch* on their own New Hormones label.'

Brian Devoil of Twelfth Night: 'When punk came in it blew apart everybody's preconceptions that only bands with major labels could make records. We were one of the few groups to make an album totally independently. We did all the artwork and packaging ourselves.'

But punk did render prog deeply unfashionable. If you were not one of the established bands, then the record labels didn't want to know. And if you were an established band but were not seen to be as commercially successful as required, more immediate success was demanded, with that flurry of hit singles at the end of the 1970s now turning into a push for further hits. This was a major misreading of the marketplace: the dedicated prog fanbase were not interested in singles. But labels lost the long-sightedness of early periods and bands such as Camel, Gentle Giant, Van Der Graaf Generator and most of the others were either pushed to release singles that flopped, or chose to go for it anyway. Camel eventually released an album knowingly called *The Single Factor* in 1982.

Martin Orford of IQ: 'Punk had come and gone, peace and love was out of fashion, and music pubs and clubs were quite often quite aggressive and violent places. Their clientele expected fast, tough music, so the prog bands had to adapt or risk not getting out alive. This brought an almost punk-like intensity to much of the music: faced with a club full of angry unemployed Welsh coal miners or a bunch of Staffordshire skinheads as the broken glass rains through the air, you have to toughen up and try to blitzkrieg them, because it's the only way you stand a chance of surviving the experience.'

As the 1980s began, the more commercially successful bands of the 1970s continued to release high profile albums and thus became even more commercially productive. Others struggled to gain a foothold with new material, gradually disbanding or turning into 'legacy' acts.

Many of the more successful progressive rock musicians of the 1970s remained active but had moved on from the styles of music that they had helped to develop. Examples include Peter Gabriel, Phil Collins, Jon & Vangelis, Genesis, Yes, Asia and Jethro Tull, each of which achieved singles and/or album chart successes during the 1980s. In live performance, many of these acts continued to perform tracks from their 1970s back catalogues, yet their focus in both live performance and their then contemporary album releases was upon shorter and more melodic songs and arrangements, as well as lyrically more accessible material. The broader scale experimentation and musical ambition that had previously been seen was reined in on albums that sought and achieved wider audience acclaim.

Chris Anderton, *Fire In Harmony: The 1980s UK British Progressive Rock Revival*, 2013

Against all of the odds, the first UK number 1 single of the 1980s was Pink Floyd's *Another Brick In The Wall Part 2*. This was, let's face it, a novelty disco inspired hit. The song stands out from its parent album, the almost unwaveringly gloomy *The Wall* like, well, a fish out of water.

Yes, meanwhile, replaced Jon Anderson and Rick Wakeman with two members of pop outfit The Buggles for their tenth album, *Drama*, their eighth consecutive Top 10 album release. They would split at the end of the year.

Steve Howe immediately formed Asia with three other prog luminaries: lead vocalist and bassist John Wetton of King Crimson and UK, keyboardist Geoff Downes of Yes and The Buggles and drummer Carl Palmer of Emerson, Lake & Palmer. Their debut, *Asia*, released in 1982, remains their bestselling album, powered by the single *Heat Of The Moment*, which sounds like none of their previous bands.

ELP had split in 1979 after the release of their 'contractual obligation' album, *Love Beach* (it is a sign of the times that the cover of *Love Beach* sees the band kitted out like disco artists). With Palmer committed to Asia, Emerson and Lake formed Emerson, Lake & Powell with former Rainbow drummer Cozy Powell. The trio toured in 1986, playing material by the Nice and Emerson, Lake & Palmer. ELP reformed (this time with Palmer back on drums) for the disappointing *Black Moon* in 1992. The dismal *In The Hot Seat* ended the band's studio career with a whimper. Their last gig together was in 2010. Keith Emerson died by suicide in March 2016. Greg Lake died from cancer in December of the same year.

The trio version of Genesis hit their stride with 1980's majestic *Duke*. All three members pushed for a more commercial sound with *Abacab* (1981), *Genesis* (1983) and, especially, *Invisible Touch* (1986). Genesis evolved to become a pop band because they were, at the root of it, songwriters and were able to adapt. They lost many older fans but gained many more new ones: their immense 1986-1987 tour ended with four sold out performances at the 72,000 capacity Wembley Stadium. Collins left Genesis in 1996, but the 1976-1996 line-up reunited for hugely successful tours in 2007 and 2021-2022. The last ever Genesis show was at the O2 (Millennium Dome) in London on 26 March 2022. Peter Gabriel was in attendance to witness the end of the band. Phil Collins joked from onstage that a heckler calling for *Supper's Ready* to be played was probably Peter Gabriel.

King Crimson reformed in 1981 with former members Robert Fripp and Bill Bruford joined by two Americans: singer/guitarist Adrian Belew and bassist Tony Levin. Their three albums in the 1980s are an uncompromising mix of Belew's melodies and Fripp's angular, precise and complicated guitar playing. They are very good albums indeed. Fripp would lead various King Crimson line-ups between 1993 and 2008 before 'retiring' to Worcestershire with his wife, pop singer Toyah Willcox. King Crimson would unexpectedly regroup in 2014, touring extensively and playing technically complex reworkings of pieces from their wide-ranging back catalogue. A seemingly permanent disbandment in 2021 has drawn a veil on one of the most musically adept and uncompromising bands of any genre. Unexpectedly, Belew and Levin joined forces with guitarist Steve Vai and Tool's drummer Danny Carey for a Robert Fripp approved Crimson offshoot called Beat, touring in 2024 and 2025.

Yes reformed in 1983 with long-time members Jon Anderson, Chris Squire and Alan White joined by guitarist Trevor Rabin and original keyboard player Tony Kaye. Their album *90125* spawned an unexpected US number 1 hit single with *Owner Of A Lonely Heart*. The follow-up, *Big Generator* (1987), gained mixed reviews. More than 30 years later, Yes are still touring and recording but without any original members (or, indeed, any from their commercially successful 1983-1990 line-up).

Steve Howe left Asia in 1984 and formed a new group with former Genesis guitarist Steve Hackett and drummer Jonathan Mover, who was briefly a member of Marillion in 1983. GTR failed to meet expectations and split after two years, one self-titled album and the minor hit single *When The Heart Rules The Mind*.

Pink Floyd's last album with Roger Waters, *The*

A PLAYGROUND OF BROKEN HEARTS

Final Cut (1983), has aged rather well: it's an intriguing and intelligent corner of their back catalogue. Waters' departure from Pink Floyd in 1985 has been well documented. David Gilmour carried on, leading the band to new commercial heights with *A Momentary Lapse Of Reason* in 1987, which was followed by a massive world tour. They did it all over again in 1994 with the much more palatable *The Division Bell*, reunited with Roger Waters for an extraordinary performance at Live 8 in 2005, released a one time listen album of outtakes in 2014 and put out a new (and presumably final) single in 2022. Waters and Gilmour continue to release infrequent solo albums and snipe at each other on social media.

After a fallow period in the 1990s, the 2000s saw the emergence of new prog bands led by Porcupine Tree and Big Big Train. All six of the main contenders from the 1980s Marquee scene remained active, despite occasional periods of inactivity and shifting personnel. In the 21st century, the likes of Progzilla Radio, the Winter's and Summer's End, Night Of The Prog, Cruise To The Edge and Fusion festivals and bands' own weekend events draw in fans from across the world.

Prog magazine sits on the shelves of every supermarket each month.

So, no, punk didn't kill prog and today's vibrant if increasingly niche prog scene proves that. However, it did help to bring about a negative change in the attitude of record labels who didn't (and don't) see immediate returns from this type of music. Business plans have needed to adapt in today's marketplace. Crowdfunding and other sources of income, such as playing in multiple bands, are key elements of the financial model. Their middle-aged audiences are quite happy to travel to concerts across the world and buy expensive physical media, but it has been difficult for the bands to extend their reach outside of the progressive rock genre.

For the rest, the DIY ethos instigated by punk still holds true, even if it's now a movement featuring musicians who are grey-haired, short of cash and sometimes out of breath.

The dichotomy of the new progressive scene of the 1980s - and the underlying whisper to the louder narrative of these two books - can be focussed on the massive success of Marillion. They were not the first of these new bands - that honour goes to either Pallas or Twelfth Night depending on when you start to count - but they had by far the biggest impact.

All of the bands profiled in these two books on the '80's prog scene were highly ambitious, perhaps with the exception of Solstice, whose hippy ideals eschewed the London 'breadheads'. We can point to Fish's incessant mixture of charm, brio and onstage charisma as the focus of Marillion's initial impact. His shameless courting of Keith Goodwin, the hot nights under the Marquee lights, their stroke of fortune with the *Friday Rock Show* session, the willingness of EMI to take a punt and his bandmates' effortless musicality to reshape old ideas into new music combined to light the fuse.

Once Marillion were through the door, many other record companies sniffed at their heels. Pallas

Closure: Impressions Lost And Overstepped

Nick Barrett and Fish,
Reading Festival, 1983
(Photograph by
Roger Morgan)

followed Marillion into the corridors of Manchester Square but were badly let down with the recording and promotion of *The Sentinel*. Twelfth Night eventually signed to Virgin, possibly as a sop to Phil Collins' management company. The foibles of their producer and utter lack of interest from their record company split the band within months of a major label debut which strayed too far from the band's roots. IQ tweaked their style just enough when they worked with Phonogram to hint at a breakthrough, and were allocated some high profile support bookings, but were dropped as soon as their second album with Paul Menel failed to chart. By the end of the 1980s, only Marillion still enjoyed a major record deal, and that would end in 1995 after the band's eighth studio album, *Afraid Of Sunlight*, which received limited promotion and no mainstream radio airplay. Pendragon and Solstice never managed to sign a major deal at all.

And yet, for a while at least, there was so much promise, a collective experience for both bands and fans, even if some of the major players tried to deny it. Malcolm Dome's two part review of the prog scene in issues 36 and 37 of *Kerrang!* includes an interview with Fish and photographs and profiles of Twelfth Night, Solstice, Pallas, Dagaband and Pendragon. The articles conclude with Marillion's singer hubristically claiming that the so-called revival was nothing more than a media invention.

'What has happened,' he said, 'is that the spotlight has just swirled around, caught us, bounced off and found some others who are working in the same area. But the media is going to destroy it because that spotlight, instead of revealing them to the public, is burning them! The whole thing has been completely blown out of proportion; it's nothing, it's half a dozen or so bands coming through, that's all. And some of them still have a lot to do; some of them realise it, some of them don't. Some of them are looking for a quick kill or this famed 'half million quid' deal. But for any one of those bands to catch up with us at the point we're in now, you'd have to put us in deep freeze for over eighteen months.'

Well, Fish *might* have thought that, but an alternative interpretation of the situation is that, having pushed hard for Marillion to break through, he was now trying to pull up the ladder behind him. As the members of the various bands attest (and the contemporary photographic evidence confirms), for a short time at least in 1983-1984, there was a tight coterie of musicians (including Fish) who would cross paths, support each other, attend each other's gigs, drink together at the St. Moritz and help to build, for want of a better word, a scene.

And, more so, the fans who travelled to The Marquee and elsewhere around the country felt a belonging which was, perhaps, more reassuring than at home, school, university or in the workplace.

'You had that excitement from the show you'd gone to see,' says Marquee regular Stephanie Bradley. 'But you also had the sense of it was your place, that it was the right place for you. It was like our home, and you went to meet your friends and hang around afterwards to chat with the bands. It felt very much like family because you would see all the same faces. It was just the best place to go to. It really was.'

As the 1980s progressed, these fans moved on to university and/or full-time jobs. Many of the bands fell apart, The Marquee moved location and the new prog scene started to fade.

A PLAYGROUND OF BROKEN HEARTS

Fish, Lowson and Mann, Reading Festival, 1983 (Photograph by Mark Hughes)

Pallas, Solstice, IQ and Twelfth Night all changed singers in the 20 months between November 1983 and August 1985. For the bands who were signed to a major label, attempts to shape the music of their progressive rock forebears of the 1970s with a more modern edge meant that their music was very difficult to market. Radio stations did not know what to make of these bands' music in the second half of the 1980s. Sometimes it's easy to imagine that the bands themselves thought the same way.

'For a time,' noted the late rock journalist Malcolm Dome, 'it seemed possible that Twelfth Night, IQ, Pendragon and Pallas would find commercial success. This is why a lot of them landed biggish deals. But these were bands dedicated to their music, and not prepared to compromise for the sole sake of commercial success, so only Marillion truly enjoyed the bigger rewards. I still feel that the likes of IQ and Pendragon, for instance, wouldn't have been best served by big success. It would last only briefly, and then what?'

'There's an enormous danger that goes with the trappings of success,' says Nick Barrett of Pendragon. 'Getting halfway there is often the breaking point, and many bands don't realise until it's too late. With the exception of Marillion, this happened with all of the prog bands of the 1980s. We never attained those dizzy heights of headlining Glastonbury and having hit singles that we all set out to achieve. Twelfth Night knew exactly where they were going and had the musicianship and ability to be able to push forward. But, ironically, getting halfway there by having Andy Sears and Tony Smith and signing to Virgin Records effectively killed them off. Twelfth Night, IQ and Pallas all came a cropper after reaching this halfway mark.'

The mid-1990s have been characterised as the low point of progressive rock. Yet some green shoots were apparent. As Marillion fulfilled their EMI contract and with Pink Floyd's *The Division Bell* at number 1, IQ's *Ever* (1993) and Pendragon's *The Masquerade Overture* (1995) established a business model – self-funding and self-management – which continues to operate successfully 30 years on. Eventually (after 13 years), Solstice's second album, *Circles*, would be released as the follow-up to *Silent Dance*. Pallas reconvened for 1998's *Beat The Drum*. Twelfth Night had seemingly ended forever: whilst the death of Geoff Mann might have brought them together, briefly, to honour his memory, it would not be until 2007 that most of them were able to sit in the same room once again.

Meanwhile, a third generation of prog bands started to grow up: Porcupine Tree (UK), Big Big Train (UK), The Flower Kings (Sweden) and Spock's Beard (US) are four examples of bands that formed or coalesced in the mid-1990s that still draw audiences, find critical and commercial success and, mostly, remain fully professional musicians. This third generation would abstract from or explore other forms such as electronica and progressive metal. Indeed, Radiohead's *OK Computer* (1997) is a prog album in almost every respect. Ozric Tentacles achieved a top 10 album and The Orb had success with a double concept album with 10-20 minute long tracks. The likes of Dream Theater, Tool and

Opeth successfully execute a progressive rock approach with a harder edge.

'The problem for the 'Big Six',' Steven Wilson says, 'was that the old seventies Genesis tropes were ultimately too retro and reductive in an era when things like electronic music, trip-hop, Brit pop and grunge were all exploding.'

It was the rise of the World Wide Web at the end of the 1990s that rekindled interest in the bands of the 1980s.

'The internet helped save the progressive scene in the UK,' suggests *Prog*'s Jerry Ewing, 'because everyone went underground and ran their news groups and mailing lists and stayed connected.'

'We could reconnect and regain our fans,' says Pallas aide de camp Mike Bentley. 'We gained an impetus that has held us in good stead ever since.'

'The really amazing thing about all of this,' says Jerry Ewing, 'is that almost all of the bands, or the people in those bands, are still alive and still playing. And that, I think, is quite remarkable. It singles out the whole 1980s scene as being something quite unique. It was a magical period. It was great being there, being part of it. I always feel that I owe a huge debt to that whole scene because I wouldn't be here now, doing what I do, if it wasn't for me going to see Marillion in December 1982 and picking up a copy of *The Web* and suddenly being able to create something that aligned with what people wanted to read. It was through luck and coincidence that I got my foot in the door as a professional writer. No careers advisor could predict that.'

Marillion's innovative business plan – pre-orders ahead of recording – coupled with the reach of the internet, the development of fan based social media and the spending power of their very devoted followings now allows the prog bands of the 1980s to take control of their own management, distribution and marketing.

'It's the craft of making the music that has become most exciting,' notes Nick Barrett. 'The road forks when you're younger. When you're faced with having to become more popular, because the industry demands commercial returns, so you tend to leave your craft a little bit behind; you end up spending too much time being famous, or trying to be famous. And that is a killer because in the end your craft becomes secondary: you don't produce anything that you like, let alone anything anybody else likes. So, as far as I'm concerned now, I'm doing this with people who I love to be with. When we get in a room, we sit round, we have a good laugh. It's an incredibly valuable thing to be able to make music with people that I cherish enormously. I don't think I'll ever stop doing it.'

There are hundreds of part-timers joining the remains of the '70s and '80s bands on a thriving small festival and concert circuit, even if their audiences are now mostly well past middle age.

Prog ain't dead, just older.

And, let's hope, wiser.

Derek Smalls: We're lucky.
 David St. Hubbins: Yeah.
 Derek Smalls: I mean, people should be envying us, you know.
 David St. Hubbins: I envy us.
 Derek Smalls: Yeah.
 David St. Hubbins: I do.
 Derek Smalls: Me too.

Sources

The majority of quotes in the book come from interviews and direct communications with the author. Sources for secondary quotes are referenced below.

1984: A Bleeding Heart Poet In A Fragile Capsule
- 'The thing is, if we could find ourselves a suitable front man…' *Afterglow* issue 13, 1983
- 'The band had matured since the first album…' interview by Marko's Marillion Museum, 2021
- 'It's about the unreality of the pop song…' *Sounds*, 18 February 1984
- 'They were also unhappy about the huge studio bill run up by our late album…' *Marillion Misadventures & Marathons: The Life & Times Of Mad Jack*, 2022
- '*Eyes In the Night* was written in a 'fit of pique'…' *The Sentinel*, vol 2, issue 3, January 1984
- 'The plot behind *The Spy Song* is loosely based on Orwell's 1984…' *The Sentinel*, vol 2, issue 3, January 1984
- 'Though I'm not sure why! …' *The Sentinel*, vol 2, issue 3, January 1984
- 'I feel great satisfaction with this track…' *The Sentinel*, vol 2, issue 3, January 1984
- 'We took enough material over to complete a double album…' *The Sentinel*, vol 2, issue 3, January 1984
- 'I actually woke up with the idea swimming about in my mind…' *The Sentinel*, vol 2, issue 3, January 1984
- '*Atlantis* appeared out of thin air…' *The Sentinel*, vol 2, issue 3, January 1984
- 'The song, on the surface, is fantasy…' *The Sentinel*, vol 2, issue 3, January 1984
- 'Having been temporarily taken under Eddie Offord's wing…' *Kerrang!*, November 1983
- 'There were a lot of people there, which was fantastic…' interviewed for *Past and Presence* DVD, 2006
- 'For me, to be playing on the same stage as all my favourite musicians have played on over the years was magical…' *Mob Mag* issue 3, 1988
- 'I actually came across 'fugazi' in Mark Baker's book…' *Sounds*, 18 February 1984
- '*Fugazi*, for reasons both good and bad, is still probably the hardest Marillion album for first-time buyers to grapple with…' *Market Square Heroes: The Authorized Story of Marillion*, 1987
- 'Remember this gig well as it was tagged on at the end of a gruelling tour…' Facebook, 2014
- 'That's the Holy Grail, isn't it, for a band?…' YouTube interview with Mark Jepson, 2021
- 'His studio was down in Cornwall in this idyllic vicarage…' YouTube interview with Mark Jepson, 2021
- 'Everything was set up in the main room…' *Prog* magazine 'The Albums That Saved Prog'
- 'The band were in a wonderful, atmospheric old building in the middle of nowhere…' *Prog* magazine 'The Albums That Saved Prog'
- 'That Solstice album bankrupted me…' *Prog* magazine 'The Albums That Saved Prog'
- 'Before we go any further, I'd better lay the cards face up on the table…' *Melody Maker*, 4 April 1984
- 'Ye Gods! It honestly frightens me to death…' *Melody Maker*, 4 April 1984
- 'God, I hate those bloody comparisons…' *Melody Maker*, 4 April 1984
- 'Pallas may be a large step behind Marillion at present…' *Melody Maker*, 4 April 1984
- 'John started a label called Elusive…' *Loudersound*, 2021 'Pendragon: the journey to The Jewel'
- 'Will was a good engineer…' *Loudersound*, 2021 'Pendragon: the journey to The Jewel'
- 'We had been playing the material live for so long …' *Loudersound*, 2021 'Pendragon: the journey to The Jewel'
- '…becoming a little too complacent, not really contributing to the songs…' *Kerrang!* February 1986
- 'Places like Germany, France, Switzerland, and Holland…' *Market Square Heroes: The Authorized Story of Marillion*, 1987
- 'Making *Real To Reel* was exciting…' interview by Marko's Marillion Museum, 2021

- 'Canada at the start of that tour was great!…' *Market Square Heroes: The Authorized Story of Marillion*, 1987
- '[These were] intended as promo for the USA…' *IQ Newsletter* number 4, 1986
- 'Working with a producer for the first time…' *Soundcheck*, 1984
- 'Nigel and Marc Elton didn't get on terribly well from the beginning' *Prog* magazine 'The Albums That Saved Prog'
- 'I don't know why they [did] it…' *The Stairway* issue 1, November 1985
- 'So we all piled in the van and drove up to Wakefield…' *Market Square Heroes: The Authorized Story of Marillion*, 1987
- 'Barwell Court was idyllic and atmospheric…' *Marillion Misadventures & Marathons: The Life & Times Of Mad Jack*, 2022
- 'We were asked by a promoter to do a tour of the South West of England…' interviewed for *Past and Presence* DVD, 2006
- 'I thought that [*Silent Dance*] was okay…' *Prog* magazine 'The Albums That Saved Prog'
- 'Most bands when mixing live recordings replace, repair, overdub or completely re-record their songs…' *Marillion Misadventures & Marathons: The Life & Times Of Mad Jack*, 2022
- 'We went to Rick Parfitt's studio in Weybridge…' interview by Marko's Marillion Museum, 2021
- 'Having Ian in the band is like knowing you carry heavy insurance…' *Market Square Heroes: The Authorized Story of Marillion*, 1987
- 'Playing with Ian means really having to be on your toes…' *Market Square Heroes: The Authorized Story of Marillion*, 1987

1985: Dawn Escapes From Moon Washed College Halls

- 'After the experience of recording the album,…' *Prog* magazine 'The Albums That Saved Prog'
- 'We didn't feel that Mark was cutting it…' *Prog* magazine 'The Albums That Saved Prog'
- 'The long and short of it is that we felt that a new bass player was the right thing to do…' YouTube interview with Mark Jepson, 2021
- 'Sandy was embracing a particular way forward with that pregnancy…' *Prog* magazine 'The Albums That Saved Prog'
- 'Sandy was another absolutely crucial part of what the band was…' YouTube interview with Mark Jepson, 2021
- 'If I was to go back and give myself some advice…' YouTube interview with Mark Jepson, 2021
- 'We approached a few respected producers…' *Marillion Misadventures & Marathons: The Life & Times Of Mad Jack*, 2022
- 'Berlin, before the Wall fell…' *Marillion Misadventures & Marathons: The Life & Times Of Mad Jack*, 2022
- 'It's a German social problem…' *Innerviews*, 1993
- 'The budget wasn't there for us to bring in an outside producer…' *Loudersound*, 'Pendragon: the journey to The Jewel', 2021
- 'Peter would do his bass parts overnight…' *Loudersound*, 'Pendragon: the journey to The Jewel', 2021
- 'I had been working so hard on my parts that I simply had to bow out…' *Loudersound*, 'Pendragon: the journey to The Jewel', 2021
- 'The writing process of *The Wake* started…' *Background*, July 2011
- 'The main theme of the album is death…' *Background*, July 2011
- 'I have to say we were fairly naïve …' *Background*, July 2011
- 'It was with only a few sleepless nights of rehearsal…' *The Sentinel* issue 10, 1986
- 'I haven't actually seen it all…' *The Stairway* issue 2, April/May 1986
- 'We had a few dates to play in Spain and Portugal…' *Marillion Misadventures & Marathons: The Life & Times Of Mad Jack*, 2022
- 'We thought that the EP would be a transitory phase…' *Kerrang!* February 1986

- 'We were looking for a producer for *Knight-moves*...' *The Stairway* issue 2, April/May 1986
- 'It sold well...' *Kerrang!* February 1986
- 'We were treated wonderfully...' *The Sentinel* issue 10, 1986
- 'By the time 1985 came around everyone knew what was going to happen...' YouTube interview with Mark Jepson, 2021
- 'I didn't really want to experience that so didn't go...' YouTube interview with Mark Jepson, 2021
- 'It isn't easy to describe what each track is about lyrically...' *Background*, July 2011
- 'The main face was inspired by a film...' *Background*, July 2011
- 'I remember just after we released *The Wake*...' The Prog Report, 'Catching up with Michael Holmes from IQ', 2017
- 'Ultimately I don't think a band can survive without it really...' *The Stairway* issue 1, November 1985
- '*Misplaced Childhood* might have been an interlinked suite of songs...' *The Quietus*, 27 October 2015 'Neo-Prog 35 Years On: Marillion, IQ, Pendragon Etc. Revisited'
- 'We had been told that on pre-order sales alone...' *Market Square Heroes: The Authorized Story of Marillion*, 1987
- 'It's funny, though, when you're still a kid...' *Market Square Heroes: The Authorized Story of Marillion*, 1987
- 'We booked The Marquee and we didn't know about this Live Aid thing...' *The Stairway* issue 1, November 1985
- 'This one was tucked into a basement flat just off Shepherd's Bush Green...' *The Sentinel* issue 10, 1985
- 'It was a very big day for us...' *Market Square Heroes: The Authorized Story of Marillion*, 1987
- 'I had many reasons for wanting to stay in IQ...' *Background*, July 2011
- 'Fish was in a party mood...' *Marillion Misadventures & Marathons: The Life & Times Of Mad Jack*, 2022
- 'There's bound to be a difference in style between two singers...' *Background*, July 2011
- 'The idea was really twofold...' *The Stairway* issue 2, April 1986
- 'The pressure was two pronged...' *The Stairway* issue 2, April 1986
- 'It's really weird...' *The Stairway* issue 2, April 1986

1986: Egos Check Cheques In Transit

- 'Alan wrote some great lyrics one sleepless morning...' *The Sentinel* issue 10, 1986
- 'A lot of the essence of the original Pallas is in *The Wedge*...' *The Stairway* issue 2, April 1986
- 'We sat down before we did the album...' *The Stairway* issue 2, April 1986
- 'We actually chose it as a single because it was the most unusual track...' *The Stairway* issue 2, April 1986
- 'We needed some B-sides quickly...' *The Stairway* issue 2, April 1986
- 'We've spent a year, almost, rebuilding...' *Kerrang!* February 1986
- 'The way we look at it...' *Kerrang!* February 1986
- 'Well, I think we've always had a chance of making it...' *The Stairway* issue 2, April 1986
- 'Well, it's the comfiest place in the house...' *The Stairway* issue 2, April 1986
- 'Basically they ran out of money...' *The Stairway* issue 2, April 1986
- 'We're pressurising them very heavily...' *The Stairway* issue 2, April 1986
- 'We did earn a lot of money from those dates...' *Market Square Heroes: The Authorized Story of Marillion*, 1987
- 'With the money we got from those shows...' *Market Square Heroes: The Authorized Story of Marillion*, 1987

Sources

- 'Soap Aid [was] a badly conceived follow up to Live Aid…' *Marillion Misadventures & Marathons: The Life & Times Of Mad Jack*, 2022
- 'Marc and I tried to get something going with Howard Rogers from Liaison…' YouTube interview with Mark Jepson, 2021
- 'Stanbridge consisted of a Tudor style house…' *Marillion Misadventures & Marathons: The Life & Times Of Mad Jack*, 2022
- 'Our records went out of stock with Elusive Records…' *The Rocking Horse* issue 2, 1987
- '[The arrangement with Awareness] was initially viewed as a stop-gap…' *The Rocking Horse* issue 2, 1987
- 'There are quite a lot of Pendragon bootlegs kicking around…' *The Rocking Horse* issue 2, 1987
- 'I expected the music press to view this album as…' *A Little Angry In A Very Nice Place*, 1987
- 'There was this girl who came on with whips…' *A Little Angry In A Very Nice Place*, 1987

1987: Building Hope On Shifting Sand

- 'We were actually going to release it as a live single…' *A Little Angry In A Very Nice Place*, 1987
- 'The whole album was about Fish's excessive drinking…' *Marillion Misadventures & Marathons: The Life & Times Of Mad Jack*, 2022
- 'We didn't expect it to be a hit single…' *A Little Angry In A Very Nice Place*, 1988
- 'I'm still not sure how or why…' *Marillion Misadventures & Marathons: The Life & Times Of Mad Jack*, 2022
- 'I'd had enough of the egos and temper tantrums…' *Marillion/Separated Out… Redux*, 2012
- 'Understandably, Steve was done with Fish…' *Marillion Misadventures & Marathons: The Life & Times Of Mad Jack*, 2022
- 'I love the music and lyrics, especially the lush chords…' *Marillion Misadventures & Marathons: The Life & Times Of Mad Jack*, 2022
- 'She added something new and different to the live set…' *A Little Angry In A Very Nice Place*, 1988

- 'We were treated like kings…' *Marillion Misadventures & Marathons: The Life & Times Of Mad Jack*, 2022
- 'We walked on to a huge roar…' *Live From Loreley* sleeve notes

1988: Indifferently Ticking In Cold Deserted Mansion Halls

- 'There's been much speculation over the years…' *Marillion Misadventures & Marathons: The Life & Times Of Mad Jack*, 2022
- 'By 1988 I had a track record as a musical director…' *If I Was…*, 2004
- 'On the day of the show, I was standing backstage…' *If I Was…*, 2004
- 'We returned from Scotland feeling demoralised…' *Marillion Misadventures & Marathons: The Life & Times Of Mad Jack*, 2022
- 'Somehow, between us, we had poisoned the well…' *Marillion Misadventures & Marathons: The Life & Times Of Mad Jack*, 2022
- 'Marillion became a really big band…' FaceCulture podcast, 2021
- 'We'd written a lot of music before Fish left…' Raised On Radio podcast, 2021
- 'I just thought nothing could get any worse…' *Loudersound*, 13 May 2016 'Are Pendragon prog's greatest unsung heroes?'

1989: Watch The Old World Melt Away

- 'I joined Marillion in January 1989…' marilliononline YouTube channel, 2021
- 'I didn't prevent them doing it…' marilliononline YouTube channel, 2021
- 'I just happened to mention to him…' marilliononline YouTube channel, 2021
- '[Pete] had got cats…' marilliononline YouTube channel, 2021

Going Underground: The 1990s and Beyond

- 'We started up again with John…' from an interview by Jurriaan Hage and Roberto Lambooy, June 1997
- 'It turns out that since the communist era…' *Loudersound*, 13 May 2016 'Are Pendragon prog's greatest unsung heroes?'
- 'I was able to buy quite a nice house in Ascot…' *Loudersound*, 13 May 2016 'Are Pendragon prog's greatest unsung heroes?'
- 'That was one night where it felt that everything was working perfectly…' marilliononline YouTube channel, 2021

Calling All The Heroes

- 'Unfortunately, the headliners' audiences took an extreme dislike…' Louderthanwar.com April 2021 'The Cardiacs – an epic overview'
- 'Dave had a plan to form a band in the vein of Hawkwind…' *Marillion Misadventures & Marathons: The Life & Times Of Mad Jack*, 2022
- 'We started up in 1982 playing gigs at working men's clubs…' *Cumberland News*, 7 May 2008
- 'The flat had nothing in it apart from equipment and us…' *Cumberland News*, 7 May 2008
- 'He agreed to pay for rehearsal time…' *Cumberland News*, 7 May 2008
- 'An unknown four-piece from Cumbria…' *The Music's All That Matters*, 2010
- 'It Bites' songs are pop songs…' *The Music's All That Matters*, 2010
- '*Once Around the World* locates the band in…' *The Music's All That Matters*, 2010
- 'People say to me that there's more guitar on this album…' *Sounds*, 17 June 1989
- 'Part of the problem was the friction between us and Virgin bosses…' *Cumberland News*, 7 May 2008
- 'Tim had a band called Plenty…' *Limited Edition Of One*, 2022

Closure: Impressions Lost And Overstepped

- 'Yes to me symbolised everything that was wrong with music…' *Record Play Pause*, 2019
- 'Punk signalled a huge shift in attitudes…' *A New Day Yesterday: UK Progressive Rock and the 1970s*, 2020
- 'The glam-rock thing was over…' *I Swear I Was There*, 2006
- 'I was not totally loath to a little bit of prog rock…' *I Swear I Was There*, 2006
- 'The weird thing is…' *Record Play Pause*, 2019
- 'Prog rock didn't fit into the backdrop really…' *I Swear I Was There*, 2006
- 'While punk had crystallised many writers' hatred…' *The Quietus*, 2015
- 'Progressive Rock is an easy pigeon-hole…' *Kerrang!* November 1983
- 'None of the bands that you and I…' *Kerrang!* November 1983
- 'A lot of people seem to think…' *Kerrang!* November 1983
- 'While the bigger progressive rock…' *A New Day Yesterday: UK Progressive Rock and the 1970s*, 2020
- 'What has happened…' *Kerrang!* issue 37, March 1983

Bibliography

Anderton, C., *Fire In Harmony: The 1980s UK British Progressive Rock Revival* (Editions Universitaires de Dijon, Dijon, 2016)

Anthony. M., *Words and Music: Excursions in the Art of Rock Fandom* (Celtic Mist Publications, 2012)

Barnes, M., *A New Day Yesterday: UK Progressive Rock and the 1970s* (Omnibus Press, London, 2020)

Burns, R., *Experiencing Progressive Rock: A Listener's Companion* (Rowman and Littlefield, Lanham MD, 2018)

Butterworth, R., *Pink Floyd On Track* (Sonicbond, Tewksbury, 2022)

Cocker, J., *Good Pop Bad Pop* (Jonathan Cape, London, 2022)

Collins, J., *Marillion/Separated Out… Redux* (Foruli Classics, Potters Bar, 2012)

Covach, J., 'Progressive Rock, "Close to the Edge" and the Boundaries of Style' in *Understanding Rock: Essays in Musical Analysis* (Oxford University Press, Oxford, 1997)

Feakes, G., *1973: The Golden Year of Progressive Rock* (Sonicbond, Tewksbury, 2022)

Garner. K., *In Session Tonight – The Complete Radio 1 Recordings* (BBC Books, London, 1993)

Hegarty, P. and Halliwell, M., *Beyond and Before: Progressive Rock Since the 1960s* (Continuum, New York, 2011)

Holm-Hudson, K. (ed.), *Progressive Rock Reconsidered* (Routledge, New York, 2002)

Kelly, M., *Marillion Misadventures & Marathons: The Life & Times Of Mad Jack* (Kingmaker, London, 2022)

Kranitz, J., *Cassette Culture: Homemade Music and the Creative Spirit in the Pre-Internet Age* (Vinyl-on-Demand, Friedrichshafen, 2023)

Lambe, S., *Citizens of Hope and Glory: The Story of Progressive Rock* (Amberley Publishing, Stroud, 2013)

Lambe, S., with Watkinson, D., *Yes in the 80s* (Sonicbond, Tewksbury, 2022)

Lucky, J. *The Progressive Rock Files* (Collectors' Guide, Ontario, 1998)

Macan. E., *Rocking the Classics: English Progressive Rock and the Counterculture* (Oxford University Press, Oxford, 1997)

Morris, S., *Record Play Pause* (Constable, London, 2019)

Nolan, D., *I Swear I Was There: Sex Pistols, Manchester and the Gig that Changed the World* (Independent Music Press, Church Stretton, 2006)

Sellers, R and Pendleton, N., *Marquee: The Story Of The World's Greatest Music Venue* (Paradise Road, Dagenham, 2022)

Smith, S., *In The Court of King Crimson* (Panegyric, Hardwick, 2019)

Stump, P. *The Music's All That Matters* (Harbour Books, Chelmsford, 2010)

Tkach, G.M, and Siekler, P.M, *Steven Wilson Footprints Volume I* (GP Publishing, London, 2021)

Ure, M., *If I Was…* (Virgin Books, London, 2004)

Wall, M., *Market Square Heroes: The Authorized Story of Marillion* (Sidgwick & Jackson, London, 1987)

Webb, N., *Marillion in the 1980s* (Sonicbond, Tewksbury, 2020)

-- *Marillion in the 1980s: Notes and Errata* (self-published PDF, 2021)

Weigel, D., *The Show That Never Ends: The Rise and Fall of Prog Rock* (Norton, New York, 2017)

Wild, A., *Play On – The Authorised Biography of Twelfth Night* (Twelfth Night, Higher Denham, 2009)

-- *One For The Record – The Authorised Biography of Galahad* (Avalon, Ferndown, 2013)

-- *Phil Collins in the 1980s* (Sonicbond, Tewksbury, 2022)

-- *His Love: Art Music and Faith – The Authorised Biography of Geoff Mann* (Sonicbond, Tewksbury, 2023)

Wilson, S. with Wall, M., *Limited Edition of One: How to Succeed in the Music Industry Without Being Part of the Mainstream* (Constable, London, 2022)